THE EQUIPPING CHURCH

GUIDEBOOK

Also Available . . .

the companion book

The Equipping Church, by Sue Mallory

YOUR COMPREHENSIVE RESOURCE

LEADERSHIP
training
NETWORK

THE EQUIPPING CHURCH

GUIDEBOOK

Sue Mallory & Brad Smith

ZONDERVAN™

GRAND RAPIDS, MICHIGAN 49530

We want to hear from you. Please send your comments about this book to us in care of the address below. Thank you.

ZONDERVAN™

GRAND RAPIDS, MICHIGAN 49530

www.zondervan.com

ZONDERVAN™

The Equipping Church Guidebook
Copyright © 2001 by Leadership Network, Inc.

Requests for information should be addressed to:

Zondervan, *Grand Rapids, Michigan 49530*

ISBN: 0-310-23957-5

Interior design by Nancy Wilson

Printed in the United States of America

05 06 /❖ VG/ 10 9 8 7

To Bob Buford, who started Leadership Network
with a vision to "turn the latent energy of
American Christianity into active energy,"
and to the growing number of pioneers
of the equipping church movement
who are turning that dream into reality—
one individual, one church, one city at a time.

Contents

PART 1

BUILDING AN EQUIPPING MINISTRY VISION AND CULTURE

PART 2

BUILDING AN EQUIPPING MINISTRY SYSTEM

Tables, Charts, and Forms

PART 1

Acknowledgments

THIS GUIDEBOOK HAS BEEN a labor of love of several people. The operative word here is *labor*. The wisdom, learning, and commitment to getting it all on paper belong to many. This guidebook is not about ideas originated in the authors' heads, but an organized journal of the ideas, practices, and movements of God that we have seen in some of the healthiest, most innovative churches in North America.

The original *Starter Kit for Mobilizing Ministry* was edited through the gifts and wordsmithing of Sarah Jane Rehnborg, Ph.D. Your years of experience in the nonprofit world and your heart for the church made you a priceless resource to Leadership Training Network (LTN).

To all of you senior pastors, directors of equipping ministries, and your team members who have persevered and shared your successes and your failures so that others might learn, this book is a reflection of your faithfulness to Scripture and to the vision of growing the church God intends us to lead. Our deep thanks for your faithfulness and shared wisdom.

To the LTN faculty, past and present—Leroy Armstrong, Sally Vasen Alter, Preston Bright, Chris Hardy, Tammy Kelley, Barbara Harris, Calvie Hughson Schwalm, Don Simmons, and Ian Stevenson, for your tenacity, your humor, and your commitment to God's call on your lives. Thank you for your leadership, your sacrifices, and your willingness to keep adapting, flexing, growing, and challenging until we got it right, and, most important, for modeling what real team commitment looks like, both to us and to those we have taught.

To Kim Clegg, whose obedience to God and loyalty to LTN has been a great gift. You have been the most tenacious, dedicated editor one could ever hope for. Without your commitment and dedication to excellence, we never would have made it. Thank you from all of us.

Thanks to Greg Ligon for your fresh energy, your "can-do" spirit, and your willingness to go the last mile—with grace, humor, and excellence. You have been a gift and a blessing. Without your gifted eye as a managing editor, this would merely be an unassembled box of great potential.

To Carolyn Cochran, our taskmaster, we are thankful for you, your heart for Christ, and your servant leadership that allows us all to shine.

To Bob Buford, for the faith to support a project that took some time to become concrete, and for the vision to expand any idea we had 100-fold.

To the rest of the Leadership Network team, for all the "scouting reports" of innovation in large churches, postmodern-transition churches, and urban churches and for the denominational leadership that provides much breadth of understanding and impact for this guidebook.

Sue Mallory and Brad Smith

Preface: What Is Equipping Ministry?

EQUIPPING MINISTRY PREPARES people to understand their gifts and live out their calling in every area of their lives—church, community, family, marketplace, and mission. It is discipleship that includes both knowledge and action, resulting in group maturity. Church leaders must count equipping ministry as their primary goal.

The Equipping Church Guidebook starts with the biblical mandate to leaders "to equip the saints for the work of ministry, for building up the body of Christ" (Ephesians 4:12 RSV). This book emerges not out of a "theory" of how this mandate should be achieved, but out of a journalistic effort to describe the best models of churches who are not just *talking* but actually *doing* healthy equipping ministry. Finally, this book translates what was found in these healthy and innovative models into transferable principles, examples, questions, and exercises to help other church leaders build an equipping ministry that is tailored to meet the needs and calling of their own church.

Every one of the churches we studied that modeled healthy equipping ministry possessed the following common factors:

- The key leaders not only understood the importance of equipping ministry, but also proactively cast the vision, built an equipping-oriented internal culture, and personally modeled an equipping-centered ministry. Their vision affected how they conducted meetings, preached sermons, wrote newsletters, hired staff members, and even how they built their buildings. Chapters 1–5 will explain this in more detail.
- Key leaders viewed equipping ministry as such an important emphasis that they appointed or hired a primary point person with the gifts and the authority to lead the effort. In smaller churches this often proved to be one of their best nonpaid leaders. In larger churches this was often a full-time staff person who possessed the essential leadership and management gifts to guide the effort. Chapters 6–8 will explain the nature of these gifts and how this person's role should be defined.
- Key leaders understood that most people require competent coaches, a supportive small group, or a series of next steps to take them from merely learning about their gifts and calling to a lifestyle of gift-based ministry. To accomplish this, these churches developed leaders and built systems that moved people from visitor through membership and all the way to involvement. These systems moved people from hearing to doing, from the classroom to the streets, from inside the church walls to living out their calling in their daily lives in every part of the neighborhood, city, and world. Chapters 9–15 will provide information about what these systems look like and how they can be built.

> Leadership Training Network strives to provide resources to churches that come out of a variety of traditions and cultures. Please consult the glossary in the back to clarify the meanings of words and terms we use in this guidebook.

WHY IS EQUIPPING MINISTRY SO IMPORTANT?

NOTHING IS MORE IMPORTANT for church leaders to focus on than how they can fulfill what Scripture defines as their primary task:

> It was he who gave some to be apostles, some to be prophets, some to be evangelists, and some to be pastors and teachers . . .
>
> EPHESIANS 4:11

God gave leaders to the church. They did not appoint themselves, no matter what the actual process looks like from our human viewpoint. They serve God by leading; they serve God's people by leading. The church is under their care, but she is owned by God, not by the leaders. Leaders should serve as *stewards* of what God has given them.

> . . . to prepare God's people for works of service, so that the body of Christ may be built up . . .   EPHESIANS 4:12

The bottom-line purpose of what leaders are to do is to prepare God's people for works of service. Of all the Scriptures that explain the qualifications of church leaders, that give them instructions in various circumstances, and that specify their attitudes, this is the primary passage that describes the essential nature of what they should be doing. Ephesians 4:12 is the mission statement for church leaders. They should return to it time after time to ask, "Do our programs and activities 'equip the saints'? If not, how do we go back to the basics and refocus our leadership and our church on this priority?"

> . . . until we all reach unity in the faith and in the knowledge of the Son of God and become mature, attaining to the whole measure of the fullness of Christ.   EPHESIANS 4:13

The end goal is not activity for activity's sake, but maturity. Our goal is not about individual growth, but about group growth. This is whole-church, community discipleship.

> From him the whole body, joined and held together by every supporting ligament, grows and builds itself up in love, as each part does its work.   EPHESIANS 4:16

Many people mistakenly define equipping by the activities they do rather than by the results that occur. Equipping is more than apostling, prophesying, evangelizing, pastoring, or teaching. A faulty understanding of equipping leads to an overabundance of programs. We know that we've equipped others when each individual does his or her part so that the whole body grows and loves. How much easier it would be if we simply measured healthy equipping by the activities we do. Scripture sets a much higher standard than merely good sermons, plans, or programs.

Equipping is not a program we ladle on to a large stack of other programs, but a "North Star" by which we measure and redirect all of our programs. It is a return to the biblical priority established for church leaders, which allows them to simplify their work around the essential tasks God has defined for them.

WHY IS EQUIPPING MINISTRY SO MUCH WORK?

IF EQUIPPING MINISTRY WERE a simple, quick task, we could describe it in a chart or in a series of five steps or in a "one-size-fits-all" program. Simple charts are great for overviews and vision clarification, but they can be misleading with respect to how this vision is actually implemented. *The Equipping Church Guidebook* is a faithful description of what the many "journalists" among the church leaders who represent numerous denominations and who make up Leadership Network and Leadership Training Network actually saw in innovative, healthy equipping churches.

At first glance, equipping ministry sounds very simple: essentially building an internal culture that values gift-based service, then creating ways to help people move from where they are now to where they should be. But the problem centers on where we start. Most people walk into your church with a consumer mind-set. We live in a consumer culture where we are used to going to megastores, Web sites, and highly specialized vendors who provide us with many choices and services so we can get exactly what we want. Many choose a church by looking for the one that gives them the best "religious goods and services," since they are a consumer of "religious goods and services." It is hard to move people from a consumer mind-set to a servant lifestyle when so much in their world militates against this transition. Yet, it is exactly this transformation that will provide them with the greatest joy and maturity. To build an equipping culture in a sea of opposing forces requires bold prayer, careful strategy, and persistent, never-ending work.

The second problem centers on how we have traditionally defined the solution. Too often church leaders are taught to address a need by importing a program or a curriculum from another church where it had been wildly successful. We then attempt to recruit people to run these imported programs. But by trying to make a task easier for people, we often lose their ownership, create a square-peg program in a round-hole need, and find that our shortcut was actually a dead end.

Often these programs can serve as excellent starting places, but they don't come already tailored to the calling of our own church, and in the attempt to "package" them, essential parts are often left out. *The Equipping Church Guidebook* is designed to provide a framework so that each church can develop her own solutions. Not only will the end results better fit the church, but the actual processes of creating the solutions will deploy gifts, develop teams, and build your church body to maturity. We've done everything we can to provide you with what you need in order to avoid the mistakes that other churches have made and to focus your work on the major issues in the right sequence, without overpackaging it so that the task fails to stimulate and incorporate your own creativity and ingenuity.

WHAT EQUIPPING MINISTRY IS NOT

EQUIPPING MINISTRY IS MORE than volunteer management. Volunteer management alone creates excellent service opportunities, but these opportunities are often disconnected from the discipleship and maturity mission of the church. Equipping ministry can be marginalized when it becomes viewed as simply one more program among many others.

Furthermore, equipping ministry is not just gifts assessment, though assessment is a critical early step. However, if we have only the knowledge and not the concrete next steps and the relational guides to apply this knowledge, people are often left sitting on the curb, desiring to serve but not actually doing it. Too much classroom without the systems to apply what is learned can create a false sense that knowing is actually doing.

Equipping ministry is not just small groups or pastoral care. Many people have gifts and a calling that are not centered in leading small groups or providing care. Small groups often provide the best place for gifts discovery, and they can become a powerful community of support as a person ministers either inside or outside of the group. However, not all gifts are best utilized in a small group. Equipping ministry looks for multiple vehicles for the growth and deployment of gifts.

Neither is equipping ministry only the carrying out of service. Gift-based service is the venue for spiritual growth, but activity alone does not produce growth. Equipping ministry creates ways for people to be cared for through small groups, Sunday school classes, and one-on-one relationships so they end up both serving and being served themselves.

WHAT EQUIPPING MINISTRY IS

EQUIPPING MINISTRY IS ABOUT . . .

- mobilizing Christians in service.
- ministry that functions through God's power and gifts to build God's kingdom.
- management systems and structures to support and enable people to come to understand their role as ministers, to identify opportunities to serve, and to communicate needs.
- sharing vision, selecting leaders, forming teams, and creating communication systems.
- hard work, prayer, fellowship, and fun.
- "walking the talk" and helping every member be a minister.
- empowering both clergy and laity to use their gifts.
- Christians becoming active in today's world.
- preparing people for whole-life ministry—in their churches, communities, families, and workplaces.

WHAT IS THE ULTIMATE GOAL OF AN EQUIPPING MINISTRY SYSTEM?

TRUE OR FALSE

The ultimate goal of an equipping ministry system is to . . .

_____ meet the need for workers in the various programs of the church.

_____ care for the underprivileged and displaced of the community.

_____ engender more ownership in the church.

_____ increase retention of and giving among members.

_____ provide personal fulfillment through ministry.

_____ help individuals mature spiritually by using their God-given gifts to serve each other and the community, so that the whole church can attain the maturity that God intended.

CORE VALUES OF EQUIPPING MINISTRY

SEVERAL CORE VALUES ARE nonnegotiable in order for equipping ministry to succeed. The embodiment of these core values into the fabric of the church is one of the most critical foundational elements of successfully shifting your church culture to one characterized by an equipping mind-set.

Prayer

The equipping church recognizes the inherent value of prayer as a means of discerning God's vision, developing leadership, and planning toward an equipping ministry model. Equipping church leaders rely on prayer to see God involved in all aspects of their ministry.

The Priesthood of All Believers and the Vision of the Church as Contained in Ephesians 4

Every member in the body of Christ is gifted and called into ministry. The church embraces people holistically in the discovery of gifts, needs, and God's calling. She seeks to equip people for ministry in the family, the church, the community, and the world.

Servant Leadership

Leaders demonstrate a genuine caring for people, a spirit of humility and authenticity, and a willingness to be accountable as they equip others to use their gifts in the body of Christ.

Team Ministry

Healthy community in team settings is built around the individuality of gifts, team accountability, and the willingness of people to work for the good of the body as a whole.

Intentionality

The church embraces equipping ministry as a value and models it through the intentional implementation of systems to prepare, connect, and equip people for ministry inside and outside the walls of the church. It calls a leader to facilitate the implementation throughout the body of Christ.

Proactive Response to Change

The church recognizes and embraces the organic characteristic of change and responds creatively and proactively to shifts in culture. She continually changes her methods, but always maintains the message of Christ regarding the church.

SHIFTING THE LANGUAGE TO AN EQUIPPING MIND-SET

AN INTEGRAL PART OF EMBRACING the core values of this ministry involves a shift in language to an equipping ministry vocabulary. Each shift in language reflects a prior shift in perspective, attitude, and action.

Here are some examples of a shift to an equipping ministry vocabulary:

From	To
Recruit	Invite
Delegate	Share the ministry
Volunteer	Serve
Volunteers	Ministers/servant leaders
Administration	Information/Communication
Committee	Team
Programs	Ministries

Pat Roth, Woodman Valley Chapel,
Colorado Springs, Colorado

WHO IS THIS BOOK WRITTEN FOR?

Independent and Denominational Churches Alike

Some churches do their work through established structures, while others are less formal. This book focuses on shared theological principles and provides a framework for discussion and strategizing, with the result that each church can develop her own customized approach.

Churches of All Sizes

Large churches may have more detail in their processes, but the basic components of the equipping ministry system as explained in this book can be as present in a church of fifty as in a church of five thousand.

Churches with a Clear Vision of Every Member as a Minister

This book is especially well designed for those churches that are ready to *implement* an equipping ministry system. Preaching and teaching the importance of gift-based ministry is vital, since an effective equipping ministry system must be built on the vision of the senior pastor, the key leaders, and church members to equip the "priesthood of all believers." This book focuses on the steps to build the system, even as the church leaders are teaching the underlying theology of equipping ministry and establishing a strong foundation that will embrace its values.

HOW CAN THIS BOOK HELP YOUR CHURCH?

THE EQUIPPING CHURCH GUIDEBOOK is a practical resource designed with two parts. Part 1 is designed primarily to allow senior pastors, governing boards, key staff members, and nonpaid leaders to think through how they can cast the vision and build the internal church culture that will serve as the foundation for healthy equipping ministry. This first section provides the "generals' guide" to creating the overall strategy. It is designed with exercises called "contractors' conferences" that can be used in elders' meetings or staff meetings, as well as at planning retreats, to foster dialogue and decisions as a leadership team. Part 2 is designed primarily for the equipping ministry director and the various people and teams that will implement the vision. This section can be viewed as the "field guide," with how-tos, application steps, models of how others have applied these principles, and a number of worksheets to serve as guides for developing your own approach.

This guidebook is the perfect tool to steer your discussion and to help lay the cultural foundation for equipping ministry systems in your congregation. Your church, for example, might want to hold a two-day retreat. Prior to the retreat, photocopy appropriate sections and distribute them to your leadership team for advance reading. Use the "contractors' conference" guides to focus your discussion.

Here's another idea: Designate a half-hour time slot at your governing board meeting to discuss specific issues raised as a result of studying this book. Purchase a copy for each board member to use in the meeting and to take home afterward.

The design reflects the construction theme of Ephesians 4:12—"so that the body of Christ may be built up." Throughout the book look for the following features:

- *Builders' Notes,* which clarify concepts and offer variations on a theme
- *Contractors' Conferences,* which offer discussion questions for the leadership and ministry teams
- *Checkpoints,* which offer related concepts, summarize key points, and make useful suggestions

AFTER THE BOOK, THEN WHAT?

AS A REVISION OF Leadership Training Network's previously published *Starter Kit for Mobilizing Ministry,* this guidebook ultimately seeks to help churches learn from each other as they begin to implement equipping ministry. In addition to providing print materials, Leadership Training Network (LTN) was formed to stimulate ongoing networking dedicated to resourcing and influencing innovative church leaders to equip and mobilize people for biblical, gift-based team ministry.

LTN services include . . .

- *Training Institutes,* which are high-energy five-day seminars led by key leaders on the front lines of equipping ministry who represent a diversity of denominations, geographical locations, and church sizes. Training focuses on the biblical foundations for building the necessary teams, communication systems, and supports to implement or enhance Christ-centered equipping churches.
- *Strategies for Equipping Ministry,* which is a comprehensive listening guide and set of six audiotapes that contain the teachings of a two-day forum. This guide is designed for use by church leaders to share the vision and teach the strategies of equipping ministry to other leaders and team members in their churches.
- *New Century: New Church,* which is a video resource featuring some of the best working models of equipping ministry and demonstrating the impact that this style of ministry has had on the church as a whole.
- *Tool Kit for Equipping Ministry,* which provides hands-on resources to enhance learning. Various training modules provide your leadership team with leader's guides, resources, tools, and exercises to use during the development of equipping ministry systems.
- *Consultants and Support Services,* which makes available skilled consultants who will work directly with churches, assisting them in the implementation stages of program development and in any troubleshooting concerns. Arrangements are negotiated individually. Contact the Leadership Training Network office for referral information.

For information about these resources or for additional copies of this guidebook, call the Leadership Training Network office at 877-586-5323 (877-LTN-LEAD), or visit the Web site at www.ltn.org.

Introduction

EPHESIANS 4:12 STATES THAT the ultimate role of church leaders at its most basic level is "to prepare God's people for works of service, so that the body of Christ may be built up." How easy it is, in the midst of managing facilities and staff and dealing with conflicts, budgets, zoning laws, and counseling loads to forget that this is what God has called you to do.

This responsibility is both exciting and challenging. *The Equipping Church Guidebook* is designed to help you focus on your role as an equipper of others and to help you and other church leaders think through how to move proactively in the direction of equipping ministry, either for the first time or as a way of enhancing an existing effort.

This book provides a plan to lead your church to a new level by . . .

- reviewing the trends that support the need for equipping ministry.
- affirming the biblical foundations of equipping ministry.
- assessing the positive outcomes of equipping ministry.
- outlining the key elements of equipping ministry.
- assessing current church culture and structure.
- formulating the vision for equipping ministry for your church.
- embodying the core values of equipping ministry as church leaders.
- developing strategies and processes to fit the unique needs of your church.
- selecting the key leaders to build and facilitate the system.
- nurturing a churchwide equipping culture.

Equipping ministry is not an easy or quick endeavor. Decisions take time and require input from an ever-increasing number of people who need to have ownership in the decision-making process. The many crises of daily church management can constantly encroach on your time as you work to develop new, proactive approaches to address reoccurring problems.

Through presenting information and raising questions, you and your leadership team can walk through a process that will help you engage in ministry that equips and releases God's people in service to your church and the larger community. What an exciting opportunity, through much prayer, hard work, and persistence, to watch your church continue to grow as a congregation where members know their gifts and are supported in ministry.

Before you begin, you must understand that equipping is *not* the purpose of the church, but rather the purpose of church leaders.

Search the Scriptures and begin to discern the theology and traditions of the larger group of churches to which you belong in order to determine the church's timeless purpose. At the same time look at your own church in order to investigate the history of God's work there and to assess the gifts God has

> "Vision is the ability to see what others may not. It is the capacity to see potential, what things *could be.* It is the ability to see what God sees, and the God-given motivation to bring what you see to pass! We need faith to see the unseen, and by seeing what God sees for your future, you begin to have vision. This is how you begin to see, not only with your eyes, but also with your heart."
>
> Wayne Cordeiro,
> *Doing Church as a Team*

As a church grows quickly, it's easy to become reactive to an increasing number of problems and rarely have time to address the underlying causes. This book is designed to provide a framework for helping "firefighters" build "fire prevention systems."

given to your people, so that you might hear God's unique calling for your church today. You can neglect neither the timeless purpose of the church nor the need to regularly update how that purpose is expressed in the changing culture around you. Your church must be rooted in God's purpose, and not in the fickle needs of the culture; yet, you must constantly translate the expression of God's timeless purpose to styles that demonstrate this truth in ways that connect with a changing world.

It's not an easy job. The faster our culture changes, the easier it is to be swept up in the changes or to retreat to obsolete expressions that worked in years gone by. The people you lead will challenge both change *and* the status quo. The fast-changing culture we live in is confusing for them, too.

STEP 1: CLARIFY GOD'S TIMELESS PURPOSE FOR THE CHURCH

AS WE SEEK TO BECOME crystal clear about God's timeless purpose, we must commit to a continual process of prayer, study, discussion, and teaching as new leaders are added, new challenges are faced, and new generations emerge with limited understanding of Scripture and of what the church is called to be. Any innovation and updating of styles, methods, programs, and strategies must come from the foundation of God's timeless purpose for the church. Part 1 of *The Equipping Church Guidebook* is not designed to help you determine this timeless purpose. The book is addressed to a variety of church leaders from many denominations, theologies, and traditions and is written by a team from a variety of church backgrounds. It emerges from a careful journalistic examination of the common principles adopted by these various traditions. You must engage in this important foundational work of clarifying the timeless purpose of the church from the vantage point of the specific denomination or larger church body to which you belong.

One example of a widely used resource for church leaders is Rick Warren's book *The Purpose-Driven Church*, which identifies Matthew 22:37–40 and 28:19–20 as critical passages for defining the biblical purpose of the church. From their study of these passages, Rick and other leaders at Saddleback Valley Community Church describe the five purposes of the church:

- Worship: "Love the Lord with all your heart"
- Ministry: "Love your neighbor as yourself"
- Evangelism: "Go and make disciples"
- Fellowship: "Baptizing them"
- Discipleship: "Teaching them to obey"

Saddleback Church then formulated a purpose statement, followed by five key words to help church members learn and remember this purpose: To bring people to Jesus and *membership* in his family, develop them to Christlike *maturity*, and equip them for their *ministry* in the church and life *mission* in the world, in order to *magnify* God's name.

- Magnify: We celebrate God's presence in worship
- Mission: We communicate God's Word through evangelism
- Membership: We incorporate God's family into our fellowship
- Maturity: We educate God's people through discipleship
- Ministry: We demonstrate God's love through service

While your church may not come to the same conclusions or use the same language, it's important that you as church leaders engage in a similar thoughtful process. Because of your church distinctives, you may have to develop a clear statement of purpose with a sacramental priority, pietistic perspective, Reformed theology emphasis, or some other distinguishing mark. The key is to articulate God's timeless purpose for the church in a clear and understandable way.

After completing this first step, many churches immediately move to address the issue of equipping, spiritual gifts, lay mobilization, volunteer management, community service, marketplace ministry, or any of the other labels used to describe the topic of this guidebook. Consequently, they often see equipping as either one of the items on a laundry list of purposes or as a program to help implement one of the items on the list—such as membership or ministry (to illustrate from items on Saddleback's list). This mistake will all too often result in a failed, or at least a prolonged, effort. Why? Because they've moved too quickly before defining another key area of purpose.

STEP 2: CLARIFY GOD'S TIMELESS PURPOSE FOR CHURCH LEADERS

AFTER DEFINING GOD'S timeless purpose for the church, step 2 is to define the role of the elders, deacons, pastors, and other key leaders. This is closely related to step 1 in that it requires prayer, study of Scripture and church tradition, discussion, and teaching. Again, *The Equipping Church Guidebook* is not designed to achieve this purpose; it must be accomplished through using resources from your particular theological perspective.

Having observed hundreds of churches undertake step 2, here is what we've seen:

- Churches define the *specific* roles of their leaders in vastly different ways. Just a brief look at the names for these roles gives a hint of the diverse viewpoints: elder, vestry, session, diaconate, council, board, minister, pastor, rector, priest, and vicar. Even within the same traditions, there is much debate about specific functions of church leaders in different geographic regions, among churches of different sizes and structures, and among people in the same church with different backgrounds or different entry points into that church. Some churches assign greater authority to international, national, regional, and local leaders (sometimes called bishops, apostles, and the like); others assign much of the authority to the local church or even to the congregational majority.
- Churches define the *general* roles of their leaders in amazingly similar ways. While there is great debate about the specific functions and even about how the biblical lists of qualities and characteristics of the leaders should be applied today, there is little debate about the underlying purpose of church leadership. Most churches uphold Ephesians 4:11–16 as the primary passage to define not the purpose of the church, but the purpose of the *leaders* of the church.

> **And his gifts were that some should be apostles, some prophets, some evangelists, some pastors and teachers, to equip the saints for the work of ministry, for building up the body of Christ, until we all attain to the unity of the faith and of the knowledge of the Son of God, to mature manhood, to the measure of the stature of the fullness of Christ; so that we may no longer be children, tossed to and fro and carried about with every wind of doctrine, by the cunning of men, by their craftiness in deceitful wiles. Rather, speaking the truth in love, we are to grow up in every way into him who is the head, into Christ, from whom the whole body, joined and knit together by every joint with which it is supplied, when each part is working properly, makes bodily growth and upbuilds itself in love.**
>
> **EPHESIANS 4:11–16 RSV**

The primary purpose of . . .

- the top leadership group is *not* to be the "business board"— although that may be a subpurpose to accomplish the goal of equipping the saints.
- the pastor is not to be the CEO, although that may be in the pastor's gift set and may be useful in some places as a means to an equipping end.
- church leadership is not to oversee programs, although programs that are streamlined to equip people may be the primary activity of the leadership.

When church leaders understand God's timeless purpose for their church (step 1) and God's timeless purpose for themselves as leaders (step 2), they are ready to develop the unique way God has called them to express these timeless purposes through the vision, strategies, programs, and activities of their church in their unique place and time (step 3).

Part 1 of this book is designed to help *church leaders* develop the following: (1) a foundation of a healthy equipping-oriented internal culture and (2) a comprehensive churchwide system to implement the vision well. Part 2 is designed to help the *implementation team* build the churchwide system, as you continue to cast the vision that undergirds this system and establish a healthy equipping-oriented internal culture that provides the nourishing environment where growth can occur.

Take some time now to think through the questions and prompts in the "contractors' conference" on pages 25–26; discuss them with other church leaders before you move on to the first chapter.

MOVING ON TO CHAPTER 1

AS YOU PROCEED to chapter 1, we assume you have completed step 1 (clarifying God's timeless purpose for the church) and step 2 (clarifying God's timeless purpose for church leaders). The task before you now is to study your time and place—what is happening in the culture around you and what is happening in your church that will affect how you translate God's timeless purposes into the unique expression to which God has called your church.

CONTRACTORS' CONFERENCE

A purpose is the *why*—the reason you are doing what you do. A means is the *what*—what you do in terms of activities. If the *whats* are not carefully connected to the *whys,* you may end up having too many programs, too many meetings, too many conflicts, and a very complicated church. As a result, you find much of your time is spent running diversely directed programs and corralling "mavericks" who aim programs toward competing or divisive purposes.

1. In addition to Ephesians 4, identify other Bible passages and church documents that address the purpose of church leadership. What do these add to what is stated in Ephesians 4:11–16?

2. The following are often included as part of the role of church leaders:

   • Guard and teach the doctrine of the church.
   • Shepherd and care for the flock.
   • Provide vision and direction.
   • Pray for the church and provide a spiritual example.

   Which of these are means that are necessary to equip the saints? What are some other means, activities, and programs in your role as church leaders? What are some other purposes of your role as church leaders?

3. Provide a few examples where the church has failed to differentiate between the "means" of your role and the "purpose" of your role. What happened? How was it corrected? How could it have been avoided with clarity of purpose from the beginning?

4. The root meaning of the Greek term translated "equip" is "to mend a broken bone" or "to repair a broken fishing net." As you equip the people in your church, what is broken that must be taken into account before they are ready to do works of service?

5. Ephesians 4:11–16 might be described in the formula: *If* leaders equip for works of service, *then* the whole church will grow to maturity. Is the purpose of church leaders (a) to mature the saints, or (b) to equip the saints so that *God* will mature them? What is the leader's role, and what is God's promise? Is the purpose of church leaders to (a) exercise their gifts, or (b) to exercise their gifts in a way that they see people doing works of service as a result? How would (b) look different from (a)?

6. The logic of Ephesians 4:11–16 might be expressed as follows:

   a. God gave leaders to the church with intentional gifts.
   b. The purpose of these leaders is to equip the saints for works of service.
   c. As these saints are equipped for works of service, the whole body will grow to maturity.
   d. Maturity results in reduced confusion, greater truth, and individuals who are connected to Christ and each other to form a whole, inter-dependent body.

   How would you restate or add to this logic? How could this be restated to become a compass to determine how to focus your time and activities as a means toward a clear purpose? Using this compass, what would be the most important items on your "to-do" list as church leaders? What would be on your "to-stop-doing" list? As you apply this compass to the church programs and activities you oversee, how do these equip saints for works of service? How would you measure this?

7. What is the difference among the following?

   - creating an equipping ministry that implements a particular church *strategy,* such as "closing the back door" through which visitors slip away without becoming members
   - creating an equipping ministry that implements a particular church *purpose,* such as "membership" or "service"
   - creating an equipping ministry that establishes the foundation and churchwide internal culture and system for every purpose, strategy, program, and ministry in order to "equip the saints for works of service"

   In what way does the third type of equipping ministry point to an important part (if not *the* most important part) of your role as a church leader?

PART 1

Building an Equipping Ministry Vision and Culture

Part 1 is designed primarily for senior pastors, governing boards, key staff members, and nonpaid leaders to think through how they can build the vision and shape the internal church culture that will provide the foundation for healthy equipping ministry. It provides the "generals' guide" to creating the overall strategy. It is designed with exercises called "contractors' conferences" that can be used in elders' meetings, staff meetings, and planning retreats to foster dialogue and decisions as a leadership team.

the natural
ride you to
evaluating
ss, remem-
ng person,
nd may be
a "10"

Do Best
ty of Christ

1

Why Equipping Ministry?

Clarify the Purpose to All Involved

PREPARING THE GROUND to either begin an equipping ministry or enhance what you already have in place is important work. It doesn't have to be complicated, but it generally is more work and takes more time than most church leaders estimate. Why? Because an equipping ministry affects every area of your church in some way. Many more people have to be brought into the dialogue than if you were simply starting a new program in one area of your church.

Many church leaders who have successfully built a churchwide equipping ministry say it is very similar in time and effort to a building program. The first step of a building program involves understanding why you are doing it and effectively articulating the purpose to the church. The case for a building program must be connected clearly to your mission, or else the congregation will not support it with the necessary funds. Even later, if the purpose of the building program is not clearly understood and monitored, the architects and contractors will likely have a field day adding gadgets and gizmos that your church doesn't really need. If you design the building without asking every major stakeholder what he or she wants in the finished product, you will likely have constant conflict and last-minute expensive additions along the way. Even after that, as unexpected costs require certain cuts from the wish list, you must keep members involved in the discussions about what changes must be made and why. If done well, in the end every person should have a high degree of ownership and excitement about the finished product. Accomplishing this often involves starting more slowly at the front end to gain ownership and clarity of vision, so that you can move more quickly later on as more people own the vision and sign on as willing participants.

> Suppose one of you wants to build a tower. Will he not first sit down and estimate the cost to see if he has enough money to complete it? For if he lays the foundation and is not able to finish it, everyone who sees it will ridicule him, saying, "This fellow began to build and was not able to finish."
>
> LUKE 14:28–30

This chapter will help you form and articulate the vision for why you are building an equipping ministry. For church leaders who are asking why, this chapter will provide some fodder for discussion. For church leaders who are saying, "We're already on board, but we need some facts, figures, and ideas on how to cast this vision to the rest of the congregation," this chapter will meet that need as well.

CHAPTER PREVIEW

IN THIS CHAPTER WE WILL reflect on the following questions:

- What are the biblical imperatives that make this purpose an important and pivotal part of your work?
- What is changing in society to make this vision more urgent?
- What is changing in the church that makes equipping ministry more of an imperative?
- How has God preceded you?
- What needs in your church will this address?

WHAT ARE THE BIBLICAL IMPERATIVES OF EQUIPPING MINISTRY?

> It was he who gave some to be apostles, some to be prophets, some to be evangelists, and some to be pastors and teachers, to prepare God's people for works of service, so that the body of Christ may be built up until we all reach unity in the faith and in the knowledge of the Son of God and become mature, attaining to the whole measure of the fullness of Christ. . . .
>
> We will in all things grow up into him who is the Head, that is, Christ. From him the whole body, joined and held together by every supporting ligament, grows and builds itself up in love, as each part does its work.
>
> EPHESIANS 4:11–13, 15–16

> Then the righteous will answer him, "Lord, when did we see you hungry and feed you, or thirsty and give you something to drink? When did we see you a stranger and invite you in, or needing clothes and clothe you? When did we see you sick or in prison and go to visit you?"
>
> The King will reply, "I tell you the truth, whatever you did for one of the least of these brothers of mine, you did for me."
>
> MATTHEW 25:37–40

ACROSS ALL CHRISTIAN denominations we find a history of theological support for gift-based service in ministry carried out by all believers. The emphasis and methods may vary, and there may be huge disparities at times between the theology and practice of equipping ministry, yet there is an amazing agreement on the central points. In large part this is due to the many scriptural references on the subject. In the pages ahead we'll refer to these texts and their significance for equipping ministry. You can build on these passages as you develop Bible studies, write sermons, and create vision pieces to educate and inspire your congregation about the importance of serving through giftedness in order to build up the body of Christ.

Seven Ways to Summarize the Biblical Imperatives

Imperative 1—A ministry of serving others is an act of love for and devotion to Christ.

Any equipping ministry system should emphasize this aspect of serving others. Ministry, above all else, is an act of *worship*. Worship is not merely an event that occurs at 10 A.M. or 11 A.M. on Sunday morning. Worship involves a minute-by-minute mind-set of acknowledging that God is the Creator, and we are the creatures. Worship is recognizing our place of submission before a God who gives us our purpose. We do not own our time, family, possessions, or even our calling. We receive these things from God and "steward" them for God. A person gifted with vision worships God by giving vision to others, while recognizing that this gift came from and is used in submission to God's purposes. People gifted to serve can worship God by serving others, not to gain human appreciation, but out of the recognition that they are created to be "serving creatures" who have God's thumbprints all over them. These thumbprints reveal God's intentionality in the way each of us was created. We worship God when we do what God created us to do.

> I urge you therefore, brethren, by the mercies of God, to present your bodies a living and holy sacrifice, acceptable to God, which is your spiritual service of worship. And do not be conformed to this world, but be transformed by the renewing of your mind, that you may prove what the will of God is, that which is good and acceptable and perfect. For through the grace given to me I say to every man among you not to think more highly of himself than he ought to think; but to think so as to have sound judgment, as God has allotted to each a measure of faith. For just as we have many members in one body

and all the members do not have the same function, so we, who are many, are one body in Christ, and individually members one of another. And since we have gifts that differ according to the grace given to us, let each exercise them accordingly.

ROMANS 12:1–6A NASB

See also Matthew 25:31–46.

Imperative 2—God has a unique purpose or calling for each of our lives.

All Christians—clergy, staff members, laypersons, leaders, followers, men, women, children, the physically fit, and those with disabilities—are priests. God knew before we were born what he intended our purpose and calling to be. Thus, we don't choose our own calling, and we cannot be "anything we want to be." The purpose God created us for is where we find the greatest rest, the greatest honor, the greatest joy, and the greatest connection to God, ourselves, each other, and the world in which we live.

In that light, consider the word *volunteer*, which is used freely in churches. It implies that you "choose" to do something optional or extraordinary. If you are created with a purpose and specifically gifted to accomplish that purpose, how is what you were created to do from the beginning of time an act of volunteerism? Gift-based service is not an optional activity, but the activity for which we were created.

> For we are God's workmanship, created in Christ Jesus to do good works, which God prepared in advance for us to do.
>
> EPHESIANS 2:10

> You also, like living stones, are being built into a spiritual house to be a holy priesthood, offering spiritual sacrifices acceptable to God through Jesus Christ. . . .
>
> But you are a chosen people, a royal priesthood, a holy nation, a people belonging to God, that you may declare the praises of him who called you out of darkness into his wonderful light. Once you were not a people, but now you are the people of God; once you had not received mercy, but now you have received mercy. 1 PETER 2:5, 9–10

> The word of the LORD came to me, saying,
> "Before I formed you in the womb I knew you,
> before you were born I set you apart;
> I appointed you as a prophet to the nations."
>
> JEREMIAH 1:4–5

Imperative 3—We all have been given gifts to fulfill our calling.

As we use the gifts God has given us, we accomplish his will. Just as God's purpose for each of us is unique, so are the gifts he gives us.

> Each one should use whatever gift he has received to serve others, faithfully administering God's grace in its various forms. If anyone speaks, he should do it as one speaking the very words of God. If anyone serves, he should do it with the strength God provides, so that in all things God may be praised through Jesus Christ. To him be the glory and the power for ever and ever. Amen. 1 PETER 4:10–11

"People led by the Spirit of God give their world to God. When the Spirit leads you, your desires are to know and please God. Spirit-directed people gear their whole lifestyle and focus toward the purpose of God."

Michael Slaughter, *Real Followers: Beyond Virtual Christianity*

"Your ministry should be the natural outgrowth of who God made you to be.... Whenever you are evaluating your ministry effectiveness, remember: You are not the wrong person, you are the right person, and may be in the wrong position. You're a '10' ... somewhere!"

Bruce Bugbee, *What You Do Best in the Body of Christ*

For you created my inmost being;
    you knit me together in my mother's womb.
I praise you because I am fearfully and wonderfully made;
    your works are wonderful,
    I know that full well.
My frame was not hidden from you
    when I was made in the secret place.
When I was woven together in the depths of the earth,
    your eyes saw my unformed body.
All the days ordained for me
    were written in your book
    before one of them came to be.

PSALM 139:13–16

See also 1 Corinthians 12–14, as well as Exodus 35–40, which tells the story of the tremendous variety of gifts and skills the Israelites offered for the building of the tabernacle.

Imperative 4—Gifts are given not to be left idle, but to be used in community, to serve God and others.

The purpose of spiritual gifts is not to build up the individual, but to serve the community. Each of us grows in spiritual maturity as we use our gifts. God has a specific purpose for every person, and in using our gifts in service we glorify God and grow in relationship with him.

We don't seek our gifts with the attitude of "tell me my gifts so I can do what fulfills me most and thereby find my calling and my joy and say to everything else, 'I don't do windows.'" Gifts are given to serve the body of Christ, not to serve ourselves.

Just as each of us has one body with many members, and these members do not all have the same function, so in Christ we who are many form one body, and each member belongs to all the others. We have different gifts, according to the grace given us. If a man's gift is prophesying, let him use it in proportion to his faith. If it is serving, let him serve; if it is teaching, let him teach; if it is encouraging, let him encourage; if it is contributing to the needs of others, let him give generously; if it is leadership, let him govern diligently; if it is showing mercy, let him do it cheerfully.   ROMANS 12:4–8

There are different kinds of gifts, but the same Spirit. There are different kinds of service, but the same Lord. There are different kinds of working, but the same God works all of them in all men.

Now to each one the manifestation of the Spirit is given for the common good. To one there is given through the Spirit the message of wisdom, to another the message of knowledge by means of the same Spirit, to another faith by the same Spirit, to another gifts of healing by that one Spirit, to another miraculous powers, to another prophecy, to another distinguishing between spirits, to another speaking in different kinds of tongues, and to still another the interpretation of tongues. All these are the work of one and the same Spirit, and he gives them to each one, just as he determines.

The body is a unit, though it is made up of many parts; and though all its parts are many, they form one body. So it is with Christ. . . .

But in fact God has arranged the parts in the body, every one of them, just as he wanted them to be.

1 CORINTHIANS 12:4–12, 18

Each one should use whatever gift he has received to serve others, faithfully administering God's grace in its various forms. If anyone speaks, he should do it as one speaking the very words of God. If anyone serves, he should do it with the strength God provides, so that in all things God may be praised through Jesus Christ. To him be the glory and the power for ever and ever. Amen. 1 PETER 4:10–11

Jesus called them together and said, "You know that those who are regarded as rulers of the Gentiles lord it over them, and their high officials exercise authority over them. Not so with you. Instead, whoever wants to become great among you must be your servant, and whoever wants to be first must be slave of all. For even the Son of Man did not come to be served, but to serve, and to give his life as a ransom for many."

MARK 10:42–44

See also Matthew 25:14–30

Imperative 5—We more deeply understand our personal relationship with Christ as we serve in community.

We do not live to ourselves, but we are called to live in community. When we express the attitude that we could walk more closely with Christ if it weren't for "other people," we counter the very purpose of our commitment to Christ, namely, to love others as Christ has loved us. The Great Commandment and the Great Commission are based on the understanding that we are called to live in community, and our personal relationship with Christ must be grounded in the accountability, grace, patience, and love that only community can provide.

God uses the relationships, challenges, and joys of gift-based service to teach us about our relationship with him. Our walk with God is not about "me and my God," but about "us and our God."

"My command is this: Love each other as I have loved you. Greater love has no one than this, that he lay down his life for his friends. You are my friends if you do what I command. I no longer call you servants, because a servant does not know his master's business. Instead, I have called you friends, for everything that I learned from my Father I have made known to you. You did not choose me, but I chose you and appointed you to go and bear fruit—fruit that will last. Then the Father will give you whatever you ask in my name. This is my command: Love each other." JOHN 15:12–17

When they had finished eating, Jesus said to Simon Peter, "Simon son of John, do you truly love me more than these?"

"Yes, Lord," he said, "you know that I love you."

Jesus said, "Feed my lambs."

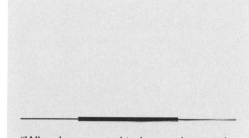

"Why do we need to know about spiritual gifts? First, we are told to be aware of them. Second, we are expected to use them. Third, we are stewards and will be held accountable for the use of our gifts."

Bruce Bugbee, *What You Do Best in the Body of Christ*

Again Jesus said, "Simon son of John, do you truly love me?"

He answered, "Yes, Lord, you know that I love you."

Jesus said, "Take care of my sheep."

The third time he said to him, "Simon son of John, do you love me?"

Peter was hurt because Jesus asked him the third time, "Do you love me?" He said "Lord, you know all things; you know that I love you."

Jesus said, "Feed my sheep."   JOHN 21:15–17

From [Christ] the whole body, joined and held together by every supporting ligament, grows and builds itself up in love, as each part does its work.   EPHESIANS 4:16

And let us consider how we may spur one another on toward love and good deeds. Let us not give up meeting together, as some are in the habit of doing, but let us encourage one another—and all the more as you see the Day approaching.

HEBREWS 10:24–25

Imperative 6—Real spiritual growth is activated as we serve others.

Spiritual growth involves many things, including Bible study, prayer, spiritual disciplines, the sacraments, fellowship, and worship. Yet, real spiritual growth is activated as we serve others.

Do not merely listen to the word, and so deceive yourselves. Do what it says. Anyone who listens to the word but does not do what it says is like a man who looks at his face in a mirror and, after looking at himself, goes away and immediately forgets what he looks like. But the man who looks intently into the perfect law that gives freedom, and continues to do this, not forgetting what he has heard, but doing it—he will be blessed in what he does. . . .

Religion that God our Father accepts as pure and faultless is this: to look after orphans and widows in their distress and to keep oneself from being polluted by the world. . . .

What good is it, my brothers, if a man claims to have faith but has no deeds? Can such faith save him? Suppose a brother or sister is without clothes and daily food. If one of you says to him, "Go, I wish you well; keep warm and well fed," but does nothing about his physical needs, what good is it? In the same way, faith by itself, if it is not accompanied by action, is dead.

JAMES 1:22–25, 27; 2:14–17

"Getting involved by using your gifts accelerates your spiritual growth immensely! God designed us that way. Don't head for the grandstands when you enter the Kingdom of God. Head for the playing field. That's where the excitement is. That's where the action is. But most of all, that's where our Coach is!"

Wayne Cordeiro,
Doing Church as a Team

BUILDERS' NOTE

A highly organized equipping ministry system does not necessarily ensure that the biblical connection between a person serving according to his or her gifts and a person growing in faith maturity is always seen. Even a heavy dose of Scripture at the front end of the program does not ensure that a participant understands the connection. It takes a proactive and ongoing effort to make sure that spiritual growth continues as a primary theme and is woven throughout the process and continually emphasized, even after a person is placed in ministry. Be sure to read chapter 15 for guidance on encouraging ongoing faith development through the process of reflection.

Imperative 7—The role of leaders in a church community is to equip others to use their gifts so that everyone can grow.

The twentieth-century church shifted away from a view of the leader as equipper to a view of the leader as manager/doer. In the twenty-first century God seems to be calling church leaders back to their primary role of equipping. This is, you must remember, not a new idea, but a return to the priority and purpose given to the first-century church leaders.

> It was he who gave some to be apostles, some to be prophets, some to be evangelists, and some to be pastors and teachers, to prepare God's people for works of service, so that the body of Christ may be built up until we all reach unity in the faith and in the knowledge of the Son of God and become mature, attaining to the whole measure of the fullness of Christ.
>
> Then we will no longer be infants, tossed back and forth by the waves, and blown here and there by every wind of teaching and by the cunning and craftiness of men in their deceitful scheming. Instead, speaking the truth in love, we will in all things grow up into him who is the Head, that is, Christ. From him the whole body, joined and held together by every supporting ligament, grows and builds itself up in love, as each part does its work. EPHESIANS 4:11–16

See also Exodus 18:13–23, as well as the "contractors' conference" at the end of the introduction (see pages 25–26).

> "A leader empowers others to serve. Jesus made extraordinary leaders out of ordinary people. He saw the potential within them, and he invested in their lives with the belief that God had something special in mind for them. As we embody the Spirit of Christ, we need to empower others to become all that God intends them to be. We need to give others opportunity to flourish under our guidance and love. We need to share the load with others who are gifted in areas where we are not as strong. We must express tangibly and intangibly that we affirm God's call on them and invest in them so that they utilize their gifts in meaningful ways. We dare not hold others back from the potential that is within them, planted there by God himself."
>
> Stephen Macchia, *Becoming a Healthy Church: 10 Characteristics*

WHAT IS CHANGING IN SOCIETY TO MAKE EQUIPPING MINISTRY MORE URGENT?

IN ADDITION TO KNOWING the timeless biblical principles that support equipping ministry, church leaders also must read the times in which they live in order to apply these principles in relevant ways. What is happening in the world that makes equipping ministry a more urgent imperative today?

This section examines a number of North American trends and considers the implications of each for the future of the church.

As the pace of change accelerates, many of the programs and methods the church has used during the last two centuries will become increasingly less effective. Some of the forecasted applications include the following:

- The "Sunday morning event" will continue to be important, but more and more of the church will be focused on how her members live out their faith in their communities and workplaces during the rest of the week.
- As those who attend church have increasing needs, there will be an increase of specialized ministries, requiring more nonpaid leaders to direct them.
- With a better educated church membership, we will see a move toward greater use of ministry teams and less hierarchical structures and fixed committee systems.

As you read about the following changes in society and in the church, what conclusions will you draw? How do these affect the urgency and importance of equipping ministry in your church?

> ... men of Issachar, who understood the times and knew what Israel should do . . ."
>
> 1 CHRONICLES 12:32

"North America is caught in the crack between what was and what is emerging. This crack began opening in 1960 and will close sometime around the year 2014. Trusted values held for centuries are falling into this crack, never to be seen again. Ideas and methodologies that once worked no longer achieve the desired results. This crack in our history is so enormous that it is causing a metamorphosis in every area of life. [The current years] are often called 'the hinge of history' or the transforming boundary between one age and another, between a scheme of things that has disintegrated and another that is taking shape."

Bill Easum,
Dancing with Dinosaurs: Ministry in a Hostile and Hurting World

Increased Needs in Society

Peter Drucker recently made the following observation: "When I arrived in America in the mid-1930s from Austria, America had a healthy society but an unhealthy economy. Today we seem to have a healthy economy, but an unhealthy society."

The Family

Increasing challenges are reducing the family's role as the central place in society where values are formed and children are equipped for life. This trend will mean that the role of the church and the educational system will take on a greater significance.

Some summary statistics are as follows:

- According to the 1994 census, 39 percent of children under the age of eighteen live in a home without a father. Approximately half of these haven't seen their father in the last year (*USA Today* 3/26/00).
- 4.2 million unmarried couples cohabited in 1998—compared with 439,000 in 1960 and up from 3 million in 1990. ("No longer undercover, living together is replacing marriage"—*USA Today* 4/18/00.)
- More than 80 percent of adults say marriage is a cherished institution, but the United States has the highest divorce rate in the world. The current divorce rate is averaged at 50 percent, and if separated couples are added, the percent rises to 66 to 70 percent.
- People living alone accounted for 83.2 percent of the 31.6 million nonfamily households.
- Approximately 12 million households have single parents—10 million with only a mother, 2 million with only a father—making up 32 percent of total households in the United States. This has increased by 10 percent since 1980.

Implications for Equipping Ministry

- People come to church with a greater number of basic relational, social, and personal needs that used to be met by healthy families. The old idea that one paid pastor could shepherd up to a hundred parishioners is obsolete. These deep and diverse needs will require more and more people in the church to pastor and care for each other.
- Small group leaders find that they often have to "re-parent" their members, requiring extensive time in counseling and relational training as part of their discipleship task. This often requires additional training, as well as resources that go beyond the traditional small group curriculum.
- People come to church in order to have a much greater variety of needs met than what can be met through Sunday morning and Wednesday evening events. This often requires people, facility, and money resources to be directed toward more of a seven-day-a-week program, thus requiring many more nonpaid leaders for additional programs.
- Churches that understand these needs have great potential to become primary centers of community health. Not many other structures in society are as effective as the church is in building

CONTRACTORS' CONFERENCE

Consider these questions as your church begins to focus her vision for equipping ministry:

1. What is the most compelling Bible passage for encouraging your leadership team to increase attention to equipping ministry?

2. Which of the biblical principles supporting equipping ministry is the most personally motivating or convicting as you consider your own ministry?

3. Which of these principles should be emphasized in your teaching as you encourage your congregation toward intentional caring for people in the body of Christ through greater involvement and gift-based service?

4. What are some of the necessary biblical components of an equipping ministry system based on these principles? How can these principles be clearly integrated and communicated in whatever system you build?

5. As you implement equipping ministry in your church, how can you ensure that, along with finding members to meet ministry needs, you emphasize the importance of personal spiritual growth through service?

healthy families and creating "villages" of families for those who don't have their own healthy families. While these needs place an increased burden on the church, at the same time numerous opportunities are opened up for the Christian message of eternal salvation to be expressed in a context of a Christ-centered model of compassionate behavior.

The Workplace

- Both men and women spend a growing amount of time in the workplace. As the strength of local communities diminishes and extended families are increasingly scattered throughout different cities, the workplace provides a growing means of primary social contact. At the same time, companies have found that providing a work environment where employees can thrive and a culture that values people more holistically gives them an advantage in retaining valuable employees. The generalized topic of spirituality is no longer off-limits in many workplaces, but is allowed or even encouraged.
- Of the 30.5 million married-couple families in the labor force, 94 percent have both husband and wife employed.

Implications for Equipping Ministry

- Churches with strong equipping ministries often help people discern their gifts in ways that not only apply to church or community service, but also to marketplace work that is best aligned with their gifts and motivations. Doing so helps them advance in their careers. More important, it provides specific connections to help people see how their work can be an act of worship, as they recognize God as the source of what they do. A strong equipping ministry extends the church's ministry beyond her walls to hundreds of workplaces that would never be touched otherwise by church programs.
- Strong equipping ministries often organize people into groups that meet throughout the week—groups organized by work location or common industry, management level, or expertise. This provides a means to explore with peers how their faith interacts with the specific ethical challenges of their work and encourages them to see their work as ongoing ministry.

Decreased Biblical Literacy

While general literacy has increased, biblical literacy has steadily declined, even among those raised within the church. Readership of the Bible has declined from 73 percent in the 1980s to 59 percent today. And the percentage of frequent readers (those who read the Bible at least once a week) has decreased slightly over the last decade, from 40 percent in 1990 to 37 percent today. People with more education are less likely to think that the Bible is a comprehensive guide to life than are the less educated. Forty-six percent of those with a postgraduate degree say the Bible answers basic life questions, compared to 72 percent of those with a high school education or less (Gallup Poll on the Web at www.gallup.com).

Implications for Equipping Ministry

- Churches cannot assume that people understand the biblical reasons for gift-based service, the fundamental elements of discipleship, or even some of the basic tenets of the Christian faith. To address the diverse needs of a Sunday morning audience, many sermons must aim toward the "middle ground" of the audience and assume at least a certain basic biblical knowledge. As a result, many people will fall through the cracks unless the church provides targeted programs for those who need this basic biblical knowledge. Often an equipping process can provide defined pathways for people to systematically increase their biblical knowledge, along with a tracking system to help church leaders encourage them to take the next step.

- Adult learning has shifted much more to application-oriented learning. New Christians who are not used to older styles of classroom-heavy Christian education provide fresh enthusiasm for new styles of discipleship that interlace knowledge and application of that knowledge. Equipping ministry provides an excellent process for both intellectual learning and heart application through service.

Increased Volunteerism

- 49 percent of respondents (93 million adults) to the 1996 Gallup Survey donated an average of 4.2 hours per week.
- Overall, 109 million adults volunteered in 1998, donating a total of 19.9 billion hours. This is a 13.7 percent increase over 1995 in the number of volunteers, but a 2 percent decrease in the number of volunteer hours contributed. The average wage for volunteers used for calculating the current 1998 value is $14.30 per hour.
- The hours donated by volunteers to formal organizations represent the equivalent of 9.3 million full-time employees, with a value of $225.9 billion.
- 90 percent of individuals volunteered when asked; only 22.3 percent of those who volunteered did so without being asked. (Those who are asked to volunteer do so at a rate roughly four times of those who are not asked.)
- 42 percent of volunteers found out about volunteer activities through personal contact, while 35 percent participated through an organization.
- Among those who reported that one or both of their parents had set an example and volunteered while they were young, 69 percent reported volunteering as adults and 75 percent reported having made charitable contributions.
- Volunteers continued to make larger financial contributions than nonvolunteers, giving over two-and-a-half times more on average.
- 46 percent of Hispanics volunteered—a 6 percent increase since 1995; 47 percent of African-Americans volunteered—a 12 percent increase since 1995.

(Statistical information gleaned from various sources.)

Implications for Equipping Ministry

- Busy people do have time to volunteer and will do so if they are asked well and organized well, and if they have the sense that they are making a contribution to needs about which they care. For the church to compete against many sophisticated volunteer causes, the church must organize herself well and continue to build into the lives of her people.

- The contributions made through people's time commitments to the church are substantial, but often overlooked. As a church grows in her ability to recognize people's contributions, she will increase the ownership and commitment levels of people who serve.

- In many communities the majority of volunteers in various agencies and programs attend local churches, yet their service is not always directly connected to local churches. Part of the reason why faith-based volunteers are so attractive to community agencies is that churches often provide the "faith teaching" that encourages people to volunteer, both inside the church and elsewhere. Those who attend churches with strong equipping ministries come to community agencies prequalified, because their passion for service is well known, their gifts are finely tuned, and their base of relational and spiritual support is strong. Equipping ministries that do a good job of preparing the church's internal programs to receive, train, equip, and recognize volunteers are often invited to do the same for community agencies.

- In several cities, churches with strong equipping ministries collaborate with other agencies on city-renewal projects, as they take what they've learned inside the church walls and apply it to service in the community.

- Finally, as noted in the statistic above, people who give of their time also give of their finances.

Halftime

An increasing number of people are reaching financial independence at a young age; at the same time, because of medical advances, they are expecting to live productive lives into their 80s. As a result, they may have thirty or forty prime working years left (without much need to make money), during which they choose to dedicate themselves to cause-oriented work. Often these people have high levels of skill development and experience. Yet, if a church limits her vision to her own internal programs, often these people are not excited or motivated by the "smallness" of the cause. But if a church is able to see the huge opportunities for local and world missions, these people can often be engaged to lead colossal efforts never before dreamed possible by a local church.

Bob Buford, founding chairman of
Leadership Network and author of *Halftime*

Implications for Equipping Ministry

The increased emotional, role, and time demands of ministry today brought about by the increased needs of church members make it easy for paid church staff people to burn out. And then when you add the huge scope of increased opportunities made available because of the effects of globalism, technology, and "halftime" revitalization, it is impossible for paid staff members to provide what is needed. If a church is to take advantage of these unprecedented opportunities, she must bring more skilled leaders into positions of significant commitment and responsibility than what any church budget can support. Equipping ministry is designed to do just this.

Welfare Reform and Charitable Choice

Writing in *The Wall Street Journal* (July 28, 1999), Gerald Seib made this significant observation: "There is a growing body of evidence to show that faith-based social services are, in fact, often more effective than non-faith-based social services in certain areas."

The United States Welfare Reform Act of 1996 transferred some of the federal government's authority for specific welfare programs to state and local governments. The Welfare Reform Act included a "charitable choice" provision designed to allow faith-based organizations and churches to be able to compete for state welfare funding at an equal level with secular groups for several specific welfare programs. Religious groups have the right to maintain a religious environment by displaying religious art, Scripture, religious apparel, and other symbols—items that previously had to be removed if the organization received federal funding. Charitable choice also protects a church's right to maintain a clear faith-based mission, including hiring practices that are limited to people who espouse their faith. The law prohibits faith-based groups from using state money to pay for worship services, sectarian instruction, or "proselytizing"—a term the law doesn't define.

While churches have been the backbone of charitable services in many communities, this opened up a new era of collaboration between churches and government welfare initiatives. Perhaps for the first time in decades, there is now widespread recognition that government-only initiatives are more effective when delivered in collaboration with local communities—especially churches that have a long-standing tradition in the community of providing holistic services to help meet people's economic, physical, emotional, and spiritual needs. Not only does government funding open up new service opportunities for churches, but it can also increase credibility with many nonchurched people, who become open to the spiritual message as they see the church involved in authentic and widespread charitable action.

Charitable choice also raises new challenges, as churches learn how to work with often debilitating bureaucratic decision processes and policies, untested legal definitions, and risks that come with being overly dependent on resources tied to the changing whims of government policies.

Implications for Equipping Ministry

- Churches will have to develop new capacities to deal with government entities, collaborating with other churches and agencies to create "mediating agencies" with specialized knowledge of government rules and with greater economies of scale.
- To take advantage of the new opportunities of charitable choice without being overwhelmed by the challenges, churches will need to greatly increase their ability to mobilize people to serve. For churches that can mobilize the necessary resources to take advantage of charitable choice, their stature in the community as a center for community health and holistic service can greatly increase. Equipping ministry provides the necessary foundation for this type of resource mobilization.

Gangs

Gangs and crimes committed by gang members are now pervasive in numerous American cities, presenting a challenge to law enforcement. A

National Institute of Justice (NIJ)–sponsored survey of metropolitan police departments in the 79 largest United States cities showed that in spring 1992 all but 7 of these cities were troubled by gangs, as were all but 5 departments in 43 smaller cities. In 110 jurisdictions where gang activity was reported, the survey found that over the previous twelve-month period there were . . .

- 249,324 gang members
- 4,881 gangs
- 46,359 gang-related crimes
- 1,072 gang-related homicides

(Statistics can be found on the Web at www.communitypolicing.org.)

Addiction

- According to a 1997 National Institute on Drug Abuse report, heroin use among American high school seniors was 100 percent higher than it was from 1990 to 1996 (*American Foundation of Addiction Research* on the Web at www.addictionresearch.com).
- In 1999 an estimated 3.6 million Americans (1.6 percent of the total population age 12 and older) were dependent on illicit drugs. An estimated 8.2 million Americans were dependent on alcohol (3.7 percent). Of these, 1.5 million people were dependent on both. Overall, an estimated 10.3 million people were dependent on either alcohol or illicit drugs (4.7 percent). (*Substance Abuse and Mental Health Services Administration* on the Web at www.samhsa.gov).

Abuse and Domestic Violence

- The Department of Health and Human Services released a survey estimating that child abuse and neglect in the United States nearly doubled during the seven years between 1986 and 1993 (see the Web site at www.prevent-abuse-now.com).
- From 1983 to 1991 the number of domestic violence reports received in the state of New York increased by almost 117 percent (according to the NYS Division of Criminal Justice Services, comparing 1983 statistics with 1991 statistics).

Increased Cases of Depression, Anxiety, and Stress

- Up to 20 percent of Americans will experience clinical depression at some time during their life. It is estimated that one out of six will experience some type of debilitating anxiety, such as panic attacks and obsessive-compulsive disorder (as observed by Dr. Timothy Clinton, American Association of Christian Counselors).
- Nearly 30 million persons in this country seek help for anxiety and depressive disorders (cited in R. L. DuPont, D. P. Rice, L. S. Miller, et al., "Economic Costs of Anxiety Disorders," *Anxiety* 2, 1996).
- Anxiety is epidemic in our culture (quoted by Dr. Archibald D. Hart, *Christian Counseling Today*, vol. 8, no. 4, 2000).

Troubled Teens

- In 1998 suicide ranked as the third-largest killer of teens (*U.S.A. Suicide Summary: 1998 Official Final Data*).

- Student fighting is perceived to be rising. Fully two-thirds of students (66 percent) say fights among students at their schools are a "very big" or "fairly big" problem. This is a sizable increase over 1999, when 52 percent of teens perceived a "very big" or "fairly big" problem with student fights. One-fifth of teens (20 percent) report that they were in a physical fight during the past year. This figure is down from the comparable period two years ago, when 23 percent of teens reported that they took part in a physical fight (Gallup Poll on the Web at www.gallup.com).
- According to the National Crime Victimization Survey (NCVS—a national barometer of crime trends), in 1997 juveniles under age eighteen were involved in 27 percent of all serious violent victimizations, including 14 percent of sexual assaults, 30 percent of robberies, and 27 percent of aggravated assaults (adapted from Howard Snyder and Melissa Sickmund, "Juvenile Offenders and Victims: 1999 National Report" [Washington, D.C.: The Office of Juvenile Justice and Delinquency Prevention, 1999], 63).

Implications for Equipping Ministry

What Christianity has to offer in terms of providing holistic help for people's economic, social, emotional, relational, and spiritual needs will increasingly be desired and valued if offered in a relevant way that doesn't diminish God's power to change lives. Neither the social gospel (physical help detached from spiritual help) nor the propositional gospel (a call for decision without demonstrating care for physical needs) will be where most of the advances will be made. Many church leaders will be treading on new ground as they develop fresh ways to address people's needs for a restored relationship with God through Jesus Christ, while at the same time addressing the need to restore people's economic and social lives.

To meet this challenge, the church will have to employ many of the gifts of her people—including high-capacity, highly educated people who have the kind of corporate experience, wealth, and professional training that has often been overlooked or underchallenged by service opportunities within the church's internal programs.

Decreasing Influence of Christianity in Forming Social Values

Christianity is no longer the dominant belief in the United States in the way it once was. The church, once the center of family and community life, competes for attention in a secular world filled with work, television, athletics, school, recreation, and other events. The percentage of the "unchurched" and "less churched" continues to grow.

Additionally, we are witnessing the increasing influence of other religions, life philosophies, and "spiritual" answers on the North American landscape. Secularization is continuing to remove many of the historic practices and evidences of Christianity from government, education, and other civil arenas. Islam has taken a strong hold in many inner cities. Various types of Americanized Buddhism provide a loose philosophy that is woven throughout business management principles, health practices, and much of popular culture.

Implications for Equipping Ministry

People are less likely to attend church for reasons of social convention, which means that more of the church's work will take place outside

"Churches see themselves as separate islands in a secular society. [Yet, in reality] they are organs of the larger society to do the social (human) job. It is the foundational job for everything else. It is their job to raise the vision and the sense of purpose for the community."

Peter Drucker, at the
Drucker Foundation Annual
Conference, October, 2000

- Only 51 percent of adults who attend Christian churches agreed that revival was the top challenge facing the church. One implication of this finding is that the job of motivating and mobilizing the laity to contribute to revival efforts may be more difficult than pastors might have otherwise expected (1998 research).
- 35 percent of Christians versus 57 percent of non-Christians said that to get by in life these days, sometimes you have to bend the rules for your own benefit (1997 research).
- 50 percent of Christians versus 25 percent of non-Christians said that there are moral truths which are unchanging, that truth is not relative to the circumstances (1997 research).

(Statistics from the
George Barna Institute
on the Internet at www.barna.org.)

"The future church will have to be even more intentional in the formation of its laity. Living in the world's ambiguous environment and attempting to act faithfully there, every church member is on the front line. . . . Laypeople in an uncertain environment will be called on for independent decision and action. Memorized answers will not be enough. Every local congregation will be called on to develop processes and programs to support laity on a lifelong basis."

Loren Mead,
The Once and Future Church

"If you are over the age of 40, you are an immigrant in a world that is changing so fast that you are no longer a citizen with the dominant worldview."

Leonard Sweet,
at Leadership Network's "Exploring off the Map" event, May, 2000

A popular illustration of the difference between modernism and postmodernism is seen in how a baseball umpire calls balls and strikes:

Modern: "I calls 'em as I sees 'em, and I sees 'em as they are."

Postmodern: "They ain't nothing until I calls 'em."

her buildings and outside her formal programs. The people of the church will assume a greater role as lifestyle evangelists, shepherds, administrators, and leaders as the work of the church moves into the community. As a result, there will be fewer "come to the church and do it" programs and more "we'll train you to go be with them" programs.

Change of Worldview from Modern to Postmodern and Beyond

Many historians have divided human history into two widely held macro worldviews. Today we are in the midst of a transition to a possible third macro worldview.

Supernatural Worldview

The supernatural worldview is sometimes labeled "premodernism," because for most of human history prior to the seventeenth century, people believed that gods or other supernatural beings caused the events that happened around them. Often the priest, medicine man, shaman, or other religious figure translated meaning out of what people experienced or could not understand on their own. For Christians, God's revelation preceded and served as the foundation for understanding.

During the Enlightenment in the seventeenth and eighteenth centuries, these long-standing beliefs were questioned and eventually overturned as the dominant way of thought in the Western world. People began to question if kings truly had a "divine right" to rule. Philosophers and scientists questioned if gods were the cause of all that we experience. As people began to rebel against the excesses of those in power during the previous age and to question the assumptions on which this age was built, a new way of thinking emerged. Divine revelation was replaced by human reason, and people undertook a search for certainty.

Rationalistic Worldview

What emerged out of the questionings of the seventeenth and eighteenth centuries has been labeled "modernism." It holds a belief that what we experience is caused by forces that are knowable—forces called "natural laws." These laws can be discovered by the five senses and understood by the human intellect. Human logic and the scientific method are the primary tools of understanding.

Postmodernism

Beginning in the mid-twentieth century in obscure philosophical writings and in fields such as art and architecture, then moving to the arenas of academic literary criticism and popular culture, a reaction emerged against the over-two-hundred-year rule of modernism. This reaction is called "postmodernism." Many historians believe we are still in a pendulum swing or "antithesis to the modern thesis." They characterize postmodernism as defining itself by means of its critique of the excesses of modernism. As this shift reaches the "tipping point" of popular culture, we are seeing in our lifetime a shift of a magnitude not experienced since three hundred years ago. What will eventually emerge as a dominant worldview may determine much of our world's thinking during the twenty-first century.

Modern Worldview	Postmodern Worldview
Determinism—all things are caused by knowable natural laws.	Knowledge is uncertain—no foundational laws exist.
Rationalism—we can discover natural laws through human rational processes and logic or through objective scientific study, and by using the five senses (empiricism).	Everyone has cultural and personal biases, so reason cannot be truly objective. Discoveries are made not simply through reason, but through other means such as intuition, emotional intelligence, and the like.
Reductionism—objectivity and precision can be attained in understanding complexities such as human behavior, social patterns, spiritual phenomena, and the like.	All-inclusive systems of explanation are impossible. Reducing complexity into understandable parts limits understanding of the whole.
Naturalism—what is real is limited to what can be observed in nature.	What is real is beyond observation. Certainty is not attainable.
Words have an inherent meaning that can be used to convey a common "absolute" truth from the speaker to the hearer.	**Deconstruction**—language is not objective. The meaning of a statement is the meaning that the hearer finds in it.
Individualism—an individual can find truth by means of his or her own efforts.	The idea that the isolated individual can find knowledge is replaced by community-based knowledge.

Neither modernism nor postmodernism is inherently Christian or anti-Christian. They simply describe the sea of cultural beliefs in which today's church lives. Currently, the postmodern worldview is dominating television, movies, music, and other media. It exerts a strong influence over education, commerce, and politics. To stop a worldview transition of this magnitude is like an ant stopping a locomotive. Yet, the forces of history are under God's control, and we can be confident that God has a plan for how the church will speak clearly the message of Christianity in this age, just as she has done in previous ages.

Since we live in an age of transitioning worldviews, it is important to understand what we must do to be the church anchored with a timeless purpose in a world in massive transition. The church rises above these changes but must speak and live in the midst of them with relevance. This creates huge challenges for church leaders—and it opens up opportunities for equipping ministry to provide critical help.

Implications for Equipping Ministry

The range of effective communication will increasingly be limited unless extended through diverse communities of age, background, ethnicity, experience, and interests. Sermons will increasingly be viewed skeptically by postmodern audiences, who cry out, "Tell me the story, and let our community draw our own conclusion rather than you forcing your all-inclusive conclusion on us." Equipping more and more Christians who live in these communities and can express the Christian message in these relationships will require more equipping of people for ministry in their environment.

People are searching for spiritual solutions, not in the sophistication of the logic but in the centeredness and authenticity of the community that

> "The world has reached a major watershed in its history, equal in importance to the turn from the Middle Ages to the Renaissance. It will demand from us a spiritual blaze; we shall have to rise to a new height of vision, to a new level of life."
>
> Alexander Solzhenitsyn

Pluralism—the emergence of new political, economic, and cultural groupings built around new affinities (such as, ethnicity, ideology, philosophy, politics, economy, religion, style), and the resulting competition for influence and power without an agreed-upon common standard.

CONTRACTORS' CONFERENCE

Changes in Our World

Discuss the evidence of the above-mentioned trends in your lives and community.

1. Which trends most affect your church? What evidence do you see of the effect of these trends in your own life, your community, and your church?

2. Can you identify other trends affecting your church that are not addressed in this section?

3. Which of these trends most excite you because of the opportunities they bring to your church?

4. Which of the implications for equipping ministry seem to be most important for your church? What are the points of urgency, if any, for increasing your commitment to equipping ministry?

5. Are there any specific trends that particularly affect your church that must be at the forefront of consideration as you build an effective equipping ministry?

holds a particular spiritual viewpoint. The apologetic, or "persuasion to faith," of the future will be increasingly less word oriented and more relational and action oriented. In this environment, where any one individual's range of personal relevance becomes lessened, the role of church leaders as the equippers of others to do ministry rather than doing ministry themselves becomes critical. The Sunday sermon is still vital, to be sure, but more as a means to equip the internal culture and community and less as a "one-to-masses" communication of argument and application.

Globalism

Globalism is a word that describes the removal of significant physical, economic, cultural, political, and technological barriers, with the result that there is significantly increased global interaction and the beginning of an enhanced global identity. Globalism means that more and more people in the church are daily, weekly, and monthly speaking with people of other nations or traveling to other countries. More and more people of other nationalities are a part of the local community of the church. Never has the spread of the Christian message had fewer geographic and communication obstacles.

Technology

Technology has opened new doors of communication, training, and economics that were impossible to imagine a very short time ago. Beyond even the impact that building the system of Roman roads had on the spread of the first-century church, the Internet provides the potential to spread the gospel to every culture on the globe.

WHAT IS CHANGING IN THE CHURCH TO MAKE EQUIPPING MINISTRY MORE URGENT?

- Is equipping ministry just another fad, or is it a major and lasting transformation that affects many aspects of the church?
- Equipping is not a new topic for the church. After decades of books and teachings on gifts assessment, volunteer management, small groups, and leadership development, what is different now?

Changes and Trends in the Lives of Church Attenders

Lifestyles of Churchgoers

People who attend church are busier than ever before and face more crises in their lives through such things as multiple careers, job transfers, forced retirements, and second careers; divorces, single parenting, and blended families; chronic illness and losses; and aging parents and returning children. They are therefore less willing to make open-ended commitments to serve without ensuring that their own personal needs are addressed.

Implications for Equipping Ministry

Crises and busy schedules actually present an opportunity for a well-run equipping ministry system. Interviewers and ministry mentors who have been trained to identify the needs and expectations of today's churchgoers can initiate a dialogue for ongoing faith development and support. An effective interview enables the person to share personal crises, as well as to examine skills and talents for possible ministry. People need ongoing

---

My church's Web site contains a Bible that is delivered to my computer monitor in the form of bits. Bits weigh nothing. They have no physical measurements. Our Bible is in six different languages and four different translations. . . .

I am planning a trip to China. I know better than to carry a dozen Bibles into that country in the form of atoms; they will be stopped at customs. . . . Think about the same information in the form of bits. Bits fly around the world without regard to borders or politics. It is estimated by authoritative sources that close to four million Chinese are now on-line. If you add Internet cafés in China I suspect that twenty million people in China might have access to the Internet. Chances are slim that we can get twenty million Chinese Bibles in atoms delivered anytime soon; however, those Bibles are already there in bits!

Walter Wilson, *The Internet Church*

On a Sunday morning, ask people to raise their hand (and keep it raised) if they've been overseas since last Sunday. Then ask those who have talked by phone to someone overseas to raise their hand; again, ask anyone who has written or received an e-mail or a fax from outside the country or visited a Web site located in another country to raise their hand. Then ask people who have talked to a person of a different nationality in your community to raise their hand. Finally, ask people who have used a product or service from another country to raise their hand. As you look around, you will no doubt be facing a sea of hands. This exercise provides a visible demonstration that almost every church member today is a "foreign" missionary, whether he or she realizes it or not.

☑ CHECKPOINT

What do members expect when they serve? An opportunity to . . .

- find personal fulfillment
- meet targeted growth objectives
- meet specific, personal needs
- build relationships
- make a difference in the lives of those served or a cause championed
- use their unique gifts and talents in a meaningful way
- fill gaps in life plans and expectations
- schedule service around the competing demands of work, family, and personal obligations
- be invited to continue
- be equipped as needed in order to succeed

When people serve in your church, do you consider their needs when you design ministry opportunities? How do you balance the needs of the person with the needs of the church?

"In the absence of community, a church might easily become a high-octane, crusade-driven ministry, or it can fall victimized by entropy and end up becoming a 'keeper of traditions.' Community is the life, the gel that fuses hearts together."

Wayne Cordeiro,
Doing Church as a Team

support and nurturing as they cautiously test the waters of Christian service and grow spiritually through ministering to others.

New Patterns of Giving

In the midst of materialistic lifestyles, increased numbers of direct-mail appeals and telephone solicitations, and highly visible scandals among Christian leaders, we are seeing a marked tendency to give less money to causes to which a person has no direct connection. People give their discretionary dollars where they give their discretionary time. The independent sector has found that persons actively engaged in voluntary service consistently give an average of three to four times the amount given by persons not engaged in voluntary service.

Implications for Equipping Ministry

Increased involvement earns people's ownership and their excitement about giving to a cause in which they can also serve. An additional benefit of meaningful equipping ministry is numerical growth. Retention of church members is increased if they are meaningfully involved in the ministries of the church and community. Involved members generally come to know and trust the decision makers, increasing the likelihood that they will stay and invest their energy and their resources in the church body for the long term.

A Quest for Community

Because our neighborhoods are characterized by constant turnover and our extended family members often live hundreds of miles away, people are looking for places where they can quickly establish community with others who share common values. Many see the church as the primary source of community for themselves and their children.

Implications for Equipping Ministry

An equipping ministry system designed to allow people to serve in groups provides a strong basis for friendships and community—a basis that surpasses the teamwork needed to accomplish a task. Many churches are combining an emphasis on small groups with a focus on lay involvement. Gifts assessment in a group setting increases self-knowledge for individuals and also provides mirrors of self-identity often absent to individuals who have not grown up in stable families. Likewise, family programs designed to incorporate assessment instruments facilitate positive communication, thereby strengthening families to work together in service projects.

New Patterns of Learning and Growth

With the plethora of new educational materials now available, many churches are responding to the overload of "head knowledge" by developing learning approaches that utilize more experiential styles of education. Members want training that will help them apply their faith in life situations, and they are looking to the church to help them examine their life experiences, set personal and spiritual growth goals, and establish career objectives.

Implications for Equipping Ministry

Equipping ministry provides a laboratory for Christian living. How can the experiences encountered in working in a soup kitchen for the

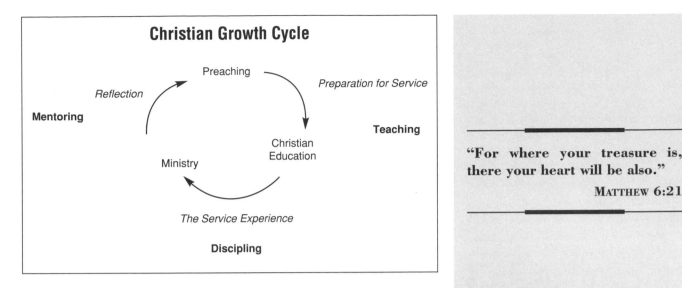

Christian Growth Cycle

Preaching

Reflection

Preparation for Service

Mentoring

Teaching

Christian
Education

Ministry

The Service Experience

Discipling

homeless be grounded in Scripture? When Jesus admonishes Peter to "feed my sheep" (John 21:17) in response to Peter's assertion of his love for Jesus, what does that directive mean to us in our daily lives? Ministry is where faith can become active in love, where head knowledge can be felt, seen, touched, and known.

The Need to Simplify

Corporate America, as well as the volunteer and public sectors, have witnessed the trend toward "downsizing" and "reengineering." Some churches face declining membership due to changing neighborhoods and consequently must downsize. In other growing churches the trend toward "excellence" in the 1980s caused congregations to expect increasing quality in programming. These same churches are now looking for ways to refocus on core issues. Downsizing in these churches often means reducing the quantity of programs, placing a greater emphasis on small groups, and maintaining quality services without producing the expectation that a youth ministry event needs to be in the same league as a rock concert in order to be considered successful, or that each Sunday must be bigger and better than the last.

Implications for Equipping Ministry

Strategically use an equipping ministry system by placing it at the core of the church's effort to simplify and gain focus. A well-run system spreads out the tasks and enhances commitment through manageable pieces of work within people's areas of interest and calling. Through intentional discovery and connection processes, each person better understands his or her gifts and is encouraged both to serve in an area of talent and interest and to be served.

When joined with a churchwide commitment to simplify, members are set free to focus on fewer activities and can develop deeper relationships in the midst of their service.

Twenty-First-Century Church Shifts

- From institution to mission
- From program to purpose
- From decision to disciple
- From doer to equipper

> "For where your treasure is, there your heart will be also."
>
> MATTHEW 6:21

> "Equipping is a fundamental change for professional clergy. Most have been trained to enable and to perform ministry for the congregation. Becoming an equipper is difficult, but those clergy who do not make this change will continue to experience burnout, stress, confusion, and a lack of success in helping people develop spiritually. . . . Leadership today is more about creating an environment than it is what you're teaching. It's in the giving of one's life to a mission that the growth really begins to happen. If you don't have the mission, you won't have the passion. . . .
>
> Life metaphors are the sum total of all that we've experienced in our lifetime. Anything other than Jesus Christ that becomes a sacred cow is almost always the metaphor that is going to keep you from being the kind of leader God called you to be."
>
> Bill Easum, *Dancing with Dinosaurs: Ministry in a Hostile and Hurting World*

> As a new movement of God is revealed, we more fully understand the purpose of a previous one. A watershed is occurring on the church landscape. We've spent the last two decades bringing more and more people into the church. We'll spend the next two decades deploying them back out.

> "Ministry is about living out one's faith. Church business seldom has anything to do with faith in God's work."
>
> Bill Easum, *Sacred Cows Make Gourmet Burgers*

> "The healthy church encourages believers to grow in their walks with God and with one another in the context of a safe, affirming environment."
>
> Stephen Macchia, *Becoming a Healthy Church: 10 Characteristics*

- From single leader to leadership team
- From denomination to local church
- From in-church concerns to community concerns

Be sure to consider this key question: How would these shifts be influenced by a church adopting a value and a mind-set of equipping?

Changes in Church Programs

Church Growth

Church growth was a major emphasis during the 1980s. The burning question was, "How do we make the church more relevant to the world around us and as a result see more unchurched people attend?" By the early 1990s many of the church leaders who were most successful at church growth realized that they had a crowd, but not a church. Many people would come, but they wouldn't stay long, or perhaps they'd never move beyond merely attending worship on Sunday morning. What's more, a change in senior pastor or worship leader often had a huge effect on attendance.

As a result, we began to hear more and more about church health. The burning question became, "How do we move people toward more involvement in the church and more progress in their spiritual growth?" Much of today's renewed emphasis on equipping ministry comes out of this shift in emphasis.

Implications for Equipping Ministry

No matter what approach people use to intentionally move people through various steps of discipleship, community, and service, an equipping system must be built to support the effort. Churches have repeatedly stated that they have too often jumped on board with a particular program, curriculum, or gifts assessment only to have to start over because they hadn't built the foundation of the teams, communication networks, and leadership development that make up an equipping ministry system.

Church Health

You can define church health in a variety of ways, from providing an intentional path of moving people to greater levels of Christian growth to a whole checklist of various characteristics needed throughout the church. Each of these lists always includes an element of lay mobilization, volunteer service, or spiritual gifts understanding.

Churches are finding, however, that if the first two or three steps of an intentional growth path emphasize the acquisition of knowledge, they have much less success in later steps when they ask people to make a commitment to changes in lifestyle, in actions, or in stewardship of their resources. Classroom programs are much easier to organize, and a church can more easily develop leaders for small group programs that focus on interactive teaching. Yet, starting with a knowledge priority, the discipleship process can create an early expectation that the crux of discipleship is knowledge acquisition. Often the next step is defined as "signing up" for another class. When the next step finally results in "becoming involved in ministry," some may feel that the game has been changed, and they may resist.

In other cases, while there may be excellent communication of the next steps of a growth plan, there are no systems of leaders, mentors, coaches, and small groups to help people take that next step. Most people are not self-starters and need help to progress along the path. A chart in a church newsletter and strong statements from the pulpit may inspire the minority who are already good at taking knowledge and moving to application on their own. The rest will know that they are supposed to do something, but they may fall through the cracks for lack of application assistance.

Implications for Equipping Ministry

An equipping ministry system is designed to overcome these challenges by creating a network of leaders and communication that undergirds every program and allows application-oriented discipleship to operate from the beginning.

The point of *church growth* is not to use church programs as a way to collect new people and put them in cages. The goal of *church health* is not to fatten church members for display at the county fairgrounds. The church exists to *equip* people in order to release them back into the world, grounded in truth and in genuine community, "dangerous" for the cause of the gospel.

Worship

For much of the 1980s and early 1990s, many churches embarked on a transition to contemporary styles of worship. Many mistakenly measured the quality of worship by the quality of the music, the degree to which they created an emotional experience, or the ability to draw crowds. What resulted was a mistaken understanding that worship was an event rather than an attitude, mind-set, and lifestyle. Instead of feeling empowered to worship throughout the week in the family, community, and workplace, people began to see Sunday morning as the "weekly fix" they needed in order to be able to truly worship God.

Today many churches are asking the questions "How can we empower our people to worship God throughout the week?" and "How do we create an event on Sunday that inspires our people to pay attention to God's presence in *every* setting?" Even liturgical churches are exploring how the liturgy and the sacraments can have meaning in weeklong reflection and anticipation. In each case a participatory environment is created on Sunday morning, drawing people into the life and work of the congregation, then continuing in a seamless flow to equip them throughout the week.

Implications for Equipping Ministry

Strong equipping ministry provides service with reflection, communities of relationships with each other and with God, and connections of learning that drive the message and the experience of Sunday morning into weeklong application.

Small Groups

The movement toward small groups originally developed as a way to increase the church's ability to provide pastoral care, nurture, interactive Bible teaching, and fellowship. Yet, over time an intense focus on the internal needs of the small group can result in an unhealthy and isolated clique mentality. Many small group ministries are shifting the emphasis toward seeing small groups as a launch pad for the formation of other groups and for evangelism or gift-based ministry opportunities.

"The point is not to get people to work, but to help them connect to the story of Jesus Christ. Our job is to develop a system of meaning and recognition that leads to a personal legacy."

Michael Foss, senior pastor, Prince of Peace Lutheran Church, Burnsville, Minnesota

"The movement of Christ is a movement of reconciliation. God is putting together a new community known as the body of Christ. It's more about connections than attendance. To join, you don't attend so much as you connect. It's not even about believing in Jesus so much as being in Jesus."

Michael Slaughter, *Real Followers: Beyond Virtual Christianity*

Proactive Cousins: Three Ways to Reach the Same Goal

A relatively small percentage of people have the gifts to develop their own path to a goal. Most people need help to establish a path to reach their goals. They need a clear statement of "what is the next step for me?" and a way to keep track of their progress along the way. What tends to happen in many churches is that people have difficulty applying the truths of the sermon to their lives. Values such as community building, discipleship, and gift-based service may be clearly preached, but without a pathway for implementation, these values may not be translated into actions. In these cases, the church begins to feel stagnant and people get used to listening to sermons without knowing what their next step should be in response to God's Word.

In the last fifteen years, three movements (the "proactive cousins") have begun to address this problem in different areas of the church. All three start with the basic assumption that people need a clear path in order to reach their goals. Also, all three movements strive for a healthy balance of community, discipleship, and equipping ministry.

COMMUNITY

Carl George developed a paradigm called "the MetaChurch," which provides clear steps for new member assimilation and progress toward small group communities. Rather than preaching about community and hoping that it will happen, the MetaChurch provides a proactive system to move each member to a small group facilitated by a trained leader.

Chart used with permission. Carl F. George, *Prepare Your Church for the Future* (Grand Rapids: Revell, 1991).

DISCIPLESHIP

The Purpose-Driven Baseball Diamond
A visual road map in moving people from conversion to mission

At Saddleback Valley Community Church, Rick Warren developed a paradigm called "The Purpose-Driven Church," which provides four clear steps through which people can advance as they grow in their commitment. Each step includes a special training class. Members are encouraged always to be thinking about when they can take the next step in their spiritual growth.

COMMITTED TO MATURITY — C.L.A.S.S. 201: Discovering Spiritual Maturity and The Maturity Covenant

COMMITTED TO MEMBERSHIP — C.L.A.S.S. 101: Discovering Church Membership and The Membership Covenant

COMMITTED TO MINISTRY — C.L.A.S.S. 301: Discovering My Ministry and The Ministry Covenant

COMMITTED TO MISSIONS — C.L.A.S.S. 401: Discovering My Mission and The Missions Covenant

Baseball Diamond Strategy Overview

First Base	To lead people to Christ and membership
Second Base	To grow people in spiritual maturity
Third Base	To equip people for ministry
Home Base	To enlist people with the mission of sharing Christ

The Christian Life and Service Seminars (CLASS) curriculum and tapes are available through Pastors.com, 20131 Ellipse, Foothill Ranch, CA 92610-3002; telephone toll-free at 866-829-0300; e-mail at info@pastors.com; or visit the Web site at Pastors.com.

LAY INVOLVEMENT THROUGH GIFT-BASED SERVICE

Through the work of Marlene Wilson, Bruce Bugbee, Paul Ford, and *The Equipping Church Guidebook,* various proactive systems have been developed to move church members toward understanding their gifts and finding a place of service.

| Assimilation | → | Biblical Foundations | → | Discovery | → | Matching & Placement | → | Growth | → | Recognition & Reflection |

Don't make the mistake of labeling any of these systems as just a small group program, or just a volunteer management program, or just a Christian education program. Done properly, each movement includes community, discipleship, and gift-based service, and together they help every person in the church realize his or her goals.

The following diagram illustrates the powerful synergy that can be created when equipping ministry balances community, discipleship, and gift-based service:

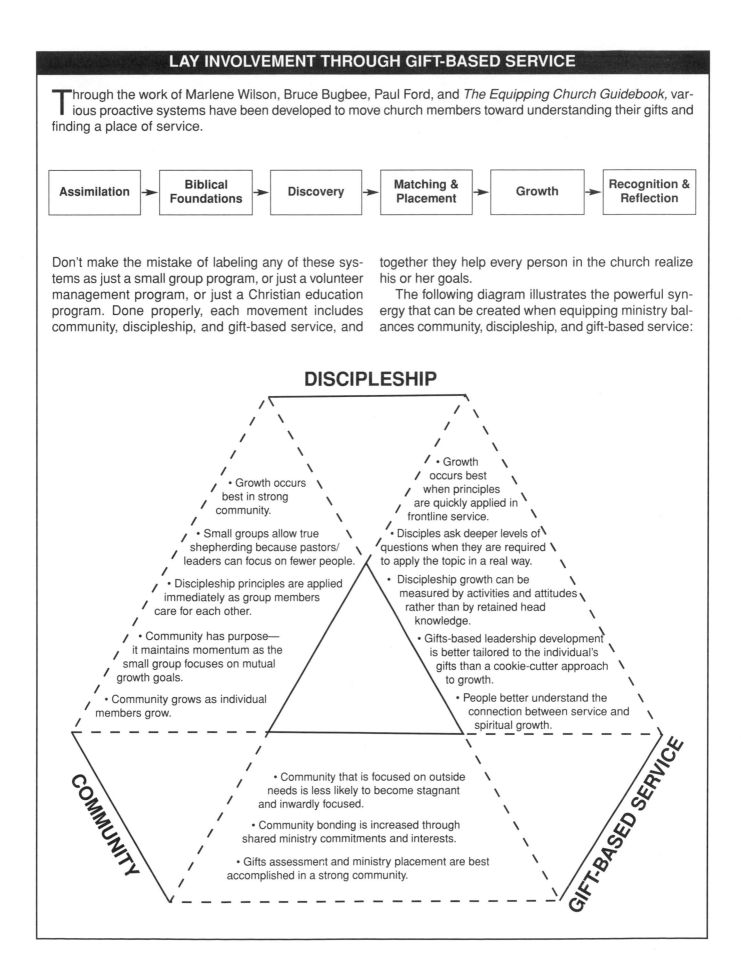

DISCIPLESHIP

• Growth occurs best in strong community.

• Small groups allow true shepherding because pastors/ leaders can focus on fewer people.

• Discipleship principles are applied immediately as group members care for each other.

• Community has purpose— it maintains momentum as the small group focuses on mutual growth goals.

• Community grows as individual members grow.

• Growth occurs best when principles are quickly applied in frontline service.

• Disciples ask deeper levels of questions when they are required to apply the topic in a real way.

• Discipleship growth can be measured by activities and attitudes rather than by retained head knowledge.

• Gifts-based leadership development is better tailored to the individual's gifts than a cookie-cutter approach to growth.

• People better understand the connection between service and spiritual growth.

• Community that is focused on outside needs is less likely to become stagnant and inwardly focused.

• Community bonding is increased through shared ministry commitments and interests.

• Gifts assessment and ministry placement are best accomplished in a strong community.

COMMUNITY

GIFT-BASED SERVICE

> "Spiritually, the only way I become a person of promise is to be connected. 'Being in' Jesus means that I am in the middle of Christ's body—a faith community. John Wesley, the founder of the Methodist movement, observed that people could quickly become converted during an enthusiastic event. But they would just as quickly fall away if they were not connected to a small group that would hold them accountable for their promises."
>
> Michael Slaughter, *Real Followers: Beyond Virtual Christianity*

> **Do not merely listen to the word, and so deceive yourselves. Do what it says. Anyone who listens to the word but does not do what it says is like a man who looks at his face in a mirror and, after looking at himself, goes away and immediately forgets what he looks like. But the man who looks intently into the perfect law that gives freedom, and continues to do this, not forgetting what he has heard, but doing it—he will be blessed in what he does.**
>
> **JAMES 1:22–25**

Working off the assumption that everyone grows best in a small group, some churches set a goal that all members would become part of a small group. Yet, frustration often set in as this goal was rarely met. Many concluded that in actuality there are a number of ways in which people grow best—some in midsize groups, some in one-on-one mentoring relationships, some through serving with others to accomplish tasks, and some within a nuclear family setting. Some people's gifts are best used to lead or serve in a small group, while others' gifts are best used outside of a small group setting.

Implications for Equipping Ministry

An equipping ministry system helps a church organized around small groups move to the next step of providing a greater variety of means for growth, community, and service that address the needs of people often missed within the small group ministry setting.

Discipleship

The last three decades have seen a renewed emphasis on spiritual formation and discipleship in many denominations. At times discipleship has been pursued through a workbook curriculum in small groups or through highly reflective and academically oriented exercises. Churches are beginning to see that classroom-oriented discipleship results in greater knowledge, but not necessarily in greater obedience and genuine, heartfelt Christian joy.

Implications for Equipping Ministry

A strong equipping ministry takes discipleship to the next step of interlacing knowledge and obedience from the start. When ministry is pursued through a holistic understanding of gifts, it allows both basic and advanced Bible knowledge to be applied through the learning styles of the individual—and applied in ways that are most powerfully effective to how God has created a specific individual to grow.

Evangelism

If evangelism is defined by what bold "I've never met a stranger" people do in elevators and on airplane flights, then most people don't have this gift. If we define evangelism as "living your life in ways that demonstrate Christ and show that you are ready to explain to people the key Christian beliefs," then people of all gifts and lifestyles can participate.

Implications for Equipping Ministry

Many of the innovations in evangelism today are centered around helping people understand what their gifts are and how they can participate in evangelism in ways that are natural to their gift mix—and then training is provided on how to express their faith in natural ways. Training people for evangelism will increasingly focus on "train and send" activities rather than on "go and get and hear" events.

Some churches follow the model of Willow Creek Community Church by creating seeker services on Sunday morning or Saturday evening. At their root, these services are not an end in themselves, but are essentially a means of equipping. They provide a way for people to casually invite someone to an event that will help deepen the relationship and center their conversation around spiritual topics.

——————— CONTRACTORS' CONFERENCE ———————

Changes in Your Church

Discuss the evidence of the above-mentioned trends in the lives of those who attend your church and in the programs and opportunities in your church.

1. Which trends do you see as most evident in your church? How would you restate the general trend to account for the specific way it is demonstrated in your church?

2. Can you identify other changes taking place in your church that are not addressed in this section?

3. Which of these trends most excite you because of the opportunities they bring to your church?

4. Which of the implications for equipping ministry seem to be most important for your church? What are the points of urgency, if any, for increasing your commitment to equipping ministry?

5. Are there any specific trends that particularly affect your church that must be at the forefront of consideration as you build an effective equipping ministry?

> The seeker service has been described as a safe place for seekers to investigate the claims of Christ. Perhaps more important, it is an "unsafe place for complacent Christians." Without some way to disrupt our attempts to go into a "holy huddle," we can too easily lose sight of the church's call to be salt (different from the world) and light (a witness in the midst of the world). By placing the seeker service in the prime time of religious activity, it stands as a constant reminder that our call is to reach out, not to cocoon in.

Church Missions

One of the goals of equipping ministry is to help each person recognize his or her calling and gifting as a minister. If missions is loosely defined as "crossing cultural barriers to demonstrate Christ," then in many ways every church member has the potential to be a missionary without necessarily moving to another country or having to raise financial support. Every city has racial, economic, gender, ethnic, and age divides that invite people to be a part of cross-cultural service. Living in a pluralistic society means that people who "look and live like us" may have radically different beliefs, perspectives, and worldviews that require us to possess cross-cultural skills that will help us communicate Christ to them. On the international front, the effects of globalism and economic and technological changes have radically opened the way to previously closed or hard-to-access countries. More and more church members are involved in daily or weekly global relationships at a level that would have been inconceivable a few short decades ago.

Implications for Equipping Ministry

While "professional" missionaries continue to play a vital role, missions is no longer about equipping a few who go and do the work and then report back what they have done. Churches that understand they exist as a mission to their own neighborhoods understand the vital urgency and potential of equipping ministry to spread the good news both far and near.

HOW HAS GOD PRECEDED YOU?

HOW EASY IT IS to waste time and effort in life! If God is not preceding your efforts at building an equipping ministry, you are wasting your time. When asking why you should embark on a new effort, it's vital that you spend time looking for signs that God has prepared the way and is calling you to join. Over the last half century, we have ample evidence that God has been working. How?

> We have seen a movement of God to create a new emphasis on equipping ministry. This "second reformation" (or "revolution," to use the language of leadership development expert Reggie McNeal) is happening across denominational lines and is an expression of the word and work of God. Successful churches are healthy churches. A healthy church takes many forms. At first glance, the churches that are the most visible and most often imitated seem to be widely different. Yet, in the midst of these differences, a common thread emerges, namely, equipping ministry. The shift to equipping ministry only makes sense if it is a movement of God. God has preceded our efforts, and this is evident as we examine the major trends of church innovation converging on the concept and practice of equipping ministry.

- He's working in the world to create increased need for more decentralized church ministry, as evidenced by the demographic statistics cited earlier in this chapter.
- He's working in seminaries and denominational offices to articulate the theological foundations for a renewed emphasis on equipping ministries. Beginning in the 1950s, the topic of lay ministry became an important discussion in theological journals. Vatican II had at its roots a call to increased lay involvement in the life and work of the church. Since then most major denominations have made lay ministry a priority in teaching and practice.
- He's working in your church as you add key programs that will form the building blocks of all your efforts to develop a church-wide equipping ministry. Early in your effort it's crucial to reflect on the way God has prepared the way for an increased equipping ministry and to seek God's guidance on the why, what, and when of your work.

CONTRACTORS' CONFERENCE

1. What evidence do you have that God has preceded your efforts in your community, denomination, and local church body?

2. What does God seem to be saying about the reasons and urgency for increased equipping ministry in your church?

3. What plans do you have to make sure your effort is undergirded with consistent prayer for and reflection on God's direction?

WHAT NEEDS IN YOUR CHURCH WILL THIS ADDRESS?

☑ **CHECKPOINT**

Reaching the Goal: Ministry in Daily Life

The ultimate objective for the Christian is that all of life—home, work, service, and leisure—grows out of a faith commitment and reflects an understanding of one's personal relationship with God. This relationship assumes that each person is gifted and called to be a part of the body. Although such a broad perspective seems natural, most people need support as their faith matures to come to the point of understanding this. Reaching this level of commitment comes through thoughtfully developed equipping ministry, undergirded by solid biblical study and Christian education. All of this requires a graduated, sequential approach. Until people actually experience themselves as gifted and see the relationship between their gifts and their service as Christians who have a calling, the larger understanding is strictly theoretical. Equipping ministry provides the foundation necessary for growth in faith.

GIVEN ALL THAT WE'VE said in this chapter, you undoubtedly have several immediate felt needs that you hope equipping ministry will address. It's important to know from the beginning what these are, because people rarely get excited about the long-term impact of a significant change unless they see the immediate practical benefit. Ask yourself the following questions:

1. What are our most immediate needs?
2. What are our most serious needs?
3. From what we understand so far of equipping ministry, what do we hope will be different if we have a healthy equipping ministry focus?

We've begun our building program in this chapter by showing the "why" of a churchwide equipping ministry. Along the way we've given you opportunities to pause and consider several "contractors' conferences." This foundation will now enable us to move ahead in the next chapter and show the "what" of equipping ministry. We invite you to join us as we look at the house plans and talk to the engineers.

2

What Is Equipping Ministry?

Look at the House Plans ... Talk to the Engineers

BEFORE YOU DEVELOP AN equipping ministry system and customize it to meet your church's special needs, you may find it helpful to examine some sample "house plans" that represent the essential components of a complete system. "The Equipping Church" chart (see page 65) allows you to examine each part of the process and its organizational relationships. This chart and much of the material in this chapter were formulated after observing hundreds of the most effective equipping churches in North America and asking, "What are the common principles shared by all these churches?" This knowledge, combined with your awareness of the unique needs and specific mission of your church, will enable you to design a customized approach for your church.

> Instead, by speaking the truth in a spirit of love, we must grow up in every way to Christ, who is the head. Under his control all the different parts of the body fit together, and the whole body is held together by every joint with which it is provided. So when each part works as it should, the whole body grows and builds itself up through love.
>
> **EPHESIANS 4:15–16 GNT**

CHAPTER PREVIEW

IN THIS CHAPTER WE WILL ...

- examine the characteristics shared by equipping churches.
- examine a chart representing a blueprint for an equipping ministry system.
- explore ways to use the chart in planning equipping ministry for your church.
- identify the elements of an equipping ministry system.
- identify the leaders of equipping ministry and clarify their roles.

CHARACTERISTICS SHARED BY EQUIPPING CHURCHES

WHETHER CONTEMPORARY OR TRADITIONAL, urban megachurch or small rural church, churches with a core value for equipping seem to share similar characteristics:

CHECKPOINT

"The Equipping Church" chart serves only as a guideline to help you visualize an equipping ministry system and then develop a model and a strategy that work for your church. In actual practice no system works as smoothly or as neatly as a chart suggests. People may enter the process at various points, stay in certain places longer than others, or skip components altogether. You have to develop people-friendly, reality-based systems that take these realities into account. The key to application is to create a system that allows each person to navigate the complete process with clear, identifiable "next steps."

Innovation, health, and effectiveness come together at the point where the gifts of many people are being prepared and released for ministry.

"No one person is meant to carry this assignment [a divine purpose] alone. It wasn't designed that way. We were created to do church as a team! A full symphony under the direction of a master conductor will always sound infinitely better than a one-man band."

Wayne Cordeiro,
Doing Church as a Team

Strong, Top-Level Embodiment of the Values and Vision of Equipping Ministry

The senior pastor, staff members, and leadership board members understand, support, and, most important, advocate and actively incarnate the values of equipping ministry. The vision is repeatedly cast from the pulpit and supported through ongoing Christian education. Church bulletins and newsletters endorse the effort. People are affirmed and recognized on a regular basis for their involvement. Bulletin boards herald new events and feature the people involved in service, both inside and outside of the church. Church leadership actively celebrates participation. The level of support also includes providing adequate resources to implement equipping ministry with appropriate churchwide visibility. In essence, the top-level leadership team is proactively involved in building a healthy church culture that creates the right environment for equipping ministry to flourish.

Comprehensive Systems That Allow Members to Grow into a Readiness to Serve and to Mature as Christians through Service

Participation is more than simply establishing a new class or a program to incorporate members into a new ministry area. New member classes, Bible studies to equip members, gifts seminars, and "matching" systems are integral parts of the process, but none is sufficient in itself. A complete system involves new and existing members, sets the context for service, supports a discovery process, matches members to service based on their gifts, places members in ministry opportunities, provides coaching for their involvement, and celebrates service as an avenue for spiritual growth. Successful lay participation is integral to the structure and operation of the church, so that equipping ministry doesn't become just one more program among many.

An Identifiable Leader and Team That Share the Vision and Facilitate the Ministry

Sometimes an exceptionally gifted director of children's ministry has organized an equipping ministry system in the children's area and then expands this skill to other areas in the church. In other cases the director of small group ministries may have expanded his or her role, implementing churchwide equipping ministry. In smaller churches often an exceptional church member—one of the most active nonpaid leaders reassigned from solving problems to building proactive solutions—organizes an equipping ministry. Many large churches hire a person to facilitate equipping ministry throughout the church and title the position one of a number of options—director of equipping ministry, volunteer ministries director, director of lay ministries, equipping pastor, or spiritual gifts minister, just to name a few. God uses many ways to lead a church into this movement, but it almost always results in a key person and team vested with the authority, responsibility, and resources needed to facilitate a churchwide equipping ministry system.

BUILDING A HEALTHY EQUIPPING MINISTRY CULTURE

Executive Summary of the Process

Culture is the environment of expectations, values, and often-unwritten rules that surround everything your church does. Your church's culture powerfully determines people's actions and their acceptance or rejection of new things. It is mostly invisible and assumed—unless the church leaders purposefully spend time discerning and defining it. Many church leaders have been taught that they must live with whatever internal culture they've inherited. However, internal culture can and must be changed and proactively built up in order to provide a healthy underpinning for the task of equipping people for ministry.

Some of the most effective cultural change agents change and build culture almost intuitively. They smell something wrong in the air that surrounds the church, and then they go about trying to get rid of what they sense as wrong and replace it with what seems right. Yet, when change agents are carefully interviewed about the process they intuitively used, there are strong similarities:

- They first *assessed* what was wrong and began to point it out to others who could then join them in the desire to create a change.
- They then *envisioned* what it would look like if the wrong were made right. They articulated this new vision in a way that increased the hunger in others for change.
- Then they *embodied* that change in their own lives and in the lives of the church's leaders. Since culture consists of so many intangible aspects, people have to live the change before they can create strategies to get others to live it as well. When it comes to cultural change, the only way to do it is by example. Trying to take a short-cut and move to words too quickly always results in a dead end.
- Next, once they saw a core group of leaders progressing toward living out the new culture, they began to *strategize* how to make this new way of living contagious to ever-larger groups within the congregation.
- The first part of the strategy was often to *lay down the biblical foundations* that illuminated what needed to be changed and what the end result should look like. They did this through a coordinated focus in sermons, newsletters, and Sunday school classes at all levels of the church.
- Then they started to *cast a vision* of what a new culture should look like, in a way that facilitated others being able to see and explain it in their own words and stories.
- Finally, they *looked for models* of people and groups already making progress toward acting out the new culture. They made heroes of them, because when people see examples of change in their leaders and others in the church, they become motivated themselves to become part of this change.

True cultural change leaders followed these steps in a loosely sequential way, but they kept interweaving the steps, always circling back to previous steps. They continued to pray for breakthroughs, because change at this level faces large and long-standing obstacles. Once they saw significant change, they maintained the process in order to keep building the culture to new heights of health.

☑ CHECKPOINT

Three Critical Components of Successful Equipping Ministry

1. *Equipping Culture:* Strong, top-level embodiment of the values and vision of equipping ministry and the provision of adequate resources for success.
2. *Equipping System:* A comprehensive system that includes preparation and development of members, thorough communication systems, staff support and involvement, and celebration of success.
3. *Point Leader:* An identifiable leader and team given the authority and responsibility to share the vision and facilitate the ministry.

The culture of a group can be defined as "a pattern of shared basic assumptions that the group learned as it solved its problems of external adaptation and internal integration, that has worked well enough to be considered valid, and, therefore, to be taught to new members as the correct way to perceive, think, and feel in relation to those problems."

Edgar Schein, *Organizational Culture and Leadership*

The Leader as "John the Baptist"

How do leaders increase people's dissatisfaction with the status quo in order to prepare the way for something new and better?

- Preaching biblical foundations to create hunger for the biblical ideal
- Vision trips with key leaders to similar churches that are several steps ahead of where you are
- Specific prayer for a hunger for a deeper life and healthier community, as well as a prayer for dissatisfaction with complacency
- "Town hall" meetings to brainstorm what the people hope their church will be three, five, and ten years in the future
- Finding and providing a platform for the "prophets" in the congregation—people who have the character and gifts to confront others by using the means God provides in order to create repentance and change

Definition of Culture

Many things make up the culture of a society, organization, or church:

- observed behavioral regularities when people interact (language, customs and traditions, rituals)
- group norms
- espoused values
- formal philosophy
- rules of the game
- climate
- embedded skills
- habits of thinking, mental models, and linguistic paradigms
- shared meanings
- "root metaphors" or integrating symbols

Among the components of culture are the following:

- *Tangibles* ("artifacts"), which are visible organizational structures and processes and tangible objects; they include such things as mission, vision, identity, relationships, spirituality, program emphasis, and budget and time emphases.
- *Intangibles* ("espoused values"), which are the core values—expressed either verbally, behaviorally, or in writing—that have become embodied in an ideology or organizational philosophy.
- *Basic assumptions,* which are the shared mental models that the members of an organization hold and take for granted.

The Role of Leadership in Culture: Dismantle, Rebuild, Maintain

The culture of an organization can almost always be traced back to the beliefs, motivations, and assumptions of the organization's founders. Throughout the life of the church, the culture is changed, either purposefully or accidentally, by each successive layer of leaders.

In an established church, the culture will only shift toward an equipping ministry culture if a large percentage of the church perceives that the current methods of ministry are no longer working. Often the leaders must first increase the level of dissatisfaction in the status quo before they can initiate the building of something new. Doing so breaks up complacency and creates a hunger for something better.

While creating dissatisfaction with the status quo, leaders must also paint a concrete picture of what the ultimate vision and next steps look like. Most churches will already have islands of strength and health in the area of equipping ministry—individuals, departments, or small groups doing a good job of equipping but needing to have their story told. You change culture primarily by example, not by words. By setting good examples the leaders should take on the role of championing the places where God has preceded change.

The ongoing "embedding and transmitting" of an equipping culture is one of the most foundational and fundamental responsibilities of church leaders—including the senior pastor, ministry leaders, and the director of equipping ministry, as well as key staff members, decision makers, and influencers.

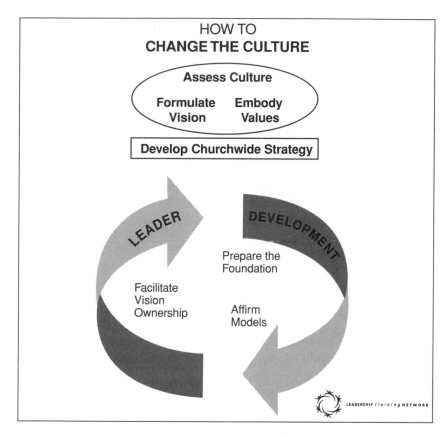

Overview of the Process of Changing Culture

At a leadership level, changing the culture involves the following steps (implemented by the church leadership team—senior pastor, governing board members, key staff members):

1. *Assess your church culture.*

- What is your church's current culture?
- How is your culture demonstrated?
- How does your existing program emphasis reflect your culture?
- What and where is your readiness for change?

The three windows we will use to help you assess and define your culture include . . .

- what you say.
- what you do.
- what you believe.

2. *Formulate your vision.*

- Where do you want to go?
- Who do you want to be?
- Who needs to be involved in formulating the vision?
- Who needs to own the vision in order for it to be realized?
- Who has the responsibility and necessary gifts to communicate and expand the vision?

3. *Embody the values.*

- How do you, your team, and the church leaders incarnate target values?
- Where do you need to change and grow?
- How do you facilitate change in your leadership team?

"The unique function of leadership that distinguishes it from management and administration is [a] concern for culture. Leaders create culture and must manage and sometimes change culture."

Edgar Schein, *Organizational Culture and Leadership*

How Much "Embody" Is Enough?

No leadership team can perfectly embody a new culture, but leaders need to feel that they have made significant enough personal change that they have a deeper understanding of the pain and joys of the changes they are asking the congregations to adopt.

The Most Important Step When Changing Culture

When changing programs, facilities, or even leadership structures, you can move quickly from vision to strategy because the critical element of change is the ability to clearly explain what is new. When changing an internal culture, however, the longest and most critical step is for leaders to *embody* or *model* what they have envisioned. Culture is changed by example, not by words, and articulating a new lifestyle is a much longer process than articulating a new idea, program, or physical location. Whenever there is a shortcut at the "embody" stage, no matter how well the change is explained and even verbally mimicked by the congregation, real change doesn't occur because people perceive from the example of their leaders that the change is more about words than about actions.

4. *Strategize about how to share the vision.*

- How do you reach your desired future state?
- How do you move churchwide culture toward the vision?

These four elements make up the necessary groundwork to prepare the top level of leadership to promote change in the wider congregation. However, even after the leaders have gained understanding and have begun to live out the changes they will be promoting, they still must continue to "sharpen the saw" by assessing, envisioning, embodying, and strategizing how to intentionally build a churchwide equipping culture.

At a congregational level, changing the culture involves the following (implemented by the church leadership team and all ministry leaders on an ongoing basis):

1. *Prepare the foundation.*

- How do you lay the biblical framework and foundation for the vision?

2. *Facilitate ownership of the vision.*

- How do you share the vision with the church body so that each person can see his or her place in it?

3. *Affirm good models.*

- How do you find and affirm the good examples and stories of equipping ministry within the church?

Laying the biblical foundation is a vital and necessary component for creating a church culture receptive to the values of equipping ministry. For strong ecclesiastical churches, your task may also include explaining the teachings of church theologians. As the church begins to embrace and embody the biblical core values of equipping ministry, it is essential for the leaders to help members make specific application to their own church by declaring a vision of what it could look like and piling up examples of where God is already creating the change. These critical mechanisms must be implemented on an ongoing basis and are the work of all program and ministry leaders, as well as the core leadership team.

IDENTIFYING THE ELEMENTS OF AN EQUIPPING MINISTRY SYSTEM

IN EVERY EFFECTIVE equipping ministry system, three broad components are found in some form or other, namely, *Prepare, Connect,* and *Equip.* The shaded boxes under each of these three broad components each represent an element that people experience as they progress through the system. The two shaded "cross beams" in the middle indicate the support and development functions necessary to create and sustain a well-functioning system. The equipping culture, once established, is the supporting foundation for the entire system.

Prepare

Assimilation

Helping new people understand the church and her equipping ministry values and helping them connect into the church community, as well as helping existing members extend their involvement beyond Sunday morning attendance and find meaningful ministry opportunities.

The Equipping Church

Providing personal, relational, Christ-centered growth through ministry in the church, community, world, and the whole of life

LEADERSHIP
training
NETWORK

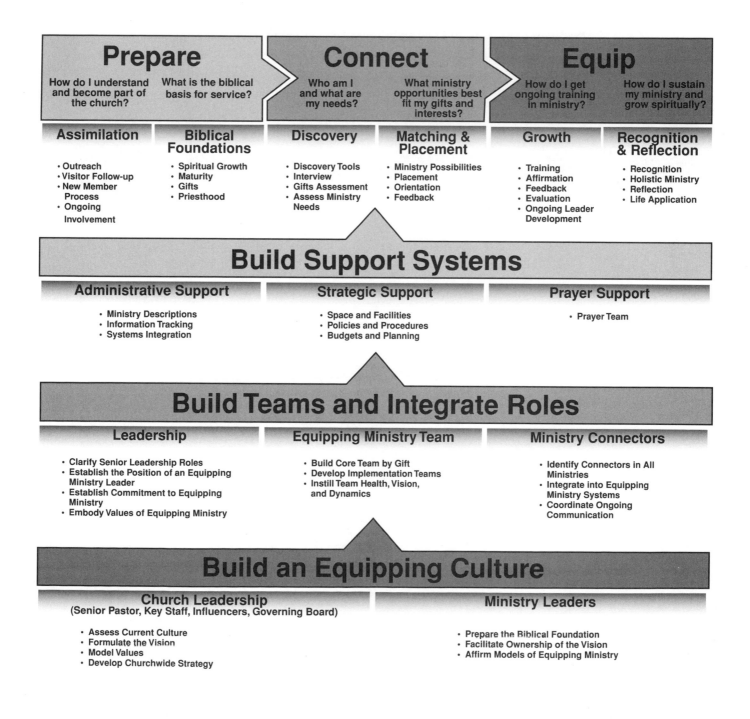

Prepare

How do I understand and become part of the church?

What is the biblical basis for service?

Connect

Who am I and what are my needs?

What ministry opportunities best fit my gifts and interests?

Equip

How do I get ongoing training in ministry?

How do I sustain my ministry and grow spiritually?

Assimilation
- Outreach
- Visitor Follow-up
- New Member Process
- Ongoing Involvement

Biblical Foundations
- Spiritual Growth
- Maturity
- Gifts
- Priesthood

Discovery
- Discovery Tools
- Interview
- Gifts Assessment
- Assess Ministry Needs

Matching & Placement
- Ministry Possibilities
- Placement
- Orientation
- Feedback

Growth
- Training
- Affirmation
- Feedback
- Evaluation
- Ongoing Leader Development

Recognition & Reflection
- Recognition
- Holistic Ministry
- Reflection
- Life Application

Build Support Systems

Administrative Support
- Ministry Descriptions
- Information Tracking
- Systems Integration

Strategic Support
- Space and Facilities
- Policies and Procedures
- Budgets and Planning

Prayer Support
- Prayer Team

Build Teams and Integrate Roles

Leadership
- Clarify Senior Leadership Roles
- Establish the Position of an Equipping Ministry Leader
- Establish Commitment to Equipping Ministry
- Embody Values of Equipping Ministry

Equipping Ministry Team
- Build Core Team by Gift
- Develop Implementation Teams
- Instill Team Health, Vision, and Dynamics

Ministry Connectors
- Identify Connectors in All Ministries
- Integrate into Equipping Ministry Systems
- Coordinate Ongoing Communication

Build an Equipping Culture

Church Leadership
(Senior Pastor, Key Staff, Influencers, Governing Board)
- Assess Current Culture
- Formulate the Vision
- Model Values
- Develop Churchwide Strategy

Ministry Leaders
- Prepare the Biblical Foundation
- Facilitate Ownership of the Vision
- Affirm Models of Equipping Ministry

—————————— **CONTRACTORS' CONFERENCE** ——————————

Responding to the "How to Change the Culture" Chart
(see page 63)

1. What has been your experience with building a healthy culture in your church, workplace, or other settings? How are the steps defined above similar to or different from your experience?

2. Sometimes you are able to begin with a healthy culture and build new values into what is already strong. At other times, some significant unhealthy areas must be addressed before starting to build in new values. In your opinion, where is your church at present?

3. If you already have a list of your church's stated values, how widespread was the effort to build the list? How widespread is the understanding of the values? If you do not have such a list, what are the significant stories being told by leaders and other church members that illustrate key values in the church?

4. How does the list of values (or the stories illustrating key values) support or not support building the next level of equipping ministry?

5. What is the one thing you most want to change in the culture of your church? What is the one thing you want to make sure to reinforce and not change?

Biblical Foundations

Helping people come to trust that God has gifted them for and called them to ministry; teaching the biblical imperatives and spiritual growth outcomes of being connected in the body of Christ in community and using their gifts in service inside and outside the walls of the church.

Connect

Discovery

An interview and assessment process to help people learn more about the unique gifts, talents, temperament, and life experiences God has given them, and then to allow them to share their needs for ministry and for support from the congregation.

Matching and Placement (Including Follow-Through)

Identifying ministry opportunities where people's unique abilities are needed within the church or community. Matching consists of connecting people with others who are interested in exploring ministry outreach. Placement involves the actual connection of the person with the ministry opportunity and includes meeting with the ministry leader and other team members, reviewing the ministry description, receiving preparation and training for service, and initiating a regular pattern of service. Follow-through includes checking back to see how the service is going and offering the opportunity to explore other options if the initial placement proves to be inappropriate for any reason.

Equip

Growth

The ongoing supportive processes of *training, affirmation, feedback,* and *evaluation* for people involved in serving in ministry ensure their success and fulfillment as they grow spiritually. The ongoing intentional leadership development of the equipping ministry team, as well as church leaders, is critical to the success of the equipping ministry system. The church needs people who have been prepared to assume leadership responsibilities for ministries and programs. The equipping ministry system is especially useful in identifying potential leaders and developing them to assume larger roles within the church.

Recognition and Reflection

The recognition and celebration of service and the opportunity to reflect on the meaning of ministry for a Christian are important elements of the *Equip* process. Recognition includes exit interviews for those leaving a particular ministry and the provision of opportunities for development for new areas of service, as well as preparation for leadership. Reflection involves ongoing development of spiritual maturity through service, as well as the integration of faith into personal life applications of Christians in service. As an important value, reflection should be part of an ongoing process for everybody throughout the process of building the culture and equipping ministry system.

Build Support Systems

Ongoing administrative and strategic support systems are essential for successful implementation of equipping ministry. An effective system

---

Push Me, Pull You

"The Equipping Church" chart can create the impression that most people are assimilated into the church through a centralized equipping ministry process, then handed off to specific ministries. In actuality, in many churches visitors are assimilated by Sunday school classes, small groups, or relationships with parents with similar age children who are involved in children's ministry. Often the leader of a particular ministry is the best person to inspire someone with a vision for serving in that ministry. In these cases, the equipping ministry system must be designed to come alongside the involvement process already in progress in the specific ministry and not take an already motivated person through unnecessary procedures in a centralized equipping ministry process. More detail on how to do this can be found in part 2 of this book.

Sports Interviews

Equipping ministry often utilizes a team of discovery interviewers who focus on a person's passion to discover if he or she is most inclined to serve in children's ministry, youth ministry, ministry to the homeless, and the like. (To use a sports analogy, it's asking, "Do you most like baseball, football, soccer, or water polo?") As this passion is discovered, a general interviewer likely doesn't know the area of ministry well enough to provide specific help. Thus, the interviewees are handed off to the ministry connector in a specific ministry area. The ministry connector is aware of the needs of the ministry and can conduct a more detailed interview. ("We need defensive players. Do you prefer to play right tackle or middle linebacker?") The ministry connector can also watch to see how the initial placement works out and coach the individual, if necessary, to a better fit within that ministry area, or if the person changes his or her mind, send him or her back to the initial interviewer for general guidance into another ministry department.

—————————— **CONTRACTORS' CONFERENCE** ——————————

Responding to "The Equipping Church" Chart
(see page 65)

- Prepare
- Connect
- Equip
- Support Systems
- Teams

1. Which of the above components already exist and are strong in your church? Describe what they look like.

2. Which do not exist? Describe in general how they might look when they are built.

3. Which exist in part and need to be either enhanced or built beyond the few programs of the church they serve now? Describe how they might look when enhanced.

—————————— **CONTRACTORS' CONFERENCE** ——————————

serves people well and is user-friendly for effective dissemination of information to teams and leaders. The best systems are invisible. While this element can include many important administrative functions, its primary role is that of facilitating effective communication and tracking among all ministries in the church.

BUILDING TEAMS AND INTEGRATING ROLES

WHEN THE RIGHT INDIVIDUAL with the right gifts has the right authority and expectations to do the job, things get accomplished. For the job of building an equipping system, the right person is a team builder, team leader, and team manager. Unlike a *group*, which is essentially defined by people hanging out together, a *team* has an agreed-upon purpose and roles for its members, as well as various assignments so that each task has a clear point person within the team. Yet, the members experience an essential interdependence so that no one person can accomplish his or her task alone.

Team ministry is an essential part of the culture and value of equipping ministry. Shifting to a team ministry model requires more than just changing the words *committee* or *department* to *team*. It requires a complete shift in culture—a move from traditional roles and processes to a more fluid, vision-driven model.

What Is a Team?

A team is a group of people with complementary and diverse skills, gifts, and strengths who are committed to . . .

- sharing a common purpose.
- loving and supporting each other.
- achieving the team's mission.
- holding each other accountable.

Clarity in working relationships and the assignment of responsibilities make a huge difference in the smooth implementation of an equipping ministry system. Discrepancies often exist between the formal and informal organizational and communication structures of the church. The more proactive the leadership is at the beginning to create clarity and common understanding of roles, the faster and easier the work of building an equipping ministry will go later in the process.

Six Critical Areas Where Role Definition Is Needed

The Role of the Director of Equipping Ministry

One of your important decisions that affects the future of equipping ministry in your church is the selection of a leader to facilitate (along with a team) the building and ongoing implementation of an equipping ministry system. This person's ability to work collaboratively with other staff members and laypeople is critical to the embracing of the vision and values of equipping ministry throughout the church. Take time to determine what characteristics are necessary before you initiate the search for the leader of this ministry.

You may be asking the question, "When should a director of equipping ministry (DEM) be hired or appointed?" Sometimes the person who eventually becomes the director of equipping ministry initiates the vision.

> Team ministry is ownership and self-initiated vision in which members carry out plans they themselves have conceived and have had a part in conceptualizing. . . . When teams take ownership of the ministry, what is the outcome for the church?
>
> - There is increased involvement and ownership.
> - Members become more positive and more open to change.
> - Staff roles are restructured to reflect each individual's gifts and each one's part in the mission of the church.
> - The foundation is laid to enable a ministry to expand without losing the depth, focus, and quality of the ministry.
>
> Daniel Reeves, "Mega-shifting to a Team Ministry Approach"

> "Since people are the most important asset of every church, a leader's primary job is to maximize the innate potential in the group as a whole. We keep searching for the perfect parishioner in hopes of cloning DNA samples. No church has ever had perfect collaborators, just as no congregation has had a perfect pastor."
>
> Alan Nelson, *Leading Your Ministry*

If God has provided the obvious leader so early in the process, it is important to establish his or her formal role as early as possible. In most cases the church leaders need time to understand the why, what, and even initial "how-tos" of equipping ministry before they are ready to commit to hiring a DEM. This book has a section in chapter 5 that provides detail on what to look for in a director. By the time you reach this section, you will have worked through most of the key issues surrounding equipping ministry, and thus you will have a good foundation of understanding as you prepare to fill this position.

Part 2 of this guidebook is essentially the director of equipping ministry's blueprint for building an equipping ministry system. It would be difficult to progress too far into the topics of part 2 without having already placed a person in this position.

A director of equipping ministry is . . .

- a facilitator of the equipping ministry systems and a supporter of other leaders.
- an equipper and leader of a gift-based team that is implementing ongoing systems and processes for equipping ministry throughout the church.
- a team player on the staff.
- a collaborator with the senior or executive pastor.
- a team leader.
- a coach, a cheerleader, and an equipper.
- a vision caster to the staff and the equipping ministry team.
- a facilitator of the core team's mission.
- a good communicator and listener.
- a strategic thinker.
- one who embraces change.
- a servant leader.

A director of equipping ministry is *not* . . .

- a gatekeeper for all the program ministries.
- an interviewer and volunteer recruiter for various ministry programs.
- a program director who manages a program.
- a data analyst who tracks people's movements in the church.
- a creator of ministry descriptions for all areas of the church.

The characteristics of successful leaders of equipping ministry are as follows:

- *Facilitative managers and leaders:* Successful leaders are able to juggle many tasks, invite people to participate in ministry service that matches their gifts, and lead a team toward a common goal.
- *Equippers and people developers:* Effective leaders have a passion and gift for helping others grow.
- *Spiritually mature role models:* Successful leaders have the spiritual grounding and character that form the basis of their credibility with the mentoring team, as well as the grace to work effectively in a fluid and ever-changing team-based work setting.
- *Change agents:* Effective leaders are flexible, able to embrace and exegete the culture of the church, and able to facilitate ownership of the vision of equipping ministry.

When in Doubt About Where to Start, Form a Team, Involve Others' Gifts, Keep It Loose Until a Plan Forms

In churches the equipping ministry team may be known as an advisory team, a task force, or a ministry mentor group. Select the title most appropriate for your church culture. In reality, the initial core team will be a "start-up" team—those involved in the building of systems and foundational work prior to equipping ministry being launched. In some cases members of this team will remain on the ongoing team, but once equipping ministry is launched, new members often will join the core team and subsequently the specialized ministry teams that facilitate the ongoing processes.

Another important question to ask is, "Where does the director of equipping ministry fit in the organization of your church?" The most successful equipping ministry systems seem to have achieved their success, at least in part, because the equipping ministry director reported to the senior or executive pastor. Why?

- Because a comprehensive equipping ministry system involves every aspect of church functioning.
- Because a comprehensive equipping ministry system represents a departure from past operational methods employed by most churches. A ministry that truly involves members according to their talents, gifts, and needs has to be continuously championed and supported by the senior pastor and requires ongoing sharing of the vision from the pulpit.
- Because a direct reporting relationship to the senior pastor communicates the importance of equipping ministry to the church leadership and encourages congregational support for the system.
- Because a close working relationship with the senior pastor is necessary if the director of equipping ministry is to be truly responsive to the needs and goals of the church. This leader must be in a position to readily inform the pastor of the issues and concerns of the people.

NOTE: Refer to chapter 5 for detailed information on hiring a director of equipping ministry.

The Role of the Core Equipping Ministry Team

The truly suitable director of equipping ministry understands the principle of Romans 12:3—"Do not think of yourself more highly than you ought, but rather think of yourself with sober judgment." This person's first step is to identify what gifts he or she does not have, and then to begin involving others who have the gifts needed to do the job.

The core equipping ministry team is the primary implementation force for the equipping ministry system. In small churches this team may consist of three to six nonpaid members. Large churches may have six to ten members, all of whom may be paid staff. Core team members will each lead the various elements of the equipping ministry components. The members of the core team, in turn, will find people with the passion and the gifts to work with them in their area as they serve on implementation teams (see "The Equipping Church" chart on page 65).

The Role of Implementation Teams (Large Churches Only)

Typically each implementation team reports to one of the core team members and helps implement one part of the equipping ministry system. While the core team's role is to build the overall system, the implementation team's role is to build a piece of the system in such a way that it fits with the other pieces. These are active teams that help develop and organize record-keeping systems, interview people, meet with groups and individuals to facilitate the writing of ministry descriptions, assist with various hospitality arrangements, and celebrate the accomplishments of those who actively serve—and the list goes on and on. The key for the core team is to develop multiple teams of people with diverse gifts who share the vision and shoulder the work.

Who Makes Up the Core Equipping Ministry Team?

- The initial team may be weighted toward people who like to create from scratch and who are gifted in designing, strategizing, and building initial pilot programs. Later on, these folks are gradually replaced with others who can develop potential, refine, standardize, and maintain.
- In larger churches the first people involved may be those who are gifted at involving others, promoting the concept, and recognizing who has the kind of skills to serve on the core team and other specialized teams.
- A basic core team for a midsize church includes at least one leader for each of these key elements: assimilation, teaching biblical foundations, discovery, matching and placement, and growth.
- Sometimes core team members are selected not just for the gifts they bring, but also for the group in the church they represent and can influence. It is helpful to make sure various age groups and influence centers of the church are included on the team.

Organized *and* Organic

Many churches create intricate tracking systems that use databases to make sure that new members receive the appropriate follow-up, are invited to the next step in their discipleship journey, and are assigned to a ministry with clear descriptions and periodic reviews to ensure that they are growing and serving well. Other churches shun such mechanistic systems, yet they, too, do not want to lose people between the cracks of a too loosely organized system. For these churches a well-developed team of ministry connectors provides the natural link between steps in the system and ways to check in with people as they grow and serve.

Examples of Implementation Teams

- *Assimilation:* a team that includes people who develop public relations ads and Web sites, who serve as parking lot traffic directors, ushers and greeters, and information desk helpers, and who serve on visitation teams
- *Biblical Foundations:* a team of teachers who teach the new member classes and who serve as guest lecturers in Sunday school classes in order to provide ongoing teaching about gifts
- *Discovery:* a team of interviewers, gifts assessors, and placement counselors who provide follow-up to new member classes and are loaned to small groups to lead them through a gifts-discovery module
- *Support Systems:* a team of database builders and data-entry workers who update member records and track where they serve
- *Recognition and Reflection:* a team that creates and organizes special recognition events for the church as a whole and for various ministries and programs

The Role of Ministry Connectors

Often concerns and misconceptions are expressed from the various departments within the church early in the process of considering an equipping ministry system:

- Children's Ministry: "This sounds great in theory, but I don't want to depend on a centralized recruiting program that doesn't work. They don't have to face a Sunday morning with classrooms full of children and too few volunteers."
- Youth Ministry: "You are hiring someone to do all my recruiting phone calls? Sounds great!"
- Men's Ministry: "If this involves writing job descriptions for all the volunteer positions in my area, then it seems like more unnecessary work and bureaucracy. Count me out."
- Sunday School Leader: "You know we recruit new people to our Sunday school, and their regular attendance is important for the relational connections that will keep them in the church. I'd prefer if you'd do your new member classes and gifts-discovery process at a special Saturday all-day retreat every six months or so rather than have our new members give up this class for eight weeks to attend your classes scheduled at the same time. By the way, can you train any of our class members to do this, or do you have to do it?"

In reality, the equipping ministry system is only viable as long as it serves the needs of these frontline ministries. To do so, it must create ongoing communication links and ways to customize what it provides in order to fit the unique needs of each ministry. One of the best ways to do this is through building a team of ministry connectors to each of the major ministries. The primary "home" of these connectors resides in the ministry area, but they are trained by and serve on a team that is connected to the equipping ministry core team.

The Role of Ministry Leaders

The leaders of the various ministries are the front line and backbone of the church. They have the most to win by having an effective equipping ministry system to support them and the most to lose by having a poor or nonfunctioning equipping system. Much of the material in part 2 is designed to make sure that this vital connection of service and communication is developed between the equipping ministry system and the ministry leaders at the very beginning and continues to grow as the equipping ministry system is built.

The role of ministry leaders is *not* to . . .

- do all the ministry themselves.
- recruit volunteers to their programs or ministries.

Rather, the role of ministry leaders is to . . .

- share and model the values of equipping ministry.
- collaborate with the equipping ministry team in living out the vision of equipping ministry.
- identify a ministry connector from their ministries to interface with the equipping ministry team.
- work through ministry connectors to ensure good placement of people into their ministries.

- provide information and feedback to the connectors regarding program needs, people placements, and successes and failures.

The Role of the Church Leadership Team (Senior Pastor, Governing Board, Key Staff)

The best news of this chapter comes at the end: *You don't have to do it all!* The role of the church leadership team in building an equipping ministry system is to set the direction, recruit the right leaders, and monitor progress—but not to serve as implementers. The ongoing role of the church leadership team is to embody and build a culture that precedes, guides, and supports the system and leaders they have empowered.

The church leadership team should . . .

- teach, preach, and cast the vision of equipping ministry.
- advocate for the role and responsibility of the equipping ministry director.
- champion the values of equipping ministry.
- educate the congregation.

The church leadership team should *not* . . .

- run the equipping ministry team.
- develop systems.
- do gifts discovery.

In clarifying the roles of leaders and the members of the equipping ministry team, you are able to define communication and interactions between the ministries and leaders in an equipping culture. The diagram below can provide a helpful picture of how the equipping ministry director and team can be integrated with all the programs in the church:

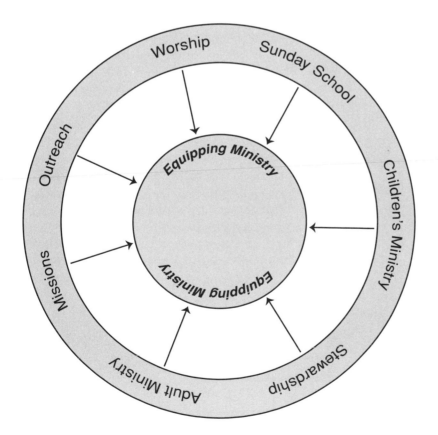

☑ CHECKPOINT

The responsibility of the ministry connectors is to . . .

- exchange information with the equipping ministry team.
- share needs, opportunities, and upcoming events (with respect to the church's human resources) with the equipping ministry team in a timely fashion.
- receive information from the equipping ministry team about people who have expressed an interest in their ministry or a desire to become involved in their ministry.
- follow up by personally connecting with every name received in order to share information about their ministry and to seek the possible connection of the person.
- inform the equipping ministry team that contact has been made, letting them know the results of the connection.

God has given each of us the ability to do certain things well. So if God has given you the ability to prophesy, then prophesy whenever you can—as often as your faith is strong enough to receive a message from God. If your gift is that of serving others, serve them well. If you are a teacher, do a good job of teaching. If you are a preacher, see to it that your sermons are strong and helpful. If God has given you money, be generous in helping others with it. If God has given you administrative ability and put you in charge of the work of others, take the responsibility seriously. Those who offer comfort to the sorrowing should do so with Christian cheer.

ROMANS 12:6–8 LB

USING GENERIC HOUSE PLANS IN YOUR CHURCH PLANNING

Monkey Teflon

A classic *Harvard Business Review* article teaches a lesson on delegation by describing unfinished and problem tasks as a monkey that clings to a person's back. When an employee approaches a boss with a problem and the boss responds, "Okay, then, I'll take care of that," the monkey jumps off the back of the employee as he or she walks out of the room, and the monkey stays with the boss. Church leaders are often poor delegators because they are gifted at caring for people and meeting needs. Yet the people who are best able to build an equipping ministry system are leader-managers, that is, people who do their best work through others. The primary purpose of *The Equipping Church Guidebook* is to serve as a tool for church leaders who need to gain the conviction to not try to do it all themselves, the confidence to understand ministry well enough to give it away without abandoning the overall direction, and the detailed blueprint to give to those who will serve in order to help ensure their success.

LISTED BELOW ARE SEVERAL suggestions for using the generic plans discussed in this chapter to encourage discussion and plan an equipping system for your church. Although you will need to customize the design to fit your church, these suggestions will help get you started and may generate other ideas:

- Make a photocopy of "The Equipping Church" chart (page 65) so people can understand the extent of the vision you are considering. Seeing a "final product" or even a sketch of a potential system is one of the best ways to get people excited about the time, money, and energy required to undertake a large initiative. The chart illustrates how equipping ministry will serve and connect the people.

- Survey what people think equipping ministry means. Develop a common understanding of what an equipping ministry system is about. Some members picture gifts-assessment seminars, others see Bible study, and still others may think they'll be getting a better way to get bulletins folded and envelopes stuffed. The chart demonstrates the "macro" scope and potential of the system.

- Create a common language. People can discuss and plan far more effectively when shared terms have shared definitions. Make sure the language reflects *your* church culture.

- Customize the chart to the needs and specifications of your church. You may currently assimilate new members effectively and thus not need to put your focus on that component. Name the programs in your church that achieve certain functions. Be sure to celebrate your successes as you identify needs.

- Develop a rough cost-benefit analysis, utilizing the visual representation. What programs and systems do you currently have? Where will new processes and systems be added?

- Focus on a particular strongly felt need, such as developing more leaders within the church. Examine how the system would help you identify these persons and provide opportunities for their development.

- Through intentional discussion, begin to define outcomes you can expect if you were to adopt a full equipping ministry system. Determine realistic timelines for research and development.

- As a discussion starter, use the chart to involve various groups or departments in the planning process. How would this system support their work? What are you already doing well? In what areas are you weakest? How can this system be adapted to best help you?

- Visit a neighboring congregation with a well-developed system. Take the chart with you. Examine how they fulfill each function. Listen to their members describe their ministry experiences.

What Is Equipping Ministry?   **75**

──────────── **CONTRACTORS' CONFERENCE** ────────────

1. What was clarified in this chapter concerning your personal role and the role of the church leadership team?

2. Of the six critical areas where is role definition most needed?
   - Director of equipping ministry (DEM)
   - Core equipping team
   - Implementation teams
   - Ministry connector team
   - Ministry leaders of various ministries
   - Church leadership

   a. Which ones need more clarification in your mind or in your church's culture? What questions do you have about the role so far?

   b. Which ones are already well developed in your church?

3. Who are the people who immediately come to mind as those who should be considered as a potential director of equipping ministry? Who are the people who come to mind as those who should be considered as part of the equipping ministry core team, specialized team, or ministry connector team?

4. What are some of the concerns or misconceptions that might arise from your ministry leaders? How can you make sure these concerns are dealt with during the design and development of the equipping ministry system?

──

3

Where Is Your Culture Now?

Survey the Site

CHAPTER 1 DISCUSSED WHY an equipping ministry is worth the attention, time, and resources needed to improve this area of your church. Chapter 2 discussed what is involved in equipping ministry:

- an internal *equipping culture*, built by the top-level leadership, that creates the environment needed to support equipping ministry
- an *equipping system* that serves each ministry of the church and each step in preparing, connecting, and equipping people for gift-based service
- a *point person* who builds the necessary teams to implement the equipping system

Now we come to the first of the "where" chapters, whose purpose is to help you assess the specific needs of your church and community. We want to avoid building a culture and system that represent a "trailer home"—built somewhere else, looks good in the "church conference" showroom, but when rolled into your church's specific location is not able to withstand the tornadoes, steep inclines, and neighborhood building codes. A good equipping ministry system is a "custom-built home"—built to accommodate the specific needs and take advantage of the unique opportunities of your site.

This chapter provides you and your leadership team with an opportunity to look at your current church culture. On the basis of this information you will begin to think through questions and solutions that support your planning efforts as you formulate the vision for equipping ministry for your church.

CHAPTER PREVIEW

IN THIS CHAPTER, you will find information and exercises to help you assess the culture of your church.

We've now arrived at the hands-on portion of this book. From now on, be prepared to roll up your sleeves. The work of asking the hard questions and making strategic decisions has begun. We assume you'll use this chapter during elders' meetings or staff retreats, as well as on other occasions where your leadership team is preparing the way for the next level of building a stronger equipping ministry. Our questions are designed to facilitate deeper discussions. The sidebar material is designed as a "quick read" to create dialogue on important points. It may be helpful to find a gifted facilitator to lead you through the exercises (and to read the chapter beforehand to select which of the many exercises would be most helpful to your team).

ASSESSING YOUR CHURCH'S CURRENT BALANCE: WHAT NEEDS ATTENTION FIRST?

Culture and System—Siamese Twins

Equipping ministry requires building both the culture and system together. If you try to build a system in a culture that is not aligned with the core values of equipping ministry, the system is quickly marginalized. If you express the values of equipping ministry without building an equipping ministry system, people can easily begin to substitute the "words" of equipping for the actions, or else their enthusiasm may explode and then wane again as their expectations are not met. The work of shifting your church culture toward an equipping vision and the task of building and implementing a system have to happen simultaneously.

Three Dramatic Scenarios of a Culture Too Far Ahead of a System

1. The program is announced from the pulpit within the first three months of the decision to pursue an enhanced equipping ministry system. A third of the congregation responds favorably. The equipping ministry team scrambles because there is no system in place. Many sign-up cards are never followed up on. Interviews are conducted hastily without any kind of connection follow-up. When the system is finally built eighteen months later, another announcement is made from the pulpit. Word spreads quickly: "I've done that, and it's no good." Few people sign up, with the result that the equipping ministry system becomes limited in its work with existing members.

2. The church's mission statement repeats the word *equipping* five times. Each year for the past decade Ephesians 4, 1 Corinthians 12, and Romans 12 have been the central passages for forty out of fifty-two sermons. People use their "Born to Equip" bumper stickers and wear name tags color-coded by their spiritual gift—but the director of children's ministry is always short of workers, the surrounding neighborhoods rarely see the church actively meeting community needs, and people are growing in knowledge but not in obedience. The church is living out the mistaken belief that equipping is about words, not action.

3. Not only is the church full of entrepreneurs and self-starters, but church leaders are effectively giving people permission to go out and use their gifts as ministers of Christ. New, creative ministries spring up throughout the church and community. Ministry fairs yield huge numbers of people who sign carbon-copy forms that indicate their commitment to serve. Who needs structure or systems when things are going so well? Then suddenly, like an exploding star that loses its center, many of the ministries begin to die for lack of people who have the gifts for ongoing ministry development and maintenance. Few of the people who signed up at the ministry fair are found serving three months later. Conflicts arise as new ministries compete for resources and demonstrate little connection to the core mission of the church.

"Why do you call me, 'Lord, Lord,' and do not do what I say? I will show you what he is like who comes to me and hears my words and puts them into practice. He is like a man building a house, who dug down deep and laid the foundation on rock. When a flood came, the torrent struck that house but could not shake it, because it was well built. But the one who hears my words and does not put them into practice is like a man who built a house on the ground without a foundation. The moment the torrent struck that house, it collapsed and its destruction was complete."

LUKE 6:46–49

Wisdom from a Chimney Sweep

To climb up the inside of a chimney, you have to move your left hand and leg upward to the point where they begin to lose the tension that holds them against the opposite wall. Next, you have to move your right hand and leg upward past the left hand and leg to the highest point where you can maintain the tension. This is repeated, left side, then right side, left side, then right side, until you reach the top. If a church allows either the equipping culture or the equipping system to get too far ahead of the other, all the effort may end in a fall into the ashes.

CONTRACTORS' CONFERENCE

(Rate first on your own, then share your answers with the group.)

1. How would you rate the health of your current equipping culture?

   • The church leaders:

1–3	**poor**—it is not a value our leadership team has discussed much
4–6	**good**—it is a value we hold, but we need to define it more
7–10	**excellent**—we are "Equipping Central" of the church and excited to make this more of a reality beyond ourselves

   • The church as a whole:

1–3	**poor**—it is not a widespread value or understanding in the church
4–6	**good**—it is a value held by many, but there's a lot of room for improvement
7–10	**excellent**—this is a church overdue for a system to implement what the members already highly value

2. How would you rate the status of your current equipping ministry system?

1–3	**poor**—very few of the "Prepare, Connect, Equip" system components are in place
4–6	**good**—we already have some of the components in place, but we need to connect them together in a comprehensive system supported by teams
7–10	**excellent**—we have most of the components of an equipping ministry system in place, connected and supported by gifted teams

3. Do any of the above dramatic scenarios sound familiar to either your church or another church you're familiar with? Describe in more detail.

4. In a midsize church (approximately 500 attendees), it generally takes a minimum of eighteen months to build an initial equipping system, complete with support teams and ministry connectors. (Don't panic; there are many ways to experience results and small wins on the way toward a complete system.) The timing of changing the culture of a leadership team (plus a whole congregation) is often impossible to estimate because it involves "heart" issues and depends greatly on where the starting place is and on God's purposes for hardening hearts and spreading flames of revival in a way and a timing that only God controls. Given all these uncertainties, where do you think is the critical path of change that needs the most immediate attention in order to undertake a balanced change process?

Three Dramatic Scenarios of a System Too Far Ahead of a Culture

1. The church possesses a comprehensive ministry catalog containing descriptions of almost every service opportunity in the church and detailed gifts and skills requirements—all matched to a perfectly maintained database that tracks people's gifts and service record. Policies and procedures abound, taking into account every possibility. Yet, only a small percentage of church members take advantage of the system. People who already know their gifts and their calling are repelled by all the hoops they must go through in order to do what they are gifted to do. The equipping ministry team has an elite air of "we know the right way to do it" that offends many other ministry leaders.

2. Groups of people are serving far and wide in the community. When asked, however, "How does this service flow from your gifts and calling?" they are confused by the question. When asked, "How does this service help you grow as a disciple of Jesus?" they reply, "Who?" When the senior pastor is asked about these groups, he responds, "This is one of the many programs of the church, sort of like our own 'junior league' for people who see church as a volunteer center to help them feel good about serving others. They are good people, and we're proud that we have this as one of our many programs."

3. The equipping ministry team functions as the volunteer gofers for the squeaky wheels of the church. They receive panicked requests for more volunteers, then work the phone banks to recruit warm bodies. People avoid equipping team members in the church hallways and program their call-recognition telephones to block their numbers (like telemarketers). Each year as the equipping team gets more sophisticated in recruiting, the congregation gets more sophisticated in saying no. Those who do serve are burned-out because they're serving long hours in areas outside of their gifts and passion.

ASSESSING YOUR CHURCH'S CURRENT CULTURE: LANGUAGE, BEHAVIOR, BELIEFS

What Do You Say? What Is Your Language?

The first part of assessing your culture, namely, looking at its current strengths and weaknesses and the things that must be built in order to increase its support of a strong equipping ministry, begins with looking at the words that both reflect and influence your internal culture. These words relate to your mission, vision, desired values, and stories.

Mission

A mission or purpose statement provides overall direction and focus for a church.

Equipping people for ministry must be part of the core purpose of the church. If it isn't, it will be seen as just another addition to existing programs rather than as a value. What's more, for people to be equipped to use their gifts within the church and community and to be in alignment with the church's mission, the mission must be widely understood and owned. In that light, you may wish to ask whether the mission statement should be adjusted and whether any steps need to be taken to increase people's understanding and ownership of the mission.

See pages 81–86 for some examples of church mission statements.

Four Key Questions about Your Mission

- Who are we?
- Whom do we serve?
- What do we do?
- Why do we do it?

———————— CONTRACTORS' CONFERENCE ————————

Mission Statement

1. What is the stated mission of your church?

2. How is your mission customized to your church?

   a. How was it developed? By whom and when?

   b. Are there words in the mission statement that have unique meaning to your congregation? Are there phrases that are borrowed from other successful churches?

3. What degree of common understanding and ownership of the mission statement is present . . .

   • among staff members?

   • among the church leaders and key influencers?

   • among the congregation at large?

   What percentage of each group above could recite it from memory?

   What percentage of each group above could restate it in their own words and illustrate it with their own stories, and be in general agreement with its intent?

   What part, if any, of the mission statement is most often misunderstood or not widely owned by each of the groups above?

4. How do the words in your mission statement, either overtly or subtly, express support of or conflict with the values of equipping ministry? Does the mission statement or statement of purpose include equipping the members to serve, be served, and grow as Christians?

ALL SAINTS CHURCH

OUR VISION

All Saints' vision is to be a progressive church of God's inclusive love, rejoicing in our diversity, ministering to one another's needs, challenging injustice and oppression, animated by the heart, mind, and ministry of Christ.

OUR MISSION

All Saints' mission is to call people, wherever they are on their journey of faith, to become agents of transformation for God's justice, peace, and wholeness.

All Saints Church • 132 North Euclid Avenue
• Pasadena, California 91101-1796 • 626-796-1172

Sugar Land First United Methodist Church

Vision

Our vision is that all people have a loving relationship with God through Jesus Christ.

Mission Statement

We are here to reach out to others, grow as followers of Christ, and go forth in ministry and service, so that all may know God's love in Jesus Christ.

OUR VALUES FOR MINISTRY*

A Dedication to Grace

God's love for all humanity is uniquely expressed through the life, death, and resurrection of Jesus Christ. "For God so loved the world that he gave his only Son, that whoever believes in him should not perish but have eternal life."

JOHN 3:16

A Dedication to the Bible

The Bible, as the living word of God, should be presented in a relevant fashion, concentrating on its application to contemporary daily life. "But be doers of the word, and not hearers only, deceiving yourselves"

JAMES 1:22

---

*All Scripture references are from the Revised Standard Version.

The Accidental Consumer Mission Statement.

Many churches have mission statements that read something like this: "The church exists to serve her members, bring them all to maturity, and spread the gospel worldwide." Often the statement is carefully constructed to reflect the primary components of the leaders' theological understanding of the purposes of the church. However, the formula of "the church exists to do X, Y, and Z to and for her members" can unintentionally reflect a mission statement structure that sounds more like a drugstore, hardware store, or country club, creating a subtle but misleading impression in a culture already predisposed to consumerism. The formula assumes that there is a group of "service providers" who do something for the "consumers." The "church" essentially becomes the paid staff members and visible leaders, while the "members" become the dues-paying recipients of the church's services. The members of one group get immersed in busily attempting to serve all the requests of the members of the other group—many of whom seem perpetually upset that the employees of the church aren't meeting their needs. To counteract this, many churches will use language in their mission statement that makes it clear that *all* the people of the church are both the service providers and the recipients:

- "We the people who make up the church exist to . . ."
- "The purpose of the church is to build itself up . . . and create a unified witness to the world."
- "The purpose of the church is to be the transforming presence of God in each other's lives and in our community."

A Dedication to Worship

Christians are encouraged to celebrate God's presence, both in personal and corporate worship. "Serve the Lord with gladness! Come into his presence with singing!"

PSALM 100:2

A Dedication to Prayer

Christians are called to focus on the power and priority of prayer in everything, both as individuals and corporately as a body of believers: "Continue steadfastly in prayer, being watchful in it with thanksgiving."

COLOSSIANS 4:2

A Dedication to Biblical Community

An authentic biblical community of faith offers loving relationships and life-changing growth through small groups, and affirms unity by embracing differences within the body of Christ. "So if there is any encouragement in Christ, any incentive of love, any participation in the Spirit, any affection and sympathy, complete my joy by being of the same mind, having the same love, being in full accord and of one mind."

PHILIPPIANS 2:1–2

A Dedication to Lay Ministry

Pastors and leaders mobilize, equip, and release believers to serve in their areas of giftedness and calling, serving God through the church and in the world. "As each has received a gift, employ it for one another, as good stewards of God's varied grace."

1 PETER 4:10

A Dedication to Stewardship

Church members are encouraged and led to discover the privilege, responsibility, and blessing of financial giving. "Each one must do as he has made up his mind, not reluctantly or under compulsion, for God loves a cheerful giver."

2 CORINTHIANS 9:7

A Dedication to Mission

The Holy Spirit will use believers as servants of God, in all areas of their lives, to reach and disciple persons for Christ. "And whatever you do, in word or deed, do everything in the name of the Lord Jesus, giving thanks to God the Father through him."

COLOSSIANS 3:17

Sugar Land First United Methodist Church • 431 Eldridge Road • Sugar Land, Texas 77478 • 281-491-6041

Eastside Christian Church

MISSION STATEMENT

Eastside Christian Church exists to glorify God.

Through the power of the Holy Spirit,
we boldly *present* Jesus Christ to all people.

Through God's Word, fellowship, and prayer,
we *equip* believers to become more like Christ.

Through our love for Christ, we work together
to *build* the kingdom of God.

CORE VALUES

Servanthood: To involve all believers as servants in the work of God's kingdom through identification, development, and expression of their spiritual gifts.

Education/Discipleship: To clearly and creatively preach, teach, and mentor the truth of God's Word by the power of the Holy Spirit, resulting in maturity.

Worship: To be a body of believers who express Christ-centered worship in every aspect of our lives.

Fellowship: To provide a loving, nurturing, healing community that meets spiritual, physical, emotional, and fellowship needs.

Evangelism: To teach and train all believers to aggressively take the gospel to all people through personal witness, community outreach, and world mission opportunities.

Eastside Christian Church • 2505 Yorba Linda Blvd.
• Fullerton, CA 92831 • 714-871-6844

UNIVERSITY PRESBYTERIAN CHURCH

Mission Statement

University Presbyterian Church seeks to know God, embracing His grace, obeying His word, loving Him. We call people of all ages to join God's family, encouraging them to mature in Christ, so together we are a people empowered by God's Spirit to use our gifts to love a world in need. We try to share God's great hope with vision, creativity, and excellence, starting in our University neighborhood and reaching to people far around the world.

**Management and Leadership Support Department
(Administration) Mission Statement**

The mission
of the Management and
Leadership Support Department (Administration)
is to enable the people of
University Presbyterian Church,
in particular the staff,
to do the work of Jesus Christ
with passion and excellence.

Mission and Vision of Lay Team

*We can,
as a Christ-centered church,
support each person in our congregation
to develop and act on the sense of God-given talent
and skill in his or her life,
so that lay ministry becomes the hallmark of UPC,
fulfilling the mandate "every member (person) a minister!"*

University Presbyterian Church • 4540 15th Ave. NE
• Seattle, WA 98105 • 206-524-7300

Trinity United Methodist Church

*Trinity United Methodist Church
guides people
of all ages
to hear and respond
to the living God's call
by using their skills,
abilities, and money
to make a difference
in the world
as disciples of Jesus Christ.*

Trinity United Methodist Church • 607 Airport Rd. SW
• Huntsville, Alabama 35802 • 256-883-3200

Westover Church

4 P's of Westover Church:

Purpose:

To develop mature followers of Jesus Christ.

Passion:

Growing tomorrow's church by reaching adults in their
twenties and thirties across the greater Greensboro area
with the claims of Christ.

Process:

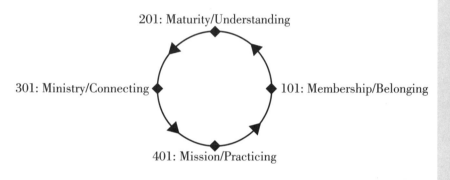

201: Maturity/Understanding

301: Ministry/Connecting

101: Membership/Belonging

401: Mission/Practicing

Priorities:

We value . . .

- practical Bible teaching where Scripture is the ultimate
  authority on all matters.
- the priority and power of prayer as an expression of our love
  and dependency on God.
- a grace-filled environment where people experience freedom
  in Christ.
- culturally relevant worship that focuses on celebrating God's
  presence in our life.
- a global perspective where people are equipped for and
  committed to local and cross-cultural outreach.
- unity in Christ where people from different backgrounds are
  welcomed and accepted.
- small groups where authentic, caring relationships provide a
  meaningful place of belonging and facilitate development in
  one's relationship with God.
- quality children's and student ministries where the church
  partners with many parents as they fulfill their God-given role.
- the ministry of all believers, who best serve according to their
  God-given spiritual gifts.
- the development of leaders who reproduce leaders.

Westover Church • 505 Muirs Chapel Road
• Greensboro, North Carolina 27410 • 336-299-7374

One of the critical cultural shifts toward equipping ministry is possess-ing a clearly stated vision that pro-vides a desired future outcome of an equipping ministry effort. Additionally, that vision must be widely understood and owned, or else people are always waiting for "someone else" to tell them the next step to take.

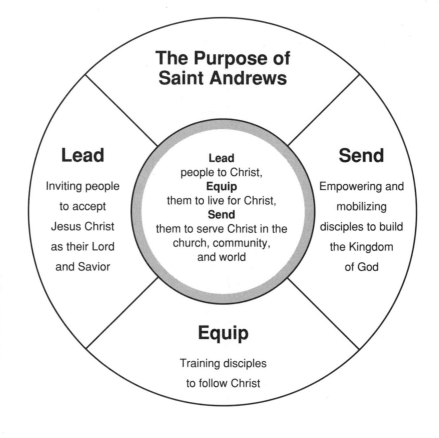

Saint Andrews Presbyterian Church

The Purpose of Saint Andrews

Lead — Inviting people to accept Jesus Christ as their Lord and Savior

Send — Empowering and mobilizing disciples to build the Kingdom of God

Equip — Training disciples to follow Christ

Lead people to Christ, **Equip** them to live for Christ, **Send** them to serve Christ in the church, community, and world

Saint Andrews Presbyterian Church • 7506 Falls of Neuse Rd. • Raleigh, NC 27615 • 919-847-1913

FIRST PRESBYTERIAN CHURCH OF BELLEVUE

Sharing Our Gifts

"Like good stewards of the manifold grace of God, serve one another with whatever gift each of you has received" (1 Peter 4:10 NRSV)

Mission Statement of Lay Ministry

To help each of us discover and develop our God-given gifts and tal-ents, empowering us for faithful and joyful ministry in every area of our lives and building up the body of Christ as we serve God and others.

First Presbyterian Church of Bellevue • 1720 100th Ave. NE • Bellevue, WA 98004 • 425-454-3082

Vision

While a mission statement focuses on the purpose of the church, the vision focuses on the projected future state of the church.

Desired Values

Values are the why behind what a church does. Desired values are statements, principles, assumptions, and beliefs about how people hope and wish things could be. All churches have certain things they value more than other things. Some churches commit to writing down the values they choose to overtly emphasize and continue to express as they build a unified and healthy internal culture. A few churches have prioritized their list of values so that when decisions arise, they can measure them against their desired values.

Examples of words often used in "desired values" lists include:

Worship	Love
Gift-based ministry	Sacraments (ordinances)
Financial stewardship	Church planting
Fellowship and authentic community	Recovery and care for the hurting
Social justice	Respect
Quality programs	Fun and excitement
People's individual needs	Truth
Prayer	Cultural relevance
Preaching	Strong relationships
Theological distinctive	Glorify God
Bible teaching	Family
Excellence	Change society and the world
Integrity	Evangelism
Creativity and innovation	Discipleship
Impact	Spiritual formation
Diversity	

Healthy equipping churches generally hold the following common values:

- *Prayer:* The equipping church recognizes the inherent value of prayer to discern God's vision, leadership, and plan toward an equipping ministry model. Equipping church leaders rely on prayer to see God in all aspects of their ministry.
- *The priesthood of all believers, and the vision of the church as contained in Ephesians 4:* Every member in the body of Christ is gifted for and called into ministry. The church embraces people holistically in the discovery of gifts, needs, and God's calling. The church seeks to equip people for ministry in the family, the church, the community, and the world.
- *Servant leadership:* Leaders demonstrate humility, authenticity, accountability, and genuine care of people, and they equip others to use their gifts in the body of Christ.
- *Team ministry:* Healthy community and teams are built around the individuality of gifts, team accountability, and the willingness of people to work for the good of the greater body.
- *Intentionality:* The church embraces equipping ministry as a value and models it through the intentional implementation of

---

Vision Is More Like Tag Team Ping-Pong Than Sporting Clays

Many church leaders hold the view that vision emerges from a single individual who casts the vision out into the congregation. In response, the congregation scatters in every direction from the impact of the vision to then go out and implement what was cast. The "vision caster" continues to cast forth, and the "vision recipients" continue to receive and do.

Some people are more gifted by God to see potential and communicate it in a compelling way. And it is also true that God often starts a vision with a single individual, although this person usually has multiple inputs from many God-directed individuals in his or her life. However, the shotgun vision caster exists mostly in church conference mythology. In reality, often a gifted visionary casts forth a vision, which is then batted around and refined by other key leaders and honed by others in its clarity and articulation. Then, once implementation starts, those with implementation gifts add a whole new level of detail and creativity to what before was only a general sketch. While the visionary may in hindsight claim, "Yeah, that's exactly how I saw it in my mind's eye," Romans 12:3–4 helps us understand that in reality this is rarely true. Vision is a team sport where each person contributes in different ways and at different levels. People own what they help create. The role of visionary leaders is to start the process and make it easy for others to join in order to hone and polish the vision.

If you don't have a current list of desired values, the book *Values-Driven Leadership: Discovering and Developing Your Core Values for Ministry,* by Aubrey Malphurs (Grand Rapids: Baker, 1996), is a good resource for creating a process for your leadership team to build a commonly owned list.

───────────── **CONTRACTORS' CONFERENCE** ─────────────

Vision

1. What is the stated vision of your church? Ask each member of the group to write down and then share how he or she would express the vision ("if the vision were to be accomplished, describe your church ten years from now"). How consistent was the expression?

2. Is the vision written down, or is it verbally expressed? Is it expressed in a story, a slogan, a metaphor, or a picture, or is it expressed through something concrete, such as building plans or strategic plans?

3. Which persons in your church would you consider indispensable to the vision? In other words, if these individuals were to leave, your church would lose a significant portion of the understanding of and energy for the vision. Is it a small or large number of people? How do you see equipping ministry expanding the number of "vision owners" in your congregation?

4. How was the vision developed—from the top down, or from the bottom up? Updated from "the vision of 1902," or "created new in 2002"? Is it unique to the church, or borrowed? If borrowed, from where?

5. What elements of the current vision demonstrate a value for equipping ministry?

6. What would you add to or change in the way your vision is expressed in order to provide greater support for equipping ministry?

7. What actions would you take to make sure the vision is more clearly understood and more widely owned?

systems to prepare, connect, and equip people for ministry inside and outside the walls of the church. It calls a leader to facilitate the implementation throughout the body of Christ.

- *Proactive response to change:* The church recognizes and embraces the organic characteristic of change and responds creatively and proactively to shifts in culture. The church continually changes her methods, but maintains the message of Christ regarding his church.

Stories

If mission, vision, and desired values are the words that create and reflect the culture of the church leaders, stories are the words the rest of the congregation uses to do the same. Stories are often the way people interpret mission, vision, and values into applications they can own and support. Stories are powerful mechanisms to shape culture, as well as to reveal artifacts about people's hopes for their culture.

What Do You Do? What Is Your Behavior?

After assessing what your church's language *says* you value, the next step is to assess how your church's behavior indicates what your church *actually* values in your internal culture.

To help translate your church's behavior, we will list the most important areas of activities for you to investigate, along with questions for your group to discuss:

What Does the Gap Look Like Between What You Say You Value and What Your Behavior Shows You Value?

A gap always exists between what we say we value as individuals and churches and what our behavior indicates as demonstrated by our actions. We need not be ashamed of it, because it is always a reality. By defining the gap, church leaders can become empowered to address the most strategic areas for changing their culture.

What Are Some of the Underlying Beliefs That Drive Your Language and Behaviors, and the Gaps Between the Two?

In addition to what you *say* and what you *do*, culture is also reflected and influenced by what you *believe*. Most churches have carefully identified what they believe in terms of their faith and doctrine, and as a result these beliefs have a huge impact on the church's internal culture. Because these are usually already linked to a wider denominational set of beliefs or to the church at large, this section will concentrate on beliefs that may be unique to your church. These often unstated but powerful beliefs also define your organizational and community identity.

Beliefs are taken-for-granted assumptions that have formed over time, often in response to problems or challenges. Depending on the history of a church community, these basic assumptions are entrenched in the culture to varying degrees. A basic assumption is formed when a leader tries out a solution to a particular problem—if it works, it will be adopted as "the way to do things," and over time it becomes a basic assumption.

Management expert Edgar Schein has studied the process and observes, "Once a set of shared basic assumptions is formed by this process, it can function as a cognitive defense mechanism." Churches, being "groups" by their nature, seek stability and meaning during their

Two Different Churches, Different Priorities of Values

Both large Suburban Church and small Urban Church had *excellence* and *authenticity* on their values lists. Both churches were set up to reach out during their Sunday morning activities to people who were not Christians. Surveys in Suburban neighborhood said the primary reason people didn't attend church was because it was "hokey and irrelevant." Surveys in Urban neighborhood said the primary reason was because it was "hypocritical and irrelevant." Suburban Church put "excellence" higher on her list of values and spent extra time practicing song arrangements and dramas—carefully planning everything, right down to the detail of how the clothing worn by people on stage complemented the lighting scheme of the week. Urban Church put "authenticity" higher on her list and spent extra time discussing as a group what the words of the songs for next Sunday's worship meant to their lives—because they knew that someone might come up after the service and ask, "What did those words you sang *really* mean?"

"Culture at this deeper level can be thought of as the shared mental models that the members of an organization hold and take for granted. They cannot readily tell you what their culture is, any more than fish, if they could talk, could tell you what water is."

Edgar Schein, *Organizational Culture and Leadership*

—————————— **CONTRACTORS' CONFERENCE** ——————————

Desired Values

1. What is included on your church's list of desired values? If you don't have a list yet, ask each individual to write down his or her top five choices and then share them with the group. Remember, at this stage these don't have to be the values you see expressed in the behaviors of your church, but the *desired* values you'd like your church to be formed around someday.

2. How many of these values directly support or require a strong equipping ministry?

3. Rate how large the gap is between where you are now and what you think is needed in order to build a healthy equipping culture. Discuss your rating and what it will take to close the gap.

    _____ Large gap
    _____ Moderate gap
    _____ Small gap

4. What would you add, subtract, or reprioritize on your current list to lend greater support to equipping ministry?

5. What steps could you take to gain more congruent understanding and widespread personal ownership of your desired values?

─────────────── **CONTRACTORS' CONFERENCE** ───────────────

Stories

1. What kind of person do your church members describe when they talk about those your church is called to serve? How do they describe the needs of this person and their hopes for how these needs could be addressed?

2. When people in your church talk about what your church does especially well, what do they say and how do they illustrate what they mean? Would you get a different message if you asked people in your community? When people join your church, what kind of language and stories do they typically use to explain their reasons?

3. When people in your church talk about what your church does poorly, what do they say and how do they illustrate what they mean? Would you get a different message if you asked people in your community? When people leave your church, what kind of language and stories do they typically use to explain their reasons? (For help on collecting these stories, see pages 262–63, 331–32.)

4. What topics are most often preached, written about in church newsletters, and taught in other teaching settings in your church?

5. What stories about the church's historical roots always seem to surface in discussions, presentations, and new member orientations?

6. When the topic of spirituality is discussed in your church, what is being described? What are some common characteristics of the "holy" people of the church? What attributes of God seem to be emphasized more than others (love, justice, faithfulness, power, forgiveness, and the like)?

7. Synthesize your findings from questions 1–6. How does the popular language that forms and reflects the culture of your church help you assess your church culture's current characteristics and its readiness to support a stronger equipping ministry?

8. What additional story-gathering activities do you as a leadership team need to do in order to better assess your internal culture?

The Bottom Line

Because of its multilevel and complex nature, culture must be analyzed at every level before it can be understood. The biggest risk in working with culture is to oversimplify it and miss several basic facets that matter greatly (these observations come from management expert Edgar Schein, *Organizational Culture and Leadership*):

- *Culture is deep.* If you treat it as a superficial phenomenon, you are sure to fail.
- *Culture is broad.* If you do not have a specific focus or reason for wanting to understand your organizational culture, you will find it boundless and frustrating.
- *Culture is stable.* If you want to change certain elements of your culture, you must recognize that you are tackling some of the most stable parts of your organization.

The assessment of your current culture can take time. Yet deep, lasting change and overall church health require an ongoing proactive effort to assess and build your internal culture.

Honesty Is a Contact Sport

One of the core values and fruits of a healthy equipping culture is "speaking the truth in love" (Ephesians 4:15). Change requires an honest evaluation of the real problems, not to pass blame but to clearly assess where change is needed. To help you prepare your list of some *actual* values in your own church, here are some candid responses from other church leaders who have done this exercise:

- *Familiarity:* "One of our highest values is to create a like-minded society so we are comfortable and can have a "country club" for us and our friends. A long time ago we effectively closed the membership so no strangers can spoil our fun. It's time to change this church into a public park with no gates."
- *Drivenness:* "We are constantly striving after bigger, better, faster. We brag about being church workaholics. We've collected a large, competitive congregation that has joined in our disease to be the best. We count and compare everything. I am tired."
- *Keep the Good Ol' Boys Looking Good:* "We are a fairly self-congratulatory bunch of longtime leaders who now, without even thinking, make decisions that keep others from questioning our authority. Most of us need to retire."
- *Don't Rock the Boat:* "Oh . . . never mind!"

Cross-Cultural Glasses Have X-ray Vision

Often one of the best ways to understand your own internal culture better is to ask someone from another very different culture to tell you what they see in yours, or go into another culture and see how it reveals new things about your own. Here are a couple of examples of what we can learn from others:

- "I never noticed the stained-glass windows that surround the worship hall of our church until a Catholic friend who was visiting asked, "Why do all of your stained-glass windows have large words from Bible verses on them rather than pictures?""
- "When I first visited the African-American church, I noticed their overly wide aisles between the pews and prided myself that our church used space much more efficiently. However, five minutes into the service as the music played and they began what would become fifteen minutes of people walking around greeting each other, hugging each other, and expressing the joy of being together in those now-crowded aisles, I was no longer so proud of the values that were so obviously demonstrated by our own narrow aisles."

existence. The defense mechanisms of the basic assumptions are entrenched in the culture to the degree that they are hard to identify without thorough analysis and discussion. In terms of "culture change," if church leaders identify the need to change basic assumptions, they should be aware that these issues have to do with defense mechanisms. Consequently, to change assumptions will result in anxiety and, in some cases, denial. At this deeper level, culture change is time-consuming and difficult. So a key aspect of changing basic assumptions would be to change the factors in a problem-solving situation.

The way to begin changing a basic assumption is by identifying a situation where the known solution is no longer working. For example, if a church has typically used the announcement time at a Sunday worship service to call for volunteers to help with children's Sunday school, and for some reason this method is no longer working, it provides a wonderful opportunity to try a different solution—one that is more congruent with the desired values of equipping ministry. If the new solution proves successful over time, it will result in a change of the basic assumption. People are far less anxious about and threatened by a change if the change provides an effective solution to a felt need or problem.

Two Observations

- Before you move ahead with strategic decisions or implementation strategies, you must ask the tough questions and make at least one pass through the processes discussed. The information gathered in this section can be used to develop your strategy, which is discussed in detail in chapter 6.
- You don't have to do it all or get it perfect the first time. This is an ongoing process that should be repeated periodically. Pick and choose the "contractors' conferences" that most apply to your situation. The gold is more in the process and the understanding gained during the discussion than in the answers that are written down.

Up to this point you've spent time surveying the building site of your church. Now it's time to look again at the general house plans to see what part of your site needs to be leveled and graded and what parts of the plans need to be adjusted in order to create a custom-built home.

"As a general principle, the way to deeper cultural levels is through identifying the inconsistencies and conflicts you observe between overt behavior, policies, rules, and practices and the . . . values as formulated in vision statements, policies, and other managerial communications. You must then identify what is driving the overt behavior and other artifacts. This is where the important elements of the culture are embedded."

Edgar Schein, *Organizational Culture and Leadership*

———————— CONTRACTORS' CONFERENCE ————————

How Does Your Behavior Reflect Your Actual Culture?

Your Programs

1. List the top ten programs in your church.

2. How do you quantify success in your programs?

3. Which programs are successful at the moment, and which are unsuccessful?

4. Which programs are given the most attention and publicity, both inside the church and in communication outside the church?

5. What percentage of your programming occurs mostly inside the church building and mostly involves church members? What percentage of your programming is conducted in the marketplace and in the community and involves individuals outside of your church or significant partnerships with community groups and agencies?

| PROGRAM EMPHASES |

The demonstration of values in a church are often expressed in the emphasis placed on various programs.

- What conclusions can you draw about your actual values after looking at your programming emphases?
- In addition to the ten programs you listed above, list the three top values that these programs promote and embody. (For example, Sunday morning worship service promotes and embodies the values of whole-community worship, Bible education, and fellowship.) Count up your answers and record the five values listed most often.
- Compare lists. How often is equipping listed as one of the top three values promoted by your programs?

Your Budget and Time

1. What are the top four areas of spending in your church budget?

2. What percentage of the budget is allocated to salaries for paid staff?

3. What percentage of your budget is allocated to equipping (training and developing) paid staff?

4. What percentage of your budget is allocated to equipping (training and developing) nonpaid staff?

5. What activity in the life of the church gets the majority of time devoted to it?

6. Roughly estimate the percentage of time spent on the following activities in your church:

   _____ Spiritual formation and prayer
   _____ Reflection
   _____ Evaluation
   _____ Meetings
   _____ Program and ministry development
   _____ Program and ministry delivery
   _____ Mentoring and discipling
   _____ Equipping staff members and laypeople in ministry service
   _____ Leadership development
   _____ Administrative activities

BUDGET AND TIME EMPHASES

The amount of resources in terms of money and time given to any particular area is a clear indicator of what is valued in a church.

- In reviewing the way you spend money and time, what are the top five values that are being promoted?
- How does the value of equipping rank in this list?

Your Relationships

1. Who are considered to be the core leaders and influencers in your church?

2. How decentralized is your decision-making authority? Rate on a scale from 1 to 10 (1 = most key decisions are made by a few of the same leaders and 10 = most key decisions are made by a variety of leaders throughout the church). Compare answers and discuss. What facts support your answer?

3. How much effort is made to continue to develop new people and place them in leadership? Rate on a scale from 1 to 10 (1 = very little effort and 10 = a great deal of effort). Compare answers and discuss. What proof can you offer for your answer?

4. If a new person with good leadership and relational skills but average ability to initiate new relationships and service opportunities for himself were to join your church this Sunday, how long would it take to become part of the inner circle of church relationships and decision makers? Why? What values are at stake here?

5. What groups would be at the center of your relational and influence community? What groups typically would be on the fringes of your relational and influence community?

6. How friendly is your church? Provide two ratings, one for friendliness toward long-standing members and one for friendliness toward visitors. Rate on a scale from 1 to 10 (1 = not friendly and 10 = very friendly). Compare answers and discuss.

7. How deep is the level of relationships within your church? Rate on a scale from 1 to 10 (1 = very shallow and 10 = very deep). Compare answers and discuss. How did you define *deep*? Does this level differ widely, depending on which group you're a part of within the church? Why? What values does this reflect?

RELATIONSHIP AND INFLUENCE EMPHASES

The depth of relationships and internal integration of people in the church is one of the key areas where values and culture are demonstrated.

- What values are reflected in your answers above?
- How do these values support or obstruct a strong equipping ministry?

Your Personnel

1. Comparing paid staff to nonpaid leaders, how would you describe differences in prestige, influence, decision-making authority, access to resources, opportunity for leadership, and level of jobs?

2. How does your church evaluate and reward paid staff? How often? How does your church evaluate and reward nonpaid leaders? How often?

PERSONNEL EMPHASES

A church's values are seen in the way she allocates and recognizes her personnel resources.

- What does your allocation of personnel resources demonstrate about your church's values?

Your Motivators and Evaluators

1. How does your church define and measure success?

   _____ in governing board meetings
   _____ at staff meetings
   _____ during worship services
   _____ in staff evaluations
   _____ in church communications (newsletters, Web sites, and the like)
   _____ in other ways

2. How does your church celebrate people using their gifts in service inside and outside the church? How often?

3. How does your church celebrate the achievement of key goals and other measurements of progress toward the stated vision? How often?

MOTIVATOR EMPHASES

The way your church defines, measures, and celebrates success is one key way of discerning what is valued.

- What do these answers reveal about your church's values?

Your Spirituality

1. What elements are emphasized as the critical ones that contribute to spiritual development in your church?

2. What biblical principles are foundational to your church's culture and taught on an ongoing basis?

3. How would you describe the overall Christian (or spiritual) maturity of those in your church?

4. Is there an intentional pathway for the new believer to follow in order to grow in the knowledge of Christ? What is emphasized in this pathway?

5. What opportunities exist for the mature believer to continue to grow and be nurtured in the body of Christ?

6. What forms of spiritual development are included in your church's programming (the teaching of prayer, discipleship programs, gifts-discovery classes, and the like)?

7. What key elements exist in worship in your church (preaching, teaching, praise, prayer, affirmations, commissioning, and the like)?

SPIRITUALITY EMPHASES

The values of equipping ministry are grounded in spiritual truths regarding individual giftedness, the importance of prayer, the fundamental biblical model of team, and a desired ever-deepening relationship with Christ for all believers through the use of their gifts in service.

- In reviewing your church's emphasis on spiritual development, what aspects of the biblical foundations of equipping are strong points in this area. What aspects are weak spots?
- What areas of spiritual growth opportunities are missing?
- What biblical principles could be preached and taught more effectively in order to strengthen the equipping ministry value?

————————— **CONTRACTORS' CONFERENCE** —————————

Defining the Gap

1. On one side of a piece of paper, list the *desired* values from the "contractors' conference" on page 90. On the other side, list what you think are the *actual* values as evidenced in the current priorities, behaviors, and assumptions of the church. After doing this as individuals, share your list with the rest of the group, telling where you see the greatest alignment and the biggest gaps between desired and actual values. What are the implications for building an equipping ministry in your church?

2. For further detail, write out what you think are the stated values and the actual values in each of the following areas, and discuss any differences you see:

    • Mission

    • Vision

    • Values

    • Programs

    • Budget and time

    • Relationships

    • Personnel

    • Motivators and evaluators

    • Spirituality

─── CONTRACTORS' CONFERENCE ───

Use the chart below to process where changes in basic assumptions might be needed. In consultation with a planning group, task force, or core leadership team, review each of your stated values that demonstrates your current culture. In one statement, verbalize what is believed to be the basic assumption. In each case, ask yourself whether the basic assumption aligns with the values of equipping ministry. The assumptions that do align are your areas of strength, and these should be built on as you proceed in your strategy. The assumptions that do not align with the values of equipping ministry can be used as a starting point in the development of a long-term change strategy.

VALUE	BASIC ASSUMPTION	ALIGN? YES/NO

Where Is Your Structure and Program Now?

Survey the Existing Structure

EACH CHURCH HAS her own way of accomplishing her mission. Your church's mission and core values should remain fairly constant, but how your church is organized to accomplish that mission can be dynamic, always adapting to different situations. In other words, the mission is sacred, the method is not. The purpose of this book, however, is not to deal with basic church structure, so for now we'll make the assumption that the basic structure of your church is effective.

Unlike the previous chapter, which discussed how you could assess your culture as a means to prepare you to proactively build and change it, this chapter will suggest that you assess your *structure* so that you don't change it unnecessarily as you build a strong equipping ministry. If your church structure is already effective for accomplishing your mission, the equipping ministry system should be custom-woven into your existing structure. If equipping ministry becomes just another program that is added on top of the pile of other programs, it may well become a "nonaerodynamic whirligig," sticking out the side and picking up wind drag as your church drives down the road toward her vision. If what you build does not serve your existing structure, it will become a distraction. It must be customized to your church's existing structure and seamlessly and aerodynamically joined with the current ministries of your church.

> "I know your deeds, your love and faith, your service and perseverance, and that you are now doing more than you did at first."
>
> REVELATION 2:19

CHAPTER PREVIEW

AS MENTIONED ABOVE, we're going to suggest ways to weave equipping ministry into your existing structure instead of adding just another program into the life of the church. Most churches have a structure that is both distinct from any other church and also fits into some general categories. We'll discuss five general categories of the way churches are structured, along with some models of how equipping ministry might work in each one. These models take advantage of the existing strengths of five basic church structures and can help you tailor an equipping ministry system to fit your specific needs:

- *The centralized model:* all departments report directly to a central staff member or leadership board

- *The department model:* primary authority lies with each department head, such as the director of children's ministry, director of worship, director of adult education, and the like
- *The Sunday school or Adult Bible Fellowship model:* organized around large adult Sunday school classes
- *The small group model:* organized so that the assimilation, teaching, and support of members occurs in small groups
- *The sacramental or liturgical model:* organized to ensure that the sacramental activities remain the center of church life and growth

ASSESSING YOUR CHURCH'S STRUCTURE

1. The Centralized Model

In the centralized model the church begins a new equipping ministry department. This department is connected in a purposeful way with almost every other ministry the church offers. A leader is selected to manage the department and to work closely with the senior pastor, staff members, and church leaders.

The equipping ministry department assumes primary responsibility for creating systems to support gift-based ministry involvement. The leader works with a team and the staff and ministry leaders to . . .

- develop a central record-keeping system to coordinate information and facilitate the connection of members with ministries that can utilize their gifts and interests.
- train interviewers and ministry mentors who meet with each person to learn his or her needs and connect the person to services, as well as to identify his or her talents and connect the person to ministry opportunities.
- teach leaders how to write descriptions of ministry opportunities in their areas.
- help coordinate churchwide programming to complement the goal of equipping ministry through developing Christian education that supports an understanding of our call as Christians to serve as God has gifted us.
- create training for existing department heads and ministry leaders that helps them invite people into ministry, place them according to their gifts and talents, train people as they begin their ministry, and affirm and recognize members for service offered.
- monitor the overall system, watching for people who are misplaced or ministries that are experiencing problems with member involvement.
- evaluate the level of member involvement in and spiritual growth through ministry.
- support the pastor and key leaders as together they continue to cast the vision of "every member a minister."
- network with groups and organizations in the community to find ways members can serve in their neighborhoods and move the church outside her walls.

The diagram of the centralized model explains the process from the point of view of someone entering the front door of your church and passing through each of the components of an effective equipping ministry system. Notice how assimilation, biblical foundations, discovery, matching, placement, training, and faith in action occur in this mode (see page 103):

THE CENTRALIZED MODEL

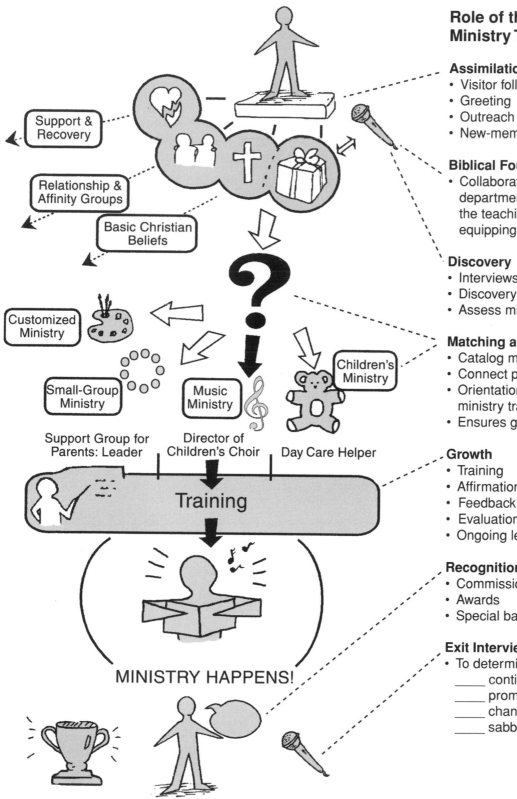

Role of the Equipping Ministry Team

Assimilation
- Visitor follow-up
- Greeting
- Outreach
- New-member classes

Biblical Foundations
- Collaborate with the continuing education department and senior pastor to ensure the teaching of the biblical basis of equipping ministry

Discovery
- Interviews
- Discovery tools
- Assess ministry needs

Matching and Placement
- Catalog ministry descriptions
- Connect person with ministry
- Orientation and customized ministry training
- Ensures good fit

Growth
- Training
- Affirmation
- Feedback
- Evaluation
- Ongoing leadership development

Recognition and Reflection
- Commissioning
- Awards
- Special banquets

Exit Interviews
- To determine ...
  ____ continue?
  ____ promote?
  ____ change?
  ____ sabbatical?

Support & Recovery

Relationship & Affinity Groups

Basic Christian Beliefs

Customized Ministry

Small-Group Ministry

Music Ministry

Children's Ministry

Support Group for Parents: Leader

Director of Children's Choir

Day Care Helper

Training

MINISTRY HAPPENS!

The Components of Equipping Ministry

Assimilation

The process begins when a new person joins your church or when an existing member tries to find a ministry opportunity. He or she participates in a seminar, new member class, or orientation organized in cooperation with the department of equipping ministry. Assimilation is about the connection between the person and the church—helping him or her feel part of the church community and providing an intentional pathway to grow as a Christian in his or her relationship with God.

Biblical Foundations

Through multiple formats that may include a centralized set of seminars or classes, each person learns the biblical basis for service and explores Christ's call for each of us to minister.

Discovery

The equipping ministry department helps each person discover and celebrate his or her unique set of gifts, skills, experiences, and interests. This involves in-depth interviews and may be supported with gifts-assessment systems. This part of the process may reveal that a person has other more urgent needs at that time than ministry involvement. These may include emotional and recovery needs, faith issues, family crises, or relationship-building needs.

Matching and Placement

In the centralized model the equipping ministry department catalogs descriptions of every available ministry opportunity in the church and uses the interview to help match the person with the best ministry opportunity. From this centralized interview the member is then directed to . . .

- a particular department of the church in which to serve.
- a community agency for ministry in the neighborhood.
- others who share dreams for new ministries.
- a mentor to help integrate ministry into the person's role at home and in the workplace.
- a counseling or support group to help the person deal with any issues that may have surfaced in the interview.

The equipping ministry department also facilitates members' placement in ministry. As ministry programs request assistance, the leader identifies members who have the requisite gifts, skills, and time, and forwards their names to the ministry area. Each program ministry is responsible for talking with prospective members and inviting them to serve. If the ministry assignment does not fit for any reason, the ministry area encourages the member to return to the equipping ministry department for guidance toward a more appropriate position.

Growth

Training people during their ministry experience is the job of the program ministry leader. The equipping ministry department provides support, feedback, and central training for the ministry leaders, as well as names of those who may be able to provide training in their area. The ongoing provision of affirmation, feedback, and evaluation is also the role of the program ministry leader, who receives support from the equipping ministry department.

Recognition and Reflection

Commissioning, awards, special banquets, and celebrations are all part of recognizing members who are involved in ministry. Through its coordination role, the equipping ministry department facilitates recognition events, ensuring that each person, no matter where he or she is placed in ministry, receives affirmation. In addition, the department ensures that ongoing reflection and spiritual growth opportunities are given to those who serve.

Advantages of the Centralized Model

- A clear point of entry ensures that all people have the opportunity both to serve and to be served. Each person progresses through the same churchwide path to opportunities to serve or to be served.
- The first emphasis is placed on the person as a child of God and only afterward on placing the person in ministry.
- Coordinated ministry descriptions enable the person to find the opportunity within the church that best suits his or her gifts and talents.
- A dedicated leader of the equipping ministry department ensures that program ministry needs will receive attention according to priority and need.

Disadvantages of the Centralized Model

- Substantial development time is required to initiate a full-scale program. Expectations need to be adjusted accordingly.
- The potential for bureaucratic structures and bottlenecks is great. The transition of members from being served by the department of equipping ministry to involvement in other departments and programs requires thoughtful coordination.
- In the early stages the process may be confusing, as program ministry leaders and other staff members shift from independent recruitment activities to a centralized "human resource" department.

How Is Equipping Ministry Staffed? An Organizational Structure

Regardless of the equipping ministry model you choose, you will need to develop an organizational chart for your equipping ministry department. The nature of your organizational structure will depend on the different organizational characteristics of the model you have chosen. Here is an example of the organizational chart from a well-developed, centralized equipping ministry system:

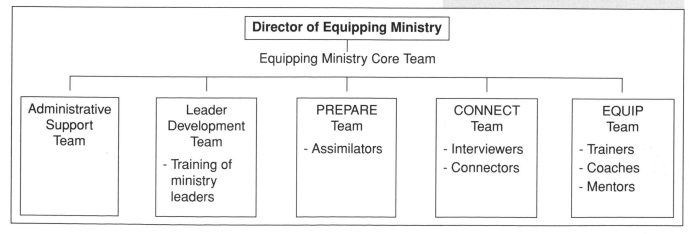

CONTRACTORS' CONFERENCE

Before You Choose Your Equipping Ministry Model, Ask Where God Has Preceded You

If a church board is planning a new emphasis on equipping ministry, in all like-lihood God has already started the movement somewhere in the church. As Henry Blackaby states in his book *Experiencing God,* "Watch to see where God is working and join him."

Staff members, key leaders, governing boards, and task forces in your church can discuss the following questions.

1. Where has God preceded your efforts to implement equipping ministry? How have you seen God prepare the way already?

2. Where have new avenues already opened?

   • through Sunday school classes

   • through small groups that have taken the initiative to help their members serve

   • through a group of entrepreneurial people who have created target ministries in the community apart from official church programs

   • through a children's ministry that has already organized its volunteers well

   • through other avenues where God has already led this movement

Identifying where God is working will help you build your equipping min-istry on a firm foundation of existing strengths.

CONTRACTORS' CONFERENCE

————————— **CONTRACTORS' CONFERENCE** —————————

The senior pastor, leadership board members, church staff members, and department heads would do well to reflect on the following questions:

1. What are the top five ways you hope the equipping ministry department will help you (or has already helped you) improve your job?

2. What are your primary concerns about how the equipping ministry department may interfere (or has already interfered) with your job?

3. If you start an effective equipping ministry department, change is inevitable. What should be done to ensure that the change benefits you and the ministry, program, or department you lead?

A Short Story of Success

Without realizing it I developed an equipping ministry system for our church. I thought your readers might find this story interesting.

I approached a large church in the southwest part of the country with a proposal for a small group program. I was hired, and the small group program went great. Lives were being changed, leadership was developing, and the idea of "customized" ministry began to blossom at the church. I soon found myself in the position of pastor of adult ministry, so I rolled up my sleeves and went to work. With my available budget, I hired people to manage the small group ministry, adult Sunday school, volunteer program, and our singles program. I devoted my time to creating a unified adult ministry. This is what happened:

I revised our new member orientation to include a comprehensive inventory consisting of life experiences, felt-needs assessment, and gifts and passion assessment. This information was used to help each new member "plug in" to our church. Future plans included conducting individual interviews with each person and then allowing existing members to experience the same process.

Instead of segmenting small groups as a separate department, I began to identify each small group as to the function it fulfilled. Support and recovery issues, Bible study, and ministry distinguished small groups. I did the same thing for the different programs of other departments, including adult Sunday school and our singles program.

I found people who wrote four-week classes on *Christian Basics.* These five classes ("Who is Jesus?" "Beginning the Christian Faith," "How to Study the Bible," "Who is the Holy Spirit?" and "How to Spend Time Alone with God") were taught on a rotating basis. The goal was to offer basic Christian teaching for people who came through our doors without a Christian background.

(continued on next page)

2. The Departmental Model

This model involves training the leaders of each ministry department so that they gain skills in the equipping ministry system. Operating as equipping leaders for their responsibility areas, the department heads assume responsibility for interviewing members, placing them in service according to their gifts and abilities, monitoring and supporting their ongoing involvement, and recognizing them for their ministry.

This approach is particularly effective in smaller churches, churches organized around strong departmental ministries, and churches unable to afford an equipping ministry director on either a full-time or part-time basis.

Practical Recommendations to Facilitate the Departmental Model

- Convene department leaders to lay the groundwork for the equipping ministry system. Thoughtful planning leads to the development of uniform ministry descriptions, coordinated training efforts, selection of gift-based educational materials, and a system for recognition.
- Create a team of ministry connectors to share departmental ministry needs and coordinate outreach efforts. The connectors facilitate churchwide interviewing efforts and provide a forum for sharing information about members who have unique gifts and interests.
- Send the ministry connectors for additional training in equipping ministry with the goal of bringing back additional knowledge to use in training each departmental director.
- Develop joint seminars and training that can be used by each department to help members discover their gifts and connect their ministry to their overall spiritual growth.

Advantages of the Departmental Model

- The leaders who are inviting people to serve understand well the needs of the departments. The point of entry is often where a person already has expressed a general interest to serve.
- When ministry connectors are used, the most critical needs of the church are the first to receive assistance.
- People can be mobilized for ministry quickly.

Disadvantages of the Departmental Model

- The focus of equipping ministry can easily shift to meeting departmental staffing needs and not to developing members as disciples.
- With limited incentive to expose members to other ministry opportunities, departments may poorly utilize members' gifts and skills.
- The needs of the surrounding community may be neglected if church programs have the inside track on inviting members to serve.
- Lack of a centralized interviewing system results in multiple entry points for service, which may confuse new members and cause them to be poorly integrated into the total ministry of the church.

See page 110 for a diagram of the departmental model.

3. The Sunday School or Adult Bible Fellowship Model

Many churches have strong Sunday school classes or Adult Bible Fellowships (ABFs) that form the backbone of their structure. The director of equipping ministry, or a designated leader, works with Sunday school teachers or ABF leaders to help them understand their role in equipping ministry. The group or class becomes the doorway to service and the vehicle for involvement within the church. The group or class leader, or someone to whom they delegate leadership, assumes equipping ministry responsibilities and supports members as he or she identifies personal needs that require support, as well as gifts and talents to utilize in service.

As illustrated in the diagram below, the Sunday school class or Adult Bible Fellowship creates time for assimilation, biblical foundations, discovery, and even ministry itself:

- *Assimilation* and *Biblical Foundations* occur as people enter groups that are active in the existing structure and learn about the role of equipping ministry in the church.
- *Discovery* is a group process where people participate in roundtable or breakout groups that help them discover their ministry.
- *Matching and Placement* occur as a group process where the class identifies the ministry it will perform as a group. The group may also choose to encourage each person to enter into ministry individually and use the group as his or her basis for support and ongoing reflection about the meaning of ministry in a Christian's life.
- *Growth* and *Recognition* happen among peers. The leader may choose to focus class discussion on people's experiences in their particular ministry.

Advantages of the Sunday School or Adult Bible Fellowship Model

- This approach takes advantage of the existing leadership structure within the church. It builds on existing Bible studies and trust relationships to encourage service through peer influence as well as through scriptural understanding.
- For some people the discovery of gifts is more effective in a group setting.
- Friends are available to participate in group projects or to develop "buddy teams" to encourage members who are hesitant to serve.

Disadvantages of the Sunday School or Adult Bible Fellowship Model

- Teachers and leaders may not feel qualified to assume this role or may not have the gifts that support this new form of involvement. You may want to encourage group leaders to delegate this responsibility to a committed assistant.
- It can be difficult to get past the needs of friends in the group in order to focus on the concerns of the church or the community.
- A centralized equipping ministry team or team of ministry connectors must be established to catalog churchwide and community ministry areas.
- Without centralized coordination it is difficult to monitor success and determine the outcome of the effort.

See page 111 for a diagram of the Sunday school or Adult Bible Fellowship model.

See page 111 for a diagram

(continued from previous page)

What's more, I began to collect information on every ministry our church offered. Each department wrote down descriptions of all its ministry opportunities and training events. We were building a ministry catalog. Ministry mentors were in the works to help nurture people as they found their ministry, received coaching, and determined their future ministries.

Finally, we began planning rallies and appreciation banquets for our volunteers in all of our ministry departments.

The result was equipping ministry! At the time, I had never even heard of equipping ministry, but suddenly there it was! By developing a process-oriented adult ministry program, which helped someone move from non-involvement to ministry, equipping ministry began. My job "accidentally" changed from pastor of adult ministry to director of lay mobilization. Each component of adult ministry became part of the process in the development of lay ministers!

I learned two very important lessons about equipping ministry. First, developing each member into a minister is a logical, natural process. Second, you can build a system without dismantling or significantly changing existing ministries. Utilize your strengths by going where God has preceded you!

Signed,
An anonymous
small group pastor

THE DEPARTMENTAL MODEL

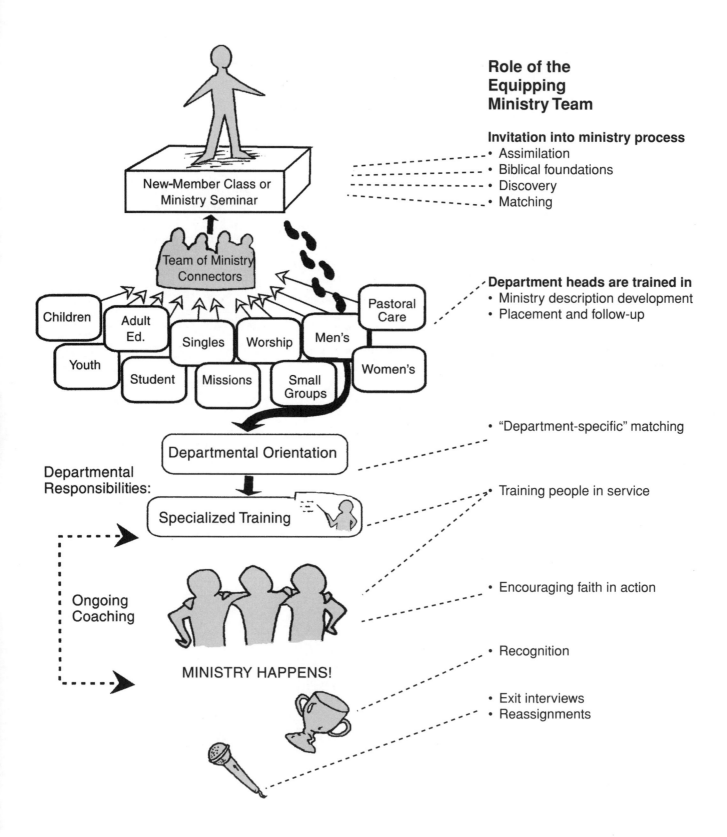

Role of the Equipping Ministry Team

Invitation into ministry process
- Assimilation
- Biblical foundations
- Discovery
- Matching

New-Member Class or Ministry Seminar

Team of Ministry Connectors

Children
Adult Ed.
Youth
Student
Singles
Missions
Worship
Small Groups
Men's
Women's
Pastoral Care

Department heads are trained in
- Ministry description development
- Placement and follow-up

- "Department-specific" matching

Departmental Responsibilities:

Departmental Orientation

Specialized Training

- Training people in service

Ongoing Coaching

- Encouraging faith in action

MINISTRY HAPPENS!

- Recognition

- Exit interviews
- Reassignments

THE SUNDAY SCHOOL OR ADULT BIBLE FELLOWSHIP MODEL

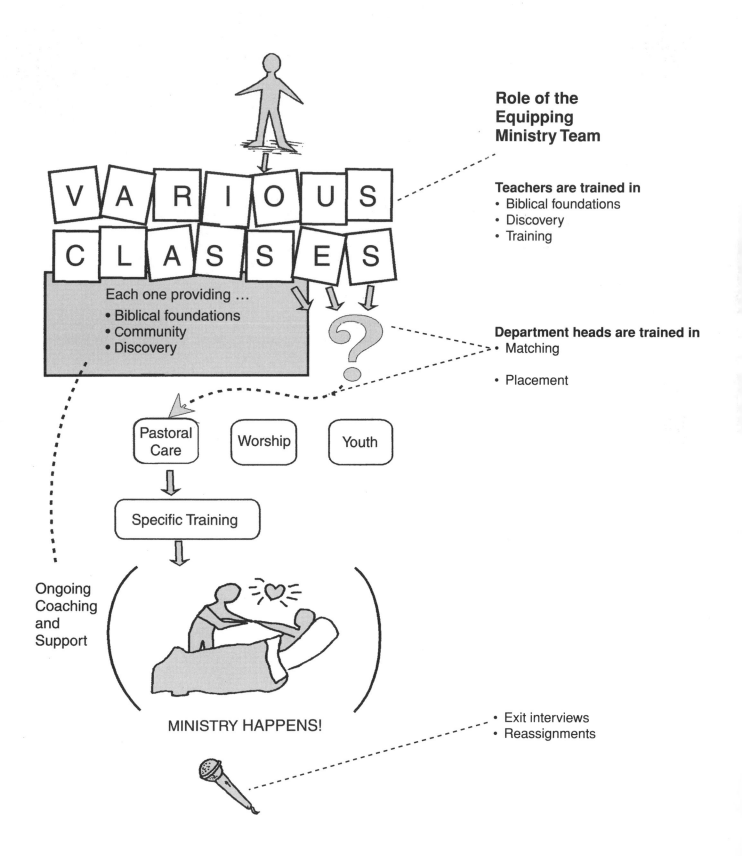

Role of the Equipping Ministry Team

Teachers are trained in
- Biblical foundations
- Discovery
- Training

VARIOUS CLASSES

Each one providing ...
- Biblical foundations
- Community
- Discovery

Department heads are trained in
- Matching

- Placement

Pastoral Care

Worship

Youth

Specific Training

Ongoing Coaching and Support

MINISTRY HAPPENS!

- Exit interviews
- Reassignments

4. The Small Group Model

The experience of community is a high priority for many churches today, which has led many churches to reorganize their entire structure around small groups. In the small group model, the equipping ministry team utilizes the existing small group structure to help groups guide people to places of ministry.

Key Features of a Small Group Model for Equipping Ministry

Small groups provide an environment where people can be nurtured, have their need for community met, and find support in their emerging biblical and spiritual understanding of themselves.

Small groups and equipping ministry can complement one another in a variety of ways:

- *Assimilation:* People assimilate more easily and make friends more quickly in small groups.
- *Biblical Foundations:* Small groups provide excellent places for interactive learning and personalized application of biblical truth.
- *Discovery:* Small groups are considered by many to be the best place to conduct gifts-assessment programs. The feedback of an intimate group of caring friends is a wonderful complement to "pencil and paper" assessments.

Equipping ministry systems can support small groups as both systems work to achieve their shared goals of building disciples in an atmosphere of support and acceptance:

- *Matching* people to ministry opportunities requires thoughtful attention to the unique needs of the individual. Many small group leaders welcome assistance with this area of responsibility. Specially trained mentors from the equipping ministry team may visit groups to guide the matching process.
- *Placement* and *Growth* are clearly enhanced by the support a person receives in the small group. Yet, as in the other models, the primary responsibility rests with the leaders of areas where people are placed for ministry. The equipping ministry team facilitates coordination between leaders of small groups and ministry areas.
- *Recognition* and *Reflection* sustain ministry efforts and build up the body of Christ. Leaders of both the equipping ministry effort and the small group effort can cooperatively ensure that people grow through ministry by providing reflection opportunities and celebration of service contributions.

Serendipity's Lyman Coleman, a pioneer in the small group movement, uses the analogy of the three-legged stool to emphasize the importance of a balanced small group: "Each small group needs to rest equally on three legs: group building, Bible study, and ministry. Any small group that keeps these three components in balance will be a healthy small group *and* a small group that is more likely to multiply in a timely way. A small group that only emphasizes one or two of the three 'legs' develops unhealthy habits, such as becoming too introspective, prone to ministry burnout, or suffering from spiritual indigestion."

BUILDERS' NOTE

Small groups can serve a vital function that many other church environments cannot. One such function includes helping people with support and recovery issues. The intimate, informal setting of a group of approximately eight people meeting together in a home can provide a powerful context for dealing with interpersonal, emotional, and historical issues. A small group equipping ministry model should recognize that some people who need what a small group has to offer might not be ready to embark on the adventure of ministry. The discovery process needs to include information gathering that can determine if someone is simply too overwhelmed with life's issues and struggles to begin serving in ministry.

Why Combine Equipping Ministry and Small Groups?

Small groups and equipping ministry can be a powerful combination. Actually, a healthy small group program *is* an equipping ministry system, because the church is inviting, training, and placing wonderfully gifted laypeople in small groups where they can exercise their gifts (gifts of pastoring, leadership, mercy, and many others, for example). Equipping ministry is enhanced in small group clusters that facilitate community, support personal growth, and encourage people to serve.

An advantage of conducting discovery in a small group context is that it provides enhanced bonding as members listen to each other's life stories and learn about others' gifts and interests. As group members help each other find a place of service, they can, from the beginning, focus on supporting each other rather than looking only for what *they* can get from the group. Mutual commitment is built around a concrete and immediate task.

Another advantage of combining equipping ministry and small group efforts is that it helps keep small groups from becoming too inwardly focused. Inwardly focused groups often become discouraged or develop unhealthy relational patterns. Many churches have discovered that once a group bonds it is very difficult to integrate new people. One alternative is to find ways the group can do service projects together; an even better

---

Team building and leadership specialist Dr. Paul R. Ford utilizes a seven-step strategic process for implementing a spiritual gifts—mobilizing emphasis in a small-group-centered church (also known as a "cell church").

1. Owning the Vision
   - Who carries the torch for cell-group gifts mobilizing?
   - How can we measure ownership among staff members, governing board members, and ministry leaders?

2. Defining Mentoring Leadership
   - Who will be the mentors: small group leader or separate role?
   - How will group leader and mentor work together if separate role?

3. Defining Small Group Leader and Mentor Training
   - What are the key issues for training?
   - How will we best use gifts-specializing, interview skills, and diagnostic assessment tools?

4. Defining Components, Ministry Identity, and Assessments
   - Spiritual gift, ministry burden and passion, plus . . . ?
   - Time availability, maturity, talents, experience, personality, and temperament

5. Planning a Curriculum
   - Should we use available resources or develop our own Bible study process?
   - Saddleback Church's "SHAPE" spiritual gifts discovery materials, Network Ministries International's "Network" spiritual gifts discovery materials, Uniquely You's "Discover Your Giftedness" material, Church Resource Ministries' "Getting Your Gifts in Gear" small group materials, and many other resources are available.

6. Placing People in Ministry in and beyond the Small Group
   - Where will group members use their gifts? Role definitions.
   - What is the best option for each—serving within the group, in a larger body ministry, or in a new small group?

7. Continuing to Mentor
   - Are there opportunities for ongoing discipling in ministry?
   - Who will check in, double-check the placement, encourage, and mentor?

Training programs and consulting on this process, including a list of churches that have adapted and used it, are available through Church Resource Ministries at 1-800-253-4276.

alternative is to help the members discover their gifts and serve in other areas, maintaining the small group as a place of support, ongoing learning, prayer, and encouragement. As individuals are focused on service in areas of giftedness outside the group, they bring back to the group the concerns of the church and community.

Equipping ministry brings broad-based coordination expertise and an awareness of all the ministry needs of the congregation. An effective leader has networks into the community and knows the areas of need where people may serve beyond the walls of the church. Through centralized management, both programs can connect with the church at large, encouraging participation in programming that supports the whole body. The equipping effort offers a central point of assimilation for incoming people, helping ensure that they are connected with small groups or other ministries of the church.

Practical Suggestions for Mutual Support of Small Groups and Equipping Ministry

- The most effective shared beginnings occur when both systems develop under the coordination of the same leader (such as the senior pastor) or the same advisory board. Otherwise, competition for the best leaders, highest visibility, and greatest number of dollars will weaken both efforts.
- Expand the training of the small group leaders. Include a comprehensive understanding of equipping ministry in the small group facilitators' training. Understanding the equipping ministry system and the importance of ministry in the life of the Christian enables the small group leader to effectively encourage and support gift-based service.
- Provide small groups with a gifts-assessment curriculum. In addition to conducting the initial interview, the equipping ministry program offers all new people and interested existing members the increased self-knowledge that comes from a good curriculum that can facilitate effective ministry placement.
- Train and develop a centralized talent bank of ministry mentors. These mentors—trained in gifts assessment, matching, and placement—can be deployed as short-term consultants to individual small groups for two- to six-month periods to support the groups in their discovery and their ministry exploration work.
- Create an information system that is easily accessible. Encourage each small group to appoint a connector to the equipping ministry team. This person can survey the needs and interests of the group and assist people with the identification of ministry opportunities.
- Work together to develop exciting churchwide recognition programs. Groups experience community as they fulfill ministry that is celebrated by the congregation. Individuals grow in their awareness of their giftedness as their ministry is affirmed.
- Encourage small groups to act as the "base camp" for people committed to ministry in the church and the community. Make the small group the vehicle for reflection and growth.
- Build task groups composed of people who are serving together in the same area of ministry.
- Focus on ministry in daily life. Encourage small group exploration of how all of life can be seen as an integrated whole for the Christian.

THE SMALL GROUP MODEL

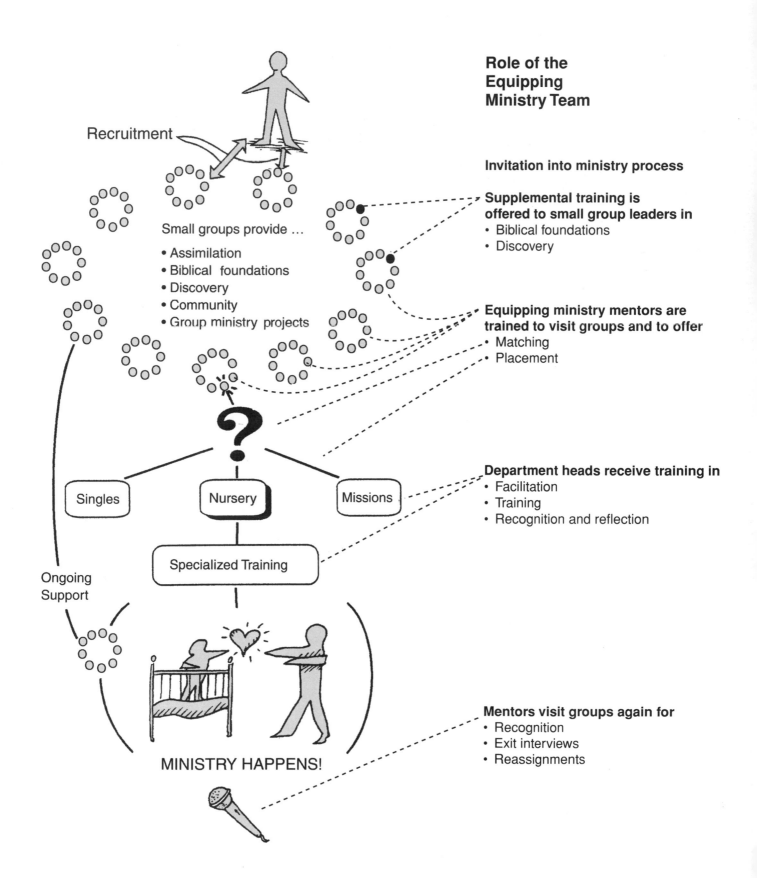

Recruitment

Small groups provide ...

- Assimilation
- Biblical foundations
- Discovery
- Community
- Group ministry projects

Ongoing
Support

Singles

Nursery

Missions

Specialized Training

MINISTRY HAPPENS!

**Role of the
Equipping
Ministry Team**

Invitation into ministry process

**Supplemental training is
offered to small group leaders in**
- Biblical foundations
- Discovery

**Equipping ministry mentors are
trained to visit groups and to offer**
- Matching
- Placement

Department heads receive training in
- Facilitation
- Training
- Recognition and reflection

Mentors visit groups again for
- Recognition
- Exit interviews
- Reassignments

——————— CONTRACTORS' CONFERENCE ———————

1. Where do your small group programs and equipping ministry overlap? Where do they have different goals and structures?

2. What steps can you take to make sure your small group program and equipping ministry are intricately coordinated?

3. What seems to be your best approach—to train the small group leaders or to develop a pool of ministry mentors? What can you do to help offset the disadvantages of the approach you've chosen?

4. What seems to be the best way to structure your groups—to serve through service projects, serve together, or act as a "base camp" of support? What can you do to offset the disadvantages of the approach you've chosen?

5. The Sacramental or Liturgical Model

For churches where the sacraments form the center of the believer's and church's spiritual growth and community life, the structure is often based on one of the other four models, but with significant modifications. The primary change results from understanding all the church's programs and practices as preparation for or reflection of sacramental worship. Other changes sometimes result from having relatively few qualified clergy and ordained leaders who can provide sacramental leadership. These folks are often overworked, and the structure of the church is built to operate most of the programs without their daily involvement, but they are included in all of the critical decisions. Depending on the number and maturity of the leaders, this can be either a refined and effective process or a sporadic and bottlenecked process.

To weave the equipping ministry system into this existing structure, it is important to make sure that service for ministry is seen clearly as an extension of and preparation for sacramental worship. Churches that do this well schedule much more time for reflection as part of the carrying out of regular tasks. Ceremonies, rituals, and visual symbols are not add-ons, but are central to serving and to fostering growth.

Advantages of the Sacramental or Liturgical Model

The sacramental model can take advantage of the central teaching of the liturgy, which focuses on being the body of Christ in the world and developing our ministry out of that mission. Furthermore, designing variations of liturgy in order to relate to many needs and styles offers the opportunity to reflect together about our different gifts, interests, and ministries.

Disadvantages of the Sacramental or Liturgical Model

The emphasis on sacramental worship can make it hard to get beyond using our gifts to serve within the liturgy or worship setting to service in the community and the world.

ASSESSING YOUR CHURCH'S CURRENT PROGRAM EMPHASIS

HAVING ASSESSED YOUR CHURCH'S structure, we move on to provide guidelines on ways to assess your current program emphasis. In addition, we have included information on updating existing equipping ministry systems and assessing the effectiveness of your current equipping ministry efforts.

The particular program emphasis and culture of your church will affect which system components receive the greatest attention. Addressing the concerns most important to your church will tailor the program to best fit and help generate excitement and buy-in. But remember, an effective and comprehensive equipping ministry system requires *all* the components presented in chapter 2.

Different Program Emphases

Evangelism

- Mission: We are a church known to be a safe place for non-Christians to hear and respond to the message of Christ.
- Strategy Implications: Emphasize *assimilation* so that casual attendees who no longer want to remain anonymous can be quickly integrated into the community.

———————————— **CONTRACTORS' CONFERENCE** ————————————

What Is Your Structure, and What Are the Implications for an Equipping Ministry System?

1. Which equipping ministry model do you think would work most effectively at your church?

    - The centralized model

    - The departmental model

    - The Sunday school or Adult Bible Fellowship model

    - The small group model

    - The sacramental or liturgical model

    - A hybrid of two or more models

2. Chart the flow that a person could take through the model that might be used in your church.

3. What will you call your equipping ministry?

4. How will you begin the equipping ministry process in your church?

Outreach

- Mission: We are a church known for sending our people out into the community with the gospel in order to help the needy.
- Strategy Implications: Emphasize *matching and placement* so that people are aware of community service opportunities throughout your city. Develop channels to connect people with community agencies and support their involvement in these agencies.

Young Christians

- Mission: We are a church known for bringing in many people who have recently come to (or returned to) the faith.
- Strategy Implications: Emphasize *biblical foundations* and *discovery* so that people learn the basic tenets of the faith, gain the necessary foundation of Bible knowledge, and acquire the knowledge of their spiritual gifts for service and growth.

Discipleship and Teaching (Bible Study Emphasis)

- Mission: We are a church known for providing good Bible teaching and opportunities for believers to grow and mature.
- Strategy Implications: Emphasize *matching and placement* so that people can apply their knowledge to practical ministry and continue their growth as Christians.

Discipleship and Teaching (Service Emphasis)

- Mission: We are a church known for helping people grow in the midst of adverse circumstances or through involvement in ongoing service.
- Strategy Implications: Emphasize *growth* and *recognition and reflection* to assist people as they make faith-based decisions in the midst of their life and ongoing service.

Community Emphasis

- Mission: We are a church known for helping people find a Christian family through involvement in small groups of various fellowship experiences.
- Strategy Implications: Emphasize *discovery* and *placement* so that people grow to learn about themselves through a group experience and find a place where they can serve as a group that is focused on a common objective.

Recovery

- Mission: We are a church known for being a safe place where those who are hurting can recover and grow.
- Strategy Implications: Emphasize *recognition and reflection* and *matching* so that people can experience both a place to recover and systems that will help them move beyond their pain to a focus on the needs of others.

Transitions

- Mission: We are a church known for a large number of people in the midst of life transitions, such as entering college, marriage, midlife, or retirement.

> You also, like living stones, are being built into a spiritual house to be a holy priesthood, offering spiritual sacrifices acceptable to God through Jesus Christ. . . .
>
> But you are a chosen people, a royal priesthood, a holy nation, a people belonging to God, that you may declare the praises of him who called you out of darkness into his wonderful light. Once you were not a people, but now you are the people of God; once you had not received mercy, but now you have received mercy.
>
> 1 PETER 2:5, 9–10

- Strategy Implications: Emphasize *discovery* because many people are making decisions that require greater self-knowledge and increased mentoring. Many will have to deal with personal transition decisions before they are ready to include involvement in service as a major part of their new direction.

Marketplace

- Mission: We are a church known for having a number of younger people who are building careers and raising children. People need help in discovering how to be more effective in using their gifts in the midst of work responsibilities and community and school activities, particularly because they have little discretionary time.
- Strategy Implications: Emphasize *discovery* so that people can better control their own careers and find pockets of fulfillment within the press of necessary tasks. By focusing on areas of gifts, *recognition and reflection* can support career decision making, relationships within work-team settings, and parenting issues.

Aging

- Mission: We are a church known for a large percentage of older members.
- Strategy Implications: Emphasize *placement* and *growth* so that people who may be motivated to serve can find the help they need to identify appropriate opportunities, as well as the ongoing support to assure that their needs are being met as they serve.

ASSESSING AND UPDATING AN EXISTING EQUIPPING MINISTRY SYSTEM

SUCCESSFULLY FUNCTIONING SYSTEMS, as well as those churches that are still finding their way, often look for new approaches to update and enhance equipping ministry processes. Here we'll address some concerns raised by experienced leaders of equipping ministry systems.

The Three Most Common Reasons Equipping Ministries Fail

Fully 99 percent of churches who are dissatisfied with their current systems can trace their disappointment to the absence of one of three key ingredients for program success. Effective equipping ministry must have . . .

1. strong embodiment of the vision and values of equipping ministry by the senior pastor and top-level leadership, along with adequate resources for success.
2. a comprehensive system that includes preparation and development of people thorough administrative systems, staff support and involvement, and celebration of success.
3. an identifiable leader and team that have the authority and responsibility to share the vision and facilitate the ministry.

An equipping ministry system will continue to produce disappointing results until a congregation is prepared to make a full-fledged, three-pronged commitment to the vision and core values of equipping God's people to serve.

Because congregations tend to emphasize certain objectives more than others, they frequently develop programs (elements within an equipping

> "As Christians, we absorb teaching, instruction, God's Word and His promises, but at some point along the way, we stop growing. We get saturated, and our capacity to absorb diminishes. Then no matter how many more messages we hear, we'll cease being able to absorb any more until we 'wring out our sponges.' Then, and only then, will our absorbency return. Wring out your sponge and serve!"
>
> Wayne Cordeiro,
> *Doing Church as a Team*

———— CONTRACTORS' CONFERENCE ————

1. What is your primary program emphasis? Rate the following on a scale from 1 to 10 (1 = the greatest current emphasis of your church and 10 = the least). Compare notes with other members of your group.

_____ Evangelism: providing a safe place for non-Christians to hear and respond to the message of Christ

_____ Outreach: sending people out into the community with the gospel in order to help the needy

_____ Young Christians: bringing in many who have recently come to (or returned to) Christ

_____ Discipleship (Bible study emphasis): providing good Bible teaching and opportunities for believers to grow and mature

_____ Discipleship (service emphasis): helping people grow through ongoing service

_____ Community emphasis: finding a Christian family through involvement in small groups of various fellowship experiences

_____ Recovery: being a safe place where those who are hurting can recover and grow

_____ Transitions: supporting people in the midst of life transitions, such as entering college, marriage, midlife, or retirement

_____ Marketplace: helping young people discover their gifts and be more effective in all facets of their life

_____ Aging: supporting and involving people in their later years

_____ Other _____

_____

_____

2. Consider the equipping ministry emphasis for each program focus. How can equipping ministry enhance your mission and help your church achieve her objectives?

☑ **CHECKPOINT**

Ask yourselves the following questions:

____ Are the vision and values for equipping ministry highly visible in the church?

____ Does the senior pastor preach the biblical principles of gift-based ministry, team ministry, and spiritual growth through service? Is equipping ministry frequently mentioned during sermons and worship services?

____ Is equipping ministry considered an integral part of the discipleship process and not "just one more church activity"?

____ Do the people participating in the ministry feel supported in and energized by their efforts?

____ Are you prepared to hire someone to lead a department of equipping ministry when the job becomes too large for a team to handle?

____ Does the person in charge of equipping ministry report to the senior pastor or the top-level management staff?

____ Is the director of equipping ministry skilled in accomplishing most of the facets of the job and capable of identifying others to augment skills he or she may be lacking?

____ Does the director of equipping ministry receive a salary commensurate with other staff positions, such as the director of Christian education or director of children's ministry? Is he or she given adequate funds for continuing education?

____ Does the director of equipping ministry have adequate secretarial support and office space, as well as access to necessary office and record-keeping resources?

____ Is the director of equipping ministry included in key planning and development meetings and retreats?

____ If the position of equipping ministry director is part-time or non-paid in your church, is increasing the funding for this position a high priority?

system) that reflect their unique concerns. While it is appropriate that a congregation support her key objectives, an equipping ministry system is only effective when all the elements are in place. Two imbalances most commonly appear: the *teaching imbalance* and the *activity imbalance.*

The teaching imbalance appears most often among evangelical churches. Many of these churches provide excellent assimilation and new member programs. Some go even further and provide in-depth biblical teaching, explaining the context for ministry and conducting sophisticated seminars to help members determine their spiritual gifts. But the track ends before the train station. Members are left on their own to figure out the implications of their gifts for ministry, and no one helps them locate a place to serve. The result is a program that gets off to a great start, but the actual number of people who are placed, trained, and serving is limited.

These congregations are encouraged to study "The Equipping Church" chart on page 65 and refer to part 2 of this book for assistance with the *Prepare, Connect,* and *Equip* processes.

Mainline churches most frequently suffer from the activity imbalance. Elaborate volunteer management systems catalog ministry opportunities with carefully developed position descriptions. They keep good records on people, and they interview and place hundreds of people. What appears to be lacking for many, however, is some connection for these individuals among their service, the mission of the church, and their own spiritual growth.

People may be matched to a ministry based on a written survey or an interview, but they don't have a sense that they've been empowered with knowledge about how God fit them for the task. They may feel that the church's priority is to fill a vacancy in a program rather than to help them grow and contribute in the unique way designed by God.

As a result, equipping ministry is sometimes seen as a program outside the central focus of the church or as something whose main value is to provide volunteers for other programs. The equipping ministry director in these churches is often placed relatively low in the church hierarchy, and much of the potential for contributing to a healthy church is lost. To use the train metaphor, the train arrives at the station, but the passengers are unclear about where they are, with the result that much of the benefit is lost.

Activity-focused churches are encouraged to study "The Equipping Church" chart on page 65 and pay close attention to chapters 5 and 6 for vision and biblical foundations support.

Ideas for Enhancing Existing Systems

Here are some practical suggestions to help you improve your existing equipping ministry system. Involve your equipping ministry director and team as you explore ways to develop and enhance your system.

1. *Add to the interview process.*

- For churches where the equipping ministry director conducts all the interviews, consider developing a team of ministry mentors who conduct interviews. The ministry mentor gives each person more time and stays with the person throughout the process of matching and placement (see page 275).

- Gifts-assessment tools can enhance the interview process and provide a common language for discussion and placement purposes. Visit the Web site at www.ltn.org for a listing of available tools.

─────────── **CONTRACTORS' CONFERENCE** ───────────

Equipping Ministry Effectiveness #1

1. In your church is there strong, top-level embodiment of the vision and values of equipping ministry and the provision of adequate resources for success? What does it mean to provide visible, ongoing support for equipping ministry? Do you have a comprehensive system in place that includes preparation and development of members, thorough communication systems, staff support and involvement, and celebration of success? Do you have an identifiable leader and team that have the authority and responsibility to share the vision and facilitate the ministry?

2. Many churches underestimate the amount of time, energy, and expertise required to implement and facilitate a comprehensive equipping ministry system. See how your church measures up as you seek to determine if your fellowship adequately supports the equipping ministry vision.

"You can inoculate people against the life of the church by throwing them into the committee structure without them seeing either the personal or organizational significance of their work. They get burned-out as they do their duty without joy. Laypeople are called to the ministry of the church, not just the business of the church. They need a personal sense that what they are involved in is making a difference."

Michael Foss, senior pastor, Prince of Peace Lutheran Church, Burnsville, Minnesota

✓ CHECKPOINT

A full equipping ministry system develops with solid organizational support and combines the strengths of both imbalances. This creates a complete track for people to be assimilated into the church, learn about their biblical calling to serve, and discover their gifts. It continues on with a system to match and guide people to potential ministry opportunities based on their gifts, calling, and life experiences. Once placed in service, people receive ongoing training, nurturing, and support, both for how their ministry is seeding their growth as Christians and how it is contributing to the mission of the church.

- If your interviewing process focuses on new visitors, consider expanding it to include longtime members and those who have served faithfully for years in one ministry area. Both groups may appreciate the attention and the opportunity to reexamine their role in the church.
- Expand your interview system to include exit interviews. People gain valuable experience and insight as a result of service. Spend time with persons completing a term of office or finalizing a ministry commitment, and learn from them.

2. *Connect equipping ministry with Christian education.*

- Help people better connect their ministry to their spiritual growth through specially designed educational programs, such as Bible studies that focus on spiritual gifts.
- Gifts assessments and personality surveys can be utilized in such a way that they can be applied to work and family, as well as to service.
- The church's social ministry and benevolence ministries may elect to offer programs that focus on community need and highlight service opportunities outside the walls of the church.

3. *Connect equipping ministry with small group ministry.* Small groups are an excellent place to administer gifts-assessment tools. Through the personal knowledge group members gain about each other, people can have their gifts recognized and validated by others and gain the support of the group to use these gifts in ministry. See pages 112–14 for more information about small group ministry and ways that equipping ministry can support and complement a small group ministry.

4. *Enhance the skills of staff members and program ministry leaders.* Time spent with staff and ministry leaders can provide them with the skills they may be lacking in order to train and affirm people in service. Allocate time at staff meetings, retreats, or in-service workshops for the director of equipping ministry to . . .

- train department leaders in how to enjoy more effective working relationships with people in ministry.
- address problems that people have shared about the church so that staff members and leaders can hear their concerns.
- teach program ministry leaders to successfully invite people into ministry.
- teach any other skills people may need in order to carry out effective equipping ministry.

5. *Set goals for system improvement.* Daily maintenance activities often demand so much attention that long-range planning is neglected. Nothing can energize a team more than setting new and exciting goals for ministry growth and development. Examine church publications, look at your mission statement, and identify new areas for exploration.

- If your system lacks strong community connections, consider ways to become "the church scattered."
- If your young people have not been a focus, look for ways to involve them in service individually, in groups, or as family units.
- Create a new recognition process, highlighting a different servant every month.

- Create plans to involve an increasing percentage of people in service.
- Have fun with your goals and watch your ministry develop!

6. *Expand the role of equipping ministry.* For church leaders familiar with the business world, the changing role of the director of equipping ministry looks similar to the expansion of human resources departments over the last few decades. As companies have increasingly recognized the value of their human resources, the departments have expanded beyond simply dealing with payroll and benefits to include career counseling, employee assistance, team development, training, and many other tasks geared to helping employees thrive. Churches with several years of experience in equipping ministry are seeing their ministry grow to include several staff members with responsibilities for leadership development, new member assimilation, gifts assessment, and small group ministry responsibilities.

> Assessing your current equipping ministry effectiveness can pose a difficult challenge for church leaders. Most leaders rarely find themselves in a situation where they are new to a church and struggling to find their place of ministry. The challenge of evaluating your strategy involves putting yourself in the place of someone who is not familiar with how to find a place in which to do ministry. For more information, refer to the in-depth assessment (for use by the equipping ministry team) on pages 196–201.

ASSESSING READINESS FOR CHANGE IN YOUR CHURCH

A CRITICAL ASPECT OF preparing the church for an equipping culture is evaluating how ready the church is for change. Be sure to read chapter 7 for more information on preparing for change.

In assessing your church's readiness for change, it is useful to apply the following model:

Dis = level of dissatisfaction with the status quo
Dsr = desirability of the proposed change or end state
Pra = practicality of the change (minimal risk and disruption)
X = cost of changing
If (Dis + Dsr + Pra) > X, then change will occur.

Level of Dissatisfaction with the Status Quo

Brainstorm a list of needs and problems that are in some way related to your church's equipping ministry. Rank them by how important you think they are, by how important the congregation as a whole thinks they are, by how important the key influencers think they are, and by how urgent they appear to both groups (1 = very little importance and 10 = great importance). Discuss as a group and rate on a scale of 1 to 10 (1 = very low and 10 = very high) what you think the level of dissatisfaction is with the status quo.

Desirability of the Proposed Change or End State

Ask yourself the question, "How well is the vision formed?" Desirability to transition to a future state is driven by understanding of, ownership of, and belief in the vision and the value of that future state. At this point, rank how desirable the future state is (1 = not at all desirable and 10 = highly desirable). What could be done to increase this number if it comes in at a low figure?

Practicality of the Change (Minimal Risk and Disruption)

As you think of the ministry being carried out at present at your church, what areas of ministry are working well, and what areas are not? Where is the most practical place to begin making changes with the minimum of disruption?

> Mobilizing people for gift-based ministry represents a significant shift from the more traditional clergy-centered model of ministry delivery. Although most churches preach the priesthood of all believers, a much smaller number have identified the process necessary to equip people for ministry. Many staff members have not been taught the steps they must take to make the transition from doing the ministry to equipping others to minister. Compounding the difficulty, seminaries have generally not taught courses in effective equipping ministry leadership (though continuing education programs have recently begun to address the issue). While denominations may want to support the vision, many are unclear how to proceed or lack the resources to initiate a major effort.

CONTRACTORS' CONFERENCE

Equipping Ministry Effectiveness #2

1. What percentage of your church members are involved in a satisfying ministry for which they have been well prepared?

   _____ percent

2. If you were to ask the people who are not currently involved in a satisfying gift-based ministry why they aren't involved, what would the three most common responses be?

   _____ I don't know what's available.
   _____ I'm not sure about my faith.
   _____ I've got too many troubles in my life right now.
   _____ I'd like to make some friends first.
   _____ I'm too busy.
   _____ I don't want to change diapers or pass the collection plate.
   _____ No one ever asked me.
   _____ I've seen too many people get taken for granted when they volunteer for something at church.
   _____ I don't know how to do anything the church could use.

3. What type of people seem to find a place to serve in your church by means of your current system? Outgoing people? New visitors? Veteran members? New Christians? Mature Christians? What can you learn from them that will help others who have been less successful in finding ministry opportunities?

4. What types of people have difficulty finding their place in ministry? What do you as church leaders need to do to help them discover their ministry?

5. Of the people listed in your answer to question 4, what reasons do you or other church leaders give for their inability to find their ministry? Mark the top three reasons below:

_____ They are not committed.

_____ They are not team players.

_____ They have too little faith.

_____ They don't like me or other staff members.

_____ The church has failed to help them find their ministry.

_____ They do not believe they have anything to offer.

_____ The church has not done a good job "giving to them" so they have nothing to give back.

_____ They are too caught up in everyday matters to make time for ministry.

_____ They have other needs that are more important, such as crisis situations, recovery issues, faith development work, and relationship building.

_____ Other.

6. Empathy is a valuable way to judge the effectiveness of your current equipping ministry system. Imagine you are Joe Q. Visitor or Josephine Q. Visitor. Mark the statements that might describe your experience during your first six months at the church:

_____ Hardly anyone spoke to me.

_____ No one invited me to an activity outside of Sunday morning worship.

_____ I had difficulty figuring out how to participate in worship. The bulletin and worship books are confusing.

_____ It isn't clear where the Bible studies or Sunday school classes are located.

_____ No one asked me what I was looking for. Instead, they assumed I wanted something based on my age or marital status.

_____ It took me over two months to find a class or group that met my needs.

_____ No one asked me about my spiritual needs.

_____ No one asked me about my relational or emotional needs.

_____ No one asked me about my spiritual gifts, skills, or areas of ministry interest.

_____ No one asked me about my previous church experience.

_____ No one explained to me the mission of the church and what gifts are needed in the various ministries.

7. Which components of an effective equipping ministry system (see "The Equipping Church" chart on page 65) is your church managing well right now? Which components do you most need to strengthen or improve?

_____ Assimilation

_____ Biblical foundations

_____ Discovery

_____ Matching and placement

_____ Growth

_____ Recognition and reflection

The practicality of change increases greatly as leaders are assigned, teams are developed, and plans are created and explained. Rate on a scale of 1 to 10 (1 = completely impractical and 10 = enormously practical) as to how practical the change is right now in any of a number of specific areas. What could be done to increase this number if it comes in at a low figure?

Cost of Changing

People often fear change because they believe they'll lose something in the process. How do you overcome this fear, which often causes resistance? It is overcome by casting the vision and creating knowledge, ownership, and understanding of what they will *gain* from the change. Only when they believe they will gain more than what they will lose will the cost of changing be a positive factor.

Ask yourself which groups in your church will bear the highest cost of change, and which will bear the lowest. Identify the primary components that make up this cost. Rate on a scale of 1 to 20 (1 = no cost and 20 = highest conceivable cost) what you think the cost of change is at this point in your church. What could be done to lessen this number if it comes in at a high figure?

Where Do You Want to Be?

Prepare the Architectural Drawings (Envision)

WHAT IS THE CRITICAL phase when it comes to envisioning the desired future state of the culture and system of your church's equipping ministry? It comes when we define the desired values and outcomes, and then formulate and strengthen the vision for equipping ministry in the life of the church. Successful implementation of equipping ministry is dependent on the vision and values supporting the biblical foundations and assumptions of equipping ministry. Vital success criteria include owning the vision and embodying the values of the ministry by everyone in the church. This chapter provides you and other church leaders with the information you need to begin defining your vision for equipping ministry.

> Then Jesus came to them and said, "All authority in heaven and on earth has been given to me. Therefore go and make disciples of all nations, baptizing them in the name of the Father and of the Son and of the Holy Spirit, and teaching them to obey everything I have commanded you. And surely I am with you always, to the very end of the age."
>
> MATTHEW 28:18–20

CHAPTER PREVIEW

- Where do you want your culture to be?
- Where do you want your system to be?

WHERE DO YOU WANT YOUR CULTURE TO BE?

Define Desired Values

An essential component of the cultural foundation for equipping ministry is for church leaders to incarnate and live out the core values gleaned from Scripture. These core values are established on strong biblical foundations. In addition, church leaders can only achieve their vision if their values are in alignment with their vision.

In chapters 3 and 4 you and your leadership team or task force had the opportunity to assess your current values and evaluate the congruency between those values and the core values of equipping ministry. At this point, the same group of people should work through the questions in the "contractors' conference"

What Is a Value?

"A value can be likened to a 'homing device,' an internal guidance mechanism that keeps you on course. A value is what helps you to make in-flight corrections to your attitudes, motives, activities, and emphases. You will need to make many in-flight corrections along the way, but if you have not clearly defined your core values, you won't know what to correct to!"

Wayne Cordeiro,
Doing Church as a Team

2020 Culture Description

The year is A.D. 2020. Assuming every one of your wildest dreams for the church were to come true, describe your church, emphasizing the values that are evident in her internal culture and how they are displayed in programs, relationships, budgets, buildings, and impact in individual people's lives, in the community, and in the world.

"I tell you the truth, anyone who has faith in me will do what I have been doing. He will do even greater things than these, because I am going to the Father. And I will do whatever you ask in my name, so that the Son may bring glory to the Father. You may ask me for anything in my name, and I will do it."

JOHN 14:12–14

☑ CHECKPOINT

Brainstorming is a valuable group process where combined creativity results in many more ideas than one person could develop on his or her own. The ideas born out of a brainstorming session often expand beyond existing boundaries because the process generates unique and innovative solutions and ideas.

---

on page 132 in order to clearly define the desired values of equipping ministry in your church—the values that currently support equipping ministry as well as the values that require some shift in emphases or basic assumptions.

A church's vision statement is an expression of her underlying core values. To realize the vision, these core values need to be in place, known by all, and demonstrated on a continual basis. If a church expresses a vision for equipping ministry but the values underlying the vision are not embodied, the vision will never become a reality.

Describe the Future State

Seeking a vision can be a creative, exciting process. As you approach the process of formulating the vision, recognize that it may not always be necessary to change an existing vision. If your current church vision is a healthy and truthful representation of the values that support equipping ministry, a simple rewording or strengthening may be the only strategy necessary.

If you determine that your church needs to formulate an entirely new vision, then this is a time to resist customary ways of solving problems and getting things done (in other words, your current basic assumptions). Think big and forget about how things have worked in the past. Imagine an equipping ministry plan where God is involved in miraculous, unexpected, and life-changing ways! Pray for faith and for discernment of God's vision for your church.

WHERE DO YOU WANT YOUR EQUIPPING MINISTRY SYSTEM TO BE?

Brainstorm the Desired System

One of the best ways to approach the vision formulation process is for a group consisting of the core leadership team, planning team, or task force to brainstorm openly. The best places to start building your equipping ministry systems are where God has preceded your efforts and where the need is felt the most.

Brainstorming Guidelines

- Brainstorming requires the freedom to suggest anything and an openness of the group's members to honor all ideas. There is no such thing as a stupid idea.
- No set pattern exists for brainstorming. Some people might begin with the finished product, while others might focus on the process.
- Brainstorming works best without structure. Some of the best brainstorming occurs in a large room with nothing more than big pads of paper and colored markers. Brainstorming cannot be scheduled and confined. For best results, allow plenty of time.
- Each brainstormer needs freedom to expand on or improve any idea on the table. Rigid ownership of ideas or oversensitivity to feelings will inhibit brainstorming.

Possible Brainstorming Questions

1. Assuming money, facilities, and involvement were unlimited, in your wildest dreams what would equipping ministry look like in your church in five years? In ten years?

2. Continue your line of thought from the preceding question. What will the different departments and ministries of your church look like after equipping ministry has taken root and made an impact on existing programs?

3. Imagine that the date is now Sunday, May 10, 2020. Jimmy and Norma Jean Swenson decide to visit your church. After visiting for several weeks, the Swensons join and become active members of your church.

Now . . . start dreaming. From first-time visitors to active, empowered ministers—imagine the Swensons moving through your equipping ministry system. Allowing yourself your wildest dreams, what experiences would you like the Swensons to have? Put yourself in their shoes and describe your ideal system from assimilation to recognition and reflection.

PREPARE

Assimilation _____

_____

_____

Biblical foundations _____

_____

_____

CONNECT

Discovery _____

_____

_____

Matching and placement_____

_____

_____

EQUIP

Growth _____

_____

_____

Recognition and reflection _____

_____

_____

4. Think about "Amy Uninvolved" church member. What would happen to her if your church developed and enacted your dream equipping ministry system? What are your dreams for how your model will connect people like Amy?

5. Consider Molly Mom, arriving at your church with three children, ages 8, 10, and 15. What experience would you want for her and her children as they become engaged in the life of the church and grow in their faith and spiritual development?

> "The process of establishing vision and values is a painful one. . . .
> We get lulled into mediocrity, we lose sight of what could be through God's power that is available to us."
>
> Bill Hybels, senior pastor, Willow Creek Community Church, Barrington, Illinois

☑ **CHECKPOINT**

Build the 50/50 Church

Often a primary motivation for a stronger equipping ministry system is a very practical one: to fill job slots in the various church departments. Yet, if the church experienced 100 percent involvement, she would still need only 25 percent of the total membership to run all her programs.

One-hundred-percent involvement is unlikely, but a 50/50 mind-set is a worthy goal. This involves trying to place 50 percent of God's people outside the church in community agencies, mission projects, and other ministry opportunities. Viewing equipping ministry from a community perspective creates a healthy outward focus. Churches that have pursued a 50/50 approach to ministry have reported increases in new members, as the church gains a reputation for being interested in the needs of the community. Evangelism happens naturally as church members build relationships with unchurched people they work with on service projects, at the office, or in neighborhood organizations.

CONTRACTORS' CONFERENCE

Defining Desired Values

1. What are your current espoused values? See the "contractors' conference" on pages 94–98.

2. Which of these values are congruent with and supportive of the biblical foundations and vision of equipping ministry? Refer again to the material in chapter 1.

3. Which of these values are not congruent with the biblical foundations and vision of equipping ministry? Are these espoused values hindering the progress of equipping ministry in your church?

4. What changes need to be made to these values? What are the basic assumptions underlying these values? How can they be changed?

5. Do you own and agree with these necessary changes?

6. In combining the values listed in your answer to question 2 with the desired new values that come out of your reflections on question 4, how would you sum up your desired core values for equipping ministry in your church?

7. How can you and your fellow leaders demonstrate these stated values in your daily lives, particularly in your ministries and in your interactions with fellow church members?

8. Of the above suggestions, which actions are you already implementing?

9. Which values need to be more strongly embodied in your leadership actions?

10. How can you hold each other accountable for the embodiment of these values?

——————— CONTRACTORS' CONFERENCE ———————

Needs, Dreams, Brainstorm

1. Begin your discussion with the following questions:

   - Where do you already see "islands of health" where God has preceded you by building the very systems you desire to be present throughout your church?

   - Where is the greatest felt need for equipping ministry in your church?

2. Use these questions to facilitate a brainstorming session on where you want your system to be.

☑ CHECKPOINT

Ministry occurs outside of ministry descriptions and organized programs. The end goal of equipping ministry is for people to develop a whole-life focus so that their gifts and purpose are lived out in every area of their lives. Brainstorm what whole-life ministry could mean to you and other members of your church. Think of the . . .

- custodian who sees attention to detail as an act of worship to God.
- homemaker who creates a safe environment in which children can stretch their creative wings and discover their own gifts.
- corporate executive who creates a company culture of integrity and justice.
- grandparent who models the grace of God by taking in an unwed mother.
- schoolteacher who encourages children to see their special potential.
- doctor who treats each patient with the compassion of Christ.
- student who swims against the tide of peer pressure and models the Christian's call to purity.

How can each of us model our calling as Christians and use our gifts in all dimensions of our lives?

6. Project a few years into the future. Sitting at a table at a local coffee shop, you unintentionally overhear two people talking in the booth next to yours. They are not members of your church (in fact, you think they may not attend a church), but you hear them talking about your church! At this point in time your equipping ministry is in high gear. What do these outsiders have to say about the ministry going on at your church?

7. Imagine that your equipping ministry system is highly successful. Some people in the church are sharing testimonials of their experience in ministry. What will they say?

8. Here are some of the many ministry possibilities, intended to inspire you as you seek your vision for equipping ministry. Which of these opportunities would you like to see included in your equipping ministry system?

Career guide for the homeless
Usher
Holiday sanctuary decoration team
Scripture reader for shut-ins
Prayer team coordinator
Banner maker
Small group outreach host
Host family for unwed mothers
Dance team director
Plant grower for patients
Grief support team
Stewardship team
New visitor contactor
Small group leader
Gifts-assessment mentor
Disaster relief food packer
Adult Bible master-teacher
Parking lot security
Sunday morning receptionist
Acolyte coordinator
Blood drive coordinator
Trustee
Mop and hammer team
Youth outreach leader
Handbell choir
Church office administrative
    assistant
Bus driver
Elder/Deacon
Small group coach
Youth chaperone
Door-to-door evangelism
New member guide
Vacation Bible school teacher
Food for the bereaved
New member sponsor
Crisis phone line counselor
Church grounds landscaper

New Christian mentor
Habitat for Humanity coordinator
Church library or bookstore clerk
Recovery ministry spokesperson
Ministry catalog editor
Scripture memory coordinator
Youth retreat helper
Greeter
Baby holder and rocker
Audio-visual assistant
Seminar organizer
Library tutor
Homeless solutions ministry
Counseling ministry
Addict support program
Outreach ministry to minority
    groups
Sports and recreation fitness
    director
New ministries assessment
    director
Church photographer
Marketplace evangelism team
Hospital visitation
Church newsletter layout
    specialist
Special events team
Prison ministry
Intergenerational ministry director
Spiritual renewal retreat director
Helper for single-parent families
Caregiver for children of divorce
Exit interviewer
Mechanic for confused car owner
Tape ministry coordinator
Crisis pregnancy center counselor
Church information center
    attendant

Youth rock band
Meals-on-Wheels driver
Nursing home ministry coordinator
Junior high "Big Brother" or
 "Big Sister"

Medical and dental adviser
Choir member
Video camera operator
Foreign mission team advocate

9. The various ministries of your church have an impact on many people. Select a person touched by one of the ministries in your actual or envisioned equipping ministry system and describe the effect this ministry can have on this person's life.

10. What about the people who indicate interest in ministry but don't see how they fit into an existing ministry opportunity? Describe your dream that these people would find a customized ministry. Describe your dream of how equipping ministry can change people's approach to their workplace, their family, and other aspects of their life outside of the church.

11. After hearing all the various expressions of the "future" vision of equipping ministry, discuss together what was most exciting about what you heard.

TRANSLATING DREAMS INTO VISION

Once the leadership has reached a common direction regarding the dream, it is important to translate the dream into a vision that can be fleshed out into a measurable plan of action that will be broadly owned by the congregation.

EVALUATING PROGRESS: HOW WILL YOU KNOW WHEN YOU GET THERE?

Once your leadership team has formulated a vision, you can establish criteria for evaluating whether you are successfully accomplishing the vision. One member of the leadership team may judge equipping ministry to be successful only when a leader development system is operating and preparing new members for team leadership roles and board responsibilities. For another, the success of the ministry may mean there are enough ushers for a three-month rotation or teacher aides who are prepared for the overflow in Sunday school. Still another may want a new Bible study curriculum or a comprehensive gifts-assessment system in place.

Here are some principles to help you sort out your expectations for your equipping ministry vision:

- Identify your expectations early on. Multiple conflicting objectives lead to frustration and ministry failure. Solid foundations are built on a clearly stated, shared understanding of the biblical imperatives central to the values of equipping ministry.
- Involve as many program directors, salaried staff members, and ministry leaders as possible in setting goals and expectations. For equipping ministry to be truly effective, it requires *churchwide* input and ownership.
- Too many goals will prevent a focused effort and result in scattered resources. Too few goals may lead to micromanagement or to a

"A dream is an 'I wish' statement. A vision is an 'I will' statement."

Howard G. Hendricks, chairman,
Center for Christian Leadership,
Dallas Theological Seminary

"How do constituents measure a characteristic as subjective as honesty? [In a leadership survey] we learned that the leader's *behavior* provided the evidence. . . .

Consistency between word and deed is how we judge someone. . . .

If leaders practice what they preach, we're more willing to entrust them with our career, our security, and sometimes even our life."

James Kouzes and Barry Posner,
The Leadership Challenge

——————— CONTRACTORS' CONFERENCE ———————

Desired Outcomes

1. Ask each member of the leadership team or discussion group to complete the following statement openings. Compile the responses and share them with the group. Discuss the implications of the various perspectives.

   • The purpose of an equipping ministry system is to

   • We will accomplish this by (broad statements of what will be done)

   • We will know it is successful when

2. From your answers and from what emerged out of your brainstorming time, list and prioritize the ten most desired outcomes of your equipping ministry system. Synthesize each into a word or short phrase (for example, community impact, whole-life ministry, and the like).

3. Using the top three or four on your list, spend no more than fifteen minutes developing a preliminary purpose or vision statement for equipping ministry in your church. NOTE: If your church has already established a leader or team to spearhead the equipping ministry effort, it is critical that they be involved in this aspect of formulating the vision if they are to own and embrace it.

weak, aimless beginning. Realistic timelines for goals must be established in order to prevent disappointment, because a shift in values and in methods of ministry can and usually does take time.

- Continue to share and discuss your goals with one another. The best way to determine if your leadership board has reached consensus is to agree on ways to measure your goals and report on the status of those goals.

In the next chapter we'll provide information and guidelines to help you establish the goals and the steps in the planning process so you can begin implementing the vision in your church.

6

How Are You Going to Get There?

Draw the Blueprints and Lay the Foundation

ONCE YOU HAVE ASSESSED and formulated your values and vision for equipping ministry you can begin the work of developing a strategy for implementation. Implementing equipping ministry in your church is dependent on a good strategy. Developing the strategy is more than planning. It involves the bigger vision—the broader focus of direction. The planning process should ensure that the strategy is being implemented and the vision realized.

Equipping ministry systems should be implemented simultaneously with the ongoing creation of an equipping culture and in a cross-functional manner. Hence, a critical success factor is infusing equipping ministry into the vision, mission, goals, and objectives of the church. An effective strategy includes maintaining the continual sense of direction toward the vision, while building and maintaining the elements of equipping ministry throughout the life of the church.

As the church embraces the values and vision of equipping ministry, there will be areas where change is necessary. But change is rarely easy—even for Christians who have a strong theological grounding for change and a sincere desire to realize the vision of equipping ministry. And for those who feel that things are pretty much all right just the way they are, the concept of change is even less welcome. This chapter addresses some of the most frequently voiced concerns about equipping ministry and offers sensitive responses to these concerns.

> "Management scholar Henry Minzberg's intensive study found strategy making to be a complex, interactive, and evolutionary process, best described as one of adaptive learning. Strategic planning, it turns out, is *not* a magic potion. It's a process that detaches strategy from operations, thinking from doing." [Successful leaders recognize that developing strategy means engaging in both the thinking and the doing.]
>
> James Kouzes and Barry Posner, *The Leadership Challenge*

CHAPTER PREVIEW

IN THIS CHAPTER YOU WILL have the opportunity to . . .

- examine the biblical foundations for developing a strategy, and then develop a strategy for implementing equipping ministry in your church.
- clarify and implement the process of hiring the director of equipping ministry.

DEVELOPING A STRATEGY

Begin with the Biblical Foundations

- Nehemiah 2:1–20

  Nehemiah provides a good example of effective planning. He clarifies the need, sets a goal, and enlists his available resources; he evaluates progress, shares the vision with others, and trusts God throughout the process.

- Psalm 33:10–11

  Discerning God's will and purpose for your church must remain central to your planning and strategy implementation.

- Proverbs 14:22; 15:22; 16:1–3

  When you involve the leadership in the planning process and jointly discern God's leadership for your church, a positive, God-honoring strategy will emerge.

- Proverbs 16:9

  Developing a strategy (a course of action) for equipping ministry needs to be grounded in prayer and continual discernment of God's will for the church.

- Luke 14:28–33

  It is wise to determine the full scope of equipping ministry prior to implementing any action steps. Laying the cultural foundation for equipping ministry involves strategic evaluation of resources, timing, and implementation actions, as well as ongoing values development. The attention of your leaders to these critical aspects will ensure that the God-given vision in your church will be realized.

- 1 Corinthians 14:33a, 40

  Developing a sound strategy is essential to achieving your stated vision in a systematic, orderly fashion. The planning of your strategy must be responsive to the needs in your church, in keeping with your culture, and focused on the long-term vision for becoming an equipping church.

Clarify the Vision and Expectations

It is critical to clarify these issues for yourselves as leaders, as well as for the director of equipping ministry, once he or she has been hired.

- Begin with prayer. Once the strategy is outlined, call all church members into the circle to begin to prepare their hearts to be open to the process.
- Develop a strategic plan that is supported with and by Scripture. Pray specifically for the development of the equipping ministry system.
- Allow creativity and flexibility in the plan. The people who lead this ministry should have freedom to put flesh on the skeleton. People commit to decisions they help make. This is true for the leadership team that develops the plan, as well as for the leaders of the ministry.
- Plan budget dollars to equip the pastor, the director of equipping ministry, and the people called to serve on the team. It is important

> The LORD foils the plans of
>   the nations;
>   he thwarts the purposes
>   of the peoples.
> But the plans of the LORD
>   stand firm forever,
>   the purposes of his heart
>   through all generations.
>
> PSALM 33:10–11

> Just each of us has one body with many members, and these members do not all have the same function, so in Christ we who are many form one body, and each member belongs to all the others. We have different gifts, according to the grace given us.
>
> ROMANS 12:4–6

> "Before you build a house, you need a blueprint. Before a plane leaves the tarmac, the pilot must file his flight plan with the tower. Before you do church as a team, there must be a clear and concise understanding of the mission and assignment the Lord has given to that specific local church."
>
> Wayne Cordeiro,
> *Doing Church as a Team*

"My first conflict with the pastor was over a measurement issue. The plan had determined the 'right' number of hours one should serve and called for me to track all volunteers' hours for the bottom-line number. I 'pushed back' on two levels. First, the standard number was totally unrealistic for the demographic makeup of the congregation, given the time availability and capability of senior citizens, single moms, college students, and the like. But more important, their hours were not the right success measure. I believed that the right fit, based on gifts and passions, the appropriate coaching for success, the follow-through and the valuing of people through various means of recognition, and the question of whether they were growing toward spiritual maturity as a result—all those things were what would honor God, the people, and the plan. This came up every year in my evaluation, and every year I 'pushed back.' I never did monitor hours."

Sue Mallory,
Leadership Training Network

that all understand the scope of the vision and the importance of their role in breathing life into it. The truth of the matter is, dollars follow values.

- Look carefully at the lines of accountability established for the director of equipping ministry. Value must be rooted from the top down, not just with the people serving but also with the staff and the leadership team. The director of equipping ministry should report to the senior pastor in a spirit of collaboration and growth development for both parties. The pastor has as much to learn from the right leader as the leader does from the pastor. Model what you value.

- The key role and expectation of the director of equipping ministry have to do with *equipping* and *releasing*. The work is about facilitating and connecting people for growth, service, and care. It is about the people, not just the paper or the systems. The systems have been created to serve and grow the people.

Establish Goals and Milestones

- Develop realistic timelines. Speed kills! It can take up to twelve to eighteen months to build or retrofit the foundation and infrastructures. This is a value you are living into, not a new program. Build consensus and teach to the biblical imperative. Remember, this is also a shift for the leadership of the church. To quote a Leadership Training Network Institute participant, "We should move only as fast as we can on our knees."

- Develop mutually agreed-on benchmarks for what the director of equipping ministry should do and for what the ministry is called to create. Think carefully about what you measure as success. Is your focus on numbers or on maturity?

- The key value of equipping ministry is broadening the base of ministry to move from 20 percent involved/80 percent uninvolved to 80 percent involved/20 percent uninvolved. This should be the focus and ongoing goal of the director of equipping ministry.

Think Through the Start-Up Needs

What You Need in Order to Get a System Started

- Office requirements for beginning a system are modest. They include a desk, telephone, and file cabinet for the director. As the program evolves, it becomes important to have an accessible office, a private space for interviewing people, and, if your church uses computers, a terminal for information management.

- Budget requirements include the salary of the director, fringe benefits, a professional development allowance, and funds to cover special events.

- Clear and reasonable expectations are critical. Most churches that start work on a comprehensive equipping ministry system allow nine to eighteen months for development activities. Think through your expectations and develop clear objectives to guide your initial system development.

Budgetary Needs

You can begin equipping ministry with a minimal budget. Other than the salary and benefits for an equipping ministry director, initial program development costs are relatively minor with one exception—providing training for the identified equipping ministry director. Few seminaries currently offer courses or workshops in leading equipping ministry. Unless the individual has directed a volunteer or community relations program in the nonprofit or public sector before accepting the position, *The Equipping Church* book by Sue Mallory, this book, and a few other books on the subject may well be all they'll have to guide their work.

As your system evolves, you will need to develop a budget to support the costs associated with the ministry. Your budget should be based on and reflect the goals and objectives of equipping ministry.

Many churches utilize a basic line-item budget system, with categories to reflect the operational systems in the church. Expense categories, such as duplicating, postage, and general office supplies, often fall within the church's general administrative or office supplies budget section. Likewise, office equipment, such as a desk, a computer, or a filing cabinet, is part of the larger church budget and is not reflected in a specific ministry budget. Personnel expenses vary. Some congregations keep all salaries and benefit packages grouped under personnel, while others allocate the expense to the appropriate department.

The equipping ministry director will want to pay special attention to the financial needs that are specific to his or her ministry. Some of these items may include the following:

- Recognition
- Professional development
- Training for laypeople
- Travel and lodging
- Special needs

No matter how carefully you plan, you will undoubtedly encounter unexpected expenses. Because you are working in an area that is by definition dynamic and flexible, you will need to be prepared for the unusual.

Be Familiar with Start-Up Strategies

Many churches may not be ready to implement a full equipping ministry effort because of budget constraints or lack of support by the staff, congregation, or top-level leadership. Consider these alternatives to pave the way for a full-scale effort down the road.

Start Slow and Pilot-Test Your Process

Start with a single department. The initial communication systems, the process of cataloging ministry opportunities, and the preparation of the ministry director to place and support people in service can be developed on small scale. Together you can brainstorm meaningful ways to recognize people who are already serving and seek their input about other people to contact to work in this ministry area. You can explore methods of discovery or gifts-assessment tools you may want to incorporate, testing their effectiveness in helping people discern their gifts and talents. As you work out the kinks in the system, you can move on to other departments.

Fix the "Squeaky Wheel" First

Many churches face the greatest crisis for member support in the children's ministry department. Select this or another high-priority area and investigate the situation. Meet with those already serving in this area

---

✓ CHECKPOINT

What Will an Equipping Ministry System Cost?

A survey (conducted in the year 2000) of 150 equipping churches across the country yielded some interesting findings:

Churches with less than a thousand in attendance at weekend services tend to employ part-time directors (29 percent of churches surveyed). Salaries and benefits for these directors averaged $18,400. "Part-time" was defined as anywhere from twenty to thirty hours of work weekly. Funds allocated for continuing education averaged $1,300. The equipping ministry budget averaged between $1,500 and $3,000.

Larger congregations (defined as more than a thousand in attendance at weekend services) generally employ full-time directors (71 percent of churches surveyed). The vast majority of directors are dedicated equipping ministry directors who are, in some cases, members of the pastoral staff. These people earn, on average, $48,700 annually.

Support funds were incrementally greater in larger churches as well. A full 98 percent of these churches surveyed showed funding of greater than $8,000 for equipping ministry and $3,000 or more for continuing education. Many also report that some expenses are absorbed in the church's operating funds.

and find out what they enjoy and what makes their commitment strong. Facilitate the development of ministry descriptions that meet the needs of the department and the concerns of the people. Develop an exciting discovery process that piques the interest of people. Recognize people currently involved in ministry and develop ways to commission new people into ministry. Promote the specific ministry and the exciting opportunities to serve there. Keep careful records of each accomplishment and highlight shared successes. Success is infectious. Find needs and meet them, department by department. Because of a good track record and needs well met, other departments will become eager to participate in the system.

Decide Where to Begin

Communication Systems

Some churches focus their initial effort on record-keeping systems to ensure that the support systems are solidly in place before people are invited to participate in the process. This makes sure that the initial participants do not suffer from partially installed systems and end up either being treated poorly or falling through the cracks. These systems operate behind the scenes for months as the hard work of designing computer programs, entering membership data, and collecting ministry descriptions occurs before the first participants start through the system.

Ministry Connectors

For other churches, the idea of complicated record keeping doesn't fit their culture. Many have an informal tradition that makes it unlikely that they will ever collect attendance records or monitor member involvement through computers. In all likelihood this will mean a loss of much of the benefit of the system, but it is better to start where the church culture allows rather than run the risk of not having equipping ministry at all.

Develop a core of trained ministry connectors and equip them to be thoroughly familiar with their responsibilities and knowledgeable about the church. The system will operate behind the scenes for several months as ministry connectors are found and trained. When ready, they can serve as follow-up consultants to a new member class or a gifts seminar, or they can be let loose throughout the church to informally help members find places of ministry that fit their gifts. As the value of equipping ministry is demonstrated through action, it will be possible to backtrack and create a system structure that will facilitate a more carefully monitored process. Few leadership boards can remain unimpressed when high levels of member involvement can be documented statistically.

Regardless of how you choose to begin, make your preparations well in advance. It is damaging to a ministry to launch an effort if you are ill prepared to meet the demand for service. Someone will always be disappointed by being left out or wrongly placed, or even worse, slip through the cracks.

Sell the Idea First to Those Most Able to Sell It to Others

It is vital that the most influential people in the church thoroughly understand and experience the process at the early stages. Their personal benefit will help them authentically convince others of the importance of a system for equipping ministry. You might wait on the results of a pilot project to yield benefits, or select a group of influential people to experience a discovery process before it is unveiled to the church at large. These people can pave a path that might otherwise have taken years of work to permeate the church. It is very important that the leadership board personally go through a pilot discovery and placement process before a launch.

Check Out the Available Tools and Resources

Several excellent curriculum resources are available to enhance your *Prepare, Connect,* and *Equip* processes. Many are listed on the resource Web site at www.ltn.org. Some churches begin their equipping ministry system with a curriculum and customize it to fit their needs. Others develop a carefully designed interview process and work hard to train the interviewer without ever incorporating a formal curriculum for discovery—a process that reflects the unique culture of their church.

Here are some of the advantages of beginning your equipping ministry initiatives without tools and resources:

- A church can concentrate on establishing the system and training the leaders without being distracted by the search for the "perfect tool." As the leaders do the work, they will define the tools they need in order to improve their efforts.
- A system initially designed without a standard curriculum can become more customized to the unique needs and language of the individual church.
- An effort designed and initiated by people in the church often leads to greater personal ownership and ongoing support of the resulting system.
- You can add a resource or tool later on, once the basic foundation is developed. This ensures that the resource is tailored to meet the needs of the congregation, not the other way around.

There are also at least two disadvantages of beginning without tools and resources:

- When a decision is made to not use a tool or existing resource, the time spent in design and adoption may appear to be reinventing the wheel.
- Some important details may be overlooked that would have been covered in existing resources.

There are several advantages of beginning your equipping ministry initiatives by using existing tools and resources:

- Someone has already carefully thought through the main issues and provided you with a step-by-step process for implementation.
- Professionally printed resources give people something they can take home and refer to on an ongoing basis.
- The church can experience a common language and a common approach and more clearly understand the terms being used by various leaders in the process.
- Some resources come with workbooks, manuals, videotapes, and audiotapes designed by professional trainers with skills that may not be available to you in your church.

Here are a number of disadvantages of beginning with tools and resources:

- Searching for the perfect tool often distracts from the main issues. The quality and comprehensiveness of tools vary greatly, and it is difficult at first to identify their weaknesses.

✓ **CHECKPOINT**

As you do your planning, be sure to remember the following:

- Drive your planning by your values and vision, not by technique. There are many useful planning tools, but none should *determine* what you want to do.
- Involve in the planning process as many of the people as possible who will end up having to implement the plan. Both empowerment and commitment are increased through choice. Involvement in planning increases people's discretion over what they do.
- Break the project into manageable pieces. One of the greatest benefits of planning is that necessary events and milestones are made explicit.
- Use the planning process as a means of getting people to mentally walk through the entire journey. This act of visualizing the events, milestones, tasks, and goals enables people to anticipate the future and imagine their success.

James Kouzes and Barry Posner, *The Leadership Challenge*

NOTE: Refer to chapter 12 for guidelines on the planning process.

- No one "perfect tool" will fit your church's unique culture.
- A published system always seems complicated until someone invests the time to understand the whole approach well enough to see where the resource fits and doesn't fit his or her church. When a church jumps into a standard curriculum without this large initial investment of time, the result often is a misfit.
- No system is perfect. Many have an emphasis that is different from the focus of your church. Beginning with an existing system may not allow you to see its weaknesses and make the necessary adjustments at the beginning.
- Many personal discovery systems were designed for business applications. They may work well in leadership development programs but be too complicated for discovery purposes. They must be checked to make sure they have multiple levels for new people and for advanced leadership development stages of your ministry. For most churches it's important to use "church" language and have biblical support. (See "Assessment Tools and the Interview Process" on pages 290–91.)

HIRING A DIRECTOR OF EQUIPPING MINISTRY

Characteristics of Successful Directors

When Birkman and Associates, an assessment organization based in Houston, Texas, profiled twenty-one leaders in the field of equipping ministry, their study uncovered the following traits, abilities, and characteristics that may help you as you search for an equipping ministry director:

Successful directors . . .

- have a positive outlook on life.
- trust other people.
- have a can-do attitude.
- thrive on responsibility and leadership.
- function as team players.
- view conflict as a result of honest people with legitimate differences trying to do their best.
- believe people are capable of self-control and can work well without constant supervision.
- describe shortcomings in others as manageable and natural.
- enjoy making things happen, especially under pressure.
- like to "sell" ideas and services.
- are generally outgoing people who enjoy contact with a wide group of people.
- operate well independently.
- tend to enjoy movies, the theater, and other literary interests.
- function with flexibility.
- like taking initiative.
- are able to deal with conflict.
- operative with creativity (although are sometimes less than organized in their efforts).
- plan well.
- possess the ability to work in the midst of multiple disruptions.

CONTRACTORS' CONFERENCE

Start-Up Strategies

1. In the space below, write down specific goals that will help determine whether your vision is being realized. Responding to the following statement may help: "We will know we are successful when . . ."

2. A handy way to evaluate your goal-setting process is the SMART acronym: Create goals that are **S**pecific, **M**easurable, **A**chievable, **R**ealistic and have a **T**imeline attached. As you set goals, ask yourself how each goal measures up to this description.

3. Consider the following questions as you decide on the goals you will use to determine the success of equipping ministry:

   • How many new and existing people do you hope to interview and involve in ministry in each of the next five years?

   • How many people are currently serving in your church and community? How many people inside and outside your church would you like to see being served?

   • What percentage of equipped people do you hope to see involved in ministry in each of the next five years?

   • How many people do you want to see trained and prepared for new leadership positions in each of the next five years?

   • What percentage of new visitors do you hope to have involved in the life of your church within six months of their first visit?

4. What progress on your goals will you ask the director of the equipping ministry system to report to the governing board or other authorities?

5. How will you reflect and communicate the importance of equipping ministry in the publications and programs of the church?

6. Outline specific strategies and goals related to the basic assumptions and core values that have been identified as needing change. Build into these goals measurable elements that can be assessed on an ongoing basis.

In addition to these traits, look for a person who . . .

- feels called to this ministry.
- communicates effectively.
- listens actively.
- shows grace under pressure.
- organizes, collaborates, and coordinates well.
- delegates capably.
- is an experienced originator of programs.
- is liked by the congregation.
- possesses a sense of humor.
- shares credit and shoulders responsibility.
- serves the church.
- believes in gift-based ministry.

Where Do You Find a Director of Equipping Ministry?

One of the best places to look for a director of equipping ministry is right within your church. To this point there are very few educational programs that formally prepare people for this new area of ministry. Most churches have hired from within their own congregation or have adapted the ministry description of a staff member who is eager to assume this new role.

It is possible to seek a candidate from the business, nonprofit, and public sectors. The characteristics listed above are equally applicable. Be sure to consider those who have experience in . . .

- *volunteer management or community relations.* The skills and the management expertise of these persons relate naturally to the management and coordination functions of equipping ministry.
- *human resource management in corporate settings.* Like managers of volunteers from the nonprofit and public sectors, these people have skills in management and training and may be seeking an alternative work setting.
- *volunteer leadership in community organizations,* such as Junior League, Women's Club, Jaycees, and the like. These persons are frequently highly capable, trained candidates who would love the opportunity to use their skills in the church.

BUILDERS' NOTE

The Question of Integrity

An energetic and skilled member arrives ready to serve. The member's particular gifts are best suited to an area where there are currently no urgent needs; however, adult ministry has a desperate need for help right now. What does the director of equipping ministry do? Which option is the best one?

1. In conformity to a truly gift-based ministry, the new member is placed according to her gifts and talents in an area other than adult ministry.
2. The director places the new member in adult ministry, convincing her that this is the best and most appropriate use of her gifts.
3. The situation is explained to the member. The member is asked if she would be willing to assist adult ministry in response to this immediate need, with the proviso that her gifts have been noted and will be exercised in a more appropriate ministry at a mutually agreed-on time in the future.

You'll undoubtedly want to employ the person who offers the third response. The needs of the church and the gifts of the members need to be held in a creative tension, balanced by honesty, a sincere desire to be of service, and a commitment to gift-based ministry.

Look carefully at people who have been served well by your church and are eager to repay a debt of gratitude. Numerous directors of equipping ministry have accepted this position so that they might serve the church and help others receive the same kind of care and support they have experienced.

What Is the Best Title for this Position?

There is no single "correct" title for this position. As a rule of thumb, titles generally reflect the function of the position, its preferred style of operation, and the culture of your church. Utilizing the list below, mix and match words and phrases to develop a title that best reflects the position in your church and its blend of responsibilities:

Operating Style	*Function*
Director	Equipping ministry
	Empowerment ministry
	Lay ministry (or Lay ministries)
	Lay mobilization
Coordinator	Congregational involvement
	Leadership development
Manager	Discipleship
	Congregational support
Minister	Congregational outreach
	Gifts ministry

For uniformity of discussion, this book refers to the position as the director of equipping ministry.

What About a Nonsalaried Director?

Some churches have been successful in locating a person who is able to assume a major professional role in the life of the church as a nonpaid staff member. If the person meets the qualifications, has the time, and is willing to make the professional commitment necessary for this leadership position, there is no reason not to use the services of a nonsalaried person in this position. Remember, nonsalaried does *not* mean nonprofessional. The same expectations and standards that apply to salaried employees should be established for nonsalaried workers as well, including standard work hours, vacations, professional development, year-end evaluation, involvement in weekly staff meetings, and the ability to be terminated.

A nonsalaried director should receive a budget for professional development and the necessary program funds to carry out the requirements of the position.

How Much Time Does This Position Require?

Centralized Leadership

1. *Full-time director of equipping ministry:* The ideal option for establishing and facilitating equipping ministry is to hire a full-time director. For churches with nine hundred or more members worshiping weekly, this option is especially effective. The position requires considerable attention to detail and full knowledge of church operations.

CHECKPOINT

Employees who split their time among competing responsibilities often find themselves squeezing equipping ministry into an already-crowded schedule, thereby short-changing support to people and skimping in the time-consuming coordination functions.

CHECKPOINT

It is important that all staff members understand how to work effectively with laypeople and become familiar with the principles of equipping ministry. There is a difficulty, however, in trying to coordinate efforts and ensure that members are placed according to their own gifts and talents and not according to the needs of the staff members who do the interview. The lack of a centralized communication system can lead to redundancy of effort and can fragment the work of the church.

2. *Part-time director of equipping ministry with no other job responsibilities:* Because of budgetary constraints or the desires of the director, many churches have initiated and continue to facilitate equipping ministry with staff persons working half-time to three-quarter-time in the position. The part-time option is particularly workable for smaller churches or during the development phases of the position in larger congregations.

3. *The full-time employee with part-time equipping ministry responsibilities:* Some churches divide the work responsibilities of an employee to include half-time leadership of equipping ministry with half-time responsibility for another work area, such as Christian education, small group ministry, and the like. Generally speaking, this option is less effective than either of the other two.

Decentralized Leadership

1. *All staff members operate as facilitators of equipping ministry:* All staff members are trained to do interviews and assist members to identify gifts and talents for ministry. Staff members develop ministry descriptions and invite members into ministry according to their interests and abilities. Each department is responsible for supporting members in ministry and for recognizing their contributions.

2. *One department manages equipping ministry for the church:* In some churches a department with high member involvement (Christian education or children's ministries, for example) assumes the role of equipping ministry facilitation. This situation has worked with varying levels of success. The responsible department usually meets most of its own needs for member involvement, while other departments may be less successful in having their concerns addressed. Periodically, the success of the organizing department becomes the catalyst for a church-wide effort to mobilize the laity. In other cases in a larger church, a department may be charged with this responsibility as a way to pilot a system.

What Is an Appropriate Salary for This Position?

The salary for a director of equipping ministry—a professional staff position—should be comparable to that of other senior-level staff positions in your church. Examine the pay scale for the directors of Christian education, youth ministries, children's ministry, or music. Consider the person's professional experience and education level as well. This information will help you identify an appropriate salary. Remember to factor health care costs, retirement plans, social security, a mileage allowance, professional development, and vacation time into the equation. (See "What Will an Equipping Ministry System Cost?" on page 141.)

The Ministry Description

Prior to interviewing to fill the position, it is essential to develop a ministry description (see chapter 12 for detailed information on ministry descriptions). This description provides clear expectations and requirements for the position. In addition, it presents the goals and purposes of the position and facilitates orientation of the director into the position. It also serves as a guide for training, feedback, and evaluation.

The First Presbyterian Church of Bellevue, Washington, strategically phased in the positions and roles of the equipping ministry director and team:

Year 1998 *(0.7 full-time equivalents)*

Director of lay ministry	part-time (20 hours)
Support staff	part-time (5 hours)

Year 1999 *(1.7 full-time equivalents)*

Director of lay ministry*	full-time
Support staff*	part-time (25 hours)

January 1999—*two elders* added to Session
June 1999—*another elder* added to Session

Year 2000 *(2.0 full-time equivalents)*

Director of lay ministry	full-time
Support staff*	full-time

Year 2001 *(2.5 full-time equivalents)*

Director of lay ministry	full-time
Associate of lay ministry **	part-time (20 hours)
Support staff	full-time

Year 2002 *(3.0 full-time equivalents)*

Director of lay ministry	full-time
Associate of lay ministry*	full-time
Support staff	full-time

* Increase in hours
** New position

A typical ministry description includes . . .

- a title for the ministry (see page 147 for help in developing a title for the position in your church).
- a purpose statement: why this position is important in the life of the church.
- a summary description of the position (see chapter 2 on the role of the director of equipping ministry):
  ___ the name or title of the person to whom the director of equipping ministry is responsible (be sure to refer to chapter 2 for ways to clarify important reporting relationships).
  ___ a list of specific responsibilities (review chapter 2 to make sure that key elements of this person's ministry are included).
  ___ the amount of time required to perform the task, usually presented on a weekly or monthly basis (for example, "two hours, one day a week," or "two three-hour meetings per month").
  ___ the skills, knowledge, and gifts needed to support this ministry.
  ___ any training needed or available to do this ministry.
- the development date, so you will know when the ministry description was created and when it should be revised.

✓ CHECKPOINT

The position of director of equipping ministry is a relatively recent one within the church. What's more, there seems to be a lack of continuing education resources for the director and team in many communities. Therefore, you would do well to allow sufficient funds for continuing education. Leadership Training Network, as well as other groups and organizations, offer seminars and training institutes in locations across the country to prepare leaders for this important work. Depending on the continuing education program selected, you will need to budget anywhere from $500 to $1,000 (plus travel expenses) to attend one of these programs.

LA CANADA PRESBYTERIAN CHURCH

626 Foothill Blvd., La Canada, CA 91011

(818) 790–6708

POSITION:
Director of Lay Ministries

EMPLOYMENT STATUS:
Full-time

ACCOUNTABLE TO:
Pastor as head of staff

COMPENSATION METHOD:
Exempt

PURPOSE:

To serve the church by developing, coordinating, and administering an effective and comprehensive lay ministry process.

PRIMARY DUTIES AND RESPONSIBILITIES: Identify and develop a core team of leaders to facilitate the process of:

DISCOVERY

1. Communicate the vision that each person is called by God to some type of ministry.
2. Listen for and respond to individual needs of members prior to ministry involvement.
3. Value the life experience of the members and help them see how that experience can be used in ministry.
4. Help members discover their gifts and discern their interests.
5. Help members see how they can use their gifts to minister to their families, in their workplace and neighborhood, as well as at church.

MATCHING

1. Maintain up-to-date descriptions of ministry opportunities within the church.
2. Maintain a network of contacts within the community, facilitating ministry to the larger world.
3. Support members as they explore the ministry opportunities where they may serve in the church and community.
4. Identify members with leadership potential and develop these persons for future leadership roles.
5. Include unique ministry opportunities in the workplace, within the family, and in the community.

PLACEMENT

1. Link members with ministry leaders to learn more about specific positions.
2. Ensure that individuals receive orientation and training for the positions in which they have chosen to serve.
3. Support members in finding new ministry experiences if the selected opportunity proves inappropriate for any reason.
4. Provide opportunities for members to serve as families or small groups.

COACHING

1. Provide members with support as they begin their ministry.
2. Provide ongoing support to members in ministry.
3. Help members reflect on their ministry experience and see the connection between ministry and faith development.
4. Help members evaluate their ministry experience.

LEADERSHIP DEVELOPMENT

1. Work closely with all programmatic areas of the church to identify ministry opportunities and needs and to provide opportunities for education, growth, and spiritual nurture.
2. Develop leaders for the lay mobilization program.
3. Administer the work of the lay ministry department by encouraging teamwork and mutual support and providing leadership and nurture to all involved with the ministry.
4. Establish departmental goals and objectives by prioritizing program needs with available volunteers.
5. Provide staff support to the appropriate Session ministry support teams. Attend Session meetings.
6. Work with the ministry support team to establish and maintain an annual budget for the department.
7. Work as a member of the ministry training team. Attend staff meetings and retreats.

RELATIONSHIP: Work in close cooperation with the senior and associate pastors and ministry support team of Session. This position must relate to all aspects of the congregation and to all ministries of LCPC.

EVALUATION: Performance reviews will be conducted by the pastor with input from Personnel and members of the ministry support teams as appropriate.

BENEFITS: Includes health insurance, vacation leave (4 weeks annually). All benefits according to policies outlined in personnel handbook.

BRENTWOOD PRESBYTERIAN CHURCH

12000 San Vicente Blvd. • Los Angeles, CA 90049
310–826–5656

TITLE: **Director of Empowerment Ministries**
STATUS: Full Time/Exempt

Purpose

To intentionally engage the people of Brentwood Presbyterian Church in spiritual growth through the use of their God-given gifts in service to each other, to the church, and to the community.

Primary Objectives

As a member of the leadership staff team, the director of empowerment ministries will assist Brentwood Presbyterian Church in broadening the base of ministry throughout the congregation by developing and leading a core team of people who are committed to creating and sustaining lay-driven systems that serve, support, and engage people in spiritual growth through the use of their God-given gifts, talents, and passions.

Key Responsibilities

1. Lead core team to facilitate the systems and programs necessary to welcome, discover, connect, equip, and call people into gift-based Christian service.
2. Be involved with staff empowerment ministries:
   - Provide ongoing support, coaching, and direction to the empowerment ministries elders: Welcome and Discovery (membership outreach), Connecting and Equipping (lay ministry and leadership support), and Calling (nominating).
   - Meet at least monthly with elders to set agendas and evaluate progress of their respective ministry teams.
3. Participate in empowerment ministries functions:

Welcome and Discovery Ministry (membership outreach)

- Attend new member classes and present empowerment ministries overview.
- Facilitate with elders the development of a system to follow up with new members to the point of connection in ministry.
- Facilitate with elders the development of an interview system to discover the needs, gifts, talents, and service interests of new members.
- Facilitate with elders and BPC support staff the computer data entry and tracking of new members.

Connecting and Equipping Ministry (lay ministry)

- Facilitate with elders the development of an interview system to discover the needs, gifts, talents, and continuing service interests of active and inactive members.
- Facilitate with elders the development of a matching and placement system to connect members into ministry service.
- Facilitate with elders the development of a liaison follow-up system.

- Facilitate with elders the development of a system to determine the training and support needs of ministry leaders.
- Attend new member dinners and desserts to evaluate assimilation.
- Participate with pastors in "new-officer orientation" annually.

Calling Ministry (nominating)

- Provide staff support to ministry team as directed by head of staff.
- Meet at least monthly with head of staff to review nominating committee process.
- Provide regular reports to leadership staff team regarding proposed officer invitations.
- Equip new leaders in the understanding of the Book of Order, church structure, and invitation and calling training.

4. Manage the administrative functions of the empowerment ministries office.
   - Develop a lay administrative staff team to work in conjunction with the empowerment ministries core team to develop and manage the computer data entry and tracking of members in ministry service.
   - Facilitate training for the team.
   - Oversee the upkeep, accuracy, and dissemination of information related to member service and participation, such as (but not limited to) rosters, ministry descriptions, files, computer data, reports, and program and event evaluations.
   - Oversee the roles and responsibilities of empowerment ministries assistants.
   - Promote teamwork and communication.
   - Facilitate monthly team meetings to discuss challenges, provide support, and promote community.
   - Provide coaching and encouragement for assistants to function as facilitators in support of lay leaders involved with the Welcome and Discovery (membership outreach), Connecting and Equipping (lay ministry and leadership support), and Calling (nominating) ministry teams.
5. Participate in regular meetings.
   - As a member of the BPC leadership staff team, participate in regularly scheduled staff meetings and retreats relating to overall church operations.
   - Meet weekly with head of staff to process all empowerment ministries progress, issues, challenges, and opportunities.
6. Pursue member involvement.
   - Become familiar with as many new and longtime church members as possible.

Personal Qualifications

Character

The position requires an engaging, compassionate, and grace-filled individual who is spiritually mature; who holds a firm belief in the priesthood of all believers and thus is committed to engaging others in spiritual growth through Christian service; who is committed to the mission of BPC; who has a heart for equipping others; and who thrives on responsibility and leadership.

Competencies

The essential skills necessary for an individual to be successful in this position are leadership, teamwork, facilitation, delegation, advocacy, motivation, presentation, communication, and organization. In addition, the individual needs the ability to facilitate the creation and management of systems, to function on computers, and a willingness to learn.

Accountability and Review

The director of empowerment ministries reports to the head of staff and is accountable to Session through the personnel committee. Performance reviews annually.

Working Relationships

Number of church employees receiving work direction	1 part-time secretary
Number of volunteer assistants receiving work direction	1
Number of seminary interns receiving work direction	As available
Number of empowerment ministries elders	4
Number of church volunteers served	1,400

The Empowerment Ministries Team

We are committed to empower the people of BPC, to live into our faith, to discover our gifts, and to actively respond to God's call. Overall, it is our collective mission to facilitate the assimilation, retention, and growth of all members through the use of their God-given gifts in service to each other, to the church, and to the community.

Welcome and Discovery Ministry Team (membership outreach)

Purpose: To identify and counsel visitors about BPC and the "new-member information seminars," and to facilitate the assimilation of new members into the life, work, and faith of the BPC community.

Objectives: Create and sustain lay-led programs that identify, engage, and inform visitors about membership, fellowship, and service opportunities at Brentwood Presbyterian Church.

Connecting and Equipping Ministry Team (lay ministry and leadership support)

Purpose: To intentionally engage the people of Brentwood Presbyterian Church in spiritual growth through the use of their God-given gifts in service to each other, to the church, and to the community.

Objectives: Create and sustain lay-driven systems that support and engage people in spiritual growth through the use of their God-given gifts, talents, and passions.

Calling Ministry Team (nominating)

Purpose: To identify and invite qualified church members into leadership positions for the offices of elder and deacon and for membership on the nominating, personnel, and endowment teams.

Objectives: Create and sustain lay-led systems to inform the congregation about leadership opportunities and qualifications. Identify and invite qualified church members into leadership positions.

Chapel Hill Bible Church

1200 Mason Farm Road
Chapel Hill, North Carolina 27514
919-968-4754

Ministry Mobilization Coordinator
Position Description

"Facilitator of shared ministry" Ephesians 4:11–12 "equip the saints" ministry

Description:

The ministry mobilization coordinator will serve the CHBC fellowship by developing and facilitating the "intentional enfolding" of people who choose to make CHBC their church home. This enfolding includes the initial acclimation and assimilation into the fellowship, as well as providing opportunities for people to discover their giftedness in ministry and service. The coordinator will function as a team leader to develop and coordinate various teams of people called to provide the hands to help enact the "intentional enfolding."

Responsibilities:

Develop and coordinate a clear path for visitors and new attendees to become a vital part of the fellowship:

- develop, coordinate, and participate in various aspects of Sunday morning hospitality/welcoming ministries (greeters, visitor welcome, and the like)
- develop and update materials, publications, and signage to assist in intentional enfolding (brochures, handbooks, Web site material, and the like)
- coordinate visitor contact ministry
- develop, coordinate, and participate in newcomer "getting plugged in" classes
- coordinate and administrate all aspects of prospective-member classes (currently two per year)

Recruit, coordinate, and oversee teams that develop, facilitate, and encourage enfolding in the following areas:

- hospitality/welcome → Sunday morning, other churchwide events
- assimilation/acclimation → "people's connections," that is, Suppers of Six, small groups
- ministry connection → interviews and systems to connect people with ministry opportunities; Ministry Sunday

Develop administrative support systems and printed materials to strive toward an "every-person enfolding and follow-up," including but not limited to . . .

- visitor information database
- gifts-assessment tools
- ministry interest surveys
- ministry opportunity/giftedness attributes resources
- ministry tracking system via modifications to church database
- churchwide photo wall
- CHBC leadership board

This position is initially a half-time position, with the potential to become full-time.

Noroton Presbyterian Church

2011 Post Road
Darien, Connecticut 06820
203-655-1451

POSITION DESCRIPTION

TITLE: Director of Lay Ministries and Program Director

ACCOUNTABLE TO: Senior Pastor and rotating Associate Pastor

THE PURPOSE OF NOROTON PRESBYTERIAN CHURCH

The Noroton Presbyterian Church—A Cross to Steer By*

We honor God by . . .
- bringing people to Jesus Christ,
- gathering in worship and prayer,
- sharing God's love with one another,
- empowering people to live their faith,
- serving our communities and the world,
    and in all things reflecting God's grace.

THE PROGRAM STAFF POSITION

The NPC program staffer is committed to the above purpose and unites with staff, session, and congregation to move toward its fulfillment. This person contributes toward this purpose by working collaboratively with the associate pastors, other office staff, the senior pastor, and the business administrator. All staff are dedicated Christians who view their positions as a ministry to the larger church.

CHRISTIAN COMMITMENT

The person is encouraged to pray for the ministry of the church and the concerns of the staff. He or she is further encouraged to be engaged in Bible study, worship, and Christian fellowship of his or her choice to build personal Christian discipleship and maturity. This person will also abide by the covenantal agreement written by staff in regard to the quality of working relationships (see attached covenant).

PRIMARY OBJECTIVES

- ❖ To broaden our base of ministry by promoting volunteerism, thereby increasing stewardship of time and personal fulfillment through ministry
- ❖ To help identify skills, gifts, and interests of all members of NPC
- ❖ To integrate new members into program delivery, thereby increasing their sense of belonging and personal contribution to the church family
- ❖ To integrate long-term members into program delivery, thereby increasing retention and developing a stronger sense of community with new members
- ❖ To expand our base of leadership by enabling leaders through regular training programs
- ❖ To increase communication among staff, session, and the wider congregation
- ❖ To understand each ministry in a "hands-on leading to training" format

PRIMARY RESPONSIBILITIES

Lay Ministry (30 hours a week)

- ❖ Meet monthly with elders (at session meetings) to assess needs and provide updates.
- ❖ Attend monthly team meetings with the lay ministry team and be available for other teams.

---

*Nautical charts of Long Island Sound mark the NPC steeple as a navigational guide.

❖ Serve as a resource to all teams and staff in their respective recruiting efforts.
❖ Attend new-member dinners to build relationships, and assist in one of the teachings of the new-member class.
❖ Work with the pastors in developing, leading, and, when appropriate, providing ongoing training opportunities for leaders of NPC.
❖ Plan and participate with pastors in the "new elder/deacon orientation" annually.
❖ Oversee the lay ministry portion of the database: personal interest and skills program results, volunteer jobs available, and recommending updates as needed.
❖ Coordinate and assist in teaching the "Stewardship of Time and Spiritual Gifts" class.
❖ Coordinate and assist the lay ministry team in the follow-up interviews with all new members.

Program Director (10 hours a week)

❖ Coordinate and help with churchwide events: potluck dinners, celebrations, and appreciation dinners.
❖ Improve communication among staff, session, deacons, teams, and the wider congregation though oversight of the material for monthly newsletter, handbook, annual report, and Web site.

Hands-On Ministry (10 hours a week)

❖ Assist with different program areas for specified projects and specified length of time to better understand programs, develop training processes, and lead the appropriate lay leaders to the given area.

PROFESSIONAL SKILL REQUIREMENTS:

1. Good communication skills
2. Personable, with the ability to motivate people
3. Strong commitment to the importance of volunteerism
4. Good organizational skills
5. Demonstrated leadership capability
6. Familiarity with members of the congregation
7. Strong computer and database skills
8. Flexibility and a sense of humor
9. Ability to work effectively with other program staff
10. Spiritually centered, committed to the mission of the church

TECHNICAL SKILL REQUIREMENTS:

1. PC-based environment: Office 97; Microsoft Word, Excel, and PowerPoint
2. Able to learn church software

CREDENTIALS REQUIRED:

References
Résumé

SUPPORT

❖ The director of lay ministries/program director attends weekly staff meetings; other meetings, monthly team meetings, and monthly session meetings as necessary.
❖ An annual review is conducted by the senior pastor and associate pastors and will include one representative from Human Relations.

PERSONNEL POLICY

All employees of the church are required to abide by the requirements listed in the session's personnel policy. If the employee is not able to abide by one or more of these policies, he or she should contact the business administrator immediately.

Questions to Ask in the Hiring Interview

Before you interview candidates for this position, identify the skills, qualifications, temperament, and gifts you would like this person to have. Consider your work environment. What type of person would work well with your existing staff members and complement the skills and gifts of your ministry team? Develop your list of questions in concert with others who know the church and the ministry.

Here are some suggested questions and prompts as you develop your own list:

1. Describe the service activities you've been involved with in the past. Tell us about the organization, the service, and the recipients. Describe your role in the organization or activity.

   Ideally, you want a person who has a desire to be involved in serving others, especially in ways that touch the lives of people directly. Look for leadership ability and the ability to coordinate multiple responsibilities.

2. This is a people-intensive position. Can you share with us situations when you have been called on to initiate conversations with strangers, or times when you've needed to persuade another person about something you believe in strongly? Can you offer some examples of types of situations with which you would feel most comfortable?

   Although few people are completely comfortable in front of audiences, you are looking for a person who is persuasive and comfortable with one-on-one interaction and talking with strangers. Public speaking ability is an added gift, although it's a skill that can be augmented by others on staff or by members of the equipping ministry team.

3. We would be interested in hearing about people you have worked with in the past. Can you share a particularly satisfying working relationship and what made the experience such a positive one?

   Equipping ministry requires teamwork, collaboration, and leadership. Look for the ability to take charge, involve others, and work effectively with groups. Look for a person with a facilitative leadership style.

4. Help us understand a work situation that you found difficult. What factors contributed to the problems? What role did you play? Explore situations where you think conflict may have occurred. How was it handled?

   You're discerning how this person has handled difficult interpersonal situations. Did the candidate manage these problems in a thoughtful and satisfactory manner?

5. From what you understand about this job, what do you think you will most enjoy?

   Look for a person who is eager to put all the pieces together, who enjoys constructing and managing systems. The management and coordination functions are more important than the ability to present gifts-assessment seminars or teach classes. You are searching for a person who can locate others to do pieces of the process, but this person needs to understand the overall process and be capable of managing a system.

6. Describe past experiences that you believe are similar to the type of work you'll be doing here.

   A person who understands the job to be a management and coordination position rather than a teaching or administrative position will more effectively grasp the responsibilities entailed.

7. Describe the first five major steps you would take as you begin the position.

   It's important to find a person who grasps the importance of building staff support and involving members in the development phases of the system. Consider how the person approaches a large management responsibility. Whom does he or she include in the process? How does he or she organize the various tasks? You're looking for a team player, but also a person who can assume responsibility, lead an effort, and involve others in planning. Be cautious of a candidate who jumps right into new member assimilation before building the foundations and support systems to uphold equipping ministry processes. Make sure the person talks about inviting and equipping others rather than doing the tasks alone.

8. When people experience equipping ministry, their concerns frequently focus on "What are *my* gifts? What is God's will for *my* life? Where is *my* place of ministry? How can the church meet *my* needs?" In the development process how do you honor these concerns while helping members begin to consider a new line of questioning, such as "How has *God* evidenced his work in my life through gifts and experiences?"

   This issue addresses the need to help people focus more on God's purposes and less on their own needs. Look for a person who recognizes the issue and is open to struggling with its implications.

9. As you look over your life, where have you seen God's hand leading you? What are your own goals for spiritual growth and development?

   Each church will have her own perspective on spiritual growth and faith maturity. It is particularly helpful if candidates understand gift-based ministry and the theological foundation for the teaching that every member is a minister.

Five Frequent Hiring Mistakes

1. *Hiring a seminar presenter.* While training and teaching skills are important, they are secondary to the ability to facilitate an equipping ministry that includes possessing interaction, collaboration, and administration skills.

2. *Hiring a career counselor.* The person you select will be training interviewers and mentors who may become ministry counselors to people in the church. You do not want a person who is more at home doing the ministry than equipping others to do the ministry. A leader who spends too much time counseling will fail to reach the goal of equipping others.

In their newsletter *The Spire* (February 2, 1999), First United Methodist Church of Mesa, Arizona, shares the announcement of the hiring of a new lay ministry director. In the column "The Pastor's Pen," the senior pastor writes the following:

Last week our staff parish committee hired Debby Elliott as our new lay ministry director. Most of you know Debby. She headed up our centennial organ drive, and she and her family have been active in the church for many years. Her first task as director will be to develop a task force to implement our lay ministry. With the task force's help, the director of lay ministries will have these primary objectives:

- develop a central record-keeping system
- train interviewers and ministry mentors to learn needs of our members and connect them to different ministries
- teach leaders to write ministry descriptions for all ministries
- help coordinate churchwide programming to complement the goal of lay mobilization
- create training for all ministry leaders
- develop an evaluation system to see how each ministry relates to our church's mission
- integrate new members into our ministry
- evaluate member involvement and spiritual growth through ministry
- help with the casting of our church's vision of "every member in ministry"
- network with community groups to find ways for members to minister in the larger community

The task laid out before us is a large task, but one that is very important for our church and her future. I would ask that you keep Debby and our lay ministry task force in your prayers as we work to strengthen our ministry.

 **CHECKPOINT**

Once a director for the ministry is appointed, the leadership team must take responsibility to implement a support and training action plan to ensure that the director is made to feel welcome and becomes quickly oriented to the new position and to the church. The second half of chapter 8 provides valuable information and guidelines for this process.

3. *Hiring an administrator.* An administrator is gifted at managing tasks and keeping the details in place, but this position needs a facilitative leader. This type of leader understands how to equip others in the ministry and how to organize and coordinate tasks, knows how to find and invite people to accomplish necessary details, and knows how to keep people motivated and on target in accomplishing the tasks.

4. *Hiring a gofer.* This is a job that should report directly to the senior or executive pastor. If placed too far down in the hierarchy, the director will be unable to accomplish the task.

5. *Hiring a part-timer.* For larger churches, the job generally requires a full-time director. Defining these responsibilities as 20 percent of another job can set up the staff member to fail.

CONTRACTORS' CONFERENCE

Hiring Worksheet for the Director of Equipping Ministry Position

This "contractors' conference" can help you begin the process of developing a ministry description for the position of equipping ministry director. Appoint a member of the church leadership team to prepare a ministry description based on the information gathered from this worksheet.

1. Where does a director of equipping ministry fit in the current organization of our church?

   The position will report to _____

2. What is the best title for this position?

   The title of the position will be _____

3. Should the position be part-time or full-time?

   The time expectations of the position will be . . .
   - this year _____
   - next year_____

4. What is an appropriate salary for this position?

   The proposed salary and benefits will be . . .
   - this year _____. The budget for this year is _____.
   - next year _____. The budget for next year is _____.

5. What are the primary objectives for this position?

   The expectations of this position are _____

   _____

   _____

6. What are the major responsibilities for this position?

   The accountabilities for this position include _____

   _____

   _____

7. What training and leadership support will be provided for this position?

   We plan to equip and support the leader by _____

   _____

   _____

8. Outline the ideal gifts, talents, and experience the leadership team members identify as important in this position.
   - Gifts _____

   _____

   - Talents _____

   _____

   _____

• Experience/Skills _____

_____

_____

• Other characteristics of importance _____

_____

_____

9. Write down names of persons the leadership team members consider to be candidates for this position. Determine a plan of action and responsibilities for the initial interview with possible candidates.

_____

_____

_____

_____

_____

_____

_____

_____

_____

10. Define the interview and selection process and determine responsibilities.

• Step 1: Identify the interviewers _____

_____

_____

• Step 2: Prepare the interview questions_____

_____

_____

• Step 3: Review the interview data _____

_____

_____

• Step 4: Make the final selection _____

_____

_____

• Step 5: Extend the invitation to selected candidate _____

_____

_____

How Will You Prepare for Change?

Get Your Hard Hat On

As YOU BEGIN TO IMPLEMENT the strategies for creating an equipping church, you will discover that change is a critical aspect of the process.

CHAPTER PREVIEW

IN THIS CHAPTER YOU WILL have the opportunity to prepare yourself and your church for change by reviewing . . .

- "protest signs and picket lines": change strategies.
- tips for managing resistance.
- cautions and suggestions to consider before you get started.
- common mistakes.

PROTESTS (OR CONCERNS) ABOUT EQUIPPING MINISTRY

Protest #1

> "With an overwhelming workload, how can this church tackle even one more new program? How can I handle even one more piece of work?"

The Problem

The perception that equipping ministry is a *program* rather than a *value* can be one of the largest stumbling blocks to moving forward. Most church staff members have position descriptions requiring 60- to 70-hour workweeks in exchange for 40 hours or less of salary. Even if things aren't perfect the way they are, a certain level of comfort comes simply through dealing with the familiar. Equipping ministry seems to add more work to this mix. One more staff person reporting to the senior or executive pastor, ministry descriptions to be written, additional training sessions to attend and additional training to deliver, a new information management system to be developed (or an existing one to be

"Change and leadership go together. There can be no real leadership without significant change. For Christians there is a strong theological grounding for change. We must change. The way things are in the world at any moment is never synonymous with God's ultimate will. There is always a 'not yet' quality and an incompleteness about things as they are. God is always pulling us into the future with a call for an order far different from the current state of things."

Lovett H. Weems Jr.,
Church Leadership: Vision, Team, Culture and Integrity

"It isn't the changes that do you in, it's the transitions. Change is not the same as transition. Change is situational: the new site, the new boss, the new team roles, and the new policy. Transition is the psychological process people go through to come to terms with the new situation. Change is external, transition is internal."

William Bridges,
Managing Transitions: Making the Most of Change

revised), and maybe some new Christian education materials to be incorporated into an established system—it's little wonder that people already on the verge of burnout find the new system slightly less than inspiring.

The Possibilities

It would be dishonest to say that equipping ministry will not bring additional work. The long-term effect, however, is to provide skilled, meaningful support to the staff and to greatly expand the base of people involved in the church's ministry. Equipping ministry is about values and principles that have to do with how the church is run. Ultimately, equipping ministry is about *stewardship*—stewardship of the time and talents of staff and church members alike. When the gifts, skills, talents, passions, and temperament of members are carefully discerned and the needs of the ministry opportunities carefully described, it is infinitely easier to connect people with opportunities that both suit and interest them. And, just as delightfully, as church members have the opportunity to pursue their gifts and interests, staff members find their time more available for those areas of ministry they most enjoy.

A comprehensive equipping ministry system brings a measure of accountability as well. When ministry is understood as an opportunity to grow in faith and as an extension of a Christ-centered lifestyle, members gain new meaning from the opportunity to be partners in the church's ministry.

Yes, there will be ministry descriptions to be developed. But with training and support from the equipping ministry team, this job will be shared among people currently doing the ministry. Likewise, as gifts and talents are discerned, those who have gifts in this area of administration will emerge to assist with the responsibility. And once the ministry description is created, with only periodic updating it will be a valuable invitation and training tool, reducing the need to explain the position over and over, plus demonstrating good stewardship of time for the church and her people.

Yes, there will be one more person on the leadership team of the church. But that person's function is to complement and support the church's ministries, not to take valuable time needed to meet other needs. This is not a staff person who will compete for members' attention but one charged with the responsibility of being a multiplier and connector by bringing in others to serve existing ministries and to build systems that communicate and embrace stewardship of gifts and time.

Protest #2

"Is my job in jeopardy? If equipping ministry is really successful, will the church still need to employ me? And what if I don't have skills in this area and don't understand how to work effectively with volunteers? Won't I look incompetent to other staff people and church members?"

The Problem

Equipping ministry is not a subject taught in many seminaries, nor are there numerous continuing education programs that address this professional development need. Some pastors feel threatened by the emergence of this new area, yet at the same time they see it as a way to bring the theology of "every member a minister" to life. It is also a concern to many support staff—administrators and secretaries—who may feel threatened by the abilities of members within their congregation. Here's how the thinking might go: If Nancy Corporate, who just resigned from her job as director of professional development for the Champions Company to be at home with her children, sees how our Christian education meetings are run, she may lobby for my resignation or even offer to take on the position as a volunteer. Involving people in ministry requires new skills and abilities, such as management, training, and supervision of those who serve—skills not possessed by every staff member.

The Possibilities

The response to this protest is that staff persons would not lose their job—although the job may change. They will be called to do *only* what they can and love to do, and then let others do the rest. Staff members become coaches to many. No one person is supposed to know how to do everything in the church that needs to be done. In the many New Testament passages about spiritual gifts, not one says, "And ye shall find the pastor and the staff that together make up the perfect and complete body of Christ so that the members can sit in their pews and pray." Every single one of these passages speaks to the importance and need for the gifts of *all*, so that *together* the parts may form one body. Relax! For a change, you are allowed to *not* be the doer of all significant things, but rather to focus on your gifts as you call others to use theirs.

Yes, it does require a new alignment of roles and responsibilities. Instead of being the ministers to all, staff and clergy are now called to *equip* the people for their positions of ministry. This is a change of thinking and behavior, and not always an easy one for staff, clergy, or laity. Not only will it take time for members to come to see each other as ministers, but it will also take time for clergy and other staff members to release people to serve through their gifts. But gradually as the vision is preached and taught, as ministries emerge and grow, and as you become more and more skilled as equippers, the whole church blossoms as the people truly become the priesthood of all believers.

And what about the "high-powered" laity, the ones who have highly developed skills beyond the ability of many church staff members? Most often these folks are looking for the opportunity to use their experiences in marketplace roles or entrepreneurial nonprofit roles. Chances are pretty good they don't want your job.

If Nancy Corporate resigned to be with her children, that is the calling she is answering at this point in her life. She may well enjoy being involved in your department. Perhaps you can release her to begin a new ministry area you've never had time to develop. But remember, Nancy didn't resign from a salaried position to assume a full-time volunteer position; she resigned to have more time with her family and to use her time in multiple ways, not just professional ways. Nancy may be able to offer you some wonderful support and growth—if you will only open your door and your heart to her experience.

Not everybody is able to or chooses to be involved in ministry within the walls of the church. Some people may have a unique mix of gifts and abilities that is best deployed in the community. Be sure to keep a finger on the pulse of your community and of the hierarchy within your denomination's administrative systems or agencies, and you will find opportunities for people whose skills and gifts lie outside the scope and needs of your local church.

"Equipping pastors are good to themselves. They have given themselves permission not to have to be able to 'do it all.' Even the superstars who run the megachurches with seeming ease have learned to play to their strengths and remain focused there. One of the most freeing things pastors can do for themselves is to accept their limitations."

Greg Ogden,
The New Reformation

Pay special attention to people at life transition points: the retired, those new to your community, those who are between jobs. For many of these people, ministry opportunities within the church allow them to utilize skills and maintain self-esteem at the same time that they explore other areas of their life. These people frequently have valuable talents, but require flexible schedules that preclude the possibility of a full-time workweek within the church. In other words, they aren't interested in your job, but they are interested in real and meaningful ministry on a short-term basis that provides a flexible schedule. Often what is equally important is the value of just being in community during their transition.

A comprehensive equipping ministry system may require you to develop some new skills or adapt some of your present skills, but you are not expected to do it on your own. One of the responsibilities of the equipping ministry team is to assist you. The equipping ministry team and people with these gifts can assist in developing ministry descriptions and equipping leaders in the skills to invite people into ministry in their areas. They can also help you learn ways to train members for ministry and ways to recognize and celebrate their involvement. Clearly, it's important to select a skilled and capable person to lead your equipping ministry system.

Protest #3

"Equipping ministry is really nothing more than just more bureaucracy. I'll have to go through another staff member or work through another committee just to get to the people I need for ministry in my areas."

The Problem

People often worry that if another department is going to be interviewing all new members, they will never get to the ones they need for ministry in their department. Conversely, people sometimes assume that someone else will do all the interviewing and that they can just tell them what they need and let the equipping ministry department fill all their needs.

The Possibilities

Equipping ministry neither prevents contact with people nor solves all your ministry needs. Rather, it focuses on the person and strives to connect him or her to the church in both a ministering and ministry capacity, based on the individual's needs and gifts. The interview process supports the person as he or she finds a base within the church home. For some people, pressing personal problems may need to be met before they can consider serving. Others may be ready to serve, but need more extensive biblical preparation or gifts assessment prior to finding a ministry. Others may be available and hungry to serve. Equipping ministry connects people within the church and creates a system where they can grow in faith maturity through ministry.

Equipping ministry, with its knowledge of the gifts, skills, personal life situations, temperament, and passions of people can supply other ministry areas with the names of people who match their ministry needs profile. Given a list of people who are strong candidates for the ministry positions, it is the responsibility of the requesting department to invite the person into ministry. Only the ministry area with the need fully understands the position and is able to answer questions and match the individual to a specific position. However, with a list of people strongly suited to the ministry and with an eye out for others, the equipping ministry department substantially streamlines the work of other ministry areas.

Protest #4

"All this is fine and good, but in all honesty, some people simply aren't qualified to do the work of the church. It all sounds great on paper, but those in ministry are really just people *volunteering*, and we all know that volunteers are unskilled, unqualified, and unreliable."

The Problem

Although few church staff people are likely to be this blatant in their objection to equipping ministry, the attitude does exist. In the past some staff members may have been forced to work with people who were in fact unskilled, unqualified, unreliable, and very possibly uninterested in their ministry. No wonder these leaders are hardly thrilled by the possibility of involving more of "these people" in their work. Bringing this type of concern to the surface is important. It is difficult to establish a new system when staff members and ministry leaders are quietly resisting your efforts for vague and ill-defined reasons. On the other hand, some staff members are not trained to equip or work with volunteers and would rather do it themselves.

The Possibilities

A good offense may be your best line of defense. Among the benefits of equipping ministry is the fact that people are carefully interviewed for ministry and ministry placements are made based on the person's gifts and talents. People suited for the ministry in question are almost always eager to be involved. A complete equipping ministry system involves preparing people for the specific ministry area, as well as providing a way to return a person to the equipping ministry department if the fit between him or her and the ministry is not good. Through vision casting and education, equipping ministry leaders can demonstrate that ministry is much more than just an obligation and another round of busywork. As people view ministry as an act of love, a living out of a call, and an opportunity to grow in faith, service assumes a new role in the life of the individual and the church.

Protest #5

"I will lose control if I turn the ministry of the church over to the people. If they are released in ministry, how will we know if they are prepared for service or if they are presenting the gospel faithfully and accurately?"

The Problem

The clergy and the staff have spent years in training for their positions within the church. It is threatening to release others to serve in capacities for which they may not be adequately prepared. In other cases, church leaders fear that they will lose their connection with the heart of their ministry if others are released for direct service to those in need.

✓ CHECKPOINT

Some Suggestions for Working with Resistant Staff Members

- Select several highly skilled people who have time to serve and are interested in the ministry of the skeptical leader, and connect the two. Often a good experience can counter a previous difficult experience.
- Encourage resistant staff persons to remember times when they served in a volunteer capacity. Ask them to remember how they felt when serving and how others supported them in their ministry.
- Involve these persons in the work of the equipping ministry department. When they see the care taken in the interview, experience the gifts-assessment instrument you use, or help with training, they often begin to recognize the attention given to match people according to their gifts and consequently become more open to member involvement.

The Possibilities

A well-developed equipping ministry system establishes processes to assist other ministries in setting up training systems to ensure that people are prepared for service. Ministries requiring considerable expertise can establish a sequence of training objectives and mentors to prepare people. A process for identifying people who are not performing well in a particular ministry allows them to be referred for service that is more appropriate for their gifts and talents. An equipping ministry system brings new and meaningful standards and guidelines that end up expanding quality ministry, not diminishing it.

As people develop and extend their reach in service, the role of the staff and pastors becomes one of equipping and coaching people. Staff members find that they can take pleasure in the opportunity to extend their reach through the work of others. Side by side, staff members and the people of the church grow in faith maturity.

Protest #6

"Will there ever be a right time to begin equipping ministry? We always seem to have something major happening in the life of the church. This new ministry will either compete with the other programs or be problematic and confusing to the people."

The Problem

When do you begin an equipping ministry system? Some churches may be between pastors, others may have just initiated a large stewardship campaign, while for others a new small group ministry system has just gotten underway. In the mix of all that is happening in the life of the church, how do you determine the best time to begin an equipping ministry system? How do you keep the system from competing with other programs?

The Possibilities

A comprehensive system needs to be part of the long-range planning process. It represents a significant new direction, and as such it should involve the leadership board and the pastors in its evolution. The system should not depend on the leadership of just one person for momentum. Rather, it represents the church's decision to involve all members in ministry and in growth in faith. It becomes a core value founded on biblical imperatives.

Many churches have several key elements of an equipping ministry system already in place. In that light it's important to evaluate existing equipping ministry activities. Building on existing strengths in the way a church is operating sets a good foundation for the expansion and enhancement of systems.

Because equipping ministry enhances the other ministries of the church, it doesn't need to compete with other programs or events. Its evolution can augment any event. It can be unveiled in support of a stewardship campaign, a new ministry area, or any other event. What is important in the evolution of equipping ministry is thoughtful planning and dedicated leadership. With those two ingredients, the system can be synchronized to the life of the congregation.

"God wants his church to grow. But long-term growth calls for assimilation and equipping skills! Churches that grow help their people find places to serve and help them get the needed skills.... Church leaders often end up doing the bulk of the service in the church, rather than equipping the rest of the Christians to do the tasks for which God has specifically given them gifts and opportunities. This factor contributes significantly to leadership burnout.... Ineffective equipping and ineffective assimilation are two of the most critical growth-stoppers in many churches today."

Lynn Anderson,
They Smell Like Sheep

—————————— **CONTRACTORS' CONFERENCE** ——————————

1. Which of the six protest statements is the biggest concern to your leadership board?

   - How can I handle more work?

   - Is my job in jeopardy?

   - Is equipping ministry more bureaucracy?

   - Are our members qualified for increased responsibility?

   - How will we maintain quality control over programs run by members?

   - Is this the right time to begin equipping ministry?

   - Other: _____

2. List the staff members and lay leaders who will be most affected by an equipping ministry system. Of the six protests, which one(s) will each staff member or ministry leader feel most strongly about? Have them express other concerns not discussed in the protests.

   Spend time with these leaders and staff people. Give them opportunities to express their concerns and fears. Simply listening to them may help to break down some barriers. It is the head of staff's role to see that the values of doing ministry together are aligned.

3. Do you plan to adapt (or have you already adapted) the methods for implementing equipping ministry in order to better meet the concerns of your staff and leaders?

TIPS FOR MANAGING THE INEVITABLE RESISTANCE TO CHANGE

NO MATTER HOW CAREFULLY you develop your plans and how intentionally you include people in the process, resistance is an inevitable part of the change cycle. These pointers may help you manage resistance to equipping ministry:

☑ **CHECKPOINT**

Equipping ministry does represent change—and change, even when planned for and embraced, is not always well received. Understanding your own method of dealing with change and identifying a model from which to understand the change process will help you appreciate how others experience times of transition. (See chapter 11 for more on facilitating change and managing transition. Based on *Managing Transitions* by William Bridges, that section presents a model for considering change and its impact on your staff and congregation.)

- *Involve a wide range of leaders in your church in the evolution of the vision and system.* The more people you involve in the planning and development phase, the more people will own the value and support your effort. A broad base of involved and supportive members also ensures systems that will meet the unique needs of your church.
- *Begin with church ministries most receptive to increased lay involvement.* Nothing succeeds like success. Showcase programs where the new equipping ministry system has demonstrated support of established priorities within the church.
- *Honor tradition.* Identify the aspects of your church culture that are important to preserve. Connect key symbols, images, and rituals to the vision for equipping ministry.
- *Seek quality over quantity.* It is better to do a few things well than to try too many new things at once. Be sure your systems are in place and working before you branch out into new areas.
- *Pilot-test your new systems.* Involve people in new practices and respond to their input and critique before you open the systems to the entire congregation.
- *Remember who your church is.* Don't abandon current needs and programs when venturing into new, challenging, or experimental ministries. For example, if you have a large number of elderly members, continue to address their needs as you reach into the community with a new ministry.
- *Be realistic.* It can take anywhere from three to five years to build a strong cultural foundation and then an effective equipping ministry system. Allow your church sufficient time to do the job right, and celebrate small wins along the way.
- *Seek necessary help.* This guidebook is designed to help you make a transition into an important biblical way of doing church. Here you will find references to other books, training methods, and resources. Take advantage of these supports as you build a strong biblical culture and foundation for an equipping church.

SUGGESTIONS BEFORE YOU GET STARTED

INTRODUCING EQUIPPING MINISTRY effectively is vital to the realization of your vision and long-term embodiment of the values. Consider all that needs to be done before you move forward. Here are some suggestions to help you start smoothly:

- Do not kick off the vision of equipping ministry to the whole church until your systems are in place to facilitate the *Prepare, Connect,* and *Equip* processes.
- Anticipate resistance to change. Refer to the earlier pages of this chapter for recommendations on managing resistance.

- Make sure that the biblical imperatives for equipping ministry have been well communicated before, during, and after the kick-off. Give special attention to communicating that the value of equipping ministry is an integral part of your church's theology of spiritual growth and not just an add-on program.
- Introduce equipping ministry by sharing stories of how people have grown spiritually through using their gifts in service.
- Avoid putting so much focus on the communication systems that it becomes tedious and bureaucratic. Think about the process from the participants' point of view, not from the perspective of the people who collect information. Remember that systems exist in order to serve the people.
- If your church holds a congregational vote before new ministries begin, make sure everyone has a crystal-clear understanding of the equipping ministry vision before any vote takes place. This is best done well in advance by means of a number of smaller forums.
- If you've already announced your vision, plan a "momentum-building event," such as a job-fair day, a celebration banquet, or a gifts-assessment seminar. Build anticipation toward this event as the "grand opening" of equipping ministry, even though equipping ministry may have been practiced for some time.
- Finally, share the vision, share the vision, share the vision. And when you finally think people understand the need for equipping ministry, start over again. People need to hear the reason for a new vision over and over again if they are going to invest in it. It must become part of the DNA of your church.

COMMON MISTAKES TO RECOGNIZE

BECAUSE STARTING WELL IS so important, make sure you are familiar with some common mistakes churches make when they develop an equipping ministry culture and system:

- Underestimating the time required for the leader to do the job well. This is a facilitative task that involves establishing a team and equipping individuals, as well as handling many administrative details.
- Not preparing other staff members to take ownership and to see the benefits of an equipping ministry team for their ministries and departments.
- Not preparing the congregation to understand the biblical foundations of using their gifts in service and to see how their service results in their growth and maturity as Christians. At first glance, many people will assume that this is just another way to increase the pressure on them to serve in order to meet the needs of church programs.
- Not placing priority on ministry connectors. Many churches begin by providing assessment seminars or computer-matching programs, or by making sure all placement opportunities are cataloged. However, the critical link is the connectors ("consultants") who come alongside people, interview them, and coach them in their ministry journey. Selecting these connectors is the most important task. Training them can take months. The strength or weakness of any equipping ministry rests on the quality of these people (see chapter 11 for more information on ministry connectors).

——— CONTRACTORS' CONFERENCE ———

Are You Ready?

Are you ready to begin equipping ministry in your church? Discuss the following to determine if you're ready:

Do you have . . .

- the willingness to honor and celebrate what was done in the past?

- the full commitment of the senior pastor and the key leaders to the vision and values of equipping ministry?

- a governing body open to a new style of operating and the idea of expanding roles for all people in leadership?

- churchwide preparation for the equipping ministry system?

- a willingness to select the right person to lead equipping ministry?

- a realistic time frame and a clear, appropriate strategy?

- the necessary financial resources to enable the ministry to succeed?

- Not giving the leadership team the opportunity to experience the process before the kickoff. For equipping ministry to be successful it must be embodied and modeled by leaders. Even if they say they support it, they need to experience the ministry firsthand in order to genuinely own and share its vision.
- Getting too complicated too fast. A communication system that is too detailed or a gifts-assessment system that is too complex will distract from the real purpose of the ministry. The purpose is not to showcase administrative technology, but to structure the system so well that it is invisible and that its participants experience focused personal attention, not bureaucracy.
- Setting expectations too high too early. Equipping ministry needs time to begin functioning properly. It will depend on many factors—size, leadership buy-in, teams, and the like. The greatest of these factors is how well the leaders process, teach, and model the new values in order to prepare the way for others.
- Not communicating that the director of this ministry is a facilitator, not a doer. When you hire a director of equipping ministry, some people think, "Great! Now we have someone to do the boring work, like telephoning people about committee meetings and recruiting Sunday school teachers." The role needs to be clearly stated and illustrated. Only occasionally will the director personally invite a person into ministry; instead, the director will train others to invite people into ministry throughout the church.
- Underestimating the need to continually share the vision of gift-based equipping ministry and to teach that this is the pathway to greater spiritual maturity. Encouraging discipleship and pointing toward spiritual growth are essential tasks in order to develop an equipping ministry that works toward maturity in the body of Christ.

✓ CHECKPOINT

Use the following questions to help you develop an effective strategy for sharing your vision with your congregation.

- Pretend you are Sally Charter-member. You've been a part of the church from the beginning. Suddenly your pastor and church leaders begin to talk about equipping ministry. How would you feel?
- Pretend you are Bob Establishedmember. You've already been involved in a variety of church programs, including serving others. What would you need to hear about equipping ministry that would get you on board?
- What methods of sharing a vision will communicate best to your church? Which methods have been overused? Which ones have not been used as of yet?
- How will you determine when your efforts to share your vision for equipping ministry have adequately prepared your congregation for kickoff?
- In your church calendar year, when would be the best time to introduce the idea of equipping ministry? When would be a good time of year to actually kick off the vision?

How Do You Lead the Equipping Church?

Oversee the Contractors

LEADING THE EQUIPPING CHURCH means embedding the core values of equipping ministry and transmitting them through words and actions into the life of all church leaders. This should be the ongoing work of the senior pastor and church leadership at large. Once equipping ministry has been implemented and the systems begin achieving the desired results, the culture must be continually nurtured through preaching and teaching. What is to be the focus of this preaching? The teaching and preaching of the biblical imperatives of equipping ministry, the creation of vision ownership, and the affirmation of those models of equipping ministry that are making an impact and transforming lives in various ministries in the church.

In addition to preaching and teaching, a key success factor in leading an equipping church is the ongoing coaching and equipping of the director of equipping ministry.

CHAPTER PREVIEW

IN THIS CHAPTER YOU WILL . . .

- prepare for ongoing development of an equipping culture by preparing the foundation, casting the vision, and affirming the models.
- equip the director of equipping ministry by training and affirmation, feedback and evaluation, and ongoing education.

PREPARING FOR ONGOING DEVELOPMENT OF AN EQUIPPING CULTURE

Prepare the Foundation by Preaching and Teaching the Biblical Foundations

In the opening chapter of this guidebook we listed in detail the biblical imperatives for equipping ministry. It was important to do so because one of the primary mechanisms available to leaders to help in embedding a culture of equipping ministry is to preach and teach the biblical foundations.

Implementing these mechanisms will to a large extent depend on the current process for providing teaching to church members, as well as on the preaching methodology and foundations used by the pastoral staff. Some pastors have found it effective to preach an entire series on the biblical interpretations and imperatives of spiritual gifts. Others have used the Ephesians 4:12 mandate to teach the importance of people using their gifts to serve in the community and in turn to be served, as the body of Christ is built up to full maturity. A majority of equipping churches provide foundational teaching on gifts and service in their Christian education, small group, adult Bible fellowship, and Sunday school programs.

The message never changes, but methods should constantly change in order for the church to remain relevant in the twenty-first century. The methods used in your church must be in alignment with your culture and systems; the mandate, however, remains the same. Until the biblical imperatives of equipping ministry are preached and taught effectively by the leaders, the church will not truly align with the values of equipping ministry.

Equipping ministry, first and foremost, is about helping people mature spiritually through the use of their God-given gifts to serve each other and the community, so that the whole church can attain the maturity God intended. Yes, we need people to serve in the church, but the real focus of equipping ministry is about faith development.

Use the information below in preparing for preaching and teaching the core biblical imperatives.

Possible Sermon Series Topics on the Biblical Foundations of Equipping Ministry

1. Ministry is an act of love for and devotion to Christ.
   Ephesians 2:14–20
   1 Peter 2:5, 9–10
   1 Peter 4:10–11

2. God has a unique purpose or calling for our lives.
   Psalm 139:13–16
   Jeremiah 1:4–5
   Jeremiah 29:11–14
   Ephesians 2:10

3. We all have gifts to fulfill our calling.
   Matthew 25:14–30
   Romans 12:4–8
   1 Corinthians 12:4–12
   Ephesians 4:11–14
   1 Peter 4
   1 Timothy 4:14

4. Gifts are given to be used in community.
   1 Corinthians 12:12–30
   Ephesians 4:11–16
   James 1:22–27

5. Gifts should be used to serve God and others and not be left idle.
   Nehemiah 1–13
   Matthew 25:14–30
   Ephesians 4:11–16
   Philippians 2:3–11

"Those who equip by establishing and laying foundations hold the person of Christ before the community. They have a facility and passion to feed people with God's Word. Paul's letter to the Galatians expresses the equipper's heart: 'My dear children, for whom I am again in the pains of childbirth until Christ is formed in you, how I wish I could be with you now' (Galatians 4:19–20)."

Greg Ogden,
The New Reformation

"We have been taught that life centers around self-focus: what I want, where I want to be, what I want to achieve, and what I want to have. That's the worldview of the predominant culture. But as you nurture God's thoughts and network with God's people, you will move in a direction counter to the rest of the culture because you will be surrendered to a God-focus."

Michael Slaughter, *Real Followers: Beyond Virtual Christianity*

"We have been grace receivers for the expressed purpose of being grace givers. Our divine endowments, or spiritual gifts, are not given for us to keep them to ourselves. They are ours to use as we further the kingdom in the world today."

Bruce Bugbee, *What You Do Best in the Body of Christ*

"There's a common misnomer that spiritual growth is measured by time spent in the church or by a person's length of stay. The truth of the matter is that in one or two years, a person who is intent on following the Lord can be much more mature with insight and wisdom than another Christian who after ten years simply cruises along without much involvement. We have to remember that Jesus turned over the responsibility for administrating the whole church to former fishermen and tax gatherers who were just 3 1/2 years old in the Lord! Christian growth is more measured by a person's willingness to apply what he has heard than it is by length of stay in the church (see John 13:17)."

Wayne Cordeiro,
Doing Church as a Team

Then Jesus came to them and said, "All authority in heaven and on earth has been given to me. Therefore go and make disciples of all nations, baptizing them in the name of the Father and of the Son and of the Holy Spirit, and teaching them to obey everything I have commanded you. And surely I am with you always, to the very end of the age."

MATTHEW 28:18–20

"A vision is a mental picture of a future reality. A leader sees a new sanctuary when it is little more than a vacant lot. The leader can describe the new church plant when there is nothing more than six people huddled together in the pastor's living room. A leader will be able to describe the growing, thriving church when it has been plateaued for the last decade. Vision is a future reality that creates present hope and direction. Although reductionistic, the primary difference between a leader and a manager is probably that of vision."

Alan Nelson,
Leading Your Ministry

6. The role of leaders in the church is to equip others for ministry.
   Exodus 18
   John 21:15–17
   2 Timothy 2:2

7. Spiritual growth occurs during service.
   Mark 10:42, 45
   James 2:14–17

Facilitate Vision Ownership

In chapter 5 we looked at ways the leadership team can formulate the vision in your church for equipping ministry. This precious vision can mobilize your people to share Christ with a hurting, broken world. Ownership of the vision by ministry leaders, pastoral and support staff, and all involved in the church is of primary importance. Facilitating that ownership is an ongoing responsibility of the senior leadership team and the director of equipping ministry. Facilitating vision ownership is a key mechanism for embedding the culture of equipping ministry in your church.

Because facilitating vision ownership is critically important, we'll provide you with insight into what it means to share a vision and suggestions on how to share a vision.

What Does It Mean to Share a Vision?

A difference exists between having the vision and clearly communicating the vision. For many of us, the theology of the priesthood of all believers is an important part of church doctrine, yet we have not been successful in moving the vision to reality.

A vision does not become a dynamic, living, breathing reality until we are able to make it specific and are able to communicate it to the church body in ways they can understand, relate to, reflect on, act on, and remember. In the shift to a new value system, a new way of "doing church," and a new scope of equipping ministry, it is vital that the vision be repeated over and over again at *every* possible occasion and in many different forms for at least the first two years. Keep repeating it until the vision becomes part of the permanent culture and language of the church.

Rick Warren, senior pastor of Saddleback Valley Community Church, identifies vision and values as principal ingredients of leadership. "People are looking for something to give their life to," says Warren. The greater the vision, the stronger the magnetism, the greater its value in attracting people. The job of the leader is to share a contagious vision. According to Warren, a leader must be able to communicate seven things:

1. *Who we are.* The leader is responsible to define why we exist, to lift up our mission, and to share it, share it, share it.
2. *Where we are going.* The leader points the direction, shares the goals, and identifies the destination. The leader knows where we are going and persuades others to follow.
3. *Why we are going there.* Stating the reason for selecting a particular destination answers the question of *why*. Why this direction, why this target and not another?
4. *What it feels like to be going there.* People want to be involved in a significant ministry. They want to feel good about where they are going. They want the journey to add meaning and fulfillment to their lives.

5. *What others can do.* People need to be able to find a place to meaningfully involve their gifts and talents. We all seek affirmation and desire belonging in a cause greater than ourselves. Individuals who want to be a part of a ministry need to be able to find their place and feel that their contributions strengthen the whole.

6. *How we're going to do it.* While there is an undisputed need for specifics and concrete directions, there is an even greater need for a work environment characterized by cooperation, unity of purpose, and the opportunity to be part of ministry that motivates.

7. *What the rewards will be.* How will I benefit from involvement? Because I chose to be involved in this ministry, what can I expect as a result of my involvement? How will I feel? The larger the potential rewards, the greater the allegiance to the ministry.

Concentric Circles of Vision Sharing

Sharing the vision is most effective when it comes from the key decision makers and core leaders outward to the congregation and community. Before you share your vision with the congregation, share it with this core group. These may be trustees, elders, deacons, secretaries, teachers, opinion leaders, or those people without formal positions who are known for their faith and commitment to the life of the church. Contact your core leaders and talk to them about their concerns and their hopes for this ministry. Keep in regular contact with them; as you keep them up-to-date, they will become carriers of the vision to other people in the congregation.

Sharing the Vision

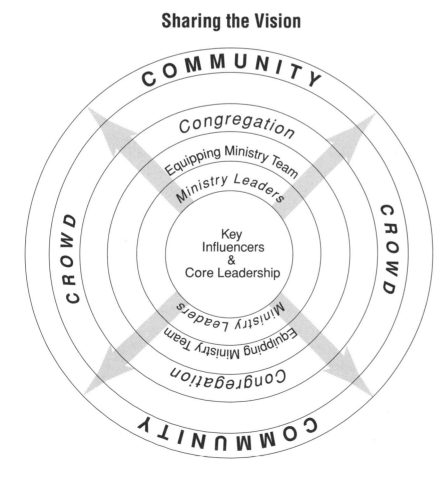

But you are a chosen people, a royal priesthood, a holy nation, a people belonging to God, that you may declare the praises of him who called you out of darkness into his wonderful light. Once you were not a people, but now you are the people of God; once you had not received mercy, but now you have received mercy.

1 PETER 2:9–10

"Unfortunately, when the need for visionary leadership is mentioned to church leaders, many call up images of Moses stepping down from Sinai with the tablets. Some church growth emphases over the past two decades have fed this unfortunate 'voice of God' approach to vision. Because this type of experience falls outside the realm of experience for most church leaders, they often feel incompetent and defeated if this is their notion of what it means to provide visionary leadership. A lot of debugging needs to be done on this issue, accompanied by an expanding attention to the processes of vision cultivation (personal and organizational) and vision casting (giving attention to both the frequency of vision casting and forums). The visioning process must be demystified for many leaders."

Reggie McNeal,
Revolution in Leadership

- Key influencers
  Who the key influencers are will differ, depending on church structure. Consider how to share the vision with this group.
- Core leadership
  This may be paid staff members, members of the board or session, and ministry leaders. How are you going to share the vision with them?
- Equipping ministry team
  How are you going to share the vision with this team in such a way that they don't lose sight of it as they get caught up in the details of building the system?
- Congregation
  These are the people who consider this their church. Maybe they are in the congregation but don't know the vision yet. How are you going to share the vision with them?
- Crowd
  People who attend services or other church events as visitors on the periphery of the church. How can you share the vision with them?
- Community
  Who are the people in the community you may be sharing the vision with? People in the community may be drawn into your church through community service.

How Do You Share a Vision?

An articulated vision needs to be communicated. Rick Warren offers seven ways to bring a vision to life:

1. *Personal example.* No one shared a vision more effectively through personal example than Jesus. If a vision is important to you, you must live it, demonstrating its significance through your own lifestyle. You must be vulnerable to others, sharing your passion, your hopes, your dreams, and your concerns for the dream you aspire to.

2. *Verbal slogans.* People remember phrases. In this age of sound bites, we must be able to succinctly capture the essence of the message. Roosevelt will long be remembered for his statement, "We have nothing to fear but fear itself." Martin Luther King Jr.'s famous speech is indelibly etched through the words "I have a dream." President Kennedy immortalized the request, "Ask not what your country can do for you, but what you can do for your country." The biggest mistake in sharing a vision is to ororverbalize.

3. *Use analogy and metaphor.* Jesus began many parables with "The kingdom of heaven is like . . ." and then wove stories based on life events familiar to all. To communicate a vision, identify an experience common to all and build on the familiar in tangible, concrete ways.

4. *Symbolism.* Symbols, logos, and visuals reach people on an emotional level. Connect symbols verbally and visually to your message.

5. *Use multimedia presentations.* Video is the communication tool of the future. Create videotapes, audiotapes, and other multimedia presentations to deliver your message. Keep presentations brief (ten to fifteen minutes in length) and crisp.

6. *Personal contact.* Spend time one-on-one with key people who are trusted and respected in your congregation. Share your enthusiasm, and allow others to catch the vision from you. Find people who confirm and extend your vision, and share it with them.

"There's nothing more beautiful than a church where everyone has the same starting point, the same heart, the same direction, and the same cadence. This is what gives the rhythm and brings harmony!"

Wayne Cordeiro,
Doing Church as a Team

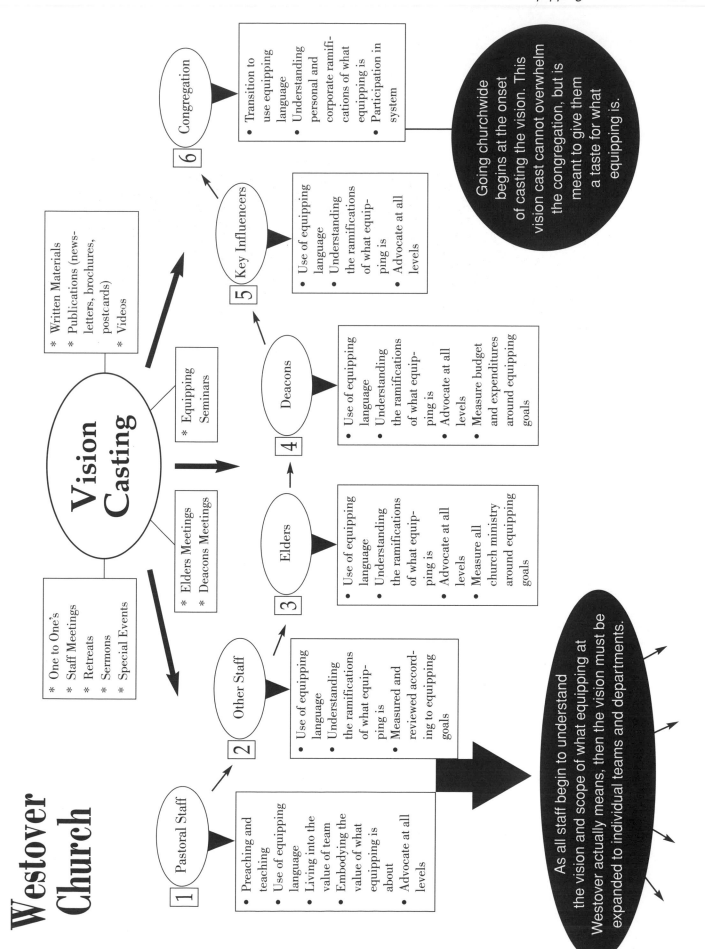

Westover Church

Vision Casting

* One to One's
* Staff Meetings
* Retreats
* Sermons
* Special Events

* Elders Meetings
* Deacons Meetings

* Equipping Seminars

* Written Materials
* Publications (newsletters, brochures, postcards)
* Videos

1 Pastoral Staff
* Preaching and teaching
* Use of equipping language
* Living into the value of team
* Embodying the value of what equipping is about
* Advocate at all levels

2 Other Staff
* Use of equipping language
* Understanding the ramifications of what equipping is
* Measured and reviewed according to equipping goals

3 Elders
* Use of equipping language
* Understanding the ramifications of what equipping is
* Advocate at all levels
* Measure all church ministry around equipping goals

4 Deacons
* Use of equipping language
* Understanding the ramifications of what equipping is
* Advocate at all levels
* Measure budget and expenditures around equipping goals

5 Key Influencers
* Use of equipping language
* Understanding the ramifications of what equipping is
* Advocate at all levels

6 Congregation
* Transition to use equipping language
* Understanding personal and corporate ramifications of what equipping is
* Participation in system

Going churchwide begins at the onset of casting the vision. This vision cast cannot overwhelm the congregation, but is meant to give them a taste for what equipping is.

As all staff begin to understand the vision and scope of what equipping at Westover actually means, then the vision must be expanded to individual teams and departments.

✓ **CHECKPOINT**

**Two Critical Components
to Vision Casting**

1. Help people feel the need.

   • Use quotes from the needs survey so people can hear what others are saying about being burned-out by serving in the wrong place or about having much to offer but not seeing a place to serve.

   • Help people understand what happens in specific ministries when they are understaffed.

   • Show the needs of the community in a way that awakens compassion and develops a passion for meeting these needs.

   • Share and preach about the Great Commission.

   • Point out the need for discipleship and the mandate to the church regarding evangelism.

2. Help people see the dream.

   • Give people clear, detailed, realistic pictures of what a better future can be.

   • As you show a better future, make it clear that current needs are tremendous opportunities to make a difference in other people's lives.

7. Always *remember the source*. Visions come from two sources: your ego or the Holy Spirit. Visions based on personal ego never last. Limited human energy wears out and the vision fails. Visions emerging from the Holy Spirit reveal God's direction and are blessed by his supporting hand. The kingdom is not ours, it is God's, and he will draw us to his plan, show us the way, and act in his time.

Creative Ideas for Sharing the Vision of Equipping Ministry

• It's hard for core leadership to get enthusiastic about equipping ministry before they've experienced it. One way to share vision is to take the key leaders and church staff members through a pilot discovery and placement process that helps them restructure their current ministry positions for a better fit. Your best vision casters will be those who know its transforming power. If you meet the needs of the influential leaders, they can help you expand the program.

• Celebrate ministry in worship services. Select a particular category of ministry. Identify a benefactor of the ministry area and ask this person to share what the gift of that ministry has meant to him or her. Honor a minister in that particular area and acknowledge all the people in the church who perform that ministry.

• Some people are natural vision casters. Find them and ask for their help. The more champions you have in various parts of the church, the more you will be able to receive input on how equipping ministry is viewed and the more you will have peers selling peers on the benefits of serving.

• Develop bulletin boards, displays, posters, bookmarks, or bulletin inserts that celebrate members in ministry. Be sure to keep a camera handy for those "Kodak moments" you won't want to miss. Have good pictures blown up to poster size to emphasize special events.

• Create a series of sermons on giving, serving, and growing through ministry. Combine the sermons with a commissioning of members for ministry, both within the church and in the larger community.

• Develop a list of hymns and praise songs that celebrate ministry and service. One song may evolve into a "theme song" for your church.

• Encourage the exploration of Sunday school materials for all ages that focus on giving, serving, and growing. Consult with your local school district for books and curriculum materials on volunteerism and service learning. Help children begin to see their natural gifts and talents in the context that God gave them for serving his purpose.

• Hold a ministry fair. Encourage each ministry area to create a booth, naming the ministry it provides and listing members involved in service. Be sure that each ministry area has a list of opportunities to invite people to participate in. Invite community agencies to the church to hold a similar festival.

• Publish a directory of ministry opportunities.

• Develop an "honor roll" of people involved in ministry. Add to the list regularly.

• Present service and ministry as an expectation of membership in your new member classes and other programs.

- Highlight the accomplishments of people, making sure to include small and big events alike.
- Develop a way to symbolize the importance of service and growth to the life of your congregation. You may want to create a "giving tree" where members place their names on leaves and place their leaves on the "ministry branch" where they serve.
- Distribute a single glove to each member who is active in ministry. The glove represents the "helping hand" they provide to others.
- Honor a "minister of the month." Involve the congregation in the selection process.
- Create a regular column in your newsletter to share stories of service and transformation in the life of the church.
- Create and distribute bookmarks with your values, vision, and mission, with supporting Scripture where appropriate.
- Do a sermon series on "lay ministers in the Bible" (for example, Priscilla and Aquila)

Affirm Models by Sharing Stories and Examples of Equipping Ministry in Your Church

Stories are probably the most powerful and wide-ranging way of casting a vision that becomes contagious. Real stories have a natural drama that needs to be clear in the retelling. Generally stories begin with a problem, followed by something happening that makes the problem greater. Next a solution is attempted, which is followed by a result. Part of the natural drama is waiting to hear how the process unfolds and what eventually happens. When people share results that include lessons learned, benefits received, and progress made, it creates a compelling motivation for others facing a similar problem to attempt a similar course of solution. ·

The Worship Service

A powerful aspect of the worship of God is telling stories of how people used their God-given gifts in everyday settings to bless others. When the story is told from a God-centered point of view, people become more aware of just how much God has designed us, our circumstances, and our world in particular ways. Sometimes these stories are told through testimonies, interviews, songs, or other creative artistic or verbal expressions. In some churches, videos are used to help hone the story to achieve just the right impact for communicating how God works in and through us.

Preaching

Illustrations are some of the most powerful communication moments in sermons. No wonder pastors are always looking for good sources of fresh and relevant illustrations. The best are often positive stories of people they know, because these stories are easy for people to relate to. They not only illustrate an idea, but they demonstrate that anybody can actually apply the principle. In churches with strong equipping systems, the word is spread among all members of the equipping team to look for success stories. Often systems come into being to collect these stories and make them available to the pastor.

Church Newsletters

Newsletters, cards, and any print, Internet, or other broadcast media can be an excellent place to tell stories. These stories should fit the

"As an assembly worker once told us, 'One of the jobs of a leader is to have a vision. But sometimes top management sees an apple. When it gets to middle management, it's an orange. By the time it gets to us, it's a lemon.' The image that constituents develop in their minds is highly dependent on the leader's ability to describe an apple so that it appears as an apple in the minds of others. Even when the leader is a master communicator, constituents won't bite from the apple if they prefer oranges—or anticipate lemons."

James Kouzes and Barry Posner, *The Leadership Challenge*

medium. Generally people remember a point made through a story much better than if it appeared in the midst of long paragraphs of points and supporting points.

Small Groups

The very best stories are not the ones people hear, but the ones they tell. Studies show that we remember 10 percent of what others say, but up to 90 percent of what we say. Small groups provide some of the best ways to ask questions, share stories, and watch the lights come on as people own the vision through seeing how their story connects with the vision.

EQUIPPING THE DIRECTOR OF EQUIPPING MINISTRY

ONE OF THE CRITICAL success factors in creating an equipping church is the relationship and interaction between the director of equipping ministry and the church leadership team (senior pastor, governing board, key staff). A crucial factor is setting up the director of equipping ministry for success from the start. Once leaders have been appointed, their ability to succeed or fail rests on the level of coaching and advocacy they receive from the senior pastor.

The following checklist provides guidelines for establishing an ongoing successful and empowering relationship of your church leaders with the director of equipping ministry:

- Establish a weekly meeting time where each person brings items to discuss.
- Ask the right questions. (You do not have to know all the answers; just pose the questions and the director will grow in discovering the answers.)
- Regularly communicate and clarify roles and expectations. With any new position, roles and structure will be nebulous at first.
- Be flexible as to new plans and role definition. Clarity comes with experience.
- Define and clarify boundaries of the new role and how this person interfaces with others on staff. Communicate this to all involved.
- Give the new director a voice in staff meetings to become known and to continually update and cast the vision as it is evolving.
- Discern how you will work together on issues of conflict. (There will be conflict!)
- Listen well to concerns and roadblocks.
- Determine together benchmarks for success.
- Give authority with responsibility.
- Declare to staff and others the value and importance of the new role. If it's important to you, it will be important to them.
- When details and strategies loom large, remind the new director why he or she is doing this, and be sure to focus on the biblical foundations and the people in ministry.
- Remind the director often that his or her job is to find a place of service and care for everyone in ministry, not just the shining stars. Help him or her learn how to look for the best in everyone God has sent to your church.
- Value and support continuing education for the director and his or her team.

- Suggest a regular study time for the director. The initial learning curve is enormous. Ongoing learning is one of the hallmarks of a good director.
- Encourage the director to find a network of colleagues to learn from and grow with, and be sure to support the connection with the appropriate time and money opportunities.
- Give permission to "push back a little" to help you see something in a new way.
- Define a phrase or signal together that will keep you aware of the need to change old habits.
- Affirm, affirm, and affirm.
- Celebrate small wins often.
- Provide ongoing feedback and evaluation.
- Equip the director to be a good steward of his or her time and talents.
- Be his or her advocate when the situation warrants.
- Pray for and with him or her on a regular basis.
- Encourage him or her to make time for ongoing reflection.

Now that you've taken this extensive journey with us through part 1 on the way toward building an equipping ministry vision and culture, you probably still have plenty of questions. That's why we urge you to turn to part 2, in which we detail the "building plans" for the construction and implementation of an equipping ministry system.

Why Are You Doing That?

"Changing behavior does not come easily to anyone. In the early months and years of this new ministry at my church, we as a staff made a covenant and defined a phrase to help us break old habits. Each time we were seen doing something that could be done by the people of the church we asked, 'Why are you doing that?' This phrase was spoken thousands of times—to the senior pastor, to me, to the church secretary, and to everyone in between. No one liked the question after a few hundred times, but it did the trick to help us change from being doers to equippers."

Sue Mallory

PART 2

Building an Equipping Ministry System

It was he who gave some to be apostles, some to be prophets, some to be evangelists, and some to be pastors and teachers, *to prepare God's people for works of service*, so that the body of Christ may be built up until we all reach unity in the faith and in the knowledge of the Son of God and become mature, attaining to the whole measure of the fullness of Christ.

EPHESIANS 4:11–13, emphasis added

Part 2 of the guidebook is designed primarily for the equipping ministry director and the various team members who will implement the equipping ministry vision.

9

Understanding the Work of the Director of Equipping Ministry and the Equipping Ministry Team

YOU HAVE BEEN SELECTED to undertake an important and challenging new ministry for your church. Whatever your title may be, you have accepted an "architectural design" position within today's church. As you work with each member to discern his or her needs and call to service, and then connect each person to a ministry opportunity that utilizes the individual's gifts or a ministry care that meets needs, you are helping to build God's kingdom.

Just as an architect needs to understand the principles of design and construction, so you need to grasp the principles and practices that will greatly facilitate your work. In his letter to the Ephesians, Paul calls us to "prepare all God's people for the work of Christian service, in order to build up the body of Christ" (Ephesians 4:12 GNT). He goes on to say, "Instead, by speaking the truth in a spirit of love, we must grow up in every way to Christ, who is the head. Under his control all the different parts of the body fit together, and the whole body is held together by every joint with which it is provided. So when each separate part works as it should, the whole body grows and builds itself up through love" (Ephesians 4:15–16). As a director of equipping ministry, you should be concerned about growing up the body of Christ through love as each of us uses for the good of others the special gift he or she has received from God (see 1 Peter 4:10).

It's hard to imagine a more exciting opportunity for a Christian. For centuries the church has talked about the priesthood of all believers and about every member being a minister, and yet she has had a difficult time bringing these words to life. You will remember from part 1 that churches that have

For as we have many members in one body, but all the members do not have the same function, so we, being many, are one body in Christ, and individually members of one another. Having then gifts differing according to the grace that is given to us, let us use them.

ROMANS 12:4–6 NKJV

successfully embraced this core value possess several common elements. Successful equipping churches have . . .

- visible support and embodiment of values by top leadership.
- a strong biblical foundation in teaching and preaching the value of equipping.
- an effective, supportive information and communication system.
- a point person and team that facilitate the communication systems.

A solid equipping ministry system involves three key processes:

- Prepare
- Connect
- Equip

Each is described in the pages that follow. As a director of equipping ministry, your job is to tailor these processes to the specific needs and culture of your church. Equipping the membership through Christian education, biblical study, and spiritual growth opportunities is foundational to any equipping ministry system.

Some congregations engage people in systematic faith development programs prior to ministry placement; others believe that serving and equipping go hand in hand. Your church will need to thoughtfully develop a system that meets her unique doctrinal considerations.

Part 2 of the guidebook is organized around the elements of church-wide development and offers information about . . .

- defining the vision.
- assessing existing ministry systems.
- building an equipping ministry team.
- defining and integrating ministry connectors.
- facilitating change in the church.
- building informational support systems.
- facilitating effective leader development.
- incorporating the elements of the *Prepare* process, namely, "Assimilation" and "Biblical Foundations."
- incorporating the elements of the *Connect* process, namely, "Discovery" and "Matching and Placement" (church and community connections).
- incorporating the elements of the *Equip* process, namely, "Growth" and "Recognition and Reflection."

What does this task require of you, the director? The answer, of course, is many things. Yet, we would like you to think about who you are as a person and the characteristics and God-given gifts that will help you succeed in this new position. This leadership position is designed for persons who . . .

- ✓ can juggle many tasks simultaneously.
- ✓ have the capacity to enjoy challenge and confusion.
- ✓ truly love others.
- ✓ desire to match people to ministries.
- ✓ are energetic, flexible, and have a sense of humor.
- ✓ are committed to the values of equipping ministry.
- ✓ are committed to prayer.
- ✓ show tact and diplomacy and can negotiate conflicting opinions.

✓ desire to serve God, to strengthen his church, and to build the kingdom.

✓ can plan, organize, work with and through others, and do consistent follow-through.

✓ value the time of others and their own.

✓ feel a calling to the ministry of releasing others in service.

✓ are patient and remember that nothing good happens either quickly or easily.

✓ seek ministry with and through people who are struggling to live out their faith in a secular world.

✓ have faith in God's steadfast goodness and an openness to his grace and guidance, knowing that "in all things God works for the good of those who love him, who have been called according to his purpose" (Romans 8:28).

You are embarking on a challenging journey, a fulfilling ministry opportunity. May God bless you as you work to help build his kingdom.

10

Defining Equipping Ministry in Your Church

As the director of equipping ministry, you are one of Christ's servants, a servant devoted to all the members of the body who serve as one in Christ. For most churches, your position is a new one—a dream come true, an opportunity to empower and support people in ministry. But a new position also represents change. It is important that you . . .

- define and clarify the vision.
- understand and embrace the culture.
- honor and work effectively with other church leaders, both paid and nonpaid.
- identify existing ministry systems, build on their strengths, and clarify where the greatest needs are.

This chapter outlines first steps to take and areas to explore as you clarify the vision for equipping ministry. Remember, when Jesus was baptized, the heavens opened and the Spirit descended on him "like a dove" (Mark 1:10) rather than like a lion. As you begin your journey, approach your church body with a loving attitude of acceptance and support and a desire to be of assistance. Seek gently to find ways to incorporate all God's children with their different gifts, that all might serve and be served in unity to the same Lord.

CHAPTER PREVIEW

In this chapter you will . . .

- seek an in-depth understanding of your church.
- examine the use of needs assessments in the planning process.
- assess existing equipping ministry systems in your church.
- begin to share the vision for equipping ministry.

EXPLORING YOUR CHURCH HOME

EXPECTATIONS ARE A PECULIAR THING. We all have them, and yet we rarely stop to identify them, discern their origins, or examine their accuracy. Just as you have expectations and dreams for your role in this ministry, others have expectations for your position as well. Even though you have a ministry description, spend time talking with people. Explore how your position and the vision for equipping ministry evolved, and try to bring to the surface and clarify the expectations and reservations others have for your position and, subsequently, for your team. This process will facilitate your ability to establish reasonable and appropriate goals and to channel your energy most effectively.

Review all the questions in the following sections. Because churches are dynamic, living organizations, you'll need the input of many people as you develop an understanding of your congregation and your position within the church. The purpose of this exploration is to develop an appreciation of your congregation and her traditions, hopes, and dreams. Because you hold a new position, other church leaders may feel threatened by your position and fearful that you will try to change or alter their work patterns. Identify these boundaries, and uncover and honor their concerns. Be prepared to encounter at least some resistance. Identify it, listen to it, pray about it, and continue forward in the ministry to which you have been called. You will surely find major pieces of work that require your attention and will not infringe on another's territory. As equipping ministry evolves, doors will open to new opportunities as you demonstrate your own trustworthiness and develop strong relationships.

Beginning with the person or leadership team members who hired you, identify key leaders with whom you should talk. Be sure to meet with staff members, governing board members, team leaders, committee chairpersons, and trustees. It is wise to ask all the leaders similar questions. At all times model a service orientation. In addition to gathering data and learning about your church, ask how equipping ministry can serve those with whom you are speaking. Two key questions that should be asked are, "How can we serve you?" and "How can we support you?" Be sure to keep track of all the information you gather. Identify additional questions, and then summarize your findings. Share these findings and concerns with your senior or executive pastor.

How to Understand Your Church

1. Read your church's mission statement and answer the following questions: What is your congregation trying to do? Who is the audience? When was this statement last revised?

2. Read your church's constitution and annual report and answer the following question: What other teams, committees, boards, or commissions have responsibilities similar to yours?

3. Identify denominational or theological statements, guidelines, or policies that affect the values of gift-based ministry. How does your church differ from others in your denomination?

This is how one should regard us, as servants of Christ and stewards of the mysteries of God. Moreover, it is required of stewards that they be found trustworthy.

1 CORINTHIANS 4:1–2 RSV

 **CHECKPOINT**

Some directors of equipping ministry may have served on staff in another capacity before assuming this new position. Even though you may know the congregation, take time to meet with key leaders and explore the dynamics of this new ministry.

Ask the pastor and church leaders to share the information gained during the assessment of the church culture and the formation of the vision.

4. Assess your congregation. What are some of her characteristics?*
   - size of membership
   - number and age grouping of adults
   - number and age grouping of children and youth
   - ethnic and racial diversity
   - economic characteristics
   - family makeup
   - educational levels
   - age of your church
   - location of your church: urban, suburban, rural
   - distance people travel in order to worship with you
   - size of staff: number of pastors, professional staff members, and support staff people
   - percentage of members who attend worship regularly
   - percentage of members who are considered active
   - other facts of interest: _____

5. What are the important traditions or customs in your church?

6. How does someone currently become a member of your church?

7. Learn about the assimilation or incorporation process. Who is involved? How effective is this system? Identify its strengths and weaknesses. What is your role in developing and managing or collaborating in this process?

How to Understand the Expectations of Your Role

1. Learn how your position evolved. Who was involved in creating this position? How was your ministry description developed? Identify the reporting relationships and expectations.

2. Examine the scope of your position. Identify all that it includes:
   - vision casting
   - team development
   - assimilation of people into the life of the church
   - record keeping
   - interviewing
   - gifts assessment
   - connecting people to ministry opportunities
   - equipping people in ministry
   - leader development
   - other: _____

3. How has the vision been shared for this ministry? What have you done to identify the scriptural basis? How are you promoting it in worship and in education? Are you using any other marketing approaches? What is your role in continuing to share the vision?

---

*Some churches have mission studies, congregational profiles, or other documents that capture much of this information.

4. How broadly has the vision been adopted?

_____ Key leaders and staff own and support the vision.
_____ Ministry leaders own and support the vision.
_____ People in the church at large understand and support the vision.

5. What immediate expectations exist for your job?

- new-member assimilation
- interviewing systems
- gifts assessment
- other: _____

6. What is the timeline for reaching goals and objectives of this ministry? Is it realistic? If not, with whom do you renegotiate?

How to Understand Your Working Relationships

1. Where does equipping ministry fit within your church's organizational structure?

2. Identify the roles and responsibilities of other staff members and key leaders. What do their jobs entail? How can you collaborate with and support each other? Clarify boundaries and identify expectations for each other. Does the staff work together effectively as a team?

3. What is your role in helping other staff members and key leaders understand and work more effectively with members who serve in their departments?

4. Seek to understand how things get done in your church. Where are the key decisions made? Who is involved? How are opinions influenced? Who locks and unlocks the church? Who controls the photocopy machine? What are the "sacred cows"?

5. Identify the key leaders in your church. Who are the formal leaders who have titles and positions? Who are the opinion leaders and key influencers? How do these people make things happen?

6. Learn about your boss. Does he or she understand the scope of equipping ministry? Does he or she prefer reports to be verbal or written? When is your boss most approachable and receptive to your concerns? What are his or her areas of passion? What are his or her spiritual gifts? What is his or her leadership style? Conversely, what issues, subjects, or even specific words are best avoided? How does your boss respond to conflict? What is the best way to respond to this style? What kinds of results does your boss most appreciate? What can other people tell you about ways to work effectively with your boss?

7. Identify your own strengths and weaknesses. What are your spiritual gifts? What is your leadership style? Are you a good team player? How do you know if you are or not? Is being a team player an important part of your job? How do you manage confusion or ambiguity? Do you delegate well? How do you respond to conflict?

8. What do you hope to accomplish in this ministry?

9. As a leader, what are your plans for professional development? What budget resources are available for your continuing education?

ASSESSING EXISTING EQUIPPING MINISTRY SYSTEMS

AS YOU SPEND TIME talking with key leaders, staff members, and members of your congregation, you are engaged in an informal needs-assessment process. Through talking, listening, and observing what's happening in your church, you have the opportunity to gather information, formulate opinions, and consider immediate and long-term goals and objectives for your program.

An informal needs assessment provides you with various personal snapshots of your church. Some of the pictures are clear and precise, while others are blurred and require greater focus. The assessment process itself is cost-effective and discrete, and while it suggests directions, it rarely obligates you to a particular action. One of the greatest benefits of the informal assessment is its relational nature. You get to know the leadership, and, more important, they get to know and trust you. On the other hand, an informal assessment can be difficult to capture in written reports submitted to church leaders, because conclusions are often subject to debate, especially by those who disagree with you.

A formal needs assessment occurs when you decide what information you need to know, and then seek to acquire that information in a consistent, reliable manner. Working with your equipping ministry team (see chapter 11), you may decide to interview each member of the church leadership team and all ministry leaders. As a team, you determine what information you want to gain from each person and develop questions designed to gather the information. You may prepare a questionnaire to distribute to each person, or you may conduct face-to-face interviews (or both). Since your questions are consistent, it is possible to organize the responses and prepare a report that reflects the opinions and judgments of the participants. Always pilot-test an assessment form. You need to ensure that your questions are clearly understood by the responder and will elicit useful information.

An assessment identifies important areas of need. Focusing your energy on a significant concern demonstrates your commitment to doing a quality job. In addition, you gather information that forms a baseline for future evaluation. If you take the time to conduct a needs assessment, honor the responders with a report of the information acquired, and act on this knowledge in your planning process.

A Few Pointers to Remember

- Don't overdo needs assessments. People want results, not just more forms and reports.
- Develop your questions carefully. Be clear, concise, and courteous.
- Know how you will use the information before you seek it.

- Be user-friendly. Ask the fewest questions necessary in order to secure the information.
- Be sensitive to age. If developing a questionnaire, be sure the print is large enough to be read by seniors and clear enough to be understood by youth. If you print your form on colored paper, check with your oldest potential responder for readability. You may need two questionnaires based on age demographics, because some seniors want to do things differently from how younger people would do them.
- Pilot-test, pilot-test, pilot-test.
- Report your results, and clearly show how this information is reflected in your planning.

A Few Words of Warning

- *Look for unrealistic expectations.* Research done through in-depth interviews with strong equipping churches shows that in a church of eight hundred or more, the director of equipping ministry should be a full-time position. It's unlikely you can accomplish the job if it's combined with a multitude of other duties. The role of director requires a singular focus on equipping ministry.
- *Look for opposition from other staff members.* Often those who are responsible for finding large numbers of people (such as children's ministries) may see the addition of a director of equipping ministry as a competitor or a bottleneck for volunteers rather than a means to free up their time to better train their teachers. Take it slowly, and work through a plan with other staff members so that they know you have considered their needs and concerns. Ongoing communication will help break down the misconceptions of this new role.
- *Look for signs that people see this as just another program rather than as a comprehensive new way of doing and being church.* A church that has truly mobilized her people in ministry is a completely different church from the inside out. Staff members become equippers of others for ministry rather than simply doing the ministry themselves. Church members begin to reach out in new ways to the community, bringing in new faces and new ideas. People take greater ownership in programs. Be patient. It will take time and some gradual successes before people understand the vision and desire these changes to take place.

An Equipping Ministry Systems Assessment Tool

Assessing what is already in place, as well as evaluating the effectiveness of each component, involves asking questions about the process, the tracking systems for each process, and the people involved in facilitating the process. Use the following assessment tool to take an in-depth look at what is currently in place in your church.

You may want to share the following questionnaire with your planning team, church leaders, committed members, and staff members. You might even convene several focus groups for a discussion of the effectiveness of your current ministry process and systems. You could adapt this questionnaire to use as a churchwide survey of equipping ministry effectiveness. Seeking broader input gives you a more accurate picture, as well as creating ownership of the outcome.

> The goal of a needs assessment is simply to determine what's working, what's not, and what's needed in order to become better equipped to serve others in the future.

> What is essential about information support systems is that they serve the people.

SYSTEM ELEMENT:

Assimilation and Biblical Foundations

A. Process	Works Well	It's OK	Works Poorly	Does Not Exist
Our church currently . . .				
involves visitors as they explore a new church home.	☐	☐	☐	☐
discerns the care needs of people who are new to the church.	☐	☐	☐	☐
quickly and effectively assimilates new members.	☐	☐	☐	☐
offers new-member classes that prepare people for their life in this church.	☐	☐	☐	☐
tells people about opportunities to learn about the church.	☐	☐	☐	☐
regularly invites inactive people to get involved.	☐	☐	☐	☐
clearly teaches the priesthood of all believers.	☐	☐	☐	☐
helps people understand the biblical basis of a gift-based ministry.	☐	☐	☐	☐
encourages people to understand the role of the Holy Spirit in the use of gifts.	☐	☐	☐	☐
helps people see the connection between ministry and their spiritual growth.	☐	☐	☐	☐

B. System	Works Well	It's OK	Works Poorly	Does Not Exist
A system is in place to track . . .				
visitor follow-up.	☐	☐	☐	☐
greeting of people coming into church.	☐	☐	☐	☐
outreach to new people in the community.	☐	☐	☐	☐
new-member classes.	☐	☐	☐	☐
Bible study attendance.	☐	☐	☐	☐
Christian education attendance.	☐	☐	☐	☐
small group attendance.	☐	☐	☐	☐
worship attendance.	☐	☐	☐	☐
people's needs for care.	☐	☐	☐	☐

C. People

Who is responsible for facilitating the systems for preparing people to join the church?

What training and support does the church provide for these facilitators?

What gifts and skills are needed for members of a team in this area of the ministry?

Whom can I think of right now who could be a member of this team?

SYSTEM ELEMENT:

Discovery

A. Process	Works Well	It's OK	Works Poorly	Does Not Exist
Our church currently . . .				
helps people discover their spiritual gifts and discern their interests.	☐	☐	☐	☐
discerns people's care needs.	☐	☐	☐	☐
listens for and responds appropriately to personal issues that need to be addressed prior to ministry involvement.	☐	☐	☐	☐
values the life experience of people and helps them see how that experience can be used in ministry.	☐	☐	☐	☐
helps people see how they can use their gifts to minister in their families, in their workplace and neighborhood, and at church.	☐	☐	☐	☐

B. System	Works Well	It's OK	Works Poorly	Does Not Exist
A system is in place to track . . .				
each person and his or her skills, interests, and abilities.	☐	☐	☐	☐
people's care needs.	☐	☐	☐	☐
training of interviewers and interviewing teams.	☐	☐	☐	☐
communication of information between the equipping ministry team and program ministry connectors and leaders.	☐	☐	☐	☐

C. People

Who is currently responsible for the interview process in the church?

What training and support is provided to equip interviewers?

What gifts and skills are needed for members of a team in this area of the ministry?

Whom can I think of right now who could be a member of this team?

SYSTEM ELEMENT:

Matching and Placement

A. Process	Works Well	It's OK	Works Poorly	Does Not Exist
Our church currently ...				
maintains up-to-date descriptions of ministry opportunities within the church.	☐	☐	☐	☐
maintains a network of contacts within the community, facilitating ministry to the larger world.	☐	☐	☐	☐
supports people as they explore ministry opportunities for service in church and community.	☐	☐	☐	☐
includes unique ministry opportunities in the workplace, within the family, and in the community.	☐	☐	☐	☐
links people with ministry leaders to learn more about specific positions.	☐	☐	☐	☐
orients people for the positions in which they have chosen to serve.	☐	☐	☐	☐
provides opportunities for people to serve as a family or as a small group.	☐	☐	☐	☐
supports people in finding new ministry experiences if the selected opportunity proves inappropriate for any reason.	☐	☐	☐	☐

B. System	Works Well	It's OK	Works Poorly	Does Not Exist
A system is in place to ...				
capture and maintain information about ministry opportunities in church and community.	☐	☐	☐	☐
provide ministry descriptions for all service opportunities.	☐	☐	☐	☐
maintain a network of contacts within the community.	☐	☐	☐	☐
maintain knowledge of community service needs.	☐	☐	☐	☐
provide needed information to church leadership for connections to be made between people and service opportunities.	☐	☐	☐	☐
capture information on new placements gained through feedback.	☐	☐	☐	☐
track information on feedback support provided to people serving in ministry.	☐	☐	☐	☐
track information on new ministry placements made if previous placements were inappropriate.	☐	☐	☐	☐

C. People

Who is currently responsible for inviting people into new ministry opportunities?

Who is currently responsible for facilitating the follow-up of people placed in new ministry opportunities?

What training and support is provided to equip these facilitators?

What gifts and skills are needed for members of a team in this area of the ministry?

Whom can I think of right now who could be a member of this team?

SYSTEM ELEMENT:

Growth

A. Process	Works Well	It's OK	Works Poorly	Does Not Exist
Our church currently . . .				
provides people with direction and support as they begin their ministry.	☐	☐	☐	☐
trains people for the work they will be performing.	☐	☐	☐	☐
provides affirmation and ongoing feedback to people as they serve, helping them be more effective in their ministry.	☐	☐	☐	☐
helps people evaluate their ministry experience.	☐	☐	☐	☐
identifies people who have leadership potential and develops them for future leadership roles.	☐	☐	☐	☐

B. System	Works Well	It's OK	Works Poorly	Does Not Exist
A system is in place to . . .				
track information about training provided to people in new ministry placements.	☐	☐	☐	☐

C. People

Who is responsible for facilitating the training and orientation for people placed in new ministry opportunities?

What training and support does the church provide for these facilitators?

What gifts and skills are needed for members of a team in this area of the ministry?

Whom can I think of right now who could be a member of this team?

Recognition and Reflection

A. Process	Works Well	It's OK	Works Poorly	Does Not Exist
Our church currently . . .				
celebrates the ministry of the people formally and informally and thanks them for contributing to the life of the church.	☐	☐	☐	☐
commissions people in the worship service for ministry in church and community.	☐	☐	☐	☐
makes heroes of people who have contributed through ministry, providing examples for others, including young people, of the importance of a life of Christian service.	☐	☐	☐	☐
provides exit interviews in order to learn from people's experience in the various ministries of the church.	☐	☐	☐	☐
allows those active in ministry to take a guilt-free sabbatical so they may be restored and have time to reflect on their spiritual development.	☐	☐	☐	☐
helps people reflect on their ministry experience and see the connection between ministry and faith development.	☐	☐	☐	☐
has one Sunday a year designated to celebrate the gifts of time and talent	☐	☐	☐	☐

B. System	Works Well	It's OK	Works Poorly	Does Not Exist
A system is in place to track . . .				
recognition of people in service.	☐	☐	☐	☐
reflection and sabbatical opportunities provided for people who have served.	☐	☐	☐	☐
exit interviews at completion of service in ministry.	☐	☐	☐	☐

C. People

Who is responsible for facilitating the systems for recognizing the gifts of service and encouraging people in their personal faith development?

What training and support does the church provide for these facilitators?

What gifts and skills are needed for members of a team in this area of the ministry?

Whom can I think of right now who could be a member of this team?

General Attributes of Current Communication Systems in Your Church

	Works Well	It's OK	Works Poorly	Does Not Exist
Our current system . . .				
is user-friendly.	☐	☐	☐	☐
maintains accurate records, allowing us to keep track of ministry opportunities and the gifts and skills needed for each opportunity.	☐	☐	☐	☐
allows us to update information easily.	☐	☐	☐	☐
allows us to meet people's care needs effectively.	☐	☐	☐	☐
allows us to pull information in useful ways in order to connect people with ministry opportunities.	☐	☐	☐	☐
is well coordinated and integrated with all ministries.	☐	☐	☐	☐
is clearly understood by the leader responsible for each area.	☐	☐	☐	☐
keeps an up-to-date schedule of events in the church and allows us to coordinate programs.	☐	☐	☐	☐
supports space and facility management consistent with our ministry needs and priorities.	☐	☐	☐	☐
is invisible and functions to serve the people.	☐	☐	☐	☐

Culture and Value-Driven Attributes of Current Ministry in Your Church

	Works Well	It's OK	Works Poorly	Does Not Exist
Equipping ministry vision and value is currently . . .				
known and understood by the leaders *and* people of the church.	☐	☐	☐	☐
firmly grounded in Scripture and preached and taught widely in the church.	☐	☐	☐	☐
embodied and modeled by church leaders on an ongoing basis.	☐	☐	☐	☐
Our church . . .				
hires staff and appoints leaders who are required to function as equippers, not doers of ministry.	☐	☐	☐	☐
has sufficient and focused financial resources to meet the objectives established.	☐	☐	☐	☐
provides continuing education funds for all leaders, paid and nonpaid.	☐	☐	☐	☐

For more information on assessment, see chapter 3 of this guidebook.

A vision without a task is but a dream; a task without a vision is drudgery; a vision and a task is the hope of the world.

A church in Sussex, England

Why Is Vision Sharing So Important?

Most churches have been preaching gift-based equipping ministry for years; yet, without a committed person to implement the vision, few have successfully seen the phenomenal energy of God's people released in powerful ways. Many underestimate the scope of the task. Some churches have seen it as purely gifts discovery and little else. Vision sharing should not be directed toward promoting your position. Rather, you are advocating something different—the necessity of an intentional, well-managed biblical approach to connecting the gifts and care needs of people in your church to the needs and ministries in the church and community, and setting people up to succeed through training and support.

YOU ARE ESPECIALLY FORTUNATE if you have been hired as a result of a key leader casting a vision for equipping ministry in your church. The groundswell of support for this vision created your position. This set of circumstances, however, is rare. Sometimes the most you will experience is that a few pivotal people in the church believe in your position. Part of your job is to increase the number of people who see the value of equipping ministry and of your role as a facilitative leader in realizing the vision for this ministry in your church. In a new ministry, especially one of this scope, it is vital that you talk about the vision over and over again at every occasion. To create an equipping culture, the vision will need to be cast year in and year out.

Where Do You Begin?

- Chapters 1, 5, and 8 include information on the formation of a vision for equipping ministry and several ways to effectively share this vision. The critical need for a director of equipping ministry to lead the vision casting and vision sharing is stressed. If you haven't already done so, you would do well to read these sections of the guidebook for information about how a vision is shared.

- Some people are natural vision casters. Find them and ask for their help. The more champions you have in various groups in the church, the more you will be able to receive input on how your ministry is viewed, and the more you will have friends selling friends on the benefits of service.

- Every church has a core of opinion leaders. These may be trustees, elders, deacons, secretaries, teachers, or people who have no formal positions but who are known for their faith and their commitment to prayer. Find out who these people are. Talk to them about their concerns and their hopes for your position. Stay in touch with them, for through them you can be in contact with the many people who are influenced by their opinions.

- Working with your pastor, the worship team, and key leaders, develop a comprehensive plan for casting the vision of equipping ministry to the whole congregation. You will want to implement your vision-casting strategy in cooperation with your equipping ministry team (see chapter 11). Initiate work on your communication systems simultaneously. It is vitally important that you have the support systems in place to enable the effective involvement of people in ministries at the very time the vision casting is igniting their desire to serve. If you don't, it will be like inviting guests to dinner before you build the kitchen.

- Remember, the vision of equipping ministry is biblical. From the outset of your planning and vision casting, be sure to ground your thoughts and actions in prayer. You would be wise to enlist the support of a prayer team or prayer partners as you embark on the critical foundation building of the ministry in your church. Continue to seek God's vision for the ministry in your church's culture, and carry out your work according to his timing.

DEVELOPING AN ATMOSPHERE OF DISCIPLESHIP

HOW EASY IT IS to see an equipping ministry system as an end in itself. Equipping ministry, however, should be part of a larger vision of discipleship and personal growth in the individual and within the fellowship of the church. The goal is not to place people in ministry slots. The goal is not even to make sure church programs are staffed. The ultimate goal is to serve God and to provide a place for people to grow spiritually through serving others and being served.

Most churches have education programs already in place. These may include Sunday school classes, small group Bible studies, catechism classes, or new-member orientations. It is important to coordinate the equipping ministry so that it becomes the avenue whereby the biblical and theological knowledge learned in these settings finds a place of application in people's lives through serving others. The end result in an effective equipping church should be whole-life ministry for people, so that who they are in and through the church permeates who they are in the workplace, in their communities, and in their families.

Our Vision

To be a community where people can . . .

- experience God
- be encouraged in their spiritual journey
- be empowered for service to others
- entrust to others a legacy

Woodman Valley Chapel, Colorado Springs, Colorado

	INVITE	CONNECT	LEAD	SUSTAIN
DEFINITION	• To motivate and move people toward involvement	• To have an intentional process through which the discovery of people's individual needs, interests, and giftedness ensure the appropriate connection into ministry	• To equip and encourage people to live out ministry by providing an environment that nurtures community, service, and personal development	• To encourage, support, and celebrate the individual's belonging and contributions to the body of Christ, keeping them participating for the long haul

CHURCHWIDE SUPPORT "Centralized"	• Platform participation
	  - Verbal announcements
	  - Teaching/stories
	• Written communication
	• Web-based communication
	• Front-door coordination (entry points)
	• Churchwide events (newcomers receptions, ministry fairs)
		• Churchwide strategy coordination
		• Reporting/tracking systems (IS support)
		• Assimilator meetings (training, communication, best-practice sharing)
		• Forms/tools
		• Reports—data interpretation
			• Understand needs of people
			• Provide leadership resources
			  - Training delivery system
			  - Information technology support
			  - Communications strategies
			  - Other resources
				• Exit interviews
				• Redirect/transfer between ministries
				• Churchwide celebrations
				• Storytelling

MINISTRY-SPECIFIC ACTIVITY "Decentralized"	• Individual recruitment
	  - each one reach one
	• Ministry-specific strategy
	  - Medium-size events (fishing ponds)
	  - Brochures
		• Assimilation strategy implementation
		• Leading individuals through process—managing the pipeline
		• Data gathering/processing
		• Reporting
		• Volunteer team development
			• Utilize centralized/decentralized resources
			• Intentionally shepherd
			  - Build the relationship
			  - Discern the need
			  - Develop next steps
			• Ensure solid experience—community, serve, develop
				• Commissioning/sending
				• Exit interviews
				• Handoffs to other ministries

INDIVIDUAL'S EXPERIENCE/ PROCESS	• Envisioned • Embrace values • Explore opportunities	• Welcomed/directed • Orientated • Understood/served • Connected appropriately	• Understand vision/their role • Resourced to carry out their role • Experience community • Personal/spiritual growth • Challenged/given feedback	• Feel valued/appreciated • Invite others into their way of life
Bill's teaching points	*"It all starts with teaching."*	*"Align with passion and gifts."*	*"Don't overwhelm/ underwhelm them."* *"Provide a real and rich sense of community."* *"Develop them over time."*	*"Remind them they're not crazy."*

Samples are as of June, 2001

Willow Creek Community Church, Barrington, Illinois

Do not merely listen to the word, and so deceive yourselves. Do what it says. Anyone who listens to the word but does not do what it says is like a man who looks at his face in a mirror and, after looking at himself, goes away and immediately forgets what he looks like. But the man who looks intently into the perfect law that gives freedom, and continues to do this, not forgetting what he has heard, but doing it—he will be blessed in what he does.

JAMES 1:22–25

BUILDERS' NOTE

Many churches live by the belief that if you teach people right behavior and biblically based values, they will be able to practice them on their own. As a result, some churches have offered gifts-assessment seminars for many years, assuming that participants are then equipped to find a place of service on their own. Other churches conclude every service with the command to serve the Lord, assuming that the command begets the action. Yet, only a small percentage of the population has the entrepreneurial ability or the initiative to launch out without further help. Only a small percentage seems capable of connecting the church's teaching with the practices of daily life. Part of your job is to link existing assimilation and education programs with a system of coaching and mentoring that will bring head knowledge to the heart, the hands, and the feet—to bring faith and life together in action.

Seven Characteristics of a Balanced Spiritual Journey

The Chapel,
Akron, Ohio

Take time to establish a solid foundation, to build trusting relationships, to honor the work that has preceded you, and to champion the vision before you. The effort will pay handsome dividends as you move into uncharted territory and unleash God's people for Christian service.

Building Relational Foundations

A KEY TO EFFECTIVE equipping ministry is building the critical relational foundations. While equipping ministry by necessity is built and facilitated as a *system*, the primary focus and value of the ministry is the *people*. Your ability to successfully implement equipping ministry is dependent on the genuine support and encouragement of your senior pastor and church leaders, combined with the hard work and advocacy of an equipping ministry team. In addition, a hugely significant factor in building successful relationships is your ability as a leader and team to facilitate the transitions involved in the change process.

> God put all the separate parts into the body on purpose. If all the parts were the same, how could it be a body? As it is, the parts are many but the body is one. The eye cannot say to the hand, "I do not need you," nor can the head say to the feet, "I do not need you."
>
> **1 CORINTHIANS 12:18–21** JB

Try visualizing the relational foundations as a three-legged stool. Each leg—the church leaders, the equipping ministry team, and the ministry connectors—must be firmly grounded in its active support of the equipping ministry system. This grounding is essential for the ministry to grow and serve the church. The church leadership includes pastors, key influencers, ministry leaders, the governing board, elders, deacons, and any other leaders who play a key part in the church operations. In addition to these leaders, ministry connectors are the people who fulfill a vital communication role between program ministries and the equipping ministry team.

Without the shared affirmation and encouragement of the leadership team, your efforts will not succeed in the long run. If you seriously question the support of any part of the leadership team, we'd encourage you to step back, examine your situation, and find ways to strengthen and balance your team before moving forward.

CHAPTER PREVIEW

IN THIS CHAPTER YOU WILL learn to . . .

- select and build the equipping ministry team.
- define and integrate ministry connectors.
- facilitate change.

"I am learning that I cannot be fulfilled apart from other people. In fact, the bottom line is this: You can't do it alone. If you want to be a successful leader, if you plan to have a successful ministry, you must develop not only your gifts, but also the gifts of others around you."

Wayne Cordeiro, New Hope
Christian Fellowship Oahu, Hawaii

When Jesus had called the Twelve together, he gave them power and authority to drive out all demons and to cure disease, and he sent them out to preach the kingdom of God and to heal the sick.

LUKE 9:1–2

TEAM MINISTRY IS an essential part of building the system and incorporating the value of gift-based ministry into your church culture. Shifting to a team ministry model requires more than just changing the words *committee* or *department* to *team*. It requires a complete shift in culture—moving from traditional roles and processes to a more fluid, vision-driven model. As director of equipping ministry, your job is to develop an effective equipping ministry team that performs several important functions.

The ministry team should work with you to . . .

- set the goals and objectives for equipping ministry.
- brainstorm and envision how equipping ministry can grow and develop.
- help prepare and educate the congregation for this new approach to ministry.
- connect every person to the church as a whole by identifying and exercising gifts in service to each other and the community.
- connect ministries with people to meet their care needs.
- support other ministry areas in the church.
- recognize and affirm people in service.

The equipping ministry team should be an active, doing, working team. Its members help develop and organize record-keeping systems, interview people, meet with groups and individuals to facilitate the writing of ministry descriptions, assist with various hospitality arrangements, celebrate the accomplishments of those who actively serve—the list goes on and on. In some churches the equipping ministry team may be known as an advisory team, task force, or ministry mentor group. Select the title most fitting for your congregation. The critical factor is to develop a team of people with diverse gifts who share the vision and shoulder the work. *You can't do it alone!* Jesus didn't carry out his ministry alone . . . and neither should you.

Determining the Ideal Team Configuration for Your Church

Spend some time looking over the examples of team configurations for large and small churches on the following pages. The larger the church,

---

☑ **CHECKPOINT**

A Few Differences between Committees and Teams

Committees	Teams
• Strong, clearly focused leader	• Shared leadership roles
• Individual accountability	• Individual and mutual accountability
• Committee's purpose same as the broader organizational mission	• Specific team purpose, which the team itself delivers
• Run efficient meetings	• Encourage open-ended discussion and active problem-solving meetings
• Measure effectiveness indirectly by its influence on others	• Measure performance directly by assessing collective work production
• Discuss, decide, and delegate	• Discuss, decide, and do real work together

the more important the creation of a core equipping team. You will have core team members who lead the various elements of the equipping ministry process (see "The Equipping Church" chart on page 65). These people will find additional people with the passion and gifts to work in their area to become the "implementation team." The smaller church will have a core team that leads ministries on its own.

An Example of an Equipping Ministry Team Configuration in a Large Church

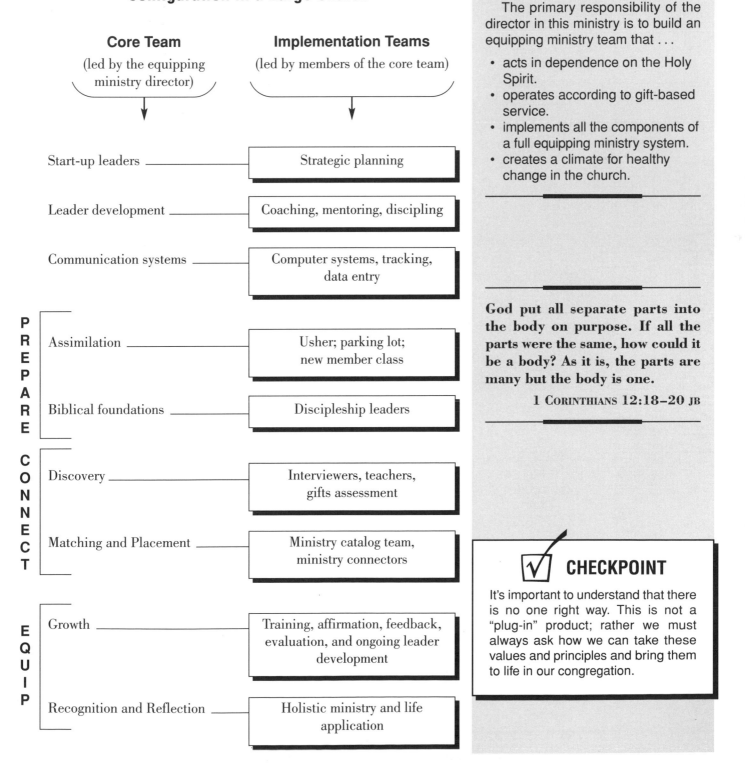

Core Team (led by the equipping ministry director)	Implementation Teams (led by members of the core team)
Start-up leaders	Strategic planning
Leader development	Coaching, mentoring, discipling
Communication systems	Computer systems, tracking, data entry
PREPARE — Assimilation	Usher; parking lot; new member class
Biblical foundations	Discipleship leaders
CONNECT — Discovery	Interviewers, teachers, gifts assessment
Matching and Placement	Ministry catalog team, ministry connectors
EQUIP — Growth	Training, affirmation, feedback, evaluation, and ongoing leader development
Recognition and Reflection	Holistic ministry and life application

A team is a group of people with complementary and diverse skills, gifts, and strengths who are committed to . . .

- sharing a common purpose.
- loving and supporting each other.
- achieving the team's mission.
- holding each other accountable.

The primary responsibility of the director in this ministry is to build an equipping ministry team that . . .

- acts in dependence on the Holy Spirit.
- operates according to gift-based service.
- implements all the components of a full equipping ministry system.
- creates a climate for healthy change in the church.

God put all separate parts into the body on purpose. If all the parts were the same, how could it be a body? As it is, the parts are many but the body is one.

1 CORINTHIANS 12:18–20 JB

☑ CHECKPOINT

It's important to understand that there is no one right way. This is not a "plug-in" product; rather we must always ask how we can take these values and principles and bring them to life in our congregation.

MINISTRY SERVICES

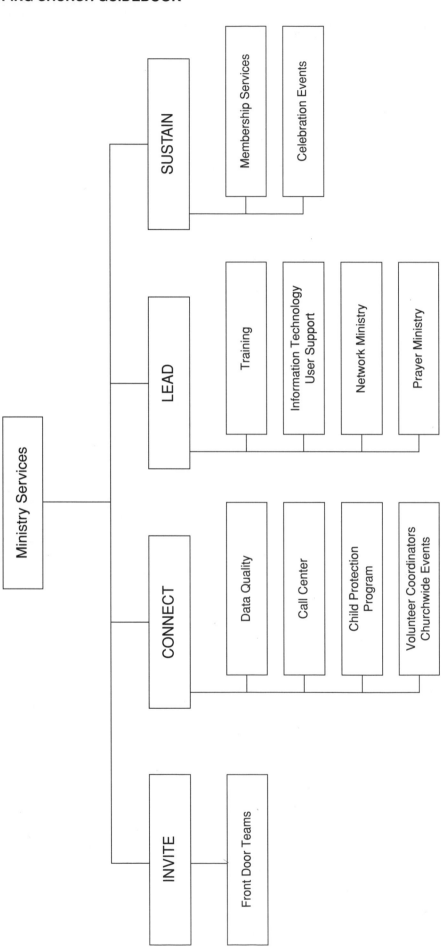

Willow Creek Community Church, Barrington, Illinois

Samples are as of June, 2001

AN EXAMPLE OF AN EQUIPPING MINISTRY TEAM CONFIGURATION IN A SMALL CHURCH (200–350 Attendance)

Approximately eight people on the team—only one staff person

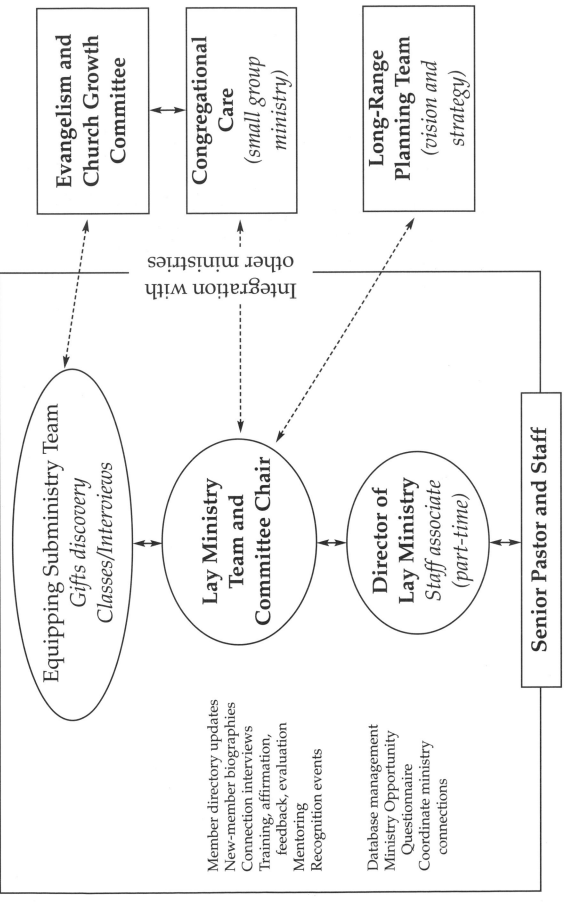

First Presbyterian Church—Kennewick, Washington

> "A team is a small number of people with complementary and diverse skills, gifts, and strengths who are committed to a common purpose, performance goals, and approach for which they hold themselves mutually accountable."
>
> Jon Katzenbach
> and Douglas Smith,
> *The Wisdom of Teams*

Here are four effective criteria for choosing leaders:

1. strength of character
2. spiritual authenticity
3. ministry fit
4. team fit

Don Cousins,
"Selecting the Right Players"

Selecting a Team

Your equipping ministry team should be made up of people gifted to carry out each of the functions in your equipping ministry system. This group is the team that's focused on facilitating the development of an authentic, gift-based equipping ministry system for all the church's ministries. If you don't take the necessary time and care to build this team, you may well slow the growth of the ministry. This team and the director are *not* the gatekeepers; they are the support and foundation that create the infrastructure for all the ministries to become healthier.

Suggested Selection Criteria

Effective equipping ministry teams are representative of the church at large. They are most effective when they reflect the demographic characteristics of your congregation. You want persons who represent your congregation in age grouping, ethnic and racial diversity, family style (traditional families, blended families, single-parent families), marital status, socioeconomic groups, geographic diversity, and the like. New members provide an important perspective, as do longtime members.

You will want to identify people with gifts, passion, and skills in equipping ministry. Seek out those who . . .

- have strong organizational abilities.
- understand equipping ministry and embrace the theology of the priesthood of all believers.
- can write well.
- understand computer systems and record-keeping concerns.
- enjoy entertaining and like to host events.
- listen well and reflect the concerns of the group.
- have had experience serving the church in other ministry areas supported by equipping ministry, such as Christian education or worship and music.

The selection grid (at the top of the next page) will help you identify potential candidates to serve on your equipping ministry team. It is essential that you interview each candidate, explaining the scope and the responsibility of the team and discerning their interest in serving (see chapter 14 for information on interviewing and on inviting people into ministry).

Tips for Selecting a Team

- *Develop a team description.* Develop this description of the team, its function, and its scope before interviewing or inviting people to join. In some churches, your governing board will need to authorize the creation of a new team.
- *Consider every person to be a potential member of the team.* While you don't want to rob other teams of their members, a person may be serving elsewhere who is ideally gifted to support equipping ministry. Allow such a person to conclude an existing commitment and serve in his or her area of giftedness and passion.
- *Consider prospective team members as potential fits in more than one category.* You may find a single person with solid writing skills or someone in your women's group who enjoys hosting events. Consider all the categories a person can cover as you look at possible team members.
- *Limit your team to eight to twelve people.* It's easier to set meeting times if you limit the size, and a smaller group encourages good

Identifying Candidates to Serve on the Equipping Ministry Team

Names of Prospective Team Members

SKILLS AND ABILITIES

Organizational skills									
Computer/Record keeping									
Writing									
Event planning/hosting									
Interviewing									
Bilingual ability (if necessary)									
Public relations/Marketing									
Creativity									
Other									

KNOWLEDGE OF THE CHURCH

Worship and music									
Children's ministries									
Adult ministries									
Youth ministries									
Christian education									
Other									

GIFTS

Administration									
Leadership									
Prophecy									
Mercy									
Giving									
Faith									
Wisdom									
Teaching									
Shepherding									
Hospitality									

attendance and closer relationships as well. Greater numbers of people will be involved on subteams that support the ministry in specific ways based on function.

- *Select carefully.* Although you need gifted, skilled, capable people who represent your church, this is first and foremost a ministry concerned with releasing the gifts of the people for strengthening the work of the church.
- *Recognize seasons of service.* Some people will simply be too busy to accept any other responsibilities, while others may have personal situations that prevent their involvement. Find ways to keep these people informed about the equipping ministry team. Keep them in mind for future service opportunities.
- *Connect with the governing board of your church.* In many churches, one member of the equipping ministry team sits on the governing board and serves in an official liaison capacity. This is an important organizational link that provides recognition, advocacy, and credibility for your work.

NOTE: The length of service on the equipping ministry team should parallel the arrangement of other key ministry teams in the church.

Start by understanding that your most important tool in the invitation process is *listening.*

Inviting People to Join the Team

A key to selecting the right people is the effectiveness of your invitation. Effective invitation requires you to . . .

- share the vision for an equipping ministry system with potential team members.
- take time to personally invite people. Get to know each one so you can affirm the gifts you believe would complement the team. You can't assess character or team fit until you really come to know them.
- ask each one to prayerfully consider joining the core team.
- let people know how important it is to have a singular focus for equipping ministry. If any of the people you invite are currently involved in other areas of ministry, ask them to pray about what they are prepared to give up in order to become part of the equipping ministry leadership team. It takes significant work and time (sometimes up to two years) to build the foundations needed for an equipping ministry, so be careful not to encourage burnout. Be a good steward of their gifts and time.

BUILDERS' NOTE

You can't give birth to something without placing a singular focus on it. You may have to let go of some other commitment in your church in order to be successful in creating or building and leading a truly effective equipping ministry team.

Building an Equipping Ministry Team

Building an equipping ministry team involves three key steps:

Step 1: Clarify the vision of the team.

As facilitator and equipping ministry team director, a key part of your job will be to clarify the team's vision. Vision casting with your team is of critical value and should be an ongoing activity for you. If team members don't understand the value, they cannot own the vision. Use meetings as an opportunity to lead brief Bible studies centered around the core values of equipping ministry. Continually share and interpret the team's purpose in equipping ministry and in the life of the church; continually clarify the purpose and progress of the team to other ministry leaders and church members.

Clarifying the vision of the team will . . .

- establish clear areas of focus for each team member.
- prevent possible conflicts with other ministries by defining and respecting boundaries and communicating them.
- establish the relationships between equipping ministry and all other existing and future ministries in the church.
- give the work of the team focus and direction.
- provide the first step toward the development of ministry descriptions.
- help team members understand the biblical foundation of team ministry in an equipping culture.

Step 2: Develop a mission statement.

Once you've selected a core team and shared the vision of the team, work together to develop a mission or purpose statement. People commit

"Building teams doesn't begin with a certain kind of technique. It begins with a certain kind of heart. Here's a key in your asking someone to join up. You must be genuinely sincere in your belief that you want to see him or her grow and be used in wonderful ways by the Holy Spirit! You must be completely authentic in your invitation."

Wayne Cordeiro,
Doing Church as a Team

to the decisions they help make. This will allow team members to develop ownership and full understanding of the ministry. By going through the process of answering four key questions a mission (or purpose) statement addresses, team members will have been part of shaping the role and value of the team. The four key questions are . . .

- who are we?
- whom do we serve?
- what do we do?
- why do we do it?

Step 3: Provide ongoing team leadership.

You can provide leadership by practicing good stewardship and management and by viewing meetings as ministry opportunities:

- Set meeting dates well in advance. To limit confusion, you may want to establish a meeting schedule, such as the first Tuesday of the month. Another approach is to set the time and date of the next meeting as you adjourn. Members are aware of their responsibility to attend when they have an equal say in setting the date.
- Be prepared. Make necessary arrangements in advance of meeting times. Check to be sure the room is set up the way you want it to be, the flip charts are ready, minutes or reports are duplicated, coffee is brewed. Phone calls or postcards serve as friendly reminders and increase attendance.
- Honor people with punctuality. Time is a valuable gift. If some members desire more time to socialize, consider serving refreshments before or after a meeting as an additional fellowship opportunity.
- Develop and work from a written agenda. Agendas identify the reason for the meeting and define what you hope to accomplish. Manage the time in such a way that you allow for adequate discussion on important or controversial issues.
- Begin meetings with Bible studies, devotions, and opportunities to pray for each other and the work of the body. If your church offers evening worship opportunities, you may want to schedule meetings so that members may worship and serve together. Select Bible studies around the meaning of gifts, calling, service, team, and so forth. You will continue to educate your team about the biblical foundations of equipping ministry (passages such as Psalm 139:13–16; Jeremiah 1:4–5; Matthew 25:14–30; John 21:15–17; Romans 12:4–8; 1 Corinthians 12:4–12, 18; Ephesians 2:10; 4:11–16; 1 Peter 2:5, 9–10; 4:10–11; James 1:22–27; 2:14–17).
- Help everyone feel comfortable and a part of the group. Take time for people to share important life events. Team-building exercises can go a long way toward helping a team come together and function effectively. Building trust, community, a shared vision, and strong relationships is the work of the team in the early stages of development.
- Involve people in their area of giftedness. Model a gift-based ministry by asking people to contribute by utilizing their God-given gifts, skills, and talents.
- Monitor group dynamics. Encourage those who are hesitant to speak. Monitor those who have a tendency to dominate the conversation. Be

---

Ministry Involvement Team Mission Statement

"Recognizing that God has given different gifts (Ephesians 4:11–13) to his children, the ministry involvement team seeks to encourage and assist individuals to mature spiritually by using their God-given gifts to serve each other and the community so that the whole church may attain the maturity that God intended."

Christ Lutheran Church,
Overland Park, Kansas

Team Purpose

To develop and implement a system to help Trinity attendees and members to become part of a gift-based team.

Trinity United Methodist Church,
Huntsville, Alabama

Mission and Vision of the Lay Team

We can, as a Christ-Centered Church, support each person in our congregation to develop and act on the sense of God-given talent and skill in his or her life, so that lay ministry becomes the hallmark of UPC, fulfilling the mandate—Every member (person) a minister!

University Presbyterian Church,
Seattle, Washington

sure each person feels heard and has the opportunity to be a contributing team member.

- Celebrate accomplishments. It's easy to become so involved in the big picture that we neglect to celebrate the many achievements or small wins of the group. Acknowledge personal accomplishments as well as group achievements.

- Record the progress of meetings. Assign a person to take notes and distribute the minutes as soon as possible after meetings. Highlight accomplishments, review assignments, and recap progress before you adjourn. As decisions are made, clarify next steps, identify responsibility for follow-up actions, define timelines, and determine who should be informed of progress and how.

- Keep good records on your people. Develop rosters with the names, addresses, e-mail addresses, and phone numbers so that people can be in touch with each other and pray for each other.

DEFINING AND INTEGRATING MINISTRY CONNECTORS

ONE OF THE CRITICAL success factors in equipping ministry is building and maintaining relationships between the equipping ministry team and the program ministry teams throughout the church. A clear understanding and ownership of the vision and values of equipping ministry by the leaders and teams involved in the ministry programs lay a foundation on which connector relationships can be built.

In every church, irrespective of structure, each area of ministry is led by a group of committed people under the guidance of a leader. "Connectors" are those people designated to provide the communication and feedback between their team and the equipping ministry team. These "touch points" between ministries are essential as equipping ministry becomes aligned with the vision of the church and infused into the operations of all the ministry programs.

The following essential questions should be asked continually by ministry connectors:

- What do we need from the equipping ministry team by way of support?

- What information do we need about people who are interested in joining our team? How successful have recent ministry placements been?

- What information do we need about other ministries and about the church at large?

- How can we serve the other ministry programs?

- What information do we have to feed back to the equipping ministry team about our ministry needs, our mission, and our activities?

- What specific activities do we need support for?

- What systems are in place to provide the information and support to our program ministry teams?

- Do we have systems in place to effectively communicate information about needs and follow-up?

The diagram at the top of the next page is an example of the relationship between the equipping ministry team and program ministry teams, using ministry connectors as the communication link.

And the things you have heard me say in the presence of many witnesses entrust to reliable men who will also be qualified to teach others.

2 TIMOTHY 2:2

Program Ministries

Implementing the ministry of the church through the
gifts of the body in order to grow people into deeper relationship with Christ

Worship

Sunday School

Outreach

Children's Ministry

Equipping Ministry

Facilitating the process
and communication systems
necessary to effectively
prepare, connect, and
equip people to serve
in your ministries

Equipping Ministry

Missions

Adult Ministry

Stewardship

← ⟶ = **Ministry Connectors**

What do we need in the way of support?
What information do we have to feed back?
How successful have recent ministry placements been?
What specific activities do we need support for?
How can we serve the other ministry programs?

Defining the ministry connector relationships involves six steps:

Step 1: Identify the program ministries of the church. Equipping ministry support systems permeate all the programs in the church. Identifying these programs, as well as their roles and functions, is the first step toward integrating the necessary values, principles, and systems into the life of the church.

Step 2: Communicate the vision and values of equipping ministry to each ministry. Effective ministry connector relationships are founded on understanding and ownership of the vision and values of equipping ministry by the ministry leaders. When leaders embody these values, they support the relationship between the program ministry they lead and the equipping ministry team. They do so by engaging in ongoing communication with and through the ministry connectors.

BRENTWOOD PRESBYTERIAN CHURCH

LAY MINISTRIES COMMITTEE

Job Description and Procedures

TITLE:

Liaison Coordinator for Lay Ministries

RESPONSIBLE TO:

Chairman of Lay Ministries Committee

Purpose:

1. To inform committees regarding the talents of church members

2. To inform lay ministries of volunteer opportunities

3. To inform lay ministries of member participation in committee-sponsored events

Responsibilities:

1. Participating on lay ministries committee

2. Distributing names of members interested in various committees to the lay ministries liaison who represents each committee. The names are gathered from . . .

   a. new member interest profiles furnished by the outreach committee.

   b. updated BPC questionnaires.

3. Sending list of names to lay ministries liaisons after each new-member class

4. Connecting with lay ministries director one month after each new-member class to obtain information.

5. Following up with liaisons to confirm they are making contact

Time Required:

1. two hours per month for committee meeting

2. one hour per week to follow up with liaisons

3. one-half hour four times per year to gather names and send to liaisons

Step 3: Identify potential ministry connectors in each program ministry. Involve the program ministry leaders in identifying people on their teams who have the gifts of hospitality and communication that would serve them well as the communication links to the equipping ministry team. In some cases, people who are not currently serving in any particular program ministry can be tapped as especially well suited to serve as ministry connectors.

Step 4: Invite identified connectors to take on the added or new responsibilities. The principles and guidelines for the invitation into ministry should be applied when inviting ministry connectors (see chapter 14, page 302).

Step 5: Define the collaboration and communication systems between the equipping ministry team and the connectors. It is essential to clearly outline the ongoing, two-way communication cycle among the connectors, the program ministries, and the equipping ministry team.

Step 6: Equip connectors to fulfill their role. In a large church a connectors coordinator, who serves on the equipping ministry team, will be responsible to train ministry connectors and ensure that follow-up systems and communication are effective and ongoing. In a small church, the director of equipping ministry may do the training and support of a team member who will be responsible for the ongoing two-way communication between program ministries and the equipping ministry team.

FACILITATING CHANGE

JUST AS EACH PERSON is a unique child of God, each person's response as you pioneer a new ministry approach is likely to be unique as well. "The church is finally serious about involving everyone in ministry in their area of giftedness," says one. Another suggests that your work was his or her idea all along, and now at last someone has listened. And some can hardly wait for you to be truly operational, because so much help is needed.

Nevertheless, sometimes your presence and persistence are considered troublesome as well. Someone might mutter under his breath, "Things are fine just the way they are," while another person never seems to find time to complete a ministry description in spite of feeling overworked and underappreciated. Or perhaps you will run across the leader who needs help on a certain committee but never calls the people who have expressed interest in this particular ministry.

As a pioneer, you are an agent of that difficult and often annoying six-letter word—C-H-A-N-G-E. The world may be full of change and people may even be calling for change in the church, but being a change agent is a very different matter indeed. This section of the book will focus on that six-letter word and offer suggestions and support as you enter the uncharted territory of mobilizing people into gift-based team ministry.

Understanding and Working with Change

This section is based on the excellent book *Managing Transitions: Making the Most of Change* by William Bridges (Cambridge, Mass.: Perseus, 2000, paperback edition). The reader is urged to consult this book for a more thorough review of the material discussed here.

As an agent of change you will encounter resistance, conflict, occasionally some support, and yes, even some joy! You need to remember that the resistance you encounter is not about you personally; rather, it is about you as the messenger of change, the person who is transforming the church

"Come follow me," Jesus said, "and I will make you fishers of men." At once they left their nets and followed him.

MATTHEW 4:19–20

"One of the distinguishing features [of self-organizing or self-renewing systems] is system resiliency rather than stability."

Margaret Wheatley,
Leadership and the New Science

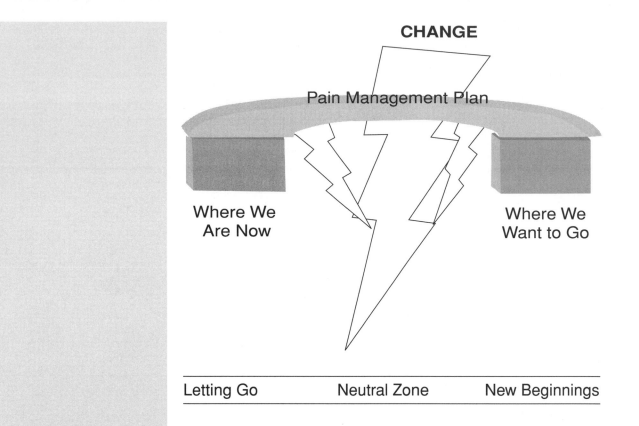

CHANGE

Pain Management Plan

Where We Are Now

Where We Want to Go

| Letting Go | Neutral Zone | New Beginnings |

through a well-thought-out, coordinated process of member involvement. Jesus was about change, too. While he was loved by his followers, he was a serious threat to the status quo. You are a threat to the status quo as well, even in churches that have prepared for and welcome equipping ministry.

Three Major Steps in the Transition Process

Transitions are a predictable journey that requires the person experiencing the change process to pass through three separate experiences. In the following pages we'll discuss each stage in greater detail and apply what we learn to the church and to the evolution of equipping ministry.

The experience of *letting go* comes first. In order for a transition to occur, the old situation must be left behind. People must identify specifically what is being lost and who is affected by the loss. Transitions begin with endings.

The *neutral zone* follows. In the neutral zone, the old reality has been left behind, but the new identity has not yet been fully accepted and embraced. It is a "limbo" stage, a type of wilderness experience when nothing seems quite right. This is the time, however, when revitalization begins and innovation and creativity are most possible. The neutral zone is, in the words of Bridges, the "seedbed of the new beginning that you seek."

New beginnings follow the ending experience and emerge from the neutral zone. The new beginning cannot really take hold without the full sequence of the transition. People pass through these zones in their own ways and at their own pace, yet each is essential to the process and to the acceptance of change.

Step 1: Letting Go

You cannot begin something new without first letting go of something old. Bridges asserts that "nothing so undermines organizational change as

---

"I tell you the truth," [Jesus] continued, **"no prophet is accepted in his hometown."**

LUKE 4:24

William Bridges reflects on the change process and its implications as he begins *Managing Transitions:* "It isn't the changes that do you in, it's the transitions. Change is not the same as transition. Change is situational: the new site, the new boss, the new team roles, and the new policy. Transition is the psychological process people go through to come to terms with the new situation. Change is external, transition is internal."

the failure to think through who will have to let go of what when change occurs." Endings must be articulated and losses specifically identified. You must ask and answer the question, "What is actually going to change?" and, as a result of those changes, "What else, what secondary things, are going to change as well?" Changes cause ripples in organizations. One thing is affected, and it in turn affects other aspects of the organization.

In addition to clarifying the specific effects of primary and secondary change, the change facilitator needs to encourage people to clarify what they individually have to let go of. In the chain reaction of events influenced by the change process, people's familiar ways of interacting and doing their jobs are affected. Naming the changes that directly impact the way you conduct yourself facilitates handling these changes. It is equally important to identify what is over for everyone as a result of the change.

One of the easiest ways to identify the changes people are coping with and the transitions they are going through is to ask three questions:

- What's different now that we have an equipping ministry system?
- With the start of equipping ministry, what did you have to give up?
- What do you miss since we established equipping ministry?

Let's look at a few of the kinds of losses that could occur with the advent of an equipping ministry system:

- "Wait, I've been on the finance committee for twenty-five years. I'm not sure about these new people you're suggesting to serve here, and what will I do now?"
- "We've always just chipped in, and somehow the work got done. Why do we need ministry descriptions and specific assignments now?"
- "The trustees normally decide who serves where. I'm not sure you have the authority to recommend someone serving in a ministry area based on a gifts assessment and an interview."

A quick read soon tells you that this is not going to be an easy transition, even if it's the desired direction for church operations. Actualizing the theology of the priesthood of all believers means that the church must begin to address what it has been doing. Is the church working to bring this theology to life, or are there certain management practices and organizational structures that need to be revised? As these changes begin to occur, the sphere of influence of equipping ministry expands. This is a time of "living in the tension" between what was and what is to come.

The question must be asked, "What is over for everyone as a result of the advent of equipping ministry?" Clearly, business as usual is over! Effective equipping ministry broadens the base of people who want to serve, enabling them to serve in their areas of talents and interests. Changes in spheres of influence and control affect everyone who has been active in the church. Even you, as the director of equipping ministry, will feel the impact on your sphere of control. For example, a member with a gift in organizational skills may suggest a new method of organizing your records. Your equipping ministry team may view the suggestion more positively than you do, so you may find yourself being affected by the decisions of others in ways you had not anticipated.

Take a moment and consider the secondary changes that could occur as a result of clarifying ministry descriptions. What will happen when new ministry areas begin emerging, especially when the ideas for these ministry areas emerge from new sources? The ripples generated by the equipping

> "With any change there is always the fear or the perception of loss. Loss of control, loss of tradition, loss of "the way we've always done it." Rarely is there a focus on what we will gain. It is important to honor the fears and honor the past, but continually in big and small ways to paint the picture of what will be gained from the change. Bathe this time in prayer. Pray for the leadership and their willingness to serve in the tension. Pray for the people, that God may soften their hearts and see his vision for the church."
>
> Sue Mallory,
> Leadership Training Network

> **Forget the former things;**
>   **do not dwell on the past.**
> **See, I am doing a new thing!**
>   **Now it springs up; do you not**
>   **perceive it?**
>
> ISAIAH 43:18–19

Your ripples are gaining strength, waves are now rolling across the operational surface of the church . . . and directly and indirectly, your work in equipping ministry is at the center of the change.

ministry system are gaining strength. As waves roll across the church's operational surface, staff members, leaders, and laypeople alike will be affected. Although many of these changes were planned and sought, they directly impact the lives of those involved.

Here are some helpful tips for managing the letting-go experience:

- *Discuss in staff meetings the phases of managing transitions.* Prepare key leaders in advance to recognize the stages of transition and to expect the waves. Consider role-playing scenarios you anticipate. Discuss helpful responses to those who undermine the change process.

- *Accept and acknowledge people's feelings, and talk about losses openly and sympathetically.* Arguing about, minimizing, and solving problems do not manage emotions. The only way to respond to an emotion is with acceptance and feeling. Look for the loss behind the emotion and empathize with the person. Listen thoughtfully. Many people just need to be heard. A wonderful children's book *There's No Such Thing as a Dragon* by Jack Kent illustrates how problems can grow out of control when denied or ignored. As the book concludes, the mother says, "I don't mind dragons [problems] THIS size. Why did it have to grow so BIG?" "I'm not sure," said Billy [her small son], "but I think it just wanted to be noticed." Pretending that feelings and problems don't exist only makes them become unmanageable. Loss is a grief process. Accept the signs of grief as a natural response to the changes you are undergoing.

- *Rely on Scripture and prayer.* Both the Old and New Testaments are overflowing with stories, advice, support, and wisdom. Can you imagine Moses leading the Israelites for forty years through a change process? And nearly everything Jesus did during his earthly ministry as described in the Gospels was about change.

- *Develop a support system for yourself.* Seek out directors of equipping ministry and ministry leaders in other churches. Share your concerns and discuss your plans with a person outside your church who can offer wisdom and balance to your thinking. Some cities have networking organizations for directors in equipping ministry. Attend their meetings or consider beginning such an organization. Visit www.ltn.org for information if you are interested in starting a local network. Leadership Training Network will provide you with resources shared by others who have gone before you. Contact your local volunteer action center for support in organizing a group. A local or regional network is an invaluable source for connecting with your peers. Share experiences, see the challenges, and learn what's working in other churches.

- *Involve key leaders and influential members in the process of transition.* In time, the changes you are making will influence the entire church. Involve as many people as possible in your deliberations, and give people as much information as possible. Assure members that the church is striving to live out her mission more effectively, which may mean some changes will have to take place. The church, however, will still be built on the foundation of Jesus Christ.

- *Continually lift up the vision.* Tell and retell your story. Uphold the vision of the priesthood of all believers. Focus on the long-term gain that the immediate changes will bring: a more effective church with members equipped to serve and to build God's kingdom together.

- *Honor and value the past.* It is important to define what is over, as well as what has not changed. Identify and honor how the equipping ministry system has grown and evolved out of the rich traditions of your church. Emphasize that you are building on the best of the past and honoring the contributions of those who have laid the foundation on which you stand.

Step 2: Entering the Neutral Zone

Bridges defines the neutral zone as the "nowhere between two somewheres." In this state of limbo it seems that nothing works quite right. Neither the old ways nor the new ways are satisfactory. Problems in the system seem to reappear, anxiety is high, signals keep getting crossed, and people are polarized, with some who want to return to old ways and others who want to rush headlong into the future.

Nonetheless, the neutral zone is a very important time in the transition experience. In spite of its chaos, the zone has many positive aspects as well. It can be a highly creative time. With proper management and encouragement, people can capitalize on the confusion by fostering innovation. Let's take a look at eight steps you can take to manage the neutral zone:

1. Explain the neutral zone experience.

Most people do not understand the neutral zone. Bridges refers to it as a journey from one identity to another—a journey that takes time. Moving from an institutional model of church to a dynamic model of the *people of God* as the church is a major readjustment. It is a paradigm shift—not, as Bridges says many people think of it, a trip from one side of the street to the other. Shifting paradigms means rethinking all of your assumptions about how you "do church." The neutral zone provides the time and space for this rethinking. The larger the shift, the greater the time and space required.

2. Provide time for the neutral zone.

Earlier we mentioned that most churches allow anywhere from nine to eighteen months before expecting to see visible results from equipping ministry. Some of this time is devoted to setting up systems, piloting various options for record keeping, and carrying out other tasks; some is devoted to working with staff members and leaders to help them understand the new way of involving people in the life and work of the church. It's also a valuable time for church members to make the transition. It's critical to allow sufficient time for this phase, in accordance with the culture and systems in place in your church.

3. View your equipping ministry team initially as a transition team.

Your team might want to develop a simple newsletter for church leaders that charts the progress, raises questions, and keeps people connected and informed. Share experiments that are working, and offer notes on ideas that seem less successful. Make this neutral zone a time of anticipation and preparation—an advent in the life of the church as one reality comes to a close and another reality breaks forth.

4. Establish reasonable goals with realistic timelines, and be sure to celebrate accomplishments.

Creating a management information system is lots of work. Securing ministry descriptions takes time and patience. Have fun, lighthearted

> "I shall provide water in the wilderness and rivers in the barren desert, where my chosen people may drink."
>
> ISAIAH 43:20 REB

> "This people I have formed for myself, and they will proclaim my praises."
>
> ISAIAH 43:21 REB

> "Starts involve new situations. Beginnings involve new understanding, new values, new attitudes, and—most of all—new identities."
>
> William Bridges,
> *Managing Transitions: Making the Most of Change*

celebrations as you achieve milestones along the way. Be sure to celebrate the small wins, as well as the large.

5. Select your language carefully.

Change brings anxiety and uncertainty. Negative talk and words loaded with negative connotations weaken everyone's efforts. Even the word *change* is a difficult one for many to accept. Consider words like *transition, advent,* or *journey.* Jesus spoke of building the kingdom and preparing the way. Be a part of that building process.

6. Encourage creativity.

The systems suggested in this book have worked for others, and they have for the most part grown out of the trials and errors of churches that have begun this work before you. Use what you find here as a guide, and hunt for even better systems and approaches. Encourage your leaders to find the best ways for *your* church to become the people of God. Experiment, embrace losses and setbacks, and look for new entry points and better solutions. Take time to brainstorm options, and find ways to solve problems collectively. Share your difficulties openly in staff meetings. Ask for assistance, support, and prayer.

7. Seize the moment.

People are most open to new learning at transition points. Look for the special leadership development opportunities that come during times of transition. Offer seminars on working effectively with teams. Consider training leaders to work as mentors to encourage the spiritual growth and development of others. One word of caution: Don't offer training or new experiences that either push the group too far or seem disconnected. People are especially fragile in times of change, and they will experience overload quickly. Be certain that new experiences build incrementally on the continuum of change that has been introduced.

8. Praise the Lord.

You are walking a difficult and rocky road. If you get to the point in your system development where you are implementing these steps, you are in fact very close to a new beginning. The neutral zone, in the words of William Bridges, "is the winter during which the spring's new growth is taking shape under the earth."

Step 3: Experience a New Beginning

Distinguishing between *starts* and *beginnings* is important in the equipping ministry system. A date can be announced when the communication system is up and running or when a new member assimilation class will begin, but until people are psychologically prepared and emotionally committed to incorporating equipping ministry values and principles into the new configuration, the transition will not occur. Starts occur on calendar or clock time, while beginnings occur according to heart-and-mind time.

Why are beginnings so difficult and so scary? Bridges identifies several possible explanations:

- A beginning requires that the person make the new commitment demanded by the new situation.
- Some of the old anxieties associated with endings reemerge. The beginning signifies that the ending really was real.
- A beginning represents a gamble: Will this approach actually work? What happens if it doesn't? What if it doesn't live up to the expectations?

- Beginnings are connected to the past. Memories of old failures may be triggered, or personal embarrassment may be resurrected.
- Beginnings signal the end of the neutral zone. Some persons may have found the chaos and ambiguity of the neutral zone to their liking. The expectations were fewer, accountability could be ducked, and, in the absence of clarity, personal agendas could be pursued.

The wisdom of Solomon applies to beginnings. Just as "there is a time for everything, and a season for every activity under heaven" (Ecclesiastes 3:1), beginnings follow a natural ebb and flow as well. Endings and neutral zones are essential if people are going to arrive at new understandings, new attitudes, and new values that will reconfigure how the church goes about being the church in the twenty-first century.

To make a new beginning happen, people need what Bridges refers to as the "Four P's" of the process: People need a purpose, a picture, a plan, and a part to play.

1. Purpose

It is *very* important to identify the idea behind the changes you are proposing. In order for people to embrace the change, they have to understand the reason change has to be pursued. Some of the reasons may be negative issues. You must communicate to people the challenges faced by the church before you propose a solution to the situation. The purpose behind a proposed change only makes sense when people understand the situation.

Bridges provides an excellent example from the story of the Exodus:

> Behind Moses' journey through the wilderness was that his people had been persecuted in their adopted home of Egypt. The idea of a land of their own, a place promised to them by their God, was something everyone could understand. It was a solution to problems they experienced. It was an answer to the question, "Why are we doing this?" It represented a clear purpose for their journey.

Your church's decision to call you to this role was likely predicated on her desire to improve on her current situation. These are some of the questions your church may be asking:

- Has there been a high turnover of new members because of inadequate involvement in the life of the church?
- Are the same people doing all of the work all of the time and burning out from overload?
- Does your church know the talents, interests, abilities, and needs of her members? If not, does this lack of information affect the church's effectiveness? How?
- What has not been working well because of a lack of human resources within the church?
- What are the problems faced by your church that your hiring is intended to help resolve?

Theology may ground the solution, but it typically takes a problem to make people look to theology for a basis for the answer. The theology of "every member a minister" is basic to the life of the church, but it was just as basic thirty years ago. Why is it necessary today to hire a director of equipping ministry to actualize this theology when it wasn't necessary to do so in the past? The answer to this question will vary from church to church. But we do know that . . .

- people experience far more competition for their discretionary time today than ever before.
- members want to deploy their talents to make a difference in situations they care about.
- people are hunting for meaning in their lives and want to find ways to live out their faith.
- churches are having difficulty finding people to carry out the work of the church.

You will need to discern the relevant issues and their answers for your church. You will need to share these concerns with church members, leaders, and staff members in ways they can relate to and understand.

2. Picture

Members and leaders need a picture in their minds of what the church will look like because of your work in equipping ministry. How will the church be different as a result of your effort? How will it feel to be a part of this new body?

Consider a number of ways to paint pictures:

- You can invite an equipping ministry director or a pastor with equipping responsibilities to come and speak at your church. Invite this person to discuss how his or her church is functioning now and how equipping ministry has affected the involvement of members and their growth in faith.
- You can tell stories of churches that have grown spiritually and numerically through active equipping ministry.
- You can "bring the idea to life," as Moses did with the promised land. He created for the Israelites a picture of Canaan as a "land flowing with milk and honey," an especially appealing picture from a desert perspective.
- You can share stories of faith that address the deep-seated values of your members, as well as speak of ideas such as the fellowship of persons united in work for Christ and dedicated to building up the body through service.
- You can create a video of events in your church that personify the best of member involvement and that raise the concerns people would like to see addressed with comparable vigor and dedication.

Pictures are vitally important. People must begin to grasp new visions if they are to give up old ways. Remember, pictures alone don't make a transition occur. People will still need time to complete the transition cycle. In their own time and their own way, people need to reach a place where they are open to a new picture—a picture that builds incrementally on the past. You want to excite people by the possibilities, not overwhelm them with a radical departure from all that they are familiar with.

3. Plan

With a clear understanding of the equipping ministry culture and system, your leadership team is ready for a detailed, step-by-step plan. Big sweeping outlines of new events may be sufficient for your trustees, but they do not answer the need of staff members and ministry leaders for information about what is going to happen next and how they can become involved in the process.

This is where you, the equipping ministry team, and this book come into play. A careful reading of *The Equipping Church Guidebook*, combined with the efforts of a dedicated team, will enable you to create a concrete action plan. Each step brings the priesthood of all believers closer to reality.

Your step-by-step plan will answer questions like these:

- Who is working on the support systems? What issues are under consideration? When will the systems be operational?
- When will a seminar on ministry descriptions be held? Who should attend? When do you need to have the completed forms?
- If your responsibility includes new-member assimilation, how will the process be organized? When will the class schedule begin? Who will interview new members?
- Who is being trained to do the interviewing? What forms are being developed or revised to secure member information?
- How and to whom will the information be communicated?

You will want to create a user-friendly plan that tells each person what to expect and how he or she can become involved in the process. People need to know when they will receive information and how they will be affected by the new equipping ministry system.

4. Part to Play

In the final analysis, we all want to be included, to feel needed, to have a part to play. As the director of equipping ministry, you should develop a plan that includes as many people as possible in specific, meaningful roles. The jobs need not be large and overwhelming to be considered important. The act of inclusion helps a person feel that he or she is a part of the process. Make a special effort to involve the people who feel most uncomfortable about the changes that will happen as a result of equipping ministry. Your adversaries become your strongest supporters when included in the process and given a role to play in the change.

Bridges offers five suggestions for facilitating transition through participation:

1. Involving people in the process gives them new insights into the challenges faced by the church. When people come to understand problems, they join in the process of seeking solutions.

2. Participation aligns the problem on one side of the equation and the members and leaders on the other side. Polarity is no longer defined as "the new way versus the traditional way," but rather as "the problem versus the solution." Participation provides the opportunity to rebuild relationships frayed by the anticipation of change.

3. Expanding your team creates a broader knowledge base from which to act and make decisions. The more firsthand knowledge and involvement you have, the more likely it is that your solutions will address real needs.

4. A broad participant base expands your knowledge about the people, their values, and their personal needs. You may be able to identify a solution to a special concern, but without firsthand knowledge about the interpersonal nature of the issue, your solution may be headed for failure. Understanding the culture of your church is as important as understanding her problems.

5. Participation implicitly involves people in the outcome. If people in the church have worked together to initiate the equipping ministry system, everyone shares in the glory of success and everyone suffers the defeat of failure.

Remember that while you are, in fact, about change in the church, you are also about making the church into the body Christ intended her to be.

Let's conclude this chapter with several tips on managing new beginnings:

1. *Be consistent.* If your church decides to build an equipping ministry system, the new processes should apply equally to everyone. If ministry descriptions are necessary in order to invite members into your church school ministry, they should be equally important for identifying the work of a trustee. One of the strongest messages your senior pastor can send to other clergy, staff members, and ministry leaders is to follow the system instituted and to promote it with zeal and enthusiasm. Likewise, if your church has a performance review system for salaried staff, the effective involvement of members in their areas of ministry should be among the evaluative measures employed in the review process.

2. *Establish reasonable goals and ensure quick successes.* You are undertaking a significant ministry in your church. Set goals with realistic timelines that are attainable, so that you and your team can measure successes along the way. Identify milestones to celebrate, and publicize these events within the congregation. People need to see progress and enjoy the opportunities to say, "This was a job well done, good and faithful servant."

3. *Find ways to symbolize the new beginning of increased gift-based involvement.* Perhaps nowhere is the importance of symbolism more significant than in the church. Find ways to symbolize the new church that is the people of God. If your church has been considering a new logo or a face-lift for the stationery or bulletin cover, encourage the inclusion of the concept of equipping ministry and the theology of the priesthood of all believers in the new look. With the equipping ministry team, brainstorm creative ideas to symbolize your ministry in the church—new name tags, a regular spot in the order of worship to address the ministry of the people, or a special bulletin board dedicated to celebrating those involved in service.

4. *Celebrate successes.* Just as people need to see successes and to find ways to symbolize the transition, special events can mark major turning points in the church's life. You may want to have a major kick-off program that signifies equipping ministry, such as an annual festival promoting ministry opportunities or a day dedicated to gifts identification and Bible study. T-shirts, mugs, or pens and pencils with the insignia of equipping ministry are valuable take-home items that keep the value of the ministry central in members' minds and hearts.

Building Strategic Foundations

LET'S RETRACE OUR STEPS. In chapter 10 you and other church members defined equipping ministry in your church. You met with people, shared your vision, assessed existing systems for equipping ministry, and gained an in-depth appreciation for your congregation. Chapter 11 introduced the critical relational foundations for the ministry and provided specific guidelines for the development of the equipping ministry team. In addition, you explored how to be a change agent and successfully facilitate the transition to equipping ministry.

Now, working in concert with church leaders and your equipping ministry team, you will establish the foundations for your equipping ministry system. Two key aspects need your attention:

- building strategic and administrative support systems
- developing your leaders

> Instead, by speaking the truth in a spirit of love, we must grow up in every way to Christ, who is the head. Under his control all the different parts of the body fit together, and the whole body is held together by every joint with which it is provided. So when each separate part works as it should, the whole body grows and builds itself up through love.
>
> EPHESIANS 4:15–16 GNT

BUILDING STRATEGIC AND ADMINISTRATIVE SUPPORT SYSTEMS

BUILDING FOUNDATIONAL SYSTEMS AND infrastructure is time-consuming. Most churches experience a lag of anywhere from nine to eighteen months from the time they begin these foundational development activities until they see visible results. Yet, careful, intentional development will pay dividends for years to come.

You and your team and ministry leaders are working toward the common goal of having everyone serve in and through their giftedness so that your church might become an equipping church. Having a system to support and integrate the plans, the people, and the processes will ensure that this goal is achieved.

Most churches are already experiencing vital ministries. Some churches, however, lack the intentional connection with and communication to one another to follow the journey of the members in such a way that ensures that they receive the care and feeding they need rather than being lost or allowed to drop through the cracks.

System describes . . .

- the processes
- the people
- the plans

that are integrated together toward a common goal.

 **CHECKPOINT**

The best system is one that serves people and is invisible.

Do not reinvent the wheel. Build on what is already in place.

**The LORD foils the plans of the nations;
    he thwarts the purposes of
    the peoples.
But the plans of the LORD
    stand firm forever,
    the purposes of his heart
    through all generations.**

PSALM 33:10–11

"Planning is a process of *clarifying* (or discerning) ultimate God-given direction(s) and *identifying* a course of action to get there."

Leroy Armstrong Jr.,
Greater Good Hope Baptist Church,
Louisville, Kentucky

Support systems in equipping ministry . . .

- are the "ligaments" Paul refers to in Ephesians 4:16 ("From him the whole body, joined and held together by every supporting ligament, grows and builds itself up in love, as each part does its work").
- serve as the supportive pillars of the ministry, built on a strong vision, wise strategy, and an intentional team focus.
- provide a means of communication between staff and ministry teams to effectively follow, grow, care for, and nurture the people.
- intentionally and invisibly prepare, connect, and equip people to serve and be served in their local church and community.

Building the Foundations

Step 1: Conduct a Needs Assessment

Completing a needs assessment (see chapter 4) of your current systems will provide you with the "gap analysis" in terms of what's working, what's not, and what's missing. In assessing existing systems, you may discover several key elements already in place that don't need changing. Other systems may need enhancements, and still others need to be created from scratch.

Identify each system that needs improvement or new development. Building your strategic and administrative systems must begin with these identified systems.

Step 2: Do Planning

Releasing people in service requires a thoughtful, well-run equipping system. You and your team are responsible to work with and through other people in such a way that members of the body of Christ are enabled to identify and use their talents in response to God's call. Just as the apostle Paul planned his work in mission and involved others in his ministry, we also are called to use the gifts of management to plan a system that will support and encourage the ministry of the faithful.

The process of planning requires four key elements:

1. Mission or Purpose

The mission, or purpose, is the broadest statement of why a church or a ministry exists. The values expressed in a mission statement are timeless and broad and give direction to the ministry. A mission statement should be one sentence (though it may be a compound sentence) and should answer the following questions:

- Who are we?
- Whom do we serve?
- What do we do?
- Why do we do it?

A mission statement does not list activities or name time frames. It is not a slogan, but a clear statement of direction. It should be forceful, lucid, and immediately understandable to all who read it.

What's more, a well-defined mission statement is one of your best invitation tools because . . .

- mission motivates; people are energized to work for something in which they believe.
- mission attracts; a clearly stated purpose, with thoughtfully developed goals and objectives, will influence people to join your effort and to invest their time and energy in the work of your ministry.

2. Goals

Goals flow directly from your mission and provide definitive direction. Goals should be assessed annually and may be modified as needed. You should limit goals to a maximum of four or five in order to maintain focus.

Here are some examples of goals from various equipping ministry teams:

- empowering and equipping each member to find his or her special way to serve
- assimilating new people through interviews and follow-up placement in fellowship, service, or study
- encouraging and coordinating the writing of ministry descriptions for all activities and programs
- assisting in the training for interviewing, ministry description writing, leadership interaction with the program, follow-up, and recognition of service

3. Objectives

Objectives are specific, result-oriented outcomes within the framework of the goals. They state what will be different, when the objective will be achieved, and how it will be measured.

Objectives should be . . .

- **S**pecific
- **M**easurable
- **A**greed to by all
- **R**ealistic and achievable
- **T**ime specific

4. Action Steps

Action steps are specific activities developed to achieve objectives. They become the working plans of teams.

Planning is critical to your success. Mission, goals, and objectives point in a clear direction, focus energy, delineate the work to be done, and serve as valuable tools to evaluate your success and establish future plans.

People work hardest on the plans they help to make. Be sure to involve your team in your goal-setting process. Revisit your mission, goals, and objectives frequently to keep everyone focused on the work to be done and to celebrate each accomplishment. Evaluate where you are, based on the timelines set in your initial plan. Don't be afraid to adjust timelines as circumstances dictate.

Step 3: Develop Information Tracking Systems and Ministry Descriptions

Information Tracking Systems

After summarizing all the information gathered during the needs assessment, and then clarifying your goals and objectives, you can begin developing your administrative support systems.

1. Clarify reporting requirements.

Clarify the information the various ministries need by asking the following questions:

- What do we need to know?
- Why do we need to know it?
- Who needs to know it?
- How will it be communicated?

The mission of Leadership Training Network is . . .

- to influence and resource innovative church leaders to equip people for biblical, gift-based team ministry.

As equipping ministry grows and evolves, so will its work. Goal statements change over time to reflect new concerns or a developing understanding of equipping ministry. Your equipping ministry team should revisit its goals on an annual basis to ensure that they reflect the current direction of the ministry.

Your mission statement and your goals and objectives form a work plan. Together they define a yardstick that measures your success.

When you plan your work and work your plan, you achieve your destination.

✓ CHECKPOINT

What are the people prerequisites for the planning process?

- Prayer
- Submission
- Patience
- Perseverance
- Flexibility
- Representation
- Faith

Leroy Armstrong Jr.,
Greater Good Hope Baptist Church,
Louisville, Kentucky

Maintain a flexible system that incorporates an openness to God's call.

✓ CHECKPOINT

Critical Elements of Effective Computer Systems

- User-friendly
- Capable of storing, sorting, and retrieving information easily
- Designed so that information is easily accessible and readily available to all who need it
- Cost-effective
- Strategically designed to expand and grow as the church expands and grows
- Easily integrated into existing tracking systems

We must think through our values and find ways to reflect what we value in the statistics we maintain. In all things systems must serve the people.

2. Establish information sources and processes.

Once you know what information is needed, the next step is to plan how to gather the information. Ask the questions:

- Does the information exist in some form already?
- How will we gather information?
- What are we currently doing? From where? By whom? How? (What method?)

3. Establish tracking methods to store and share information.

Deciding which tracking and communication methods to use depends largely on the church culture, existing resources, and budgetary constraints. Visit Leadership Training Network on the Web at www.ltn.org for valuable resources on existing systems and methodologies being used by other churches.

The following questions will guide you in your tracking system development:

- Computer systems: Are we ready to go to technology? If so, what type? If not, what's the alternative?
- Who will do input?
- Who will receive output?
- Who will have access to the tracking system?

It takes a great deal of time to think through the ramifications of a comprehensive tracking system. Pilot-testing a system allows you to refine your system and work out kinks before oversights cost you time and money. Pilot-test and refine your system before going churchwide.

As you acquire information, remember that it will need to be entered into a database of some kind. Develop approaches that ensure accuracy, reasonable speed of entry, and ease of access. As you create your tracking system in order to capture the skills and interests of people, remember that this information will be optimally useful only if there is a system whereby you can match abilities and interests with opportunities.

Eight Tips for Creating an Equipping Ministry System

1. Select a dedicated and talented individual who is interested in systems to serve on your equipping ministry team. Working with this person, select a knowledgeable subteam to investigate and create a system for your church.
2. Interview other churches that use software systems. Identify what they are using and its effectiveness in managing equipping ministry information.
3. Explore management information software, looking at what your church currently utilizes and the other systems that are available (remember to consult the LTN resources at www.ltn.org).
4. Finish reading this guidebook to be sure you've considered all the areas where information may be useful to you.
5. Become thoroughly familiar with your system support needs. What do you need to know to connect people's talents with ministry opportunities? Interview other staff members to discern their needs. Develop a "wish list" of everything you want your system to accomplish. Develop several trial ministry descriptions, and pilot-test an interviewing format. What information did you acquire and how can you connect the pieces? Be sure your system is capable of meeting your needs.
6. Exciting ministry opportunities emerge from the unique life circumstances of people and their call to serve. Develop a system with sufficient flexibility to meet unanticipated demands.
7. Pilot-test, pilot-test, pilot-test.
8. Remember, developing a good system will take time. Building strong foundations is hard work. Invest the time wisely, and you will be well rewarded.

Information Records

Consider how you will use the information you acquire. What type of reports will you need to generate? If other people look at your information system, will they understand your categories and symbols? Develop a user's guide as you create the system.

Most church leadership boards and senior pastors want some type of monthly report from staff persons. Usually such reports reflect how time has been allocated and describe the results of efforts. It is only fair that the director of equipping ministry comply with this expectation as well. The question then is how best to reflect the fruits of your labor. An important place to begin is with the biblical basis of your program.

If your program is based on Ephesians 4:12 ("to prepare God's people for the works of service"), you would be expected to measure and report on such things as . . .

- the number of people interviewed and placed in service.
- the types of training programs and numbers in attendance.
- the number of people currently involved in ministry.
- the care needs and support provided to people.

Keeping these kinds of records will provide you with an outline for your annual report (see sample below).

If your system is rooted in Romans 12:6 ("the gifts we possess differ as they are allotted to us by God's grace, and must be exercised accordingly"—NEB), you may want to report on . . .

- the range of gifts identified through interviews.
- the number of people using their gifts in a related ministry.

Reflect carefully on your reporting system. In secular volunteerism it is common to report on the number of hours contributed in service. Churches can utilize this approach, but should avoid the temptation to confuse number of hours with the value of the service rendered. How does one equate the relative value of sitting with a terminally ill patient and family during the last hours of life and the same number of hours spent on the telephone reminding young people to work at a car wash fund-raiser? Hours, though important, seldom adequately reflect the value of service.

In the beginning, the development of record-keeping and information systems will be a large and time-consuming part of your job. There truly are so many issues to consider. Yet, your information system is the foundation on which you will build your ministry. As your ministry evolves and you get your systems in place, other church members and support staff will help you maintain and update the system.

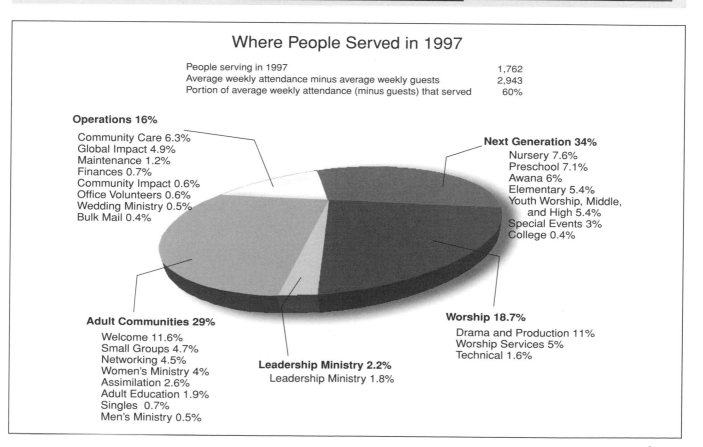

Where People Served in 1997

People serving in 1997	1,762
Average weekly attendance minus average weekly guests	2,943
Portion of average weekly attendance (minus guests) that served	60%

Operations 16%

Community Care 6.3%
Global Impact 4.9%
Maintenance 1.2%
Finances 0.7%
Community Impact 0.6%
Office Volunteers 0.6%
Wedding Ministry 0.5%
Bulk Mail 0.4%

Next Generation 34%

Nursery 7.6%
Preschool 7.1%
Awana 6%
Elementary 5.4%
Youth Worship, Middle, and High 5.4%
Special Events 3%
College 0.4%

Adult Communities 29%

Welcome 11.6%
Small Groups 4.7%
Networking 4.5%
Women's Ministry 4%
Assimilation 2.6%
Adult Education 1.9%
Singles 0.7%
Men's Ministry 0.5%

Leadership Ministry 2.2%
Leadership Ministry 1.8%

Worship 18.7%

Drama and Production 11%
Worship Services 5%
Technical 1.6%

source unknown

"Whoever would be great among you must be your servant, and whoever would be first among you must be your slave; even as the Son of man came not to be served but to serve."

MATTHEW 20:26–28 RSV

Just as you need to know who your people are and the gifts and talents they bring, you also need consistent, up-to-date information about ministry opportunities. Ministry opportunities include such things as serving as a Sunday school teacher, working with teams, and serving as greeters and ushers, to name just a few possibilities. You need to know who is responsible for each ministry area, details about the program or project, and the available service opportunities.

Not all ministries emerge from programs that currently operate within the church. The unique life situation of a person, a community crisis, or God's special call can each create new service opportunities. Consider ways to build flexibility into your communication system in order to capture these special talents and situations.

As your system develops, you'll want to expand ministry opportunities to include programs within your community. Some congregations arrange to send people out to groups and organizations that are supported through their benevolence funds. Others select areas of special needs and focus the energy of their people on a particular cause or problem area, such as delinquent youth, unwed mothers, or homeless people. Building growth possibilities into your record-keeping system allows for expansion and retards obsolescence.

Your equipping ministry system should help you define the scope of your ministry opportunities. As a rule of thumb, it's usually advisable to organize the opportunities available within the church before you expand your reach into the community. All community agencies have catalogs of opportunities readily available.

Ministry Descriptions

Ministry descriptions present the opportunities to serve within the church and the community. A ministry description is essentially a description of the work to be performed, the expectations for the position, and the relationship of the position to the mission of the congregation and to other programs or ministries within the church. Although ministry descriptions are one of the more routine aspects of the job, they are an indispensable component of the system.

A typical ministry description includes . . .

- a title for the ministry.
- a purpose statement: why the position is important in the life of the church.
- a summary description of the position.
- the name or title of the supervisor to whom the member is responsible (that is, the one who will supervise this ministry area).
- a list of specific responsibilities.
- the amount of time required to perform the task, usually presented on a weekly or monthly basis (for example, "two hours, one day per week," or "two three-hour meetings per month").
- the length of commitment (for example, six months, or two years).
- the gifts and skills needed to support this ministry.
- any training needed to do this ministry.
- the development date, so you'll know when the ministry description was created and when it should be revised.

A ministry description serves several very important purposes:

- It provides comprehensive knowledge of the ministry, its expectations, and its requirements.

- It presents the goals and purposes of the position.
- It facilitates orientation.
- It serves as a guide for training, feedback, and evaluation.
- It is the "what," not the "how," and it allows people to use their gifts in accomplishing the task.

A ministry description is stewardship of time to . . .

- the person making the invitation (has all necessary information).
- the person being invited (it is a road map with a clear description of the task and the available training and support).

Ten Steps to Building Good Ministry Descriptions

1. Together with your equipping ministry team, determine a ministry description format that meets the needs of your church (see the sample forms on the pages that follow). Be sure to pilot-test any format you select. Does it meet your communication needs? Does it help you effectively invite people to serve? Is the form sufficiently user-friendly? Is it compatible with your record-keeping system?

2. It is *not* your job to create the ministry descriptions for each ministry area; rather, it is your responsibility to ensure that each ministry area completes the task. Along with your team, you will want to meet with other teams to train them in the details of writing ministry descriptions.

3. Start the development process with your highest-level board or team. Through their participation, key leaders model the importance of ministry descriptions.

4. Develop ministry descriptions for all projects and teams, as well as for individual ministry opportunities. The coordinator of Vacation Bible School, the director of the annual Christmas pageant, and each ministry leader should develop an overall description of the project to guide the work and to invite people to serve.

5. Strongly resist providing names of potential candidates for a position that does not have a written ministry description. If the requester does not have the time to create the description, he or she may not have the time to orient, train, or supervise the one who will do the ministry either. In the long run, the creation of ministry descriptions saves time with regard to both invitation and training.

6. Review each ministry description carefully. These documents will alert you and the interviewing team to the special gifts and talents to took for as you talk with people.

7. Maintain *two* copies of every ministry description. Always keep the original in your office. All ministry descriptions should be stored, by ministry, in the computer.

8. Organize the ministry descriptions in a notebook to make it easy for people to review. As your system grows, you may want to develop a ministry opportunities handbook.

9. Use each ministry description as a working guide to the task. Make notes on it, record new duties and responsibilities, and enhance it to fit the realities of the ministry.

10. As a person provides feedback and reflection on a ministry experience, revise the description to more accurately reflect the nature of the ministry and the work associated with it. This is a very simple process when the ministry descriptions are stored in the computer. (NOTE: Always date the revision.)

A Process Suggestion

Schedule a meeting with all ministry leaders. Explain the ministry description process and its importance to the church. Share the fact that it encourages the stewardship of time through the clear definition of the work to be performed for the church. Remind them that a ministry description describes *what* you do, not how you do it. Stress that it is an excellent training and invitation tool. Indicate that people cannot offer themselves in service if they are unaware of the ministry opportunities available to them.

Begin by asking each person to complete a blank ministry description form. (You may want to have a sample form projected on a screen. Consider sharing a completed form by way of example.) Allow each one's creativity to enhance the task. Allow people sufficient time to complete their own ministry descriptions, and then collect the forms.

How to Title a Position

Title a position by its function. If the work is greeting, call the person a "greeter"; if it involves reviewing educational materials, then use the title "educational materials reviewer." The fact that most positions will be non-salaried is no reason to call a person a "*volunteer* greeter," any more than you would call your senior pastor a "salaried pastor." A title reflects a function, not a salary classification.

Sample Ministry Description Form

Title: _____

Purpose of Ministry:

_____

_____

_____

Responsible to (or relationships with):

_____

_____

_____

Ministry Description:

_____

_____

_____

Desired Results:

_____

_____

_____

Time Commitment (amount of time, length of service):

_____

_____

_____

Skills, Talents, Gifts, Qualifications:

_____

_____

_____

Training Opportunities:

_____

_____

_____

_____

Date: _____

Tailor the ministry description form to the needs and expectations of your church.

CRYSTAL CATHEDRAL
Garden Grove, California

LAY MINISTRY SERVICE DESCRIPTION

JOB TITLE: Graffiti Paint-Out Worker

DATE OF REQUEST: 3-20-99
DATE NEEDED: 4-24-99
REQUESTED BY:
PHONE NUMBER:

TASKS: (PLEASE BE SPECIFIC)

- Bring roller handles (they will not be provided)
- Wear old clothes that cannot be ruined by paint (no open-toed shoes)
- Parents must accompany juveniles
- Bring your own drinking water
- Be prepared to sign two (2) release of liability forms
- Arrive at 76 S. Claudia (the paint house shed)
- Carpool with others from church

LENGTH OF COMMITMENT: One day

HOW MANY VOLUNTEERS? Seeking 50

TIME TO REPORT: 7:30 A.M.

WHERE TO REPORT: Church parking lot
for car pool

TRAINING BY: Ministry requestor
and on-site staff

ON-SITE SUPERVISION: City of Anaheim
staff

SKILLS AND SPIRITUAL GIFTS NEEDED: service; evangelism; wisdom; a positive, helpful attitude

BENEFITS:

- You will beautify God's world while possibly touching a life for Christ.
- You will receive a certificate of appreciation from the city of Anaheim.
- You will be blessed.

- -

LAY MINISTRY OFFICE INFORMATION

VOLUNTEER ACCEPTING POSITION:_____
POSITION TITLE:_____
PHONE NUMBER: (Home): _____ (Work): _____
CHURCH MEMBER? Yes ___   No ___

Has he or she completed a skills and interest indicator for our database? Yes ___ No ___
(If no, please obtain one from the Tower lobby or from the volunteer ministry office for him or her to complete and return to the volunteer ministry office.)

PLEASE DETACH AND RETURN THIS INFORMATION TO DIRECTOR OF LAY MINISTRY.

MINISTRY DESCRIPTION FORM

POSITION: St. Gerard Majella Choir

PURPOSE OF POSITION:

Must be able to commit to one rehearsal weekly, usually Thursday evenings from 8:00 P.M. to 9:30 P.M. and singing at the 11:00 A.M. Mass and other special celebrations.

QUALIFICATIONS:

A good musical ear coupled with the ability to learn and sing music as taught by the choir director. Some singing experience and knowledge of music reading is helpful but not required. This ministry is open to all persons from fifteen years of age and up.

AMOUNT OF TIME REQUIRED: About four hours per week

WHEN MINISTRY IS PERFORMED: At the 11:00 A.M. Mass

LENGTH OF COMMITMENT: One year

RESPONSIBLE TO: Ministry coordinator

TRAINING PROVIDED: At weekly rehearsals

SUPPORT PROVIDED:

The Community of St. Gerard Majella appreciates the gifts of this ministry, and our co-pastors encourage and support all members of the music ministry all year long.

gifts

Step 4: Secure Personnel and Facilities

1. Invite people to operate and maintain the systems.

In order to develop and operate each support system or process, you will need . . .

- a point person and team responsible for the system or process.
- people with the gift of administration.
- systems thinkers.
- church leaders who understand the *need* and *value* of the process.
- computer "junkies" (experts)—those who totally uphold the value of computers as a support and communication system.
- willingness to be flexible and adaptive as ministries change.

2. Secure space and facilities.

Let's look at your basic needs:

- a desk with a telephone
- a few drawers to begin to file and organize information
- basic office supplies—pens, pencils, stationery, paper clips, and the like
- convenient access to copy machines and postage

As your ministry grows, you will begin to develop other needs:

- an accessible, inviting office where people gather
- a computer networked with other terminals in your church
- file cabinets and storage space

You will need access to church facilities:

- work space for projects
- meeting and training space
- a private location for interviewing people
- bulletin board space
- sufficient parking spaces

Step 5: Build a Realistic Budget

You can begin equipping ministry with a minimal budget. Other than your salary and benefits package, initial program development costs are relatively minor with one exception—your own training and development. Few seminaries currently offer courses or workshops in equipping ministry leadership. Unless you have directed a volunteer or community relations program in the nonprofit or public sector before accepting this position, this book and a few others on the subject are most likely all you have to guide your work.

Planning for the Future

As your system evolves, you will need to develop a budget to handle the costs associated with the ministry. Your budget should be based on and reflect the goals and objectives for equipping ministry.

Many churches utilize a basic line-item budget system, with categories that reflect the operational systems in the church. Expense categories such as duplicating, postage, and general office supplies often fall within the church's "general administrative" or "office supplies" budget

---

It takes amazingly little space to get equipping ministry off the ground!

Learning events and tools available through Leadership Training Network can be accessed by calling 1-877-LTN-LEAD (586-5323) or by visiting the Web site at www.ltn.org

Consult with your church's business manager or treasurer on how your church develops a budget and the process and timeline for submitting financial requests.

category. Likewise, office equipment (such as a desk, computer, or filing cabinet) is part of the larger church budget and is not reflected in a specific ministry budget. Personnel expenses vary. Some congregations keep all salaries and benefit packages grouped under "personnel," while others allocate the expense to the department.

As the director of equipping ministry, you will pay special attention to the financial needs specific to your ministry:

- *Recognition.* It is very important to celebrate people's ministries. Pictures, certificates, and punch and cookies (*not* brought by those you are thanking) are inexpensive forms of recognition. Be sure to set aside funds for developing photos (and even having some photos enlarged as posters). You may want to consider sending actively involved people to training programs that will enhance their skills as a way of affirming their commitment to ministry.

- *Professional development.* This category includes money for memberships in professional organizations and registration fees for workshops, conferences, and training institutes. While professional development is an ongoing need for all staff persons, most of them will be able to take part in programs close to home. As a person in a relatively new profession, your opportunities for training will undoubtedly be significantly more limited. Be sure to budget adequate funds to attend workshops, institutes, and conferences where you can learn from others in your field.

- *Training for laypeople.* As you involve more people in ministries and help them live out their gifts and calling, remember to set aside funds for training and development that will enhance their ministry experience.

- *Travel and lodging.* This line item covers the cost of travel to conferences and training institutes, as well as the traveling you do around town as part of your job. For many conferences, lodging and meals are an additional charge over and above registration fees.

- *Special needs.* No matter how carefully you plan, you will most likely encounter unexpected expenses. Because you are working in an area that is by definition dynamic and flexible, you will need to be prepared for the unusual. For example, you may decide to conduct a ministry fair where you will showcase the opportunities for service in your church. You select a "fiesta" theme. Are you ready with the crepe paper and piñata? Budget some funds that enable you to start your ministry with a bang.

For some church members, ministry opportunities stretch an already tight budget. Assistance with child care, carfare, parking, or meal expenses may make the difference in someone's ability to serve voluntarily. Create a line item in your budget to assist those who have fixed or limited incomes, or work with your senior pastor to secure discretionary funds. Brainstorm other creative options that do not require your volunteers to spend in order to serve.

Step 6: Develop Policies and Procedures

Although many churches operate without formal written policies and procedures, usually certain actions and behaviors are considered acceptable and others taboo. These may be doctrinal issues, such as who may partake of the sacraments, or selection procedures for certain boards or committees. They may be less formal (but still important) organizational concerns, such as how the kitchen is managed or what is acceptable attire at the reception desk.

As you establish the equipping ministry system, spend time talking about baseline expectations. For example, at what age should a person be interviewed for a ministry experience: at the time of confirmation, or at eighteen, or at twenty-one, or at their parents' request? When are new people interviewed: as soon as possible following membership, or after they've completed certain preestablished course work, or no later than three months after membership? When do you rotate out of or into a new ministry? Formulating answers to questions such as these creates the basis for good policies.

Procedures are the steps one follows in implementing a policy. For example, your policy may be to interview people as soon as they join the church. Your procedures may include sending a letter that explains the interview process, describes the types of questions you will be asking, and provides information about scheduling the interview. Additional procedural issues may apply to data entry and placement in ministry opportunities.

In early stages of system development you may want to . . .

- explore what, if any, policy and procedure guidelines are currently operational in your church. As a rule of thumb, equipping ministry policies should parallel general church policies.
- maintain a notebook of policy and procedure issues. As you resolve questions and establish protocols, begin creating a book of "guidelines"—a less threatening title for a policy and procedure manual. Make sure that staff members and ministry leaders also have a copy of this notebook.
- explore the concept of policies and procedures in volunteer management literature. A useful booklet by Steve McCurly (1990), "Volunteer Management Policies," is available from the publisher (VM Systems/Heritage Arts Publishing, 1807 Prairie Ave., Downers Grove, Illinois 60515; 708-964-1194). This booklet outlines a complete policy system for a volunteer program in the nonprofit world. It covers many areas—confidentiality, health screening, interviews, evaluation, insurance, and the like—that emerge as a program grows and evolves.

Step 7: Manage Risk

The title alone is "cause to pause." Risk management in the church world? "All we're trying to do," you say, "is identify the gifts and talents of our people and release these skills in service to others. Why do I need to know anything about risk management?"

Let's suppose for a moment that you have a bake sale that is open to the public. One of the patrons purchases a cheesecake and returns the next day to say the cake was spoiled and a member of her family became sick. You offer to refund her money, but she wants the cost of the visit to

Establish solid systems, maintain good records, and seek expert counsel if you believe an action or program represents a significant risk to your church or one of the members.

a local hospital emergency room covered as well. Or perhaps your youth group organizes a wilderness hike. On the way to the state park, one of the church's drivers is in an accident that results in serious injuries. Who is liable? Or again, your church organizes a "mop and hammer" crew to make minor repairs at the church. A ladder is left lying on the ground, and an elderly person trips and is injured in the fall. Who is responsible? Situations like these raise the issue of liability. Lawsuits occur, even in the world of the church.

As you develop your system, what steps should you take to manage risk?

- Talk with your senior or administrative pastor and identify who in the church is responsible for these concerns. Examine the precautions your church currently takes and the rationale for these actions. Are "assumption of risk" forms signed before groups leave the building to travel in cars? Who designed the form? Who researched the system?
- Determine your responsibility for managing the risk associated with equipping ministry operations. You may want to identify a person willing and qualified to handle this concern for you.
- Access the resources that are available to you. Many resources are available in the nonprofit arena. For example, *Energize* is an organization that provides such resources on the Web at http://www.energizeinc.com (1-800-395-9800).

DEVELOPING YOUR LEADERS

LEADER DEVELOPMENT IS one of the cornerstones of equipping ministry. Developing ministry leaders, staff and pastoral leaders, the leaders on the core equipping ministry team, and potential future leaders is critical to the ongoing success of equipping ministry.

The role of the equipping ministry team is to facilitate the equipping ministry system, not to do the entire ministry themselves. Just as the equipping ministry team models the values of a gift-based team, so they need to model the value of "equipping" by providing the training and support for church leaders to enable them to implement the various processes and elements of equipping ministry, as well as to develop leadership maturity.

In this section you will learn to . . .

- develop a team of people with the skills, gifts, and passion to provide ongoing support for the leadership of the church.
- build a leader development and support system that becomes a consistent part of every leader's experience in ministry service.
- ensure that systems and processes are in place to develop leaders at four levels: staff leaders, ministry leaders, equipping ministry team leaders, and identified potential future leaders.

The Role of Equipping Ministry in Leader Development

While the equipping ministry team is primarily responsible for equipping the leaders in skills and knowledge to implement equipping ministry processes, the additional responsibility includes facilitating ongoing leader development in the church at large.

And the things you have heard me say in the presence of many witnesses entrust to reliable men who will also be qualified to teach others.

2 TIMOTHY 2:2

"Future innovative leaders will receive training, not in seminary, but in their ministry placement."

George W. Bullard Jr., columnist, *Net Results* magazine

Patterns for Leadership Development

What Are You Trying to Develop?

COMPETENCIES

"What can you do?"

This refers to the skills, tasks, and management of the ministry on a day-to-day basis.

CONVICTION

"What do you believe?"

All of us know far more than what we really believe. Knowledge does not dictate values or central beliefs. These are formed from our relationship with Christ and our convictions in living out the gospel. The test is, "What are we willing to die for?"

CONTENT

"What do you know?"

We need a certain amount of information and knowledge.

COMPASSION

"Whom do you care for?"

When you study the biblical passages on the role of a shepherd, you can understand the need to have compassion for people. This speaks to the level of involvement we have with others within the body, within the family.

CHARACTER

"Who are you?"

You want to develop men and women who have character in two areas:

a. their inner life (vertical relationship with God)
b. their interpersonal life (horizontal relationship with others within the body of Christ)

Without character, you don't have a spiritual leader. You have leadership the way the world views it, but spiritual leadership requires character, first and foremost.

Rev. Leroy Armstrong of Greater Good Hope Baptist Church in Louisville, Kentucky, teaches that in developing leaders in our churches, we need to be developing all five "C's" of spiritual leadership, beginning with the bottom of the pyramid.

Most churches may focus on one or two of these to the exclusion of the others. Most leader development programs focus on content and competencies and leave out the others. In the five-level pyramid above, at the bottom is character and at the top is competencies. Competencies in and of themselves are not sufficient unless they are laid on a foundation of character and genuine compassion for people. And on that foundation, then tell me what you know. And after you've told me what you know and what you're willing to die for and go to the wall for, then I want to know, 'What can you do?'"

The goal of leader development is to intentionally guide the experiences and education of people in order to prepare them for servant leadership. Leader development is part of building relational foundations, and it is about ongoing leader development of current and future leaders. Be sure to review chapter 14 for valuable information on creating programs that support current leaders and develop future leaders.

"[Twenty-first century] leadership is about providing an atmosphere in which people are transformed and empowered.... Leaders are people who transform people into disciples rather than merely taking care of people."

Bill Easum, at Leadership Network's "Leadership in the 21st Century" event

No one ministry has greater ability and more strategic importance in coordinating leader development than that of the equipping ministry team. This requires effective and essential collaboration with staff members and other ministry leaders.

Include planning for leader development as you build your equipping ministry system. This means including both tracking systems and a team to continually facilitate ongoing opportunities for development for leaders.

The Key Elements of Leader Development

1. Determine the attributes or qualities you want in your ministry leaders. Decide what you want leaders in your church to be about. Whatever you decide is important, because your church leaders can become the filters through which you identify future leaders. Here's an example of the filter one church uses:

People who are . . .

- *faithful*   They consistently attend church and meetings.
- *available*   They make time to meet with me when asked.
- *influential*   People listen to them and ask for their opinions. People follow them.
- *teachable*   They ask questions and are hungry to grow and learn. They demonstrate a cooperative attitude.
- *honest*   They are genuine and transparent in sharing their life.
- *spiritual*   They demonstrate strength of character.
- *mature*   They exhibit the fruit of the Spirit. They demonstrate compassion toward others.

2. Define the role staff members will play in developing current and future leaders. Determine who will work with whom—clergy and laypeople, paid and nonpaid staff—and who's responsible for developing leaders in each ministry or program area.

3. Determine the kind of investment you're willing to make in current and future leaders. Explore the investment in terms of dollar costs, staff time, intensity of effort, available resources, and the like.

4. Establish the program component of your plan for equipping leaders. Decide what *content* knowledge and skills your leaders need in order to be successful, what *competencies* need to be enhanced in your leaders, and what *character qualities* need to be developed in your leaders.

5. Develop a process for identifying and equipping potential future leaders. Explore the systems and practices you will need in order to achieve your long-term goals for identifying and equipping future leaders. Identify people with leadership potential. Create opportunities to observe people with leadership potential. Determine who will be responsible for this aspect of leader development.

BUILDERS' NOTE

As the equipping ministry director and team you do not *do* all the training of leaders yourself. Your role is to *facilitate* the process and draw attention to the importance of leader development as a *value* in an equipping culture.

6. Develop these people for future leadership roles. Using the fundamentals you employ for developing your current leadership, create a process through which potential future leaders can develop the skills, knowledge, competencies, and character your church believes are essential for those who serve in leadership roles.

These are the core skills of leaders now and in the future:

- the ability to understand systems in terms of the great primacy of relationships—always looking for connections
- realizing that you will not do most of the work of the organization; it will be done by people within the organization
- having a deep belief in the capacity of people to solve problems, to set new directions, and to determine a vision that is worthy of them

These are things that leaders can set in motion, but can't impose on an organization.

Margaret Wheatley,
Leadership and the New Science

13

Building the Equipping Ministry System: *Prepare*

IN PREVIOUS CHAPTERS YOU'VE had the opportunity to define equipping ministry and begin to build both relational and strategic foundations for equipping ministry in your church. In the guidebook's final three chapters, the three critical elements of the equipping ministry process are discussed in detail, describing the process a person experiences when becoming part of an equipping church.

Prepare:

- Assimilation
- Biblical Foundations

Connect:

- Discovery
- Matching and Placement

Equip:

- Growth
- Recognition and Reflection

Prepare is the first of three key processes through which new people are assimilated into the church and through which you come to know people so that they may serve and be served. *Prepare* involves informing new people about the church, discovering information about them, and teaching the biblical foundations of gift-based ministry.

You may be asking, "What is involved in intentionally preparing people for service?" Make sure you remember this caution: If you assimilate people into the church and plug them straight into service, you might not meet their spiritual growth needs. Effective equipping ministry is more about spiritual growth, discipleship, and faith development than simply filling ministry slots. People typically don't come to a church just so they can serve.

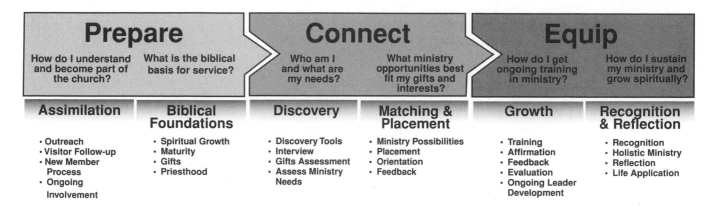

Prepare		Connect		Equip	
How do I understand and become part of the church?	What is the biblical basis for service?	Who am I and what are my needs?	What ministry opportunities best fit my gifts and interests?	How do I get ongoing training in ministry?	How do I sustain my ministry and grow spiritually?
Assimilation	**Biblical Foundations**	**Discovery**	**Matching & Placement**	**Growth**	**Recognition & Reflection**
• Outreach • Visitor Follow-up • New Member Process • Ongoing Involvement	• Spiritual Growth • Maturity • Gifts • Priesthood	• Discovery Tools • Interview • Gifts Assessment • Assess Ministry Needs	• Ministry Possibilities • Placement • Orientation • Feedback	• Training • Affirmation • Feedback • Evaluation • Ongoing Leader Development	• Recognition • Holistic Ministry • Reflection • Life Application

Service can also be an outgrowth of faith maturity, which is a result of a strong relationship with Jesus Christ. We first need to connect with God, then we are able to experience joy and the filling of the spiritual emptiness within us through that spiritual connection. Once we experience this, we worship and celebrate God's love. Out of worship and celebration comes the desire to serve others and share the love we experience from being in a right relationship with God.

It may be a different scenario for others. Some come to know Christ *through* service—in a landfill in Mexico, in a homeless shelter, or in other settings. Then these folks seek to know Christ at a deeper level and begin their "learning" journey.

No matter where the starting point of a person's journey, we make a common mistake when we overlook the vital element of faith development before we invite people into significant service.

Prepare includes . . .
- Assimilation: Helping new people understand the church and helping existing members extend their involvement beyond Sunday morning attendance or find more meaningful ministry opportunities.
- Biblical Foundations: Helping people understand Scripture and come to trust that God has gifted them and called them to ministry and that they will grow spiritually as they use their gifts in service.

ASSIMILATION

ASSIMILATION—THE PROCESS OF integrating people into your church culture—occurs when a person feels like a valued, connected, and vital part of the church. They know they belong if they are missed when they are not there. Effective assimilation goes a long way toward "closing the back door"—where people join and then leave in a short period of time. Churches may use different terms for this process and have different criteria by which to evaluate the effectiveness of assimilation activities. Whatever term is used, however, the end goal of the process is the same: that people will feel valued and connected in the church.

What can assimilation look like?

- New-member classes
- Placement in small groups
- Outreach to visitors
- Orientation to church ministries
- Outreach to existing and inactive members

The following pages include some examples of assimilation methods and different systems and documents. It is essential to select an assimilation process that is compatible with your church culture. Assimilation systems are one of the processes that are often already successfully implemented in churches even before an equipping ministry program is launched.

☑ CHECKPOINT

What systems should be in place to track information and communicate people's care needs, as well as their gifts and interests?

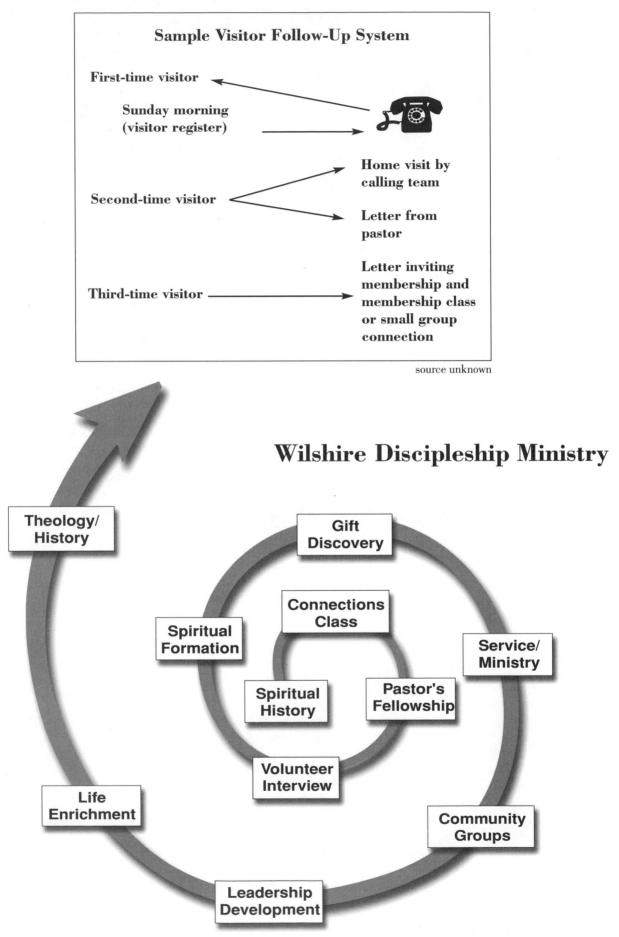

Sample Visitor Follow-Up System

First-time visitor

Sunday morning
(visitor register)

Second-time visitor → Home visit by calling team

Letter from pastor

Third-time visitor → Letter inviting membership and membership class or small group connection

source unknown

Wilshire Discipleship Ministry

Theology/History

Gift Discovery

Connections Class

Spiritual Formation

Service/Ministry

Spiritual History

Pastor's Fellowship

Volunteer Interview

Life Enrichment

Community Groups

Leadership Development

Wilshire Baptist Church, Dallas, Texas

  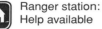 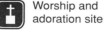

Church of the Resurrection, Leawood, Kansas

ST. MONICA VOLUNTEER MINISTRY PROGRAM

Share with us your skills.

Share with us your gifts.

Share with us your interests.

Let Us Serve Together!

Our mission is to help parishioners discover rewarding and fulfilling opportunities to grow spiritually, to serve our Lord, and to help others according to their skills, gifts, and interests.

Name _____ Today's Date _____

Address _____ City _____ Zip _____

Home Phone _____ Work Phone _____

Fax _____ E-mail _____

Do you have any special need with which the parish may assist you?

_____

_____

Please check the boxes next to the areas of ministry/volunteer service and spiritual development in which you may like to participate.

LITURGY

☐ Choirs
☐ Eucharistic ministry
☐ Hospitality
☐ Instrument
☐ Lector
☐ Liturgical dance
☐ Liturgy planning
☐ Music librarian
☐ Sacristan

OUTREACH AND HEALING/PEACE AND JUSTICE

☐ AIDS ministry
☐ Bereavement ministry
☐ Big Brother/Big Sister
☐ Build houses for the poor
☐ Care for elderly/homebound
☐ Care for terminally ill/life-threatening illnesses
☐ Counseling skills
☐ Detention ministry
☐ Eucharistic ministry to hospitals and homebound
☐ Feed homeless
☐ Food and clothing collections
☐ Holiday outreach (Toy Drive/Adopt a Family)
☐ Orphanage in Mexico (El Hogar)
☐ Thanksgiving dinner for homeless

EDUCATION AND SPIRITUALITY (ADULTS)

☐ Bible study
☐ Catholic social teaching/education
☐ Contemplative prayer
☐ Ecumenical/interfaith sharing
☐ Engaged couples sponsor
☐ Hospitality for baptism class
☐ Parish mission
☐ Prayer groups
☐ RCIA participant
☐ RCIA sponsor
☐ Retreat participant
☐ Retreat leader
☐ Returning Catholics eight-week small group sharing (Landings)
☐ Rosary
☐ Small group facilitator
☐ Speaker series
☐ Spiritual direction
☐ Welcome home Catholics

RELIGIOUS EDUCATION (CHILDREN)

☐ Babysitting during 9:30 Mass
☐ Babysitting during other parish events
☐ Crafts preparation (at home)
☐ Parking assistance
☐ Special events (help two–three times per year)
☐ Summer Bible camp
☐ Teacher assistant
☐ Teacher early childhood (three–five years old)
☐ Teacher grades 1–6
☐ Teacher grades 7–8

TEEN MINISTRY

☐ Confirmation core team
☐ Youth ministry core team
☐ Special events (help two–three times per year)
☐ Driver to youth events
☐ Newsletter editor
☐ Baking team
☐ Retreat team

OTHER EDUCATION

☐ Language translator
☐ Teaching computer skills
☐ Tutoring/literacy

COMMON INTEREST GROUPS/ FELLOWSHIP ORGANIZATIONS

☐ Activities for families
☐ Boutique
☐ Divorced and Separated
☐ Entertainment Faith Fellowship
☐ Gay and Lesbian Outreach
☐ Grief Support
☐ Italian Catholic Federation
☐ Legion of Mary
☐ Men's Ministry
☐ Mommy and Me Baby Groups
☐ Older adult monthly luncheons and retreats (Always Beginning)
☐ Older adult day bus trips and tours
☐ Respect Life
☐ Sierra Club
☐ Small group faith sharing
☐ Women's group
☐ Young Adult, Singles/Couples 20s/30s (YMA)
☐ Middle Adult, Singles/Couples 40s and over (ZMA)
☐ Teen confirmation participant
☐ Youth ministry participant

LARGE PARISH EVENTS

☐ Octoberfair
☐ Silent and live auction
☐ Rummage sale

Please check the boxes next to the areas of ministry/volunteer service and spiritual development in which you may like to participate.

PARISH SUPPORT

- ☐ Altar linen pressing
- ☐ Archives/parish records
- ☐ Automobile repair and maintenance
- ☐ Parish bookstore attendant
- ☐ Bulk mail postal knowledge
- ☐ Church pew envelope stuffing
- ☐ Computer repair and maintenance
- ☐ Corporate trainer/group facilitator; area of specialty _____
- ☐ Event coordinator
- ☐ Facility management
- ☐ Fine arts specialty _____
- ☐ Fire fighting/safety (for large parish events)
- ☐ Food service; specialty _____
- ☐ Fund-raising
- ☐ General office work/filing
- ☐ Golf tournament
- ☐ Interior design
- ☐ Interviewing skills
- ☐ Leadership development
- ☐ Mailings
- ☐ Marketing
- ☐ Nursing (for large parish events)
- ☐ Office equipment repair
- ☐ Parking design or management
- ☐ Parking ministry (Sunday mornings)
- ☐ Phone committee
- ☐ Public relations
- ☐ Printing and mailing services
- ☐ Risk management
- ☐ School library support
- ☐ Setting up chairs and tables
- ☐ Socials (organizing dances and other get-acquainted activities)
- ☐ Votive candle replacement in church

COMPUTER SKILLS

- ☐ MAC
- ☐ PC
- ☐ Data entry
- ☐ Database management
- ☐ Graphic design
- ☐ Hardware knowledge
- ☐ Software
- ☐ System/network administration
- ☐ Word processing
- ☐ Other _____

PERFORMING ARTS

- ☐ Actor
- ☐ Choreographer
- ☐ Clowning
- ☐ Costume
- ☐ Dancer
- ☐ Director
- ☐ Lighting/set design
- ☐ Producer
- ☐ Stage manager

MULTIMEDIA ARTS

- ☐ Audio production
- ☐ CD-ROM design
- ☐ Copyrighting
- ☐ Editing—AVID
- ☐ Powerpoint presentations
- ☐ Video production
- ☐ Web site design

BUILDING AND GROUNDS

- ☐ Carpentry
- ☐ Electrical
- ☐ General maintenance
- ☐ Handy work
- ☐ HVAC
- ☐ Landscaping maintenance
- ☐ Landscaping engineers
- ☐ Landscaping design
- ☐ Painting
- ☐ Plumbing
- ☐ Security

OTHER HOBBIES AND INTERESTS

- ☐ Athletics
- ☐ Baking
- ☐ Calligraphy
- ☐ Ceramics
- ☐ Cooking
- ☐ Crafts
- ☐ Creative writing
- ☐ Gardening
- ☐ Illustration
- ☐ Journalism
- ☐ Needlework
- ☐ Photography
- ☐ Public speaking
- ☐ Sewing
- ☐ Other _____

What is your specialty? (This would be something specific you do particularly well and are at least somewhat passionate about; for example, knowledge about a certain topic or hobby, proficiency in a certain sport or art form, a particular area of study, and the like.)

_____

_____

_____

Would you offer your professional services to the church? Explain.

_____

_____

_____

The best days and times for me to volunteer are (check days and times)

	Sun	Mon	Tues	Wed	Thurs	Fri	Sat
Mornings							
Afternoons							
Evenings							

I am available to volunteer (circle one):

once or twice a year   once or twice a month   weekly

❏ I am <u>interested</u> in volunteering at St. Monica as soon as possible. Please call me for an interview to explore where my gifts can best be put into service.

❏ I am interested in <u>receiving</u> more information about the ministry/spiritual development opportunities I checked. Please call me to discuss further.

Please return to: St. Monica Parish Community
Attention: Volunteer Ministry
725 California Avenue, Santa Monica, CA 90403

Please list your current volunteer involvement at St. Monica.

_____

_____

Please list previous volunteer involvement with other parishes.

_____

_____

_____

Please list your volunteer experiences within civic, community, or professional organizations.

_____

_____

_____

Please describe your dream volunteer opportunity.

_____

_____

_____

Lake Pointe Assimilation System
Follow-Up Process

The purpose of assimilation is to assist the new member/new Christian to become a fully developing follower of Christ. The system has frequent checks to keep a person from lapsing in his or her attendance and growth. When a person joins the church, there is a process of assimilating him or her into the life of the church and the life of Christ. Follow-up checks help us keep people moving through the assimilation process.

FIRST WEEK: *Introduction*

1. A letter from the associate pastor's office is mailed, welcoming the person to the church and encouraging him or her to find a Bible study small group. Also included in the letter is an invitation for the next baptism service (if necessary) and an invitation for the next membership workshop.

2. A team member makes a personal phone call to encourage the new member to make a baptism reservation and membership workshop reservation.

QUARTERLY FOLLOW-UP: *Progress Report*

1. A ministry team member takes the folder of new members who have yet to attend an ABF, be baptized, or attend the membership workshop, and records the information on a quarterly progress report (see sample form).

2. Assignments are made by the minister of assimilation.

3. Schedule for quarterly follow-up:

January:	October, November new members
March:	December, January new members
May:	February, March new members
July:	April, May new members
September:	June, July new members
November:	August, September new members

ANNUAL FOLLOW-UP: *Inactive Net*

1. A ministry team member (elders, servants, staff) contacts members who are inactive in Bible study and worship, who have not been baptized, or who have not attended the membership workshop.

2. A phone call is made to troubleshoot why they have not been assimilated.

3. An annual progress report is completed on each person contacted, and returned to the minister of assimilation's office for follow-up.

Membership Candidate Follow-Up

```
┌─────────────────────────────┐
│                             │
│       Attach label here      │
│                             │
└─────────────────────────────┘
```

Person doing follow-up: _____

Date of calls: _____

Comments from call:

    Registered for membership workshop; date: _____

    Scheduled for baptism; date: _____

    Staff member will contact for a personal workshop by appointment

    No longer lives at this address

    No longer at this phone number

    Attending _____church and does not
    intend on returning to Lake Pointe

    Does not desire to complete the membership process
        List as "Bible Study Only"

    Remove from database per their request

    Other/Comments: _____

_____

_____

_____

_____

_____

Action Taken by Office:

_____

_____

_____

_____

_____

_____

_____

Lake Pointe Baptist Church, *Rockwall, Texas*

Communication Card

Grace Fellowship Church

Please complete the following information and place in the offering basket or drop off at the info. counter.

DATE: _____ ❏ NEW ADDRESS

MR. MRS. MS.

NAME: _____

ADDRESS: _____

_____

CITY: _____

STATE: _____ Zip Code: _____

E-MAIL
ADDRESS: _____

HOME
PHONE: _____

WORK
PHONE: _____

BIRTHDATE: _____

I am   ❏ unmarried   ❏ married

SPOUSE'S
NAME: _____

Please check the appropriate box(es) below:

❏ I am visiting today
as a guest of _____

❏ I am a regular attender

❏ I am a member of a housechurch
My leader is _____

❏ I am currently serving in a ministry
My ministry is _____

Please list the names and birthdates
of your children who reside in your home:

NAME	BIRTHDATE
_____	_____
_____	_____
_____	_____
_____	_____
_____	_____
_____	_____

Communication Card

Grace Fellowship Church

Read the items below and check the appropriate box if you would like to take the next step.

I. Faith

If you confess with your mouth, "Jesus is Lord," and believe in your heart that God raised him from the dead, you will be saved. —*Romans 10:9*

❏ I would like to know more about what it means to be a Christian.

II. Life in Christ

Be imitators of God, therefore, as dearly loved children and live a life of love, just as Christ loved us and gave himself up for us as a fragrant offering and sacrifice to God. —*Ephesians 5:1–2*

❏ I have recently made a decision to follow Christ. What is the next step?

III. Community

And let us consider how we may spur one another on toward love and good deeds. Let us not give up meeting together, as some are in the habit of doing, but let us encourage one another. —*Hebrews 10:24–25*

❏ I would like to know more about what it means to participate in Christian community.

IV. Service

It was he who gave some to be apostles, some to be prophets, some to be evangelists, and some to be pastors and teachers, to prepare God's people for works of service, so that the body of Christ may be built up. —*Ephesians 4:11–12*

❏ I would like to know more about the gifts God has given me to serve by attending a spiritual gifts workshop.
❏ Please contact me regarding serving in one of the areas listed on the right. _____

Comments, Requests, or Prayer Needs

❏ Comment   ❏ Prayer request
❏ Request for counseling
❏ financial   ❏ crisis/marriage   ❏ other

_____
_____
_____
_____
_____

If you indicated an interest in serving in a ministry at GFC, please select one or more ministry areas:

❏ Nursery   ❏ Preschool   ❏ Elementary
❏ Middle school ❏ High school   ❏ College
❏ Young adults   ❏ Men's ministry ❏ Women's ministry
❏ Housechurch   ❏ Marriages   ❏ Premarital
❏ Support groups ❏ Parenting   ❏ Single parents
❏ Missions   ❏ Usher/greeter   ❏ Hospitality
❏ Office support ❏ Technology
❏ Other _____

_____
_____
_____

Grace Fellowship Church, Timonium, Maryland

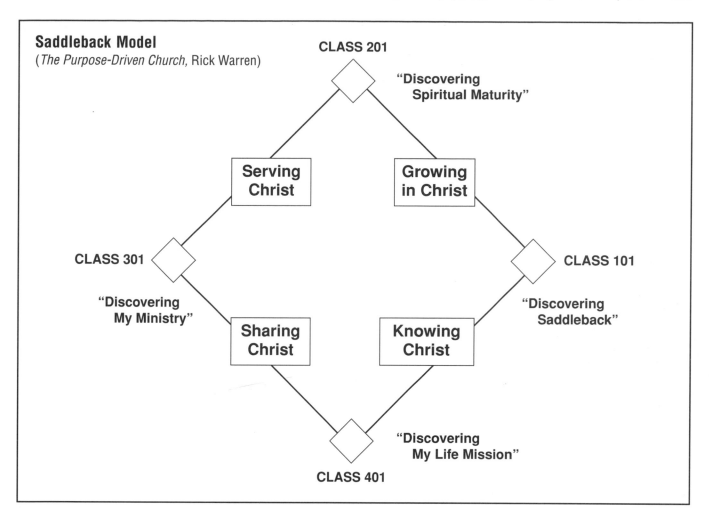

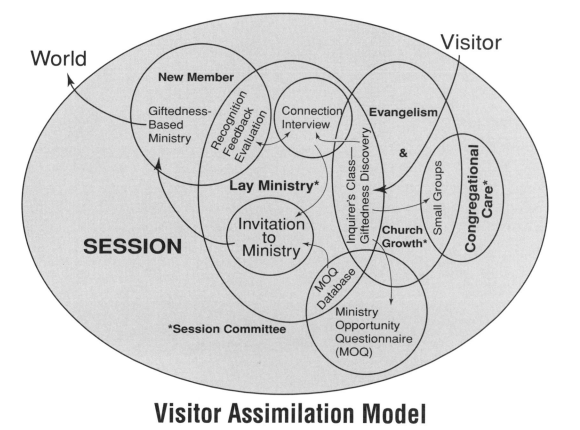

Visitor Assimilation Model

First Presbyterian Church, *Kennewick, Washington*

TEACHING THE BIBLICAL FOUNDATIONS of gift-based ministry is one of the critical components of a successful equipping ministry system. Much of the teaching can come from the pulpit in the form of one or more sermon series, annual vision reflections, and regular sharing of the value of gift-based service to spiritual growth in the life of a Christian.

Many churches provide ongoing classes and Bible studies that focus on the passages related to gifts and to our call to serve, both in the church body and in the community.

The Biblical Basis for Gift-Based Team Ministry

Consider the following important theological principles:

- Every believer is a minister.
- Each person is uniquely gifted.
- Service is a means for spiritual growth.
- Maturity factors are needed in order to serve.

What can biblical foundations look like?

- Sermon series
- Bible study
- Small group gifts curriculum

☑ **CHECKPOINT**

What systems need to be in place to track the involvement of people in "biblical foundations" activities, small groups, classes, and the like?

Spiritual Gifts Preaching Series

January 3, 1999: first of five sermons on spiritual gifts
Ephesians 4:7–13
"Gifted for Serving"

Paul does not use *charismata* here for gifts, but rather *charis* for grace. Saving grace is given to all who believe (Ephesians 2:5, 8), but serving grace is given differently according to the measure of Christ's gift. From this language the charismatic movement has been named. But no group can claim this as its own—the whole church is a charismatic community. It is the body of Christ, and every single member is gifted to exercise or function in a particular way. If the sixteenth century discovered the priesthood of all believers, maybe now, at last, by the twentieth or twenty-first century we will discover the ministry of the whole people of God.

January 10, 1999: Spiritual Gifts # 2
1 Corinthians 12:1–13
"Spiritual Gifts for Spiritual Work"

Every believer is gifted. The gifts come in all sorts and sizes. We are each gifted for the common good. The one force that is beyond this diversity and interdependence is God and the multiple gifts given by God to every one of us in the church family, the body of Christ.

January 17, 1999: Spiritual Gifts # 3
1 Corinthians 12:14–31
"All Gifted, All Needed, All Equal"

Paul's counsel on how we can get along with our diverse gifts. The gifts may be diverse, but they are not ranked by superiority. Body talk reveals we need each other; we are in this thing together. Our problem today comes from ignoring our gifts, not ranking them. The sad side of this is what we are missing when we neglect God's gifts.

January 24, 1999: Lay renewal weekend: Guest preacher

January 31, 1999: Spiritual Gifts #4
Ephesians 4:11–16
"Oh, Grow Up!"

Two things to focus on here until we attain to the whole measure of the fullness of Christ: *We are his body,* and *we are to continue his presence and his work.* He was sent to us, and he sends us—it is a missionary posture. We are literally to grow up—into him! Luther uses the stunning phrase that we are to become "little Christs." We represent him by being an exhibition of the kingdom of heaven to the world. We represent him by being an agent or servant of God's reign in the world. We represent him by being God's messenger to the world.

February 7, 1999: fifth in the Spiritual Gifts series
Romans 12:3–8
"Follow Your Passion"

Now the practical question: *How do we know our gifts?* Our gifts don't depend on us; they are God's to give according to the measure of his grace and the measure of our faith. Though we are many, we are one body in Christ, and individually we are members one of another. Spiritual gifts need to be understood as different from talents, skills, personality, and temperament, but not in opposition to those.

First Presbyterian Church of Bellevue, Bellevue, Washington

The Discovery Series

(4 books, 12 issues each = 48 lessons to spiritual maturity)

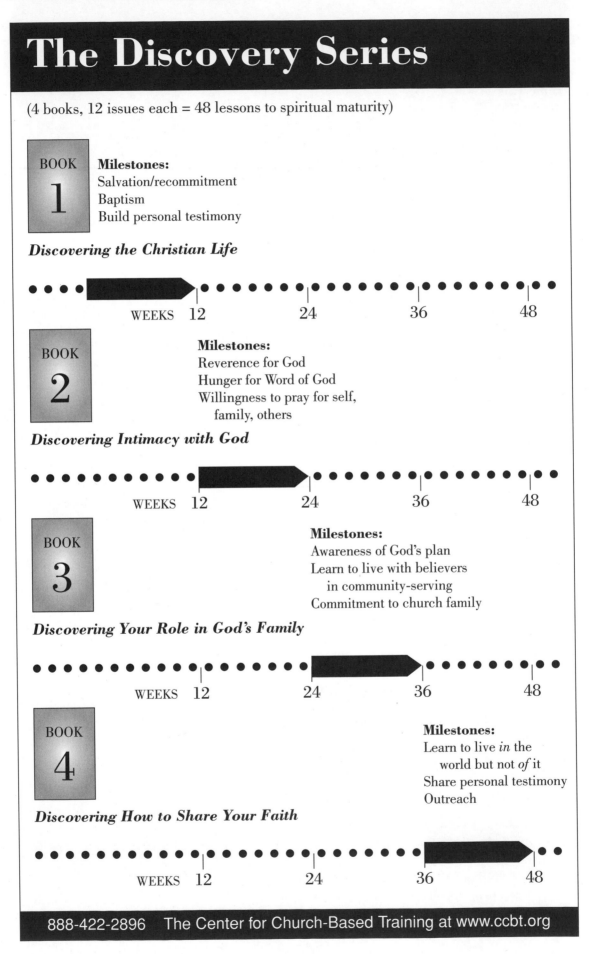

BOOK 1

Milestones:
Salvation/recommitment
Baptism
Build personal testimony

Discovering the Christian Life

WEEKS   12   24   36   48

BOOK 2

Milestones:
Reverence for God
Hunger for Word of God
Willingness to pray for self,
    family, others

Discovering Intimacy with God

WEEKS   12   24   36   48

BOOK 3

Milestones:
Awareness of God's plan
Learn to live with believers
    in community-serving
Commitment to church family

Discovering Your Role in God's Family

WEEKS   12   24   36   48

BOOK 4

Milestones:
Learn to live *in the*
    world but not *of* it
Share personal testimony
Outreach

Discovering How to Share Your Faith

WEEKS   12   24   36   48

THE FIVE LEVELS BUILD ON EACH OTHER

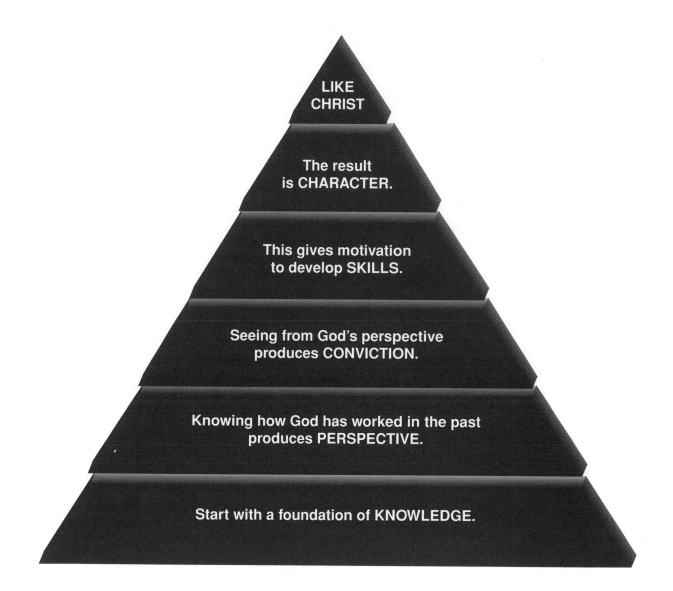

FIVE VITAL QUESTIONS TO ASK

1. What do our members have to KNOW in order to grow?
2. What PERSPECTIVES do we want them to have (about God, the Bible, themselves, Satan, the world, and so forth)?
3. What CONVICTIONS do we want them to hold?
4. What SKILLS do they need for life and ministry?
5. What CHARACTER qualities do we want them to exhibit?

THE GOAL

Know the Word of God.

Have the mind of God.

Have the heart of God.

Do all to the glory of God.

Have the character of God.

Remember that people learn in different ways!

Provide as many options as possible for people to grow.

Saddleback Valley Community Church (The Purpose-Driven Church, Rick Warren)

Building the Equipping Ministry System: *Connect*

THE SECOND OF THREE key processes in your system involves *connecting* people, church, and community. Using our gifts in service requires systems to invite people to serve and to ensure that the ministry experience enables the giver to utilize his or her gifts to the fullest. We need to support people as they discern their call and help them find opportunities to serve. The connections process includes developing an interview system, matching people to ministry opportunities in the church and community, and subsequently placing people in those ministries.

In this section we'll discuss the elements of discovery and matching and placement.

DISCOVERY

AS THE BODY OF CHRIST, we are called to care for one another and to know one another. It is important to see discovery as a value. What do you want to know about me that is useful to the church and beneficial to me and to the kingdom? How are we going to share that? Discovery is bigger than a gifts assessment, a time and talent sheet, and a subsequent conversation. Rather, it's discovering people's stories. It is holistic and dynamic—discovering what brought them to your church, what their needs are, and what concerns they bring—and how these needs and concerns change over time. It's important to make sure that systems are in place to capture information during the various phases of discovery. In this section, we'll include examples of some systems, types of assessment tools, and helpful information on the interview system.

The Interview Process

The interview process is the cornerstone of an effective equipping ministry system. The interview is simply an intentional conversation, and it serves many vital purposes:

- Paul writes in his letter to the Romans, "The gifts we possess differ as they are allotted to us by God's grace, and must be exercised accordingly" (12:6 NEB). Through the interview, we learn of the wondrous uniqueness of each member of the body of Christ.

- Each of us wants to be valued and affirmed as people of our congregation. The interview demonstrates the commitment of our faith community to provide a doorway to involvement, to meet a need, and to offer an opportunity to share our faith story and spiritual journey.

- The interview allows people to discuss why they've come to your church at this time in their lives and what they need to receive from the church. In addition, the member learns of available services, programs, and educational resources.

- The interview provides an opportunity to discern the personal concerns and need for ministry of people coming into the church.

Multiple Uses of the Interview Process

1. Start-up Interviews with Staff and Leaders

As you develop your system you will engage in many interviews. Your initial conversations or interviews will be with other staff members, ministry leaders, and senior clergy. Together you will be casting the vision for equipping ministry and exploring how equipping ministry can complement and enhance other ministries in the church. Your purpose is to build bridges, develop team relationships, and strengthen the vision of "every member a minister."

2. Entry Interviews with People

Along with trained interviewers, you will be engaging new and existing members in conversations for the purpose of learning more about the individual's gifts, desire to serve, and need to receive care and support from the congregation. For new people, the interview is a key component of the assimilation process and serves as a welcome to the church. For established members, the interview often opens the door to involvement or to a deepening of their spiritual journey.

The interview begins the equipping ministry process. It is the church's opportunity to discover another person's faith history and the life experiences he or she brings to his or her community of faith. As you come to know another member of the body of Christ, you begin to discern how each person can work together to build the church and to spread her impact in the community.

For many churches, interviewing people is a new practice. Some people may be surprised by the practice and perhaps even a bit uneasy about the process at first. However, congregations with equipping ministry systems report very positive results with the interviewing system. People come to look forward to their time to talk about their faith and their personal response to God's redeeming love.

> **Just as each of us has one body with many members, and these members do not all have the same function, so in Christ we who are many form one body, and each member belongs to all the others. We have different gifts, according to the grace given us. If a man's gift is prophesying, let him use it in proportion to his faith. If it is serving, let him serve; if it is teaching, let him teach; if it is encouraging, let him encourage; if it is contributing to the needs of others, let him give generously; if it is leadership, let him govern diligently; if it is showing mercy, let him do it cheerfully.**
>
> **ROMANS 12:4–8**

> **I will praise you, for I am fearfully and wonderfully made. Wonderful are your works, that I know very well. My frame was not hidden from you, when I was being made in secret, intricately woven in the depths of the earth.**
>
> **PSALM 139:14–15 NRSV**

An interview is a sacred opportunity to come to know a fellow Christian, to experience God's grace, and to share in another's faith journey.

BUILDERS' NOTE

Discovery occurs in many other ways as well. New-member classes and other assimilation programs will serve to spread the word about the equipping ministry. These opportunities will prepare new people for the equipping ministry interview and will answer many questions about your church and the opportunities for involvement.

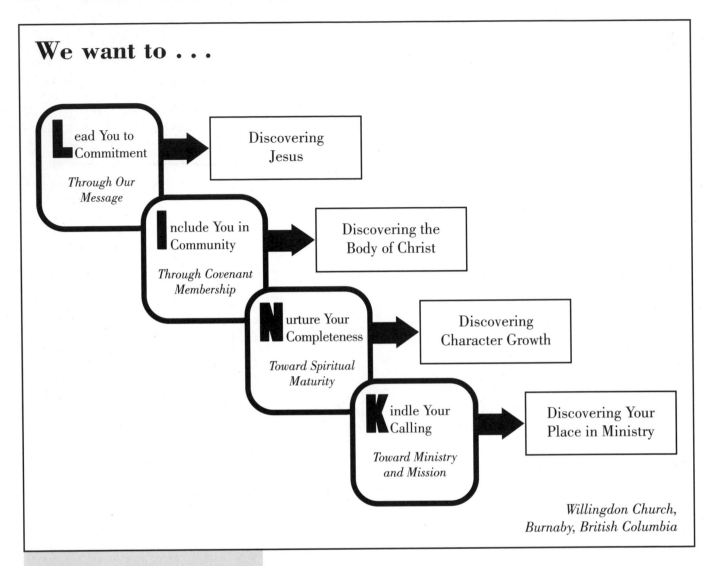

We want to . . .

Lead You to Commitment
Through Our Message
→ Discovering Jesus

Include You in Community
Through Covenant Membership
→ Discovering the Body of Christ

Nurture Your Completeness
Toward Spiritual Maturity
→ Discovering Character Growth

Kindle Your Calling
Toward Ministry and Mission
→ Discovering Your Place in Ministry

Willingdon Church, Burnaby, British Columbia

3. Placement Interviews

The interview used most often in an equipping ministry system, the placement interview provides a person with the opportunity to discover the best place to serve in terms of his or her spiritual gifts, experiences, passion, and talents. Equipping interviewers to facilitate this process is a key element to the success of a placement interview.

4. Reflection Interviews

Interviews provide the opportunity to reflect on service experiences. A critical outcome of effective equipping ministry is that people would see their connection with God through their service. During a person's service commitment, an interview can be used to enrich the ministry opportunity, help a member change to another area of service if necessary, reinforce a decision to continue with the ministry, identify the need for a sabbatical, or encourage a decision to seek a mentor to support spiritual growth. The interviewers ask the questions, "Where did you see and experience God in this service? Where did you see God in the lives of the people?"

5. Exit Interviews

An exit or closure interview can be used to learn about the person's ministry experience and its challenges and rewards. You learn about the person's life in the church, explore high points and low points, and glean recommendations to present to church leadership. The exit interview provides you and others with the opportunity to affirm the individual and show your appreciation for his or her witness to Christ.

Here are a few suggested exit interview questions and prompts:

- Describe your experience with the team/program/ministry with which you served.
- What were the challenges you faced when you joined this ministry?
- Were your talents and abilities appropriately utilized in this ministry?
- Did the ministry description adequately reflect the opportunity? What changes, if any, would you make in the description?
- How well organized was the opportunity?
- Were adequate resources available? If not, what was missing?
- Describe the degree of staff support and nurturing you and your project received.
- What did you like best about serving?
- What did you like least about serving?
- What training, education, or developmental experiences were helpful for you? What opportunities would have been helpful?
- In what ways do you feel you made a contribution through your involvement in this service area? Was your time well spent?
- Based on this experience, what suggestions do you have for the pastors, the staff, future leaders, and the board of trustees?
- In what other areas of ministry are you considering serving?
- How might the church help you with your ongoing faith development at this time?
- How can the church serve you in this transition from leadership?

Designing an Interview Process for Your Church

Process comes from the Latin word meaning "to go forward." The word has evolved to mean a set of operations for doing something. Let's look at a few of the issues you and your team will need to consider as you create the interviewing process.

1. What is your primary goal for the interview process?

- discern needs of those in your midst
- increase new member retention
- learn of people's gifts, interests, and skills
- assist persons in learning about service opportunities
- increase the person's commitment to the church
- gain feedback on the person's feelings about the church
- carry the person all the way to being placed and serving in ministry
- start an ongoing discipleship or mentoring relationship between the interviewer and the person
- other: _____

2. Whom are you going to interview?

- all new people and regular worshipers
- a combination of new and established members, experienced leaders, and inactive members
- prospective members

"One of the ongoing challenges of the church as the body of Christ is for its members to know each other as persons—individuals who are unique and important."

Marlene Wilson,
Volunteer Management Associates

An interview process is an organized, intentional plan to meet people along their path.

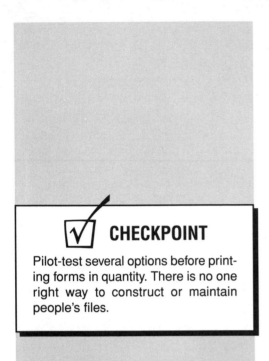

CHECKPOINT

Pilot-test several options before printing forms in quantity. There is no one right way to construct or maintain people's files.

You want a system that . . .

- meets the needs of the church and the equipping ministry process.
- is user-friendly and easy to access.
- provides you with the information needed to care for and involve people in ministry.

3. How will the people you want to interview learn of the process?

- through new-member classes or programs
- through gifts ministry classes or workshops
- from the assimilation team
- from the pastors
- from the pulpit
- from a letter sent to members or prospective members
- through bulletin announcements or newsletters
- other: _____

4. How will you schedule the interviews?

- individually, according to the schedule of the interviewer and the interviewee
- as a special event in a new-member class
- as part of a gifts-assessment program
- as a special event after joining the church
- following a gifts assessment or service preparation program
- other: _____

5. What type of interview form do you plan to create?

- Determine the type of information you want to collect on each member.
- Work with others involved in the assimilation process to create a form that meets the needs of the church. (A number of sample forms are shown on the following pages.)
- Teach the art of flexibility when the interview takes the discussion to a difficult place.

Consider these questions as you design your form:

1. When will the form be completed?

- before the interview
    - in a new-member class
    - as part of joining the church
    - on an anniversary of membership
    - in connection with a gifts-assessment program
    - in preparation for the interview
- during the interview process
    - with assistance from the interviewer
    - as part of the conversation
- after the interview is completed

2. How will information collected during the interview be managed?

- The interviewer will complete all necessary forms and file them as appropriate.
- The interviewer will meet with the leader or core team member of equipping ministry to discuss results.
- Information will be given to a data entry person for record-keeping and referral purposes.
- Other: _____

Wilshire Baptist Church, *Dallas, Texas*

VOLUNTEER MINISTRY INTERVIEW FORM

Interviewer _____

Home Phone _____

Office Phone _____

Date _____

A. Personal Information

Name _____ Title _____ Name used _____

Home Address _____

Home Phone _____ Home Fax _____ Home E-mail Address _____

Profession _____

Business Name _____

Business Address _____

Business Phone _____ Business Fax _____ Office E-mail Address _____

Date of Birth _____ Sex _____ Educational Experience _____

Hobbies _____

Foreign Languages Spoken _____

B. Family Information

Marital Status _____ Spouse's Name (if applicable) _____

Wedding Anniversary _____

Other Family Members:

Name	Relationship	Age

Date Joined _____ Method: ❑ Baptism ❑ Statement ❑ Transfer of Letter

Church _____

Reason(s) for Joining Wilshire:

❑ Preaching ❑ Bible Study ❑ Sunday School ❑ Music Ministry ❑ Location

❑ Preschool/Children's Ministry ❑ Student Ministry ❑ Friends ❑ Relatives

❑ Other _____

➪

C. Sunday School Participation

Do you attend a Sunday school class?   ❑ Yes   ❑ No   Which one? _____

Would you like more information on available classes?   ❑ Yes   ❑ No

D. Volunteer Ministry Opportunities

Please review the **yellow volunteer ministries brochure**. Answer any questions and give the new member an opportunity to complete it.

E. Volunteer Experience

Have you been ordained as a deacon?   ❑ Yes   ❑ No   If so, where? _____

Please list your volunteer involvement before coming to Wilshire:

1. **At or through church** (committees, Sunday school, teaching, off-campus ministries such as Habitat for Humanity, Interfaith Housing, and so forth):

Activity	Years of Experience	Desire to Continue at Wilshire?

a. _____

b. _____

c. _____

d. _____

2. **In the community** (not connected with church—PTA, hospitals, Meals on Wheels, and so forth):

Activity	Years of Experience

a. _____

b. _____

c. _____

d. _____

3. List the **other highlights** of your volunteer history:

Activity	Years of Experience	Desire to return?

a. _____

b. _____

c. _____

d. _____

Which were very **satisfying** for you? Why? _____

With what **age groups** do you enjoy working?

❑ Birth–2 yrs.   ❑ 3–5 yrs.   ❑ Grades 1–3   ❑ Grades 4–6   ❑ Grades 7–8   ❑ Grades 9–12

❑ College   ❑ Singles   ❑ Young Adults   ❑ Median Adults   ❑ Senior Adults

When are you *not* available to volunteer? _____

Wilshire Baptist Church, *Dallas, Texas*

VOLUNTEER MINISTRY INTERVIEW FORM

We can learn much about one another when we share stories that describe turning-point events as well as day-to-day issues. The four "H"s listed below give you a starting point for meaningful, relational discussion.

New Member's Name _____ Date _____

Highs (the best times in life)

Hurdles (single or ongoing struggles)

Hopes (dreams, driving forces)

Healings (victories, times of receiving ministry from God through others)

Wilshire Baptist Church, *Dallas, Texas*

VOLUNTEER MINISTRY REFERRAL FORM

★ To be completed by **interviewer**

_____ has been interviewed by the volunteer ministry program. This member has expressed interest and/or experience in your area of ministry. The member has been told that you, or a person you designate, will contact him or her to explore this ministry area further.

Please return the interview form and this form by _____

★ Name: _____

★ Address: _____

★ Phone: Home _____ ★ Office _____ ★ Fax _____

★ Best time to contact: _____

★ Date interviewed: _____

★ You may request additional information about this member from the volunteer ministry interviewer:

★ Phone: Home _____ ★ Office _____ ★ Best time to call _____

- -

Volunteer Ministry Response Form

❤ To be completed and returned by **minister**

Member Referred _____ Date _____

Ministry Area _____

Contact Person _____

❑ For information only

❤ Member placed in service   Position _____

❤ Member not placed in service Reason _____

❤ Other _____

❤ Member expressed an alternative interest _____

Please return this response section by_____

About Me

Name: _____

Date: _____

I am especially good at this:

1. _____
2. _____
3. _____
4. _____
5. _____

I am not so good at this:

1. _____
2. _____
3. _____
4. _____
5. _____

Things I enjoy doing:

1. _____
2. _____
3. _____
4. _____
5. _____

What would your dream occupation be if money and location were not an issue?

_____

_____

—source unknown

Brentwood Presbyterian Church
Los Angeles, California

Gifts, Skills, and Interests Survey

At BPC, we believe that we are *all* ministers and that you will be spiritually fed when you live into the "worship, plus two" formula (participate in weekly worship with your faith family, find an area of nurture, and serve in ministry). So that we can help get you connected to fulfilling areas of ministry, please complete this form and return it to the church office. May you be blessed on your journey. —*Connecting and Equipping Ministries Team*

NAME: _____ DATE: _____

PHONES: Home: _____ Work: _____ E-mail: _____

Nurture—I am interested in receiving more information about the following opportunities for nurture and spiritual growth:

❑ Mustard Seed Groups (Small Group Ministry)
❑ School of Christian Learning (Adult Education)
❑ Men's Bible Study (Wednesday mornings)
❑ Women's Bible Study (Thursday mornings)
❑ All-Church Bible Study (Thursday evenings)
❑ Meditation (Tuesday evenings)

Service—I would like to receive more information about the following ministry opportunities:
Please note which worship service: 8:00 A.M., 9:15 A.M., 11:00 A.M., 6:00 P.M.

❑ Usher—Service: ____
❑ Greeter—Service: ____
❑ Audio/Video Team—Service: ____
❑ Patio Hosts—Service: ____

Other:
❑ Nursery Volunteer
❑ Sunday School Teacher's Assistant
❑ Youth Sponsor/Mentor
❑ General Office Help (mailings, data entry, etc.)

Mission in Society:
❑ Angel Store
❑ Adult Mexico Work Camp
❑ Bluefields, Nicaragua Covenant Partnership
❑ CASA (Court-Appointed Children's Advocates)
❑ Chrysalis
❑ CLARE Foundation
❑ Common Ground AIDS Ministry
❑ Dinner for People without Homes

❑ Embangweni, Malawi Hospital
❑ Habitat for Humanity
❑ My Friend's Place
❑ Ocean Park Community Center
❑ 650 Westminster

Spiritual Gifts—I have completed a Spiritual Gifts inventory and know I am gifted with the following:

SPG01 ❑ Administration
SPG02 ❑ Creative Ability
SPG03 ❑ Encouragement (Exhortation)
SPG04 ❑ Evangelism
SPG05 ❑ Faith
SPG06 ❑ Giving
SPG07 ❑ Healing
SPG08 ❑ Helping
SPG09 ❑ Hospitality
SPG10 ❑ Intercession

SPG11 ❑ Knowledge
SPG12 ❑ Leadership
SPG13 ❑ Mercy
SPG14 ❑ Miracles
SPG15 ❑ Missionary
SPG16 ❑ Prophesy
SPG17 ❑ Service
SPG18 ❑ Shepherding
SPG19 ❑ Teaching
SPG20 ❑ Wisdom

❑ *Please contact me with information about the next Spiritual Gifts Discovery Class.*

Fellowship—Please contact me with information about the following groups and their upcoming activities:

❑ College Age Fellowship
❑ Common Threads (singles and couples, ages 20s–40s)
❑ Singles
❑ Couple's Garden (meets quarterly)
❑ Moms 'n' More (mothers of young children, ages 5 and under)
❑ Women's Ministry
❑ Men's Ministry

❑ Seniors
   ❑ TOPS (Terrific Outstanding Presbyterian Servants)
   ❑ Young At Heart (Seniors' Ministry and Fellowship)
   ❑ Friendship Builders
❑ Chain of Prayer (weekly prayer for the BPC family)
❑ Chancel Choir (Thursday evening rehearsals, sings in worship most Sundays)

Events—I'd like to participate in the following events:

❑ Christmas Caroling

❑ All-Church Retreat (Fall)

❑ Women's Retreat (Winter)

❑ Men's Retreat (Spring)

❑ Spiritual Life Retreat (Spring)

❑ Ski Trip (February)

❑ Golf Tournament (Fall)

❑ Thanksgiving Breakfast (November)

❑ All-Church Picnic (Summer)

Ministry Teams—Please contact me with information about the following ministries:

❑ Adult Ministries (Family, Mustard Seed Groups, School of Christian Learning)

❑ Connecting & Equipping (Gifts Discovery, Leadership Training & Support)

❑ Congregational Life (Singles, Common Threads, Women's & Men's, Moms 'n' More, Seniors)

❑ Children's Ministry

❑ Communications (publications, Web site)

❑ Empowerment

❑ Endowment

❑ Facilities

❑ Finance

❑ Mission in Society (local and international)

❑ Nominating (calls members into leadership)

❑ Planning & Organization

❑ Stewardship

❑ Welcome & Discovery (Patio Hosts, New Member Discovery Classes)

❑ Worship & Music (Choirs, Creative Arts Network)

❑ Youth Ministry (Jr. & Sr. High, College Fellowship)

❑ *Please contact me. I have more questions.*

Skills—I have the following skills and would like to use them in ministry:

MUSIC

SK001 ❑ Soloist

SK002 ❑ Choral Singing (Circle: SATB)

SK003 ❑ Song Leading

SK004 ❑ Banjo

SK005 ❑ Bass

SK006 ❑ Brass

SK007 ❑ Drums

SK008 ❑ Guitar

SK009 ❑ Harmonica

SK010 ❑ Mandolin

SK011 ❑ Organ

SK012 ❑ Piano/Keyboard

SK013 ❑ Strings

SK014 ❑ Woodwinds

SK015 ❑ Other Instrument

SK016 ❑ Composing/Lyric Writing

SK017 ❑ Conducting—Choral

SK018 ❑ Conducting—Orchestral

DANCE

SK019 ❑ Choreography

SK020 ❑ Ballet

SK021 ❑ Ballroom

SK022 ❑ Folk

SK023 ❑ Gymnastics

SK024 ❑ Hip Hop

SK025 ❑ Jazz

SK026 ❑ Liturgical

SK027 ❑ Martial Arts

SK028 ❑ Modern

SK029 ❑ Tap

SK030 ❑ Western

DRAMA

SK031 ❑ Acting—Comedic

SK032 ❑ Acting—Dramatic

SK033 ❑ Mime

SK034 ❑ Narration

SK035 ❑ Public Speaking

Please list topics:

SK036 ❑ Storytelling

SK037 ❑ Voiceover

SK038 ❑ Interviewing

SK039 ❑ Game Leader

TECHNICAL ARTS

SK040 ❑ Producing

SK041 ❑ Directing

SK042 ❑ Stage Manager

SK043 ❑ Production Artist

SK044 ❑ Stage Hand

SK045 ❑ Art Direction

SK046 ❑ Set Design

SK047 ❑ Special Effects

SK048 ❑ Sound Design

SK049 ❑ Lighting Design

SK050 ❑ Videotaping

SK051 ❑ Videotape Editing

SK052 ❑ Costume Design/Sewing

SK053 ❑ Makeup

SK054 ❑ Hairdressing

FACILITIES

SK055 ❑ Construction

SK056 ❑ Painting—Facilities

SK057 ❑ Electrical

SK058 ❑ Plumbing

SK059 ❑ Carpentry

SK060 ❑ Architecture/Interior Design

SK061 ❑ Landscaping/Gardening

VISUAL ARTS

SK062 ❑ Calligraphy

SK063 ❑ Cartoon

SK064 ❑ Illustration

SK065 ❑ Crafts

SK066 ❑ Drawing

SK067 ❑ Fiber/Textile Arts

SK068 ❑ Needlework

SK069 ❑ Painting/Artistic

SK070 ❑ Photography

SK071 ❑ Sculpting/Ceramics

(List of skills continued on the next page.)

HOME
SK072 ❑ Baking
SK073 ❑ Cake Decorating
SK074 ❑ Cooking
SK075 ❑ Flower Arranging
SK076 ❑ Food Art
SK077 ❑ Kitchen Aid
SK078 ❑ Sewing
SK079 ❑ Table Decorations
COMMUNICATION
SK080 ❑ Bulletin Board Design
SK081 ❑ Desktop Publishing
SK082 ❑ Editing
SK083 ❑ Graphics/Layout Design
SK084 ❑ Poetry
SK085 ❑ PR Writing

SK086 ❑ Publicity
SK087 ❑ Sign Language
SK088 ❑ Script Writing/Teaching
SK089 ❑ Training/Teaching
SK090 ❑ Web Page Design
SK091 ❑ Web Site
Programming/Mgmt.
SK092 ❑ Writing
LEADERSHIP
SK093 ❑ Accounting
SK094 ❑ Auditing
SK095 ❑ Employee Benefit Admin.
SK096 ❑ Financial Planning
SK097 ❑ Leading Small Groups
SK098 ❑ Personnel Management
SK099 ❑ Project Management

SK0100 ❑ Serving on Boards
SK0101 ❑ Strategic Planning
OFFICE
SK0102 ❑ Data Entry
SK0103 ❑ Front Desk Receptionist
SK0104 ❑ Organizational/Filing
SK0105 ❑ Phone Receptionist
SK0106 ❑ Shorthand/Fast Longhand
SK0107 ❑ Spreadsheets
SK0108 ❑ Ten Key
SK0109 ❑ Typing
SK0110 ❑ Word Processing
OTHER
SK0111 ❑ Class B Van License/
Driving
SKxxx ❑ Any we left out?

Other

Have you ever been ordained as an Elder or Deacon? ❑ Yes ❑ No
If yes, please complete the following:

Position: _____

Where: _____

When: _____

You've been coming to BPC for a while. What groups/activities/ministries have you already been involved in? _____
_____

Would you like information about Sunday morning child care, Covenant Club (Sunday school), or youth ministry? Please list the names, ages, and grades of your children:

Name: _____ Age: _____ Grade: _____

Name: _____ Age: _____ Grade: _____

Name: _____ Age: _____ Grade: _____

Name: _____ Age: _____ Grade: _____

If you have any questions, please call the office of empowerment ministries.

*To empower the people of Brentwood Presbyterian Church
to live into our faith together,
to discover our gifts,
and to actively respond to God's call.*

Entered Date: _____ Connecting Date: _____

By: _____ By: _____

Revision Date: 01/07/2000

File Name: GSI Survey

National Presbyterian Church
Washington, D.C.

gifts
ministry

_____   _____
(Title)   (First)   (Middle)   (Last)   (Familiar name/Nickname)

Address: _____   Other address (PO Box/Seasonal):

_____   _____

_____   _____

Home phone: _____   Dates of above address: _____
(If home phone shouldn't be printed in directory, print NO DIRECTORY by number.)

Business Phone: _____

Other Phones: _____   (car, fax, private line)

Occupation: _____   (Retired? Please state former occupation[s].)

Business Title: _____

Business Organization _____   (Federal employees put agency; students put school)

Business Address: _____

Sex: _____   Marital Status: _____   (Married, Single, Widow[er], Divorced, Separated)

Birth Date: _____

NPC member since: _____

Foreign languages spoken: _____

Name of spouse: _____

Is spouse NPC member?   Yes _____   No _____

Children at home (Please list)   Birth Date   Status: (Circle)

_____   _____   confirmed/not confirmed

_____   _____   confirmed/not confirmed

Other children or family ties to NPC:

_____   _____   confirmed/not confirmed

_____   _____   confirmed/not confirmed

Have you served in any of the following capacities? (Please check)

___ Elder ___ Minister ___ Deacon ___ Trustee ___ Presbytery ___ Synod ___ General Assembly

When? _____ Where? _____ Denomination: _____

....

Interviewer: _____   Date: _____

Profile Codes: (Eg., WU2) ____ ____ ____ ____ ____ ____ ____ ____ ____ ____

____ ____ ____ ____ ____ ____ ____ ____ ____ ____ ____

Permission to enter data into church computer is given by: _____

This member's priorities for service are:

1. _____   Notes:

2. _____

3. _____

Codes:

1 = Will do, haven't done before   3 = Will train/teach others to do/do not wish to do myself   5 = Doing at NPC now

2 = Will do, have experience   4 = Sabbatical—How long? _____

Current National Presbyterian Church Ministry Needs

I. MISSIONS:
- SB ____ Third Street
- SC ____ Food/Hungry
- SL ____ Campus Ministry
- SE ____ IONA House
- SF ____ Int'l Students
- SG ____ Latin America
- SH ____ Africa
- SI ____ Asia
- SK ____ Inner City
- SA ____ Help Anywhere

II. WORSHIP:
- HB ____ Choir
- HC ____ Instrumental Music
- HD ____ Special Events
- HE ____ 8:15 Service
- HF ____ Prayer Service
- HG ____ Flower Arrangements
- HH ____ National Singers
- HA ____ Help Anywhere
- HN ____ Usher

III. HOSPITALITY:
- HK ____ Table Setting
- HL ____ Food Preparation
- HM ____ Food Service

IV. EVANGELISM:
- JB ____ Track Visitors
- JC ____ Greeters
- JD ____ Telephone Prospects
- JE ____ Visit Prospects
- JF ____ Write Letters
- JG ____ NPC and Me
- JA ____ Help Anywhere

V. CONGREGATIONAL CARE:
- VA ____ Help Anywhere
- VB ____ Home Visits
- VD ____ Provide Transportation
- VE ____ Presby. Home
- VF ____ Stephen Ministry
- VH ____ Meals on Wheels
- VC ____ Military Ministry

VI. SUPPORT AND SERVICE:
- VG ____ Ask Me Desk
- VJ ____ Stewardship
- VK ____ Communication
- VL ____ NPC Tour Guides
- VM ____ NPC Directory

VII. GROWTH GROUPS
- LA ____ Any Small Group
- LB ____ Covenant Group
- LC ____ Prayer Group
- LD ____ 12-Step Support Group
- LE ____ Bible Study Group

OTHER GROUPS:
- LG ____ Gifts Ministry
- LH ____ Library

Christian Ed.: (Birth–11 years)
- CA ____ Nursery Committee
- CB ____ Teaching Assistant
- CD ____ Substitute
- CF ____ Crafts
- CG ____ Vacation Bible School
- CH ____ Child Care
- CY ____ Event Coordinator
- CZ ____ Dept. Chairperson

Children's Choir:
- FB ____ Choir Teacher
- FC ____ Choir Assistant
- FD ____ Choir Mom/Dad
- FE ____ Accompanist
- FA ____ Help Anywhere

Youth: (12–18)
- YB ____ Junior Choir
- YC ____ Senior High
- YD ____ Scouting
- YE ____ Athletics
- YF ____ Events/Retreats
- YG ____ Teach
- YH ____ Organize Parent Support
- YA ____ Help Anywhere

VIII. CHURCHWIDE EVENTS:
- KK ____ Annual Clothing Sale
- XX ____ Annual Bazaar
- ZZ ____ Alternative Christmas
- VV ____ Manual Arts Project
- FF ____ Annual Picnic
- GG ____ NPC Retreat

Gifts, Talents, and Abilities

I. EXECUTIVE & ADMINISTRATIVE SKILLS
- WA ____ Home Typing
- WB ____ Filing
- WC ____ Telephoning
- WD ____ Conceptualizer
- WE ____ Note Taker
- WF ____ Library Skills
- WG ____ Data Entry
- WH ____ Reception
- WJ ____ Registration
- WK ____ Management
- WL ____ Personnel Mgmt.
- WM ____ Computer

II. GROUP COORDINATION
- WN ____ Event Planning
- WP ____ Group Leader
- WQ ____ Group Convener
- WK ____ Devotions
- WS ____ Prayer Leader
- WT ____ Recreation/Sports
  (Specify) _____
- WU ____ Interview
- WV ____ Training
- WW ____ Work with Disabled
- WX ____ Song Leader
- WY ____ Enabler/Facilitator
- WZ ____ Fund-raising

III. COMMUNICATIONS
- XA ____ Publicity
- XB ____ Displays
- XC ____ AV Equipment Operator
- XD ____ Speaking Skills
- XE ____ Storytelling
- XF ____ Presentations

IV. CREATIVE ARTS:
- XK ____ Art and Design
- XL ____ Poetry
- XM ____ Editing
- XP ____ Proofreader
- XR ____ Needlepoint
- XS ____ Sewing
- XT ____ Calligraphy
- XU ____ Painter
- XV ____ Sculptor
- XW ____ Photography

V. MANUAL SKILLS:
- PA ____ Carpentry
- PB ____ Electrical Work
- PC ____ Painting
- PC ____ General Repair
- PE ____ Yard/Garden

VI. DRAMATIC ARTS:
- ZA ____ Dance
- ZB ____ Acting
- ZC ____ Directing
- ZD ____ Costumes
- ZE ____ Makeup
- ZF ____ Performer
- ZG ____ Set Design
- ZH ____ Lighting
- ZJ ____ Sound System
- ZK ____ Video

VII. OTHER TALENTS:
- QA ____ Play Piano
- QB ____ Play Guitar
- QC ____ Other Instrument
  (Specify) _____
- QD ____ Hobbies
  (Specify) _____
- QE ____ Singer
- QF ____ Youth Singer

VIII. TEACHING
- QK ____ Adult Teaching
- QM ____ Sign Language
- QN ____ Hearing Impaired
- QP ____ Visually Impaired
- QQ ____ Physically Impaired
- QR ____ Mentally Impaired

IX. OTHER MINISTRY TALENTS:
- RA ____ Nurturing
- RB ____ Caregiving
- RC ____ Giving Vocat. Counsel
- RD ____ Aging Care/Issues
- RE ____ Providing Housing
- RF ____ Driving to/from Church
- RG ____ Delivering Meals
- RH ____ Helping Unemployed
- RJ ____ Jobs Network
- RK ____ Financial Benefactor
- RL ____ Willing Hands

Conducting the Interview

Much of the success of equipping ministry depends on developing a team of interviewers to connect with people and support them as they seek ministry opportunities and become a part of the church body. Along with your equipping ministry team and your senior pastor, you will want to determine the type and level of assistance needed for this pivotal role in the equipping ministry system.

Here are three options to consider:

1. The equipping ministry interviewer will interview people, provide follow-up information to appropriate persons, and serve as an ambassador of equipping ministry to the congregation at large. The interviewer will be carefully selected and trained and will commit to a specified number of interviews.

2. The equipping ministry sponsor, who is a carefully selected and trained person, agrees to interview a specified number of persons and to follow through with them until they have connected with the church, either through service opportunities or in programs designed to meet their needs. The sponsor commits to either a time expectation or to establishing relationships with a specified number of interviewees.

3. The equipping ministry mentor (the most involved of the three options) establishes an ongoing relationship with the persons interviewed. The mentor assumes the responsibility to interview a person and to support him or her in his or her faith journey. The mentor works closely with the individuals as they identify their gifts, assists them in finding a placement, and maintains contact as the experience unfolds.

The process for identifying and developing interviewers is detailed on the following pages. It is imperative that you develop ministry descriptions, carefully select for the position the individuals who have the right gifts and temperament, train them thoroughly, and provide ongoing supervision. These persons represent the church to new, prospective, and established members.

What Qualities and Gifts Do You Look For
in an Interviewer?

- A pastor's heart, spiritual maturity and wisdom, a desire to help people and meet needs. This position helps people grow spiritually through guiding them to a place of service that fits their gifts. This person is a discipler, not a "slot-filler."
- An ability to listen well, plus an ability to ask good questions.
- An ability to see a person's potential and encourage him or her to see it as well.
- An ability to synthesize information. This person must create bridges in his or her mind between the person's gifts and the available opportunities for service, and then guide the person to a point of seeing that bridge.
- Willingness to take the time to invest in the lives of other people, including patience to deal with the interruptions and winding paths a person takes as he or she considers significant changes in his or her life.

The Characteristics of a Good Interviewer

- *A thoughtful listener who sincerely values others and encourages the person to share his or her story.* A good listener does not finish a sentence for the speaker. A good listener focuses on what the other is saying, listening carefully to hear the story unfold. A good listener seeks to understand the speaker and to experience life from the "frame of reference" of the person being interviewed.
- *A patient and understanding person.* A good interview cannot be rushed. A good interviewer is relaxed and puts others at ease.
- *A Christian committed to helping others find their place in the body of Christ.* An interview in the church is not the same as a job interview. While you sincerely hope to begin to identify a person's giftedness for ministry, the interview itself is a ministry opportunity—the church's opportunity to learn the needs of a fellow Christian. A person may be facing a life crisis, overwhelmed by life circumstances, or simply caught in the throes of transition over a move, a new job, or a new baby. An effective interviewer provides the member with an opportunity to share what is happening in his or her life of faith and to learn of his or her needs and desires.

On pages 287–88 you'll find a series of sample interview questions that may assist you as you formulate your own questions.

Who Make Good Interviewers?

- Counselors who have a desire to help people realize their potential, but often grow tired of long-term, problem-oriented counseling
- People who are employed in human resources fields
- Small group leaders who have indicated a particular bent for behind-the-scenes facilitating of the growth of others, rather than teaching or organizing responsibilities
- People who are proficient in the use of gifts-assessment instruments and who understand the benefits and limitations of these instruments
- Trained Stephen ministers

How Do You Train Interviewers?

- If you select the right people, they already have the inherent gifts of a good interviewer. The key is to train them in skills of gifts assessment and placement and to provide plenty of opportunities to role-play and practice in guided exercises.
- Don't be surprised if you invite fifteen interviewers and more than half decide during the training they don't have time to follow up with the commitment, or need to be reassigned because they don't have the necessary skills or maturity. These are key positions and require high standards.
- Continually identify new interviewers. It is an ongoing process. Many who have benefited from the entry interview feel a call to do the same for others.

A number of topics should be covered during interview training:

- What is interviewing all about?
- Whom will you be interviewing?
- What expectations do you have about the process?
- What purposes does interviewing serve?
- The qualities of a good interviewer.
- What listening skills will you need?
- What nonverbal communication skills will you need?
- What questioning skills will you need?
- Preparing for the interview.
- The interviewing process.
- The process for referrals.
- Practicing interviewing skills.
- A sample interview.

What Questions Do You Intend to Ask during the Interview?

Your goals and objectives for the interview process will help you determine the questions to ask during the interview. Your overriding goal is to make the person feel at ease in the interview.

A few pointers as you consider what questions to ask:

- Ask open-ended questions that encourage discussion rather than yes or no responses.
- Tailor your questions to the person with whom you are speaking.
- It is more important that the person feels cared for than it is that you leave your time together with every question answered. This is, first and foremost, a ministry experience. If a person needs to share a life situation that is not part of your interview format, follow the person's lead.

Because you will be asking people to tell you a great deal about themselves, it sometimes helps if you go first, sharing something about yourself for five minutes. Perhaps you could explain why you chose to be an interviewer and tell a personal story about how discovering your gifts helped you serve more effectively; or perhaps you could discuss how the interview experience helped you become a contributing part of the church. If applicable, you can share how the interview experience resulted in a need in your life being met. Sharing a personal story, especially one that demonstrates your own vulnerability and how you have grown and learned from this process, will help a new person feel less uncomfortable about not knowing where he or she wants to serve or not having a good grasp on his or her own gifts and talents. Personal sharing creates bridges of understanding that allow people to see interviewers as being on their side.

Here are some tips for conducting a successful interview:

Preparation . . .
- Prepare the way by sending a letter or calling the person to be interviewed. Discuss the process and provide the member with sufficient information to prepare for your time together.
- Allow at least one hour for each interview. Try to arrange a private location free of interruptions. Schedule someone else to handle your phone calls. If possible, provide child care for mothers with toddlers.
- You are "the church" to the person with whom you will be speaking. Your timeliness, courtesy, and follow-through reflect on the entire congregation.

As the Interview Begins . . .
- Remember that you've been given the great privilege of talking with fellow Christians about their life journeys, their special gifts and talents, and their unique concerns. Acknowledge this privilege. Thank each person for taking the time to talk with you.
- Determine how you intend to record and remember the information the person shares with you. If taking notes during the interview is necessary, let the person know what you plan to do with your notes.
- Put the person at ease. A good interview is like a comfortable conversation with a friend. You may want to talk about the weather, sports, or current events before easing into the questions that shape the interview.

Closing the Interview . . .
- Be sure the person feels that his or her needs have been addressed during your time together. Ask the person if he or she has other questions or concerns to discuss with you.
- Consider concluding with a word of prayer, a brief selection from the Bible, or a spiritual reading.
- Give the member a card with your name and phone number in case the person has additional questions or concerns to share.

After the Interview . . .
- Complete the necessary paperwork and forms or data entry responsibilities.
- Follow through as promised.
- If possible, maintain periodic ongoing contact with the person you interviewed.

"What process do we use for inviting interviewers onto our team? After all, our interviews will only be as effective as those conducting the interviews. How do we find the best people for this ministry? Think for a moment: Who has interviewed you during your life experience? Mentally move outside the walls of the church, and the following people may come to mind: college recruiters, employers, human resource people, counselors, volunteer coordinators from community service organizations, receptionists at various offices, and even sales representatives.

"All of these people do some type of interviewing. Why don't we seek out these kinds of people already in our churches? If they also have the spiritual gifts of encouragement, leadership, and service, along with these other skills, we can feel affirmed in asking them to join our team."

Calvie Hughson Schwalm,
Crystal Cathedral

An Added Benefit of the Interview Process

For some people service may not be an immediate option. You may find people who are exhausted from serving in other situations, who are experiencing a personal crisis, who are involved in a significant life transition, or who are overwhelmed with responsibilities. The interview provides the person with the opportunity to reflect on his or her situation. The individual may need permission to take time for a sabbatical or to engage in study and reflection. Allow people the opportunity to rest, after which they can return to their church family renewed, refreshed, and ready for service.

Interview Techniques for Ministry Exploration Team Consultant Positions

Prior to the Interview:

- Review each applicant's ministry information form.
- Pray for God's wisdom during the interview.
- Pull the ministry exploration consultant job description.

Welcome the candidates to the interview. Tell them you would like to ask some questions first and then speak more about the specific job duties for this position. Inform them that the committee will be interviewing all of the candidates, contacting references, praying about the people God wants to bring to this ministry, and then getting back to them. Tell them that at the conclusion of the interview you will also discuss the training requirements for those people who join the ministry. Inform the candidates that you will only be selecting four to six people at this time and that you will keep everyone in mind for future needs of the ministry. Give them a timeline for getting back to everyone who interviewed for the ministry.

During the Interview:

Ask the following questions. Italicized questions are very important.

1. How long have you been a member at _____?
2. How did you come to _____?
3. How and when did you develop a relationship with Jesus Christ?
4. *What are the things you do in your life to keep growing and connected to Jesus Christ?*
5. What ministries have you been involved in at _____?
6. How has God used you in service? What kinds of roles and types of circumstances has he placed you in in the past?
7. *What has to be in place for a ministry to be meaningful to you?*
8. If you were in the ideal ministry, what would be happening?
9. *What are the rewards you expect from this ministry?*
10. What kind of environment do you feel most comfortable working in?
11. What parts of this ministry would you see as challenging?
12. What do you feel you would contribute to this role?
13. *What would you see as your mission behind this ministry?*
14. What do you see to be the ingredient for success in this potential role?
15. *Do you have any strong causes or beliefs that might interfere with your effectiveness in this role?*
16. Is there anything taking place currently in your life that could embarrass the church?
17. *Do you have any unresolved issues or incidents we need to know about before we contact the staff members, pastoral staff, or personal references on your application?*
18. If someone were to share a concern about a particular staff member during a consultation, how would you handle it?
19. Do you have any further questions for us?

After the Interview:

Share with the candidates the specific job description and requirement to complete the ministry exploration seminar. Inform them of the training requirements.

After you finish interviewing the candidates, thank them for coming in. Encourage them to pray about the position. Give them a specific timeline for getting back to them. Tell them when the next training sessions will take place.

As you interview the candidates, look for the following:

- Is this person impartial and an ambassador for all the ministries in the church?
- Does this person have some knowledge of the happenings or ministries at _____?
- Does he or she have good communication skills?
- Does this person seem to have an enthusiasm for the ministry?
- Do his or her spiritual gifts match the needs of the role (encouragement, communication, good listening skills, discernment, counseling, good self-esteem)?
- Does this person come across as opinionated, nondirective, or open?
- Has this person talked to you about various staff members or laypeople in the past?
- Has this person pushed causes in the past that could prevent him or her from being impartial or nondirective with candidates?
- What is this person's track record regarding ministry? Was he or she dependable? Was he or she a team player?
- Is this person approachable? Does he or she come across as teachable?
- Does this person possess good counseling skills?
- Has this person completed the ministry exploration class or Christianity 301? If not, is he or she willing to go through the ministry exploration class?
- Were the values or items he or she indicated for a meaningful ministry in harmony with what this ministry would provide?
- Has this person's past performance indicated that he or she can maintain confidentiality? Do his or her references feel this person can maintain confidentiality?
- Does this person seem to have self-confidence and a genuine interest in people?
- Were there any concerns with the training requirements for this person's role?

Complete the necessary paperwork on the bottom of the application information form. Contact the appropriate references for past ministries and personal recommendations. Send a letter to the candidates regarding the status of the process.

source unknown

First Presbyterian Church of Bellevue
Bellevue, Washington

MINISTRY DESCRIPTION
LAY MINISTRY INTERVIEWER
(Excerpts)

Purpose of Ministry: Assist FPCB members in understanding lay ministry, identifying spiritual gifts, and connecting with ministry opportunities.

Ministry Description:

1. Attend training to develop skills and techniques for small group leader in the discovery class and as an interviewer.
2. Participate as a small group leader in the discovery class.
3. Follow up with members of small group to assist them in understanding the ministry opportunities and seeking out their preferences for lay ministry.
4. Facilitate gifts assessment and conduct one-on-one interviews.
5. Follow up with committees to ensure candidates have been connected to their ministry opportunities.
6. Follow up with candidate to aid as needed for additional information or direction and to ensure committee connection is completed.
7. Assist in assessment of process and refinements as needed.

Desired Results:

1. Interviewers are trained as small group leaders and interviewers.
2. Interviewers have an in-depth understanding of ministry opportunities at FPCB.
3. Interview process is a positive and rewarding experience for FPCB members.
4. Existing and new ministries of FPCB grow internally and throughout our community and are staffed by FPCB members whose spiritual gifts and talents are suitably matched to the specific ministry needs.

Amount of Time and Frequency: Initially weekly for training and participation in discovery class sessions as small group leaders. Thereafter, time commitment will vary, depending on need for small group leaders and to assist in one-on-one interviews.

Length of Service: Two years. May volunteer for longer period

Skills, Talents, Qualifications:

- Communication (good listening and speaking skills)
- Personable and caring
- Diversity of experiences in working with persons of varied backgrounds and interests
- Intuitive, able to discern people's interests, gifts, concerns, and potential
- Knowledge of ministry opportunities at FPCB
- Committed in his or her own faith and in bringing new people into the life and heart of the church.

Training That May Be Needed:

- Interviewing techniques
- Leading small groups
- Interpreting assessment tools
- Understanding of ministry opportunities and spiritual gifts

Wilshire Baptist Church, *Dallas, Texas*

MINISTRY DESCRIPTION
VOLUNTEER MINISTRY INTERVIEWER

VISION: We are matching and developing gifts of volunteers and staff for ministry.

IMPORTANCE TO OUR CHURCH: Every member of Wilshire has gifts to offer to the kingdom of God, and each person needs an opportunity to give his or her gifts. Wilshire, as a local congregation, needs these gifts to carry out her mission and vision.

TASK DESCRIPTION:

- Interview people as requested.

- Complete an assessment of each person's gifts, interests, and abilities.

- Communicate results of interview to the director of volunteer ministry.

- Follow up with interviewee by phone for six months to ensure assimilation.

- Conduct up to six interviews per year.

STAFF LIAISON: Associate Pastor

TIME FRAME: Two hours training annually; two or three hours monthly for interviews and follow-up

SKILLS TO BE USED:

- Thoughtful listener

- Warm, hospitable, and trustworthy

- Patient and understanding

- A Christian committed to helping each of us find our place in the body of Christ

- Discovery and assessment of gifts but not enlistment

NUMBER OF VOLUNTEERS NEEDED: 50 to 60

BENEFIT FOR THE VOLUNTEER: The joy of helping a person find his or her place in the life of Wilshire and in the kingdom of God. Meeting new people.

Establishing a Ministry Placement

SADDLEBACK'S PROCESS

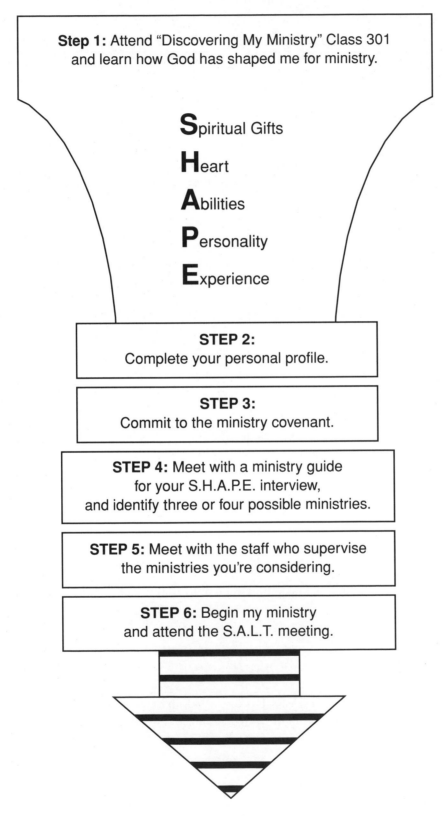

Step 1: Attend "Discovering My Ministry" Class 301 and learn how God has shaped me for ministry.

Spiritual Gifts

Heart

Abilities

Personality

Experience

STEP 2:
Complete your personal profile.

STEP 3:
Commit to the ministry covenant.

STEP 4: Meet with a ministry guide for your S.H.A.P.E. interview, and identify three or four possible ministries.

STEP 5: Meet with the staff who supervise the ministries you're considering.

STEP 6: Begin my ministry and attend the S.A.L.T. meeting.

LAY MINISTRY GENERAL FLOW

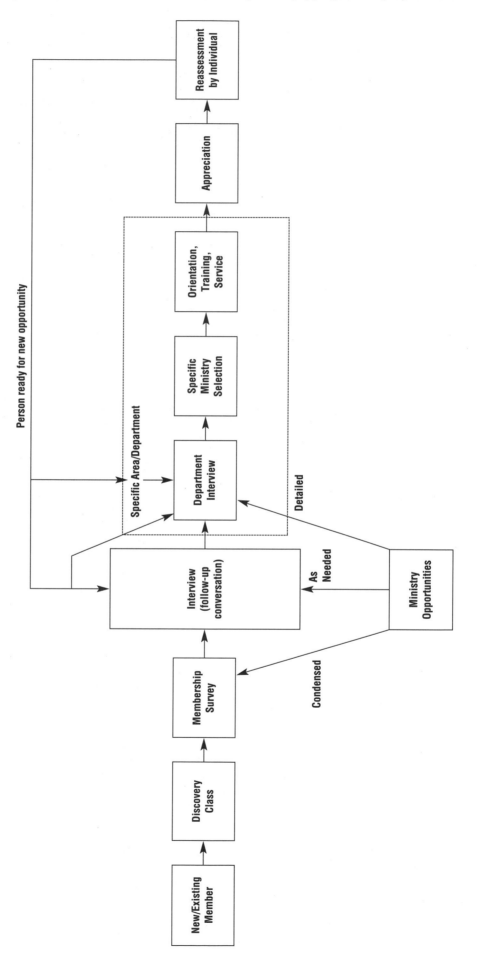

First Presbyterian Church of Bellevue, Bellevue, Washington

AN OVERVIEW OF THE LAY MINISTRY SYSTEM

DISCOVERY	INTERVIEW	CONNECTING TO MINISTRY	SHARING YOUR GIFTS IN MINISTRY	APPRECIATION	REASSESSMENT
Discovery is exploring who you are in Christ. This includes exploring and sharing your spiritual gifts; your passions, abilities, and talents; and your experience.	The interview is a continuation of the discovery process.	Each department identifies and describes current and new ministry opportunities.	It is each department's responsibility to provide orientation and training.	Celebration of service will be expressed regularly for those who serve inside the church as well as out in the community and around the globe.	At the completion of the term for ministry, the department in which a person has served asks him or her to evaluate and assess the experiences in ministry and to give feedback to the leaders in this area.
Discovery is facilitated as we build lay ministry concepts, language, and emphasis into our church culture. God created us for ministry, and we should be encouraged in this area in all facets of church life.	Schedule a one-on-one interview. This is an intentional and relaxed conversation of about an hour in length with a caring, trained member of our church. The purpose is to help each person recognize his or her spiritual gifts, talents, and experience and to find a direction for area of ministry.	The interviewer informs three people about the ministry area choice of the participant: director of lay ministry (DLM), the staff person, and the elder in charge of that ministry.	Some ministries will require additional or specialized training.	Appreciation is shown in creative ways throughout the year.	If the person wishes to continue in this ministry, he or she discusses this with the staff/elder/leader in charge of this area.
In lay ministry, discovery happens primarily in two ways:		The staff/elder/leader in charge of that area (as determined by each individual department) meets with the person to make sure that the specific match is a comfortable one for both parties.	As the person serves and uses his or her gifts in ministry, spiritual growth takes place and a greater sense of community develops.	Fellowship of the Ordained event—Once a year, all current and past deacons and elders (whether ordained in our church or in their former church) gather for dessert and discussion of topics concerning our church.	Exit interviews will be given to deacons and elders after completion of their term of service.
1. In the discovery class through teaching, scriptural context, spiritual gifts assessment, and small group experiences. This class will be offered several times each year.		The staff/elder/leader informs the DLM that a match is made or that the person will be seeking something different.	The staff/elder/leader who supervises the volunteer periodically checks in to answer questions, offer guidance, encourage, and show appreciation.		Ministry is a lifelong pursuit. Lay ministry will help each person connect to new ministries, continuing on the exciting and rich journey of services to our Lord. Let us allow God to stretch us so that we can experience his enabling power!
2. Through participation in ministry, which stretches us and allows God to work through us as our faith grows.					

First Presbyterian Church of Bellevue, *Bellevue, Washington*

FIRST PRESBYTERIAN CHURCH OF BELLEVUE
Bellevue, Washington

Guidelines for Gifts Discovery Conversation

Small Group Leader _____

> (responsible for bringing ministry opportunity matrix, if appropriate, and completing the ministry referral form after the conversation)

Small Group Participant _____

> (responsible for bringing gifts-assessment results)

General reminders: Smile with genuine warmth; use their name occasionally in the conversation, and look them in the eye.

Welcome

- This is basically "ice-breaking" time. Small talk about family, job, church activities. Hopefully, the small group leader has taken a few notes and is able to refer to things participants discussed in the small group sessions.

Purpose

- Let them know that the discussion is intended to help them process what they've discovered about their gifts and passions and explore some of the ways we might help them use their gifts in ministry, if they are not already doing so. We are not there to slot them into openings at the church or elsewhere.

Conversation

- Create an opportunity for *inner viewing.* This is the appropriate time to discuss their experience with the gifts-assessment and passion surveys. Now that a little time has passed, do they feel any differently about the results than when they first learned them? You can let this conversation move around a little bit. Explore how they feel about the results of the surveys. Try to use open-ended questions to help them reflect on their previous use (or lack thereof) of their gifts and passions. (Example: How do you think your gifts relate to your involvement with the PTA? [or whatever they might have been doing].)

  The basic focus of this time is to help them really think about their gifts and passions and whether or not they are ready to try something new or different that might use those gifts. Another good area to tackle here is a discussion of what phase of life they are in, how busy they are, how full their plate is, how ready they are to tackle a new ministry. Other possible questions to stimulate this inner viewing are: "Have you ever felt God's call in your life? Do you feel a particular call to ministry now? What do you enjoy doing? What gives you joy? What has been your faith journey?" Note the open-ended approach to all these questions—all require some thought and introspection.

Closure

- Sum up the discussion and let them know what will happen next. At the very minimum, the next step will be for you to fill out the referral form for submission to lay ministry. It might be helpful to go over this form with them, partially so they can see clearly what is going to happen, but also to make sure that the information on phone numbers, best time to call, and the like is correct.

Ending

- Thank the person for spending time and sharing thoughts, ideas, information, and feelings. Stand up and extend your hand for a concluding handshake.

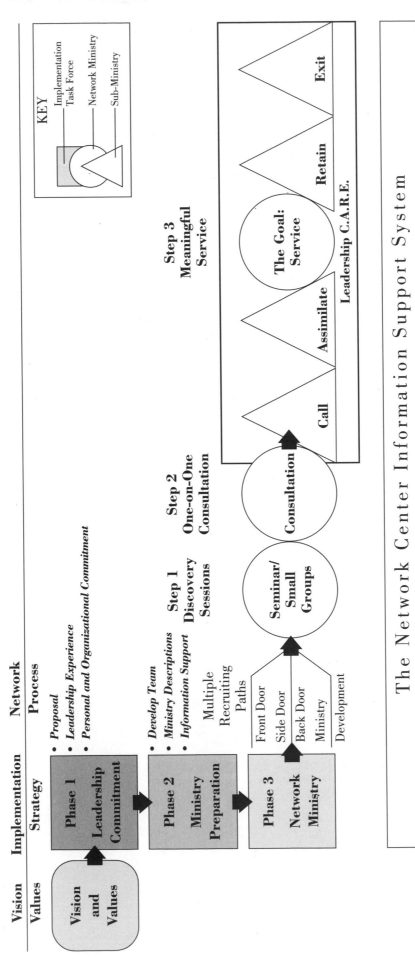

THE NETWORK PROCESS

• *Training Leaders to Develop the Right People in the Right Places for the Right Reasons* •

The Network Center Information Support System

Network Ministries International • PMB #217, 25108-B Marguerite Pkwy., Mission Viejo, CA 92692
800-588-8833   949-588-1533   Fax 949-768-8076   E-mail: nmi@networkministries.com
Web site: www.networkministries.com

Sample Interview Questions

These questions are designed to stimulate your thinking as you create your interview format. Some questions may need to be reworded to address the specific concerns of new members, and others to meet the needs of existing members.

The challenge behind the interview process is for the church, as the body of Christ, to come to know her people as important, gifted, and unique creations, each in need of nurture and each capable of caring and serving.

Here are some questions that focus on the person:

1. I would be interested in learning about your family. Tell me about ...

   Very often our experiences with our family and significant others provide opportunities for ministry. We grow through the situations or problems we have experienced. A widow may want to minister to others who are facing the loss of a spouse, or a parent of a child with physical or mental disabilities may feel called to help others. Listen for these life experiences, and determine if these are experiences a person feels called to share.

2. What do you do (or what have you done) to earn your livelihood? How do you feel (or did you feel) about your job?

3. If a person is new to the community, you might ask about his or her former home, previous church affiliations, and friendships. How can the church be helpful during this time of transition? What fellowship opportunities is he or she looking for?

4. How do you spend your leisure time? What are your hobbies, favorite sports, favorite books, and so forth?

5. What do you love doing? What brings you the greatest joy? What feeds your soul?

6. What do you dislike doing and hope you *never* have to do again?

Here are questions that focus on the person's expectations for his or her church home:

1. How did you find our church and what made you select us as your faith community?

2. What would you like to see happen in our congregation that would meet your needs and the needs of your family?

3. How can the church minister to your special concerns?

4. Have you encountered any difficulties or problems in the church that you feel comfortable sharing?

5. How can the church work with you to help you develop your spiritual life?

6. Can you share some of your most memorable experiences in this church or other church homes? What made these experiences special to you?

Here are some questions that focus on the person's gifts, abilities, and passion for service.

1. We seldom have the opportunity to share with others those things we most enjoyed doing and felt we did well. Are there things you've accomplished that you're really proud of? I'd like very much to

An interview becomes ministry when it is an intentional conversation of the head and heart that . . .

- shares the person's personal journey.
- affirms and celebrates.
- hears the person's stories—the highs, hopes, hurts, and healings.

hear about them. (This question is based on the Gifts Identification System developed by Arthur F. Miller and Ralph T. Mattson. You can read more about the System for the Identification of Motivated Abilities [SIMA] in their book *The Truth about You.*)

If you listen carefully to the answer, you'll learn a great deal about a person. The answer may well tell you about the type of situation a person is naturally drawn to, the kinds of things a person enjoys working with, and how much he or she likes to work with others. Seek a couple of situations, and look for similarities and differences in the stories the person shares. This question can be used with persons of any age. It is not important that others noticed the situation. A person may share the experience of building a model car, running a meeting, or organizing a closet. What is important is that the person enjoyed the experience and felt good about his or her work. This information will point you to his or her God-given gifts and talents.

2. What do you most enjoy doing in your free time? Would this be something you'd like to share with others in your church? Do you have any thoughts about how you might do so?

   Very often, a person's passion is evident in his or her avocation.

3. Do you have a particular talent or ability you'd like to share with the church? How have you used this ability in the past?

4. There are times in our lives when we feel that God has called us to specific ministry. Have you ever experienced God's call? Can you tell me about the situation and what you did? Do you feel called by God to a particular ministry now?

5. Often we have dreams or specific concerns for our congregation. Do you have any special thoughts or ideas you'd like to share? How can we help you explore these dreams?

   This question would be most appropriately used with an active member. A new member may not feel comfortable responding.

6. Sometimes certain events happen in our lives that create a greater sensitivity to the needs of others. For example, the mother of a child with disabilities may feel called to help others who have children with special needs. Have you experienced any life situations that give you a passion to support others in specific ways?

7. Just as we feel called to share certain parts of ourselves, there are often areas in life that we feel a particular desire to avoid for whatever reason. Are there any requests for service that you'd especially like to avoid?

8. What concerns do you have as you join? Is there any information you've received that you don't understand?

   In assimilation interviews it's critical to ask new members about their expectations, their needs to be met, and their concerns about their new commitment. For established members, you can reword this question to learn about their experiences with the church to date and how you might help them gain more from their involvement.

It is not necessary that you be able to answer every question a new or existing member asks; it is vital only that you commit to following up with an answer or having someone else supply an answer in a timely manner.

Alert

In some interviews you may learn of a crisis or problem in the life of the interviewee. This is where you transform from an interviewer to a minister. Ask if you may share this information with one of the pastors, and be sure to do so if permission is granted. It is especially important to follow up in this situation, and to close your time together in prayer.

Interview Questionnaire

> *Called to Serve Ministries*

Name of Interviewee: _____

Name of Interviewer: _____

- Briefly introduce yourself/your family/your career and any community involvement or interest.
- Share about your spiritual gifts discovery or service at your church.
- Let the person know why you are taking notes.

1. I would be interested in hearing about you and your family. _____

   _____

2. For your spiritual growth, what can the church do to meet your needs or your family's needs? _____

   _____

3. What do you love doing? What brings you the greatest joy? _____

   _____

4. Is there a spiritual gift or a particular talent or ability you have that you would like to share with this church? _____

   _____

   _____

5. Have you ever felt you experienced God's call? Do you feel called to a particular ministry now? _____

   _____

   _____

6. Approximately how much time would you like to serve:

   each week _____ month _____ preferred days _____

* Discuss ministry opportunities based on specific jobs from the ministry position descriptions, brochures, and so forth. Give your top three selections.

1. _____

2. _____

3. _____

Do you want to hear from ministries 1, 2, and 3 to learn more about these opportunities, or are you just interested in your first choice? _____

_____

- Thank the person for his or her time and interest. Let the person know that someone from the selected ministry area will be contacting him or her within two weeks.
- Give your name and phone number so the person can call with any questions.
- Close in prayer.

* If the interviewee is interested in serving in a community organization or agency, write out the organization's name, contact person, and phone number. The interviewee is responsible to make the connection.

Walnut Creek Presbyterian Church, Walnut Creek, California

Assessment Tools and the Interview Process

Many churches have found that using an assessment tool augments the one-on-one interview. Here are some of the types of assessment tools:

- Spiritual Gifts: These assessments are inventories based on the lists of spiritual gifts in Romans 12, 1 Corinthians 12, and Ephesians 4.

- Natural Gifts: These assessments tools measure gifts and motivations present from birth, as indicated usually through an autobiographical interview and observation of consistent behavior.

- Personality and Behavioral Style Assessments: These examine various aspects of the personality such as temperament, role preferences, leadership style, learning styles, and other areas.

- Interest Inventories: These tools compare a person's level of interest in various fields and cover areas such as values, career interests, and work-space and lifestyle desires.

- Skill Assessments: These tools measure acquired skills and learned abilities, usually through experience questionnaires or the measurement of physical abilities.

- Motivational Abilities: These tools measure methods of thinking and problem solving and assess a person's natural motivation toward performance.

- Other: Many churches have developed their own assessments, while others utilize tools developed for specific business or community service needs.

Advantages of Assessments

- Assessments support the program emphasis of helping individuals discover their God-given gifts and calling rather than emphasizing what the church needs and which people can be found to fill a volunteer "slot." People appreciate discovering more about themselves.

- Most assessments use a professional format and contain materials that a person can keep and continue to reread and learn. The use of a common assessment tool or tools throughout the church provides a common language for discussing team building, ongoing training, and continued placement.

- Assessment tools can save interview time, since the member determines interest or skill areas prior to the interview.

- Assessments add an element of objectivity, since most have been carefully designed and thoroughly field-tested by psychologists.

- Assessments can greatly enhance a good fit by providing the information necessary to focus on where a person will serve well. Feelings of failure and possible de-motivation that result from too many "trial runs" in unsuccessful service ventures are avoided.

- Assessments can provide ongoing empowerment to guide the individual to make better decisions in areas such as marriage, parenting, career, and leisure, as well as church or community service. Some assessments have been used to help a person develop customized approaches to personal worship and Bible study in order to create a spiritual formation experience that uniquely fits the God-given design of the person.

Cautions in Using Assessments

- Assessments should never be used by themselves. The value of a good equipping ministry system is the "people contact" the interview provides. Most assessments are designed only to provide a trained assessor with the language and information he or she needs in order to help the person, but few are designed to be a paper-only experience.

- Assessments can be overused. If people receive too much information too quickly, information overload may paralyze their decision-making ability. Often the excitement of self-discovery can draw a program off the track into introspection, and the goal of preparation for ministry service can become lost. Many churches use layered assessments, which allows certain simple assessments to be used initially, then as a person progresses to leadership levels of service, more in-depth assessments can be added.

- You can pigeonhole someone by gift just as easily as by vocation. It is important to consider all you know about a person and not just his or her gifts.

- No assessment is a magic wand. Each has some level of subjectivity, although many have report formats that increase the scientific impression of complete objectivity. The question "What am I going to do with my life?" requires more than a $25, 25-minute, fill-in-the-blank questionnaire. It involves much prayer, much introspection, continuing interaction with others, and the hard work of trial and error.

Sample Assessments Used in Churches

See the following pages (pages 292–98) for sample assessments used in churches. (Note: In some cases only excerpts are shown.)

Volunteer Ministries Survey

Thank you for taking time to inform us of the ways in which you are willing to volunteer your time and talent.

Please check the areas in which you are interested in becoming involved or continuing to serve.

Returning this form to the church at your earliest convenience is greatly appreciated.

Wilshire Baptist Church,
Dallas, Texas

Evangelism and Visitation

VAA000 ____ Visit first-time worshiper
VAB000 ____ Telephone guests
VAC000 ____ Contact new members
VAD000 ____ Contact newcomers
VAE000 ____ Greeter
VAF000 ____ Usher on Sunday morning (men & women)
  VAF100 ____ 8:30 A.M.
  VAF200 ____ 11:00 A.M.
  VAF300 ____ Special events
VAH000 ____ Parking lot ministry

Congregational Care

VBA000 ____ Homebound ministry
VBB000 ____ Sunday morning prayer ministry
VBC000 ____ Divorce recovery workshop
VBD000 ____ Grief recovery workshop
VBE000 ____ Women's ministries
VBF000 ____ Hospital visiting
VBG000 ____ Nursing home

Outreach Ministries

VCA000 ____ Friends Who Care
VCB000 ____ Literacy program
VCC000 ____ Meals on Wheels
VCD000 ____ Sewing group
VCE000 ____ Bryan's House
VCF000 ____ Exodus ministry
VCG000 ____ Habitat for Humanity
VCH000 ____ Interfaith Housing Coalition
VCI000 ____ Stewpot
VCJ000 ____ Resource Dallas Job Finders
VCK000 ____ Klubhouse Kids

Teaching Ministry

VEA000 ____ Teach Sunday school
VEB000 ____ Substitute teacher
  VEA100 ____ babies or toddlers
  VEA200 ____ two- or three-year-olds
  VEA300 ____ four- or five-year-olds
  VEA400 ____ grades 1 and 2
  VEA500 ____ grades 3 and 4
  VEA600 ____ grades 5 and 6
  VEA700 ____ grades 7 and 8
  VEA800 ____ grades 9 and 10
  VEA900 ____ grades 11 and 12
  VEA110 ____ college
  VEA120 ____ single adults

Music Ministry

Participate in:
VJA000 ____ Sanctuary choir (adults)
  VJAA00 ____ alto
  VJAB00 ____ bass
  VJAS00 ____ soprano
  VJAT00 ____ tenor
VJB000 ____ Youth music
VJC000 ____ Handbells
VJD000 ____ Wind ensemble
VJE000 ____ Organ/piano/synthesizer
Assist in:
VJF000 ____ Preschool choir (four- and five-year-olds)
VJG000 ____ Children's choir (grades 1–6)
VJH000 ____ Music library

Activities Ministry

VKA000 ____ Drive church vans (certified driver's license needed)
  VKA100 ____ day trip
  VKA200 ____ evening trip
  VKA300 ____ other trip
VKD000 ____ Teach craft class
VKE000 ____ Teach a class in your area of expertise

Building and Property

VLA000 ____ Participate in work days at church
VLB000 ____ Maintenance and beautification of the church
VLC000 ____ Minor repairs to houses of elderly and shut-ins
VLD000 ____ Plumbing
VLE000 ____ Carpentry
VLF000 ____ Painting
VLG000 ____ Electrical
VLH000 ____ Landscaping

Sports and Recreation

VMA000 ____ Golf
VMB000 ____ Basketball
VMC000 ____ Volleyball
VMD000 ____ Softball
VME000 ____ Fishing
VMF000 ____ Bowling
VMG000 ____ Camping
VMH000 ____ Backpacking
VMI000 ____ Canoeing

Diagnosis: Ministry

Name _____ Date _____

Home Phone _____ Adult Bible Fellowship _____ ❑ Saturday ❑ Sunday

Business Phone _____ E-mail _____ Permission to: ❑ Call ❑ E-mail

Discover Your GENES

Gifts *List your top three spiritual gifts:*

1. _____ 2. _____ 3. _____

Energy

List the top two selections in each category:

Motivated: _____

People: _____

Issue: _____

Natural Abilities

List three abilities you really enjoy using:

1. _____ 2. _____ 3. _____

Experiences

List your significant life experiences (with key words) that may affect your ministry selection:

Important life experiences: _____

Ministry experiences: _____

Availability: _____ hours per week ❑ Daytime ❑ Evening ❑ Weekdays ❑ Weekends

Maturity: ❑ M1-New Believer ❑ M2-Stable Believer ❑ M3-Growing Believer ❑ M4-Leading Believer

Style *List your behavioral blend:* _____

List numbers and charts: "M" Graph: __ __ __ __   "L" Graph: __ __ __ __
                                         D I S C   D I S C

Navigate Your Opportunities

List current and/or potential ministry teams below. Please check "C" for Current Teams and "P" for Potential:

1. _____ ❑ C ❑ P Contact: _____ Ph.#: _____

2. _____ ❑ C ❑ P Contact: _____ Ph.#: _____

3. _____ ❑ C ❑ P Contact: _____ Ph.#: _____

Apply Your Faith

I will commit to . . .

◆ find or affirm my place of ministry at Lake Pointe according to how God has designed me through my GENES.

◆ demonstrate a servant's heart by being available to serve when the body of Christ needs me, regardless of ministry fit.

◆ work with other ministries to build up the entire church.

◆ take advantage of opportunities offered by the church leadership to become better equipped to serve.

_____
Signature

S.T.E.P.P
Into
Ministry

Date: _____

Your Name: _____

Address: _____

City: _____

State: _____ Zip: _____

Home Phone: _____ Work Phone: _____

Place of Employment: _____

Occupation: _____

Using Your . . .

Spiritual Gifts
Time and Availability
Experiences
Personal Style
Passion

Spiritual Gifts

"Now about spiritual gifts, brothers, I do not want you to be ignorant"
(1 Corinthians 12:1).

From the results of the spiritual gifts graph, the spiritual gifts I seem to have are

1. _____ 2. _____ 3. _____

Please check the answer that seems to most accurately state your thinking:

This information ❑ confirms what I have thought.
❑ is different from what I have thought in the past.
❑ I have no previous information or impressions about my spiritual gifts.

Time and Availability

I am available for volunteer ministry involvement:

❑ Sundays ❑ Mondays ❑ Tuesdays ❑ Wednesdays ❑ Thursdays ❑ Fridays ❑ Saturdays
❑ Mornings ❑ Afternoons ❑ Evenings . . . are better for me

I am usually available ❑ year-round ❑ only at these times of the year _____

My schedule ❑ is fairly regular
❑ changes often

The following must be considered when I think about becoming involved in volunteer ministry opportunities:
(Please tell of any schedule or physical limitations.)

_____

_____

Experiences and Abilities

EXPERIENCES

A. Spiritual Experiences

   1. I see myself as

      ❑ a new Christian.
      ❑ growing toward maturity in my faith.
      ❑ a mature believer.

   2. This is how and when I became a Christian and what it has meant to me since then:

      _____

      _____

B. Educational Experiences

     This is what I might bring to volunteer ministry involvement from my education:

      _____

      _____

C. Employment Experiences

   1. My current vocation is _____

   2. This is what I might bring to volunteer ministry involvement from this or past work experience:

      _____

      _____

D. Volunteer and Ministry Experiences

     I have served in the following volunteer and or ministry positions:

Organization or Church Name	Position Held	Length of Time Involved

ABILITIES

Using the following list as an "idea base," in the space below tell what abilities you have that you enjoy using. Feel free to write ones that are not on the list.

Abilities and skills in which I have experience and that I enjoy using are:

_____

_____

_____

_____

EXAMPLES OF ABILITIES/SKILLS

1. *Entertaining:* to perform, act, dance, sing
2. *Recruiting:* to enlist and motivate people to become involved
3. *Interviewing:* to discover what others really like
4. *Researching:* to read, gather information, collect data
5. *Artistic:* to conceptualize, draw, paint, photograph
6. *Artistic:* to lay out, design, create visual displays or banners
7. *Evaluating:* to analyze data and draw conclusions
8. *Managing:* to supervise people to accomplish a task or event and coordinate details
9. *Teaching:* to explain, train, demonstrate, tutor
10. *Writing:* to compose articles, letters, or books
11. *Promoting:* to advertise or promote events and activities
12. *Repairing:* to fix, restore, and maintain
13. *Feeding:* to create meals for large and small groups
14. *Mechanical operating:* to operate tools, equipment, or machinery
15. *Resourcing:* to search out and find inexpensive materials or needed resources
16. *Counting:* to work with numbers, data, or money
17. *Classifying:* to systematize and file books, data, or records so they can be easily retrieved
18. *Computer:* to enter data, do word processing
19. *Computer Web site:* to create or update
20. *Welcoming:* to convey warmth and make others feel comfortable
21. *Composing:* to write music or lyrics
22. *Decorating:* to beautify a setting, possibly for a special event
23. *Landscaping:* to do gardening and work with plants
24. *Sports:* to play or coach a sport. Name the sport: _____
25. *Speaking to a group*
26. *Acquire:* to shop, collect, or obtain things, getting the highest quality for the price

Personal Style

Your "personal style" is the way in which you are the most comfortable being involved in ministry. Your preferred style may be to take charge and make decisions for a group. It may be inspiring and enthusiastic, steady and stable, or competent and compliant. More than likely it is a combination of these traits. Whatever your preferred personal style, it is important to remember that just as all spiritual gifts are needed, all personality styles are created by God. None is more important or better than the others. Just as our spiritual gifts are to be controlled by the Holy Spirit, so our personality and behavior are to be submitted to God's control.

From the results of the Natural Giftedness "M" graph, the highest letter points are _____ and _____.
(Some people have a third high point on the graph. If that is true for you, what is that letter point? _____)

From the results of the Natural Giftedness "L" graph, the highest letter points are _____ and _____.
(Some people have a third high point on the graph. If that is true for you, what is that letter point? _____)

In the "Discover Your Giftedness" booklet I have read the explanatory information.
This information (❑ was) (❑ was not) clear and understandable.

       ❑ I agree with the results.
       ❑ I disagree with the results.
       ❑ I'm not sure I agree or disagree.
       ❑ I'd like to talk more about the results

Passion

*"Delight yourself in the LORD and he will give
you the desires of your heart"* (Psalm 37:4).

Your "passion" in ministry consists of those areas of ministry that motivate or pull you toward involvement. These are *not* the "shoulds"; rather, they are the areas you'd choose if you weren't limited by anything and knew you couldn't fail.

Use the following list to start your thinking:

I love to . . .
  1. *design/develop:* make something out of nothing or get something from scratch
  2. *pioneer:* test and try out new concepts; be unafraid to risk failure
  3. *organize:* bring order out of chaos or keep something going once it is started
  4. *serve/help:* assist others in their responsibility; help them succeed
  5. *improve:* make things better; improve what has already been started or developed
  6. *lead/be in charge:* lead the way, and oversee and supervise; determine how things will be done

The age group(s) I prefer to work with is

❑ Infants (age 0–1)   ❑ Junior highs   ❑ Adults
❑ Toddlers (2–3)   ❑ Senior highs   ❑ Single adults
❑ Preschool (3–5)   ❑ College   ❑ Senior citizens
❑ Children (elementary)   ❑ Young marrieds

Special groups I feel drawn to work with are

❑ Homebound   ❑ Incarcerated   ❑ Missionary families
❑ Nursing home   ❑ New believers   ❑ Families of incarcerated
❑ Impoverished   ❑ Physically challenged

What I have a passion to do or what motivates me is

1. _____

2. _____

3. _____

Asbury issues, ministries, or possible needs that excite or concern me most are

1. _____

2. _____

3. _____

– 5 –

Asbury United Methodist Church, Tulsa, Oklahoma

MATCHING AND PLACEMENT: CHURCH CONNECTIONS

THIS IS WHERE what has been learned about the people and what is known about the church's ministries are matched in such a way that effective placement in ministry service occurs.

One of the most exciting parts of leading equipping ministry is the opportunity to connect the gifts of the Spirit with the work of building up the body of Christ. It is only as we help a person identify his or her gifts and release him or her in service that we can help to create the transforming Spirit-filled community that is the church. As we connect people to ministry opportunities, we allow our collective evangelistic lights to shine before all people in glory to the Father.

In order for this to happen, there are bridges that need to be built and systems that need to be developed to manage the connections between gifted people and ministry opportunities that need those very same gifts.

Effective communication and information-tracking systems are essential to the ongoing success of connections between people and ministries. Some examples of these tracking documents are included in this section.

Developing the Connection Process

As an equipping ministry team, it is your job to create a process that connects people with ministry opportunities. Systems build the bridges that make the connections possible. Yet it takes time, patience, and meaningful participation to build effective bridges. If you want staff members and key leaders to buy into the equipping ministry system, they will need to participate in its development.

Review the five steps below for developing a process and preparing leaders to involve people in ministry opportunities.

1. *Work through the rest of this chapter* to develop a feel for the process involved in connecting people to ministry opportunities.

2. *Create a team of staff members and ministry leaders* to help you develop a connecting process that meets the needs of your congregation. Remember the acronym "KIS"—keep it simple. Develop the least complex process possible. Review your process periodically to revise and refine it. Make it easy for people to connect.

CHECKPOINT

To what degree do you prepare the individual to take the initiative for his or her own placement through . . .

- new-member classes—invitations to visit any area of ministry?
- newsletters?
- gifts-education sessions or seminars?

Caution: Placement should never be the sole responsibility of the individual. Only 8 percent of the population are self-initiators by nature, according to Myers-Briggs statistics.

> For as in one body we have many members, and all the members do not have the same function, so we, though many, are one body in Christ, and individually members one of another. Having gifts that differ according to the grace given to us, let us use them: if prophecy, in proportion to our faith; if service, in our serving; he who teaches, in his teaching; he who exhorts, in his exhortation, he who contributes, in liberality; he who gives aid, with zeal; he who does acts of mercy, with cheerfulness.
>
> ROMANS 12:4–8 RSV

"One of the most common excuses people give for not getting involved in ministry is that they just don't have the abilities to offer. Nothing could be further from the truth: Many national studies have proven that the average person possesses from five hundred to seven hundred skills! The real problem is twofold. First, people need some process of skill identification. Most people are using abilities that they are unaware that they have. Second, they need a process to help them match their abilities with the right ministry."

Rick Warren,
The Purpose-Driven Church

BUILDERS' NOTE

The processes described in this section reflect an ideal model. In reality, your process will be somewhat different from the design suggested. For smaller churches, much of your connecting work will occur over the phone and in the hallways. In this case, you may want to extract ideas and management systems to help you organize your work and keep track of requests and recommendations. Larger churches will benefit from the more structured process outlined here; however, they may need to move into the process gradually in order to gain staff acceptance and the support of key leaders. In any case, adapt this material to the needs, the culture, and the special concerns of your church.

Independent Sector, 1999: 90 percent of individuals volunteered when asked; only 20.3 percent volunteered without being asked—roughly a 4:1 ratio.

The Highly Qualified Person

Some members may come with exceptional skills and abilities. While these persons are a blessing, they can pose a few challenges. A department head or ministry leader may want time to get to know the person better before directing him or her to a position commensurate with his or her skills and abilities. Another person may be in line for the position the highly qualified member seeks. The ministry leader may feel threatened by the member's skills and resist involving him or her in the ministry area.

When challenged with the placement of a highly skilled, energetic, and capable person, prepare the person's way thoughtfully and thoroughly. You may want to involve your senior pastor or equipping ministry team in your deliberations. Explore the best possible placement for the person before initiating a follow-up interview sequence. Explore new opportunities that the person may be called to begin.

Remember, truly capable people are in demand. If there is no suitable ministry in the church (for whatever reason), consider community service options or new leadership positions where their skills and abilities will be utilized and appreciated. These people are a gift to your church.

3. *Prepare staff members and ministry leaders* (especially ministry connectors, see chapter 11) to receive people. Utilize training programs that prepare leaders to . . .

• understand the connection process and the leader's responsibility to notify you when a match is not made so that you can connect the person elsewhere in service.
• conduct meaningful interviews with people, discerning both the needs and abilities of the person and the requirements and expectations of the position.
• use the ministry descriptions as a tool for training and for inviting into ministry.
• invite people to serve in ministry.

4. *Prepare the congregation to serve.* Promoting ministry opportunities must be an ongoing process that extends well beyond interviews and new-member classes. As the director of equipping ministry, it is your job to orchestrate an ongoing campaign that alerts all people to their giftedness and the opportunities available for service. Involve your equipping ministry team in organizing and developing a creative year-round invitation campaign.

Be sure to work with the pastoral staff and key leaders to continually lift up the vision of an active people who are living out their faith in service. Promote service opportunities by emphasizing their importance in the life and work of the church, the impact on those they serve, and the opportunity to grow through caring and serving. There are several ways to promote and describe the connection process and service opportunities:

• newsletters
• various group meetings and fellowship gatherings
• announcements in worship or celebration services and Sunday school classes
• attractive bulletin board displays
• Sunday school classes, Wednesday night programs, gifts-assessment programs
• new-member classes and assimilation programs
• small group ministry experiences

Celebrate people in service on a regular basis by . . .

• commissioning people for service.
• praying by name for people who serve.
• preaching about service, stewardship, and faith development through service.
• recognizing in creative and meaningful ways people who serve.

Involve all ages and groups in service by . . .

• providing family service opportunities.
• sponsoring field trips and projects for youngsters.
• offering service experiences and trips for teens.
• developing service and fellowship events for singles.
• alerting seniors to new ways to contribute.
• recognizing service as a career exploration tool for those in transition.

Shown on pages 303–309 are examples of what some churches do to announce their ministry opportunities and connections process.

5. *Continually fine-tune your connections process.* On pages 310–21 are examples of models and tools various churches have used to ensure a seamless, effective connection process. Be sure to select a connection process that is consistent with your church culture. In smaller churches, or when an equipping ministry system is just getting underway, much of this work occurs over the phone or through informal conversation. Your role as director is to develop a system to keep track of requests, to secure sufficient information in order to respond, and to keep your work current.

BUILDERS' NOTE

The ultimate goal of the connection process, regardless of how your particular church creates and implements the system, is to facilitate gift-based ministry. Your job is to help match the unique gifts, skills, talents, abilities, passion, and temperament of the member to the ministry opportunity that will best utilize the gifts of that person. This is not about filling slots; the process is about growing people and helping them to perceive and realize God's plan for them.

The Mismatch

When you prepare staff members and leaders to work with people in ministry capacities, be sure they know how to redirect people back to the equipping ministry office if the match is not appropriate for all concerned. Again, ministry connectors are key for making this process work smoothly. Sometimes the position may not be what the person expected, schedules may conflict, personality styles may clash, or timing simply may not be right. Just because a connection isn't perfect doesn't mean anyone is a failure; it simply means the right ministry position hasn't been found. Advise your ministry leaders to direct people back to your office graciously, without damaging the person's ego or communicating a sense of failure. There is a place for everyone in the body of Christ.

Delicately ... So Delicately

Connecting a person to ministry sounds so easy—even pleasant. You have been eager to arrive at this part of the job. Then why is it that people seem to be wounded so easily through their involvement with the church? We all know the stories—

- Mary Jones offered to help in the nursery, but no one called. You haven't seen Mary for weeks now.
- Jim Albertsen, an active member serving on several committees, was offended when the men's morning prayer group called and reprimanded him for missing several meetings. Jim is considering looking for another church.
- The Jacksons aren't happy with the youth pastor; they're church hunting, but the youth pastor doesn't have a clue that something is wrong.

As you start connecting people to ministry experiences, you will quickly learn of many problems in the church. Although some may seem more significant than others, remember that each problem is very real to the person who shares his or her story with you.

There are no easy answers to these kinds of problems, but a genuinely sympathetic listening ear often goes a long way to solving a problem. We all want to feel significant, needed, and appreciated—especially in our church home. You, and all who work with you, are ministers. It is your job ...

- to listen.
- to respond thoughtfully.
- not to take sides, but to seek resolution.
- not to "fix" problems, but to give guidance and offer support.
- to pray.
- to seek counsel from other church leaders.
- to speak honestly and with fairness in each situation.
- to work with ministry leaders, sharing with them the impact their actions have on others.
- to remain sensitive.
- to work for unity in the body of Christ.

Your job won't always be easy, but it will be gratifying and vitally important to the life of the church.

The Invitation to Ministry

It is the responsibility of the requester—senior pastor, chairperson of your board of trustees, Sunday school teacher requesting an aide, whomever it may be—to ensure that an effective invitation is extended as soon as possible to the person referred to them.

In evaluating ministry invitations, be sure to ask the who, when, what, and how questions:

Who?

Be sure you are the right person to extend the invitation. The right person is someone who . . .

- has an accurate understanding of the ministry area and the most enthusiasm for the ministry.
- knows the availability of training and support, scheduling, and growth opportunities.
- has had good experiences while serving in ministry.
- is a good communicator.
- values the process of helping people make satisfying connections in the church.
- exhibits joy in serving.

When?

Ideally, people should be invited to a ministry opportunity well in advance of the requested time frame. If you must ask someone at the last minute, be candid. Let him or her know that it's not the church's regular practice to ask people to consider an invitation into ministry on such short notice.

Be sure to consider the schedule of the person you're calling:

- Seniors likely don't want to be called after 8:00 P.M.
- Families with young children don't want to be called at mealtimes or bedtimes.
- Singles generally won't be available during the day.

Remember the "courtesy factor" as well. We are in the business of ministry. Whether you phone a person or initiate a conversation face-to-face, determine if it is a good time to talk; if not, schedule a time when you can visit with each other. During your conversation, you will have an opportunity to learn about what is happening in the other person's life. You can abort your invitation request if you sense that the person is experiencing trying times. If the timing and the request are right, most people desire the opportunity to serve.

What?

People should be asked to prayerfully consider an invitation to serve in a specific area of ministry. Do all you can to be prepared. Know the gifts, knowledge base, and time necessary for this ministry. Understand and communicate why this ministry is necessary. Use ministry descriptions to explain . . .

- specific areas of responsibility.
- specific periods of time.

- the people who have served in this area who could be a resource.
- the nature of the training that would be provided.
- the kind of orientation provided for new leaders.

Be realistic with your expectations. A newly retired person may need a flexible schedule. Asking a fifteen-year-old to make a year's commitment is the equivalent of asking a forty-five-year-old for three years of service. A divorced parent searching for a family ministry opportunity may need an alternating weekend schedule.

How?

- *Personalize your invitation.* Why do you want the particular person you are inviting? What makes this person right for this ministry? Talk about how this opportunity will meet an important need he or she may have expressed, or will provide an opportunity for involvement, or will offer a chance to give something back to the church.
- *Think about how the invitation will sound to the prospective minister.* Ask positively and enthusiastically. Don't apologize for the position, distort the facts, or ask negatively ("you don't want to, do you?" or "you're the last person on my list—would you . . . ?"). And don't beg.
- *Be enthusiastic.* Your best inviter values the work of the church and genuinely and joyfully supports this ministry effort. Remember, enthusiasm is contagious.
- *Bring closure to the conversation.* A person may want to pray about the request or may need to consult with family members or clarify a work schedule. Agree on a time when you will complete the discussion and hear the person's decision.
- *Follow up quickly.* If the person is willing to serve, be sure that the necessary orientation or training is readily available. Introduce the people to others so that newcomers to a ministry feel welcome and included.
- *Accept a "no" answer graciously.* The time and situation may not allow a member to accept a ministry opportunity, even one that seems perfect for the individual. If the person does decline the invitation, try to capture the reason. Is the request outside of his or her area of giftedness? Has a personal crisis caused the person to say no? Is the particular ministry too similar to what goes on in the person's workday to be enjoyable? Gift-based ministry is about joy in service; it is about unleashing a person's talents. Your job is to find the area that best uses the person's skills and accommodates his or her life situation. Allow a person the opportunity to serve at another time or in another way. Feel free to redirect him or her back to the equipping ministry office if the fit just isn't there. There is a place for everyone in the body of Christ, but careful discernment is required to make the most appropriate match for all concerned.

How to Fly A Kite
Remember the fun of kite flying?

From your friends in Lay Ministry　　　　　May, 2000

Yo-Yo Champ Becomes Kite-Flying Expert

Not only is **John Huffman** a yo-yo champ, but after taking the lay ministry discovery class he has some reflections on kite flying. Here are John's three points for kite flying:

1. If you let go of the string, the kite will go out of control and fall down.
2. If there's no wind and you find yourself running in circles, get a friend to help.
3. The purpose of kite flying is to see how high and how far the kite can go.

FOUR KITE FLYING TIPS

TIP #1
Consider the shape of your kite.
They come in all shapes and sizes. Some kites are simple and some are more complicated.

Ministry translation: God has given you spiritual gifts. Do you know what yours are? Spiritual gifts are divine abilities distributed by the Holy Spirit to every believer—according to God's design and grace for the common good of the body of Christ.

Location, Location, Location!

It's important in kite flying to avoid power poles and trees that are too high to climb. The wind is key to successful kite flying.

TIP #2

Ministry translation: Knowing where to serve is important. God gives each of us a part of his heart, which we call passion. Passion is the desire that compels us to make a difference in a particular area of ministry. The Holy Spirit (wind) is key to successful ministry.

TIP #3

The key to kite flying is catching the wind.

Some prefer running along a stretch of beach or heading for a windy bluff. Do you like flying solo, or do you prefer flying kites with a group? The point is—what's **your** preference?

Tip #3 continued . . .

Ministry translation: We've all been gifted with different personal styles, and the good news is that there's no right or wrong personal style. What's your style?

TIP #4

Go for it!

Spring is here. Let's go kite flying. It's time to go for it. Let all your string out . . . it's the only way to reach the clouds.

Ministry translation: Experience the joy of doing ministry with others. Make this the year you get connected, challenged . . . and involved.

Remember?

Remember the last scene in Mary Poppins? **Everyone** was flying their kite. They were enjoying the moment, which is God's reward!

You're invited . . .
Lay Ministry Kickoff
"Let Your Gifts Soar"
Come and see what all the excitement is about . . .
May 20 and 21
(at the worship services)
Curious? We hope so! Call for the inside scoop.

CALVIE'S CLASSIFIEDS

To volunteer, call Calvie Hughson Schwalm. See Roto-Rack on the Plaza every Sunday for a complete listing.

RHS Institute Helpers
(Gifts: Leadership, Service, Helps, Encouragement, Wisdom)
We need you to help with this year's Robert H. Schuller Institute for Successful Church Leadership. Assorted skills needed:  professional phone skills, 35-wpm typing using WP 5.1, packet assembly, registration, security, meeting, greeting, giving directions, being an encourager. Call today to see how you can help, January 1–30.

Many volunteers needed for 1/26 - 30 event

Music Librarian
(Gifts: Helps, Service)
Help the music librarian get organized in the new year. He needs your help to re-file and maintain his music library. Need to have some knowledge of musical instruments ... very basic. Start immediately by calling the volunteer office for further details.

Community Outreach Opportunities
(Gifts: All needed)
- *Wycliffe Associates*—Needs lay workers to assist accounting, communications, and computer systems departments. Know UNIX system administration, or Oracle database programming (SQL), or consultant for PC network. Also need warehouse manager, receptionist, construction workers for building mission housing.
- *Habitat food service helpers*—Help feed the Lord's workers by bringing ice, fruit juice, water, cookies, sandwiches, veggies to workers on Saturdays. Locations in Huntington Beach and Irvine. Call Calvie for more info.
- *Feeding disadvantaged and homeless*—Help on the fourth Thursday and Friday of each month with the "Food in the Afternoon" program. Times: Thursday 12:00–1:30 P.M. and Friday 1:30–3:00 P.M.

Sunday Greeters
(Gifts: Hospitality, Service)
In the new year exercise your gifts of hospitality! Are  you an extroverted, sunny, warm person who loves to make people feel at home, whether at church or in your home? If you can say "yes," we want you to sign up for one Sunday per month to greet at the doors

of the Crystal Cathedral prior to the service you attend on the same Sunday each month. Seeking energetic people, aged 17–60, once a month for twelve months.

Tower 11 Office Helper
(Gifts: Service, Helps, Leadership)
Varied assignments in a busy office with laughter, fun, and interesting work (including data input/typing—training by Calvie) using WP 5.1, and receptionist and phone skills. One half day each week on Wednesdays, Thursdays, or Fridays. Start out your new year in service to our Lord.

Blood Drive Workers
(Gifts: Service, Encouragement)
 Sign on to help sign up members and visitors to donate blood at our annual Red Cross blood drive in March. If you are a registered nurse, we need your help on the day of the drive to greet people and work at the cookie and juice table where donors sit after giving blood. Call today to get involved.

At-Home Phone Volunteer
(Gifts: Helps, Service, Encouragement)
We schedule interviews with all new members to learn more about them and help them become involved in our church. Be our "new-member interview scheduling person" on Monday evenings and report results to Volunteer Office on Tuesday mornings. A scheduling calendar will be provided.

Tenth-Floor Input Helper
(Gifts: Service, Helps)
Help by doing computer input of names, addresses, and so forth on the tenth floor of the Tower of Hope. This will be great help for the upcoming Caregivers Conference in March. Choose your days and hours. Short-term assignment.

Bible Study Leader
(Gifts: Evangelism, Teaching, Encouragement)
Do you have a heart for the elderly? Leisure Court is seeking a Bible study leader to minister to older adults on Sundays at 1:00 P.M. for forty-five minutes. Please call the volunteer office to meet with Calvie regarding this assignment.

Crystal Cathedral, Garden Grove, California

Gifts in *Action!*

First Presbyterian Church,
San Antonio, Texas
Volume 2—Issue 7,
November 17, 1998

"I don't know what your destiny will be, but one thing I know: the only ones among you who will be truly happy are those who will have sought and found how to serve."—Albert Schweitzer

This issue: Christmas Gifts that make a difference!

Gifts in *Action!* *is an outreach of our lay ministries program to empower each member of FPC to recognize and use their gifts.*

Lay Ministries is . . .

"It is more blessed to give than to receive" (Acts 20:35).

It is our commitment as members to serve and to encourage others to use their gifts as they serve.

Your lay ministries team actively encourages you to identify your gifts and to use your time and talents in ministry. This insert informs you about avenues for service in our church and community.

Is serving the Lord a "job" or a "ministry"?

Some people have a job in the church; others involve themselves in a *ministry.* What's the difference?

- If you're doing it just because no one else will, it's a job. If you're doing it to serve the Lord, it's a ministry.

- If you're doing it just well enough to get by, it's a job. If you do it to the best of your ability, it's a ministry.

- If you do it as long as it doesn't interfere with your other activities, it's a job. If you are committed to staying with it even when it means letting go of other things, it's a ministry.

- If you do it because someone else said it needs to be done, it's a job. If you do it because *you* think it needs to be done, it's a ministry.

- People will say, "Well done," when you finish a job. The Lord will say, "Well done," when you complete your ministry.

An average church is filled with people doing a job. A great and growing church is filled with people who are involved in a ministry!

Gift Opportunities

On any Sunday . . .

Worship is an activity. We invite God to talk to us. He talks. We listen and respond. In any given worship service, there are many members of the congregation who help each of us prepare to worship Almighty God. How are these assistants chosen? They *ask* for the opportunity to serve. You can be an assistant. Consider the following list of tasks that are done to prepare worship at First Presbyterian Church, San Antonio:

Ushers

Caregivers for small children whose parents are in worship

Communion service preparation

Choir members

Instrumentalists and soloists

Flower arrangers for members in hospitals

Greeters at the Avenue E entrance

Greeters at the Alamo Street entrance

Receptionist

Fellowship hour hosts

Cookie bakers

Bridge Sunday cooks and servers (breakfast for those in need under the expressway)

Loaves and Fishes cooks and servers (dinner for those in need)

Bread bakers and deliverers to visitors

Church attendance recorders

Car parkers

Sound booth monitors

Sermon tape duplicators

YELLOW PAGES

The Chapel

Ministry	Ext
A	
Adult Bible Fellowships (ABFs)	3078
ACMC	3801
Adult ministries (our philosophy)	3800
Aerobics (women)	3085
Allies	3803
Anniversary receptions	3151
B	
Baby dedications	3058
Backpacking (youth)	5444
BAPTISM	
• Adult	3120
• Children	3323
BIBLE STUDIES	
• Essentials	3338
• Men (Quarterback Club)	3053
• Women	3084
• Junior High (Breathe Deep)	3081
Birth announcements	3120
Building maintenance, properties, and supplies	3800
C	
CAMP CARL	3322
College ministry (campus focus)	3120
CAPS (Chapel adult program for seniors)	3120
Chapel Business Breakfast	3053
Chapel Christian Study Center	3054
CHAPEL NEWS	
• General Information	3060
• Mailing list	3166
Chapel Productions	3102
CHILDREN'S MINISTRY	3323
• Camp Carl	3322
• Children's bulletin	3323
• Club programs (Pioneer Girls, Brigade Boys, Space Cubs)	3323
• Kids of the Kingdom (choir)	3323
• Policies	3321
• Sunday school (birth–grade 6)	3323
• Vacation Bible School	3321
• Winter Weekends	3323
• Workers and teachers	3321
Chinese Church	4858
CHOIR	
• Adult	3101
• Children (Kids of the Kingdom)	3323
• Handbell choir	3106
• Junior High choir	3401
• Senior High choir	3401
Christian faith (fundamentals)	3330
Christians Involved	3801
Communion	3120
Computers	3421
Contagious Christians	3330
COUNSELING	
• Adult, couple, and family	3058
• Children	3323
• Financial	3058
• Premarital	3050
• Training	3058
D	
Deacons	3120
Deaths	3120
Disability ministry	3321
DISCIPLESHIP	3330
Divorce Recovery	3338
Drama ministry	3102
E	
Emergencies (church-related)	3800
Employment (support staff)	3150
English language classes	3338
Essentials	3338
EVANGELISM	
• Contagious Christian studies	3330
• Saltshakers	3330
F	
FAMILY LIFE	3060
FAX for Living	3166
FINANCE	
• Contribution info. and statements	3322
• Financial assistance	3120
• Sales tax exemption	3163
• Memorials	3161
• Tithe envelopes	3166
Firm Foundation	3338
First Call	1427
Flowers (pulpit)	3150
Food closet	3150
Food service for events	3120
Funerals	3120
G	
God's StoryLine	3330
Greeters	3800
Guest reception	3800
H	
Harvest Room counselors	3330
Homosexuality support group	3058
Hospital visitation	3120
I	
Information Center hosts	4913
INTERNATIONAL STUDENTS MINISTRY	
• General information	3803
• Friendship Partners	3803
• Friday night dinners	3803
• Furniture needs and donations	3338
Internship program	3400
J	
Job Seekers	3150
Just Me & the Kids	3058
L	
Labor of Love Run	9078
Library	3303
Life skills course	3058
M	
M.A.R. program	3054
MARRIAGE	
• Marriage classes	3058
• Marriage Enjoyment weekends	3058
• Mentoring Couples	3050
Membership class	3301
MEN'S MINISTRY	
• New Men ministries	3058
• Promise Keepers	3338
Military ministry	3800
MINISTRY SERVICES	3801
MISSIONS	
• Local/national	3330
• Medical Missions Team	3956
• Missionary support	3801
• Muslim Outreach	3801
• Short-term trips	3079
• Youth missions	
Grade 9 - Andrew	3401
Grade 10 - Barnabas	3401
Grade 11 - Cephas	3401
Grade 12 - Doulos	3401
Monday Morning Men	3917
Mothers' Club	9932
Music	3102
N	
NewComers Orientation	3330
O	
Orchestra	3106
P	
Parenting courses	3058
Pastors "on duty"	3120
Pastor's Prayer Partners (men only)	3053
Personnel	3800
Perspectives on the World	3801
Policies	3800
Prayer requests	3120
Printing guidelines	3060
Prime Time	3301
Prison ministry	3801
PROCLAMATION	3053
R	
Racial reconciliation	3803
Radio "spots"	3051
Real Life	3338
Refugee ministry	3801
S	
Saltshakers	3330
School of Fine Arts	3106
Security	3800
Seminary studies	3054
Shut-ins ministry	3120
Sign language interpretation	3101
SINGLES	3338
Singles Plus (45+)	3058
SINGLE PARENTS	
• Just Me & the Kids	3058
• Parenting Solo	3077
Small groups	3112
Social issues and action	3801
SPORTS (adult)	3085
• College basketball or "3 on 3"	3338
• Men's basketball league	3085
• Men's noon basketball (M & Th)	3401
• Golf league	3917
• Softball	4527
• Volleyball (adult coed)	3085
Sunday school (birth–grade 6)	3323
Super Monday	3053
SUPPORT GROUPS	
• A.D.D.	3323
• Aging parents	3120
• Cancer	3120
• Chronic fatigue syndrome	3120
• Fibromyalgia	3120
• Genesis support group	3058
• Genesis hotline	3952
• Grief support group	3120
• More Than Conquerors	3058
• Widows and Widowers	3120
• Women	3058
T	
Table Talk	3330
• Reservations	1190
Tapes (music or sermon)	3111
Trinity Evangelical Divinity School	3054
Trustees	3051
TV "minute spots"	3051
TNT (Thursday Night Thing)	3802
U	
Ushers	3800
V	
Vacation Bible School	3321
Video production	3101
Vietnamese Church	2077
Volunteering	3400
W	
Web site	3401
Wednesday Night Connections	3800
Weddings	3050
"Witness Stand"	3501
WOMEN'S MINISTRIES	3084
• Bible studies	3084
• Mothers' Club	9932
• Precept Ministries	3084
Workers for Christ	3801
WORSHIP/MUSIC	3102
• Banner ministry	3102
• Concerts	3102
• Music lessons	3106
• Slides	3101

Excerpted from The Chapel's Yellow Pages (omitting Youth Ministry entries)

The Chapel, Akron, Ohio

The Chapel,
Akron, Ohio

CHAPEL CLASSIFIEDS

Help Wanted

INFORMATION CENTER HOSTS

Our Information Centers need more people who want to make The Chapel a friendly, helpful place to visit. Training is provided and plenty of current information is given to help you; we just need your presence! Men and women are needed to serve at all hours on Sunday mornings, Sunday evenings, and Wednesday evenings. Good for couples, singles, or friends! Serve every week, every other week, once a month . . . we'll be glad to have you.

SUNDAY NIGHT NURSERY

The littlest Chapel attenders need your loving hands to hold and rock them! Please help parents who attend on Sunday evenings by offering to care for their babies. Weekly or monthly positions available.

CHAPEL WEB SITE MANAGERS

Do you have personal or professional experience in Web site design or management, or are you willing to learn on your own? The Chapel needs capable managers to update pages of our Web site.

COMMUNION SERVERS

Men, your help is needed for serving communion once a month during the worship service you currently attend or another service of your choice. Serving communion to fellow worshipers is a simple task but so important to worship!

JUNIOR HIGH TEACHERS

Join a growing group of people who enjoy seeing God work in the lives of young teens. Teachers and leaders are needed for junior high boys at 10:40 A.M. each Sunday.

GARDENERS

Landscape volunteers needed! If you enjoy outside gardening work in the spring and summer—planting flowers, weeding, trimming—and have an hour or two a week to offer, we need your help for one Chapel "blooming season." Hours will be flexible.

URGENT: CHILDREN'S DEPARTMENT, SUNDAY EVENINGS

We need teachers, helpers, and caregivers for all ages of children for our Sunday evening worship service and Adult Bible Fellowship times. Please help!

CHOIR MEMBERS

Help us lead the congregation in worshiping our Lord. Sing in the choir during the service you attend.

ELECTRICIANS, PLUMBERS, CARPENTERS, PAINTERS, AND AUTO MECHANICS

If you are willing to help single mothers of the Chapel neighborhood through your vital skills, we need you. We hope to share Christ's love through meeting single mothers' physical needs.

GIRLS' BASKETBALL STAFF

Help provide a way for high school girls to develop their game of basketball while learning more about Christ from their coaches, other staff, and peers at The Chapel.

ADULT BIBLE FELLOWSHIP PROMOTER

You will use your creative skills to promote our small church communities (ABFs). If you enjoy creating bulletin boards, photography, writing, or have a promotion idea of your own, your help is greatly welcome!

STRAIGHT-AHEAD MANAGER

Are you an "organizer?" This might just be for you! Assist in implementing the design, organization and management of a new cerification program of Discipleship courses to be offered to Chapel attenders. Introduce and promote the certification program in tandem with individual course/group opportunities. Design and manage attendance system for "certifying" participants. Involves 2–3 hours of time per week.

GREETERS

Please help us make The Chapel a friendly church to visit. Offer a smile and a handshake to guests as they enter. Choose to serve one or two Sundays per month at a service convenient to you.

"ESSENTIALS" LEADERS

If you have a desire to share with a newer believer how to grow in Christ, consider leading a small discipleship group: 5–8 individuals eager to learn and integrate the spiritual disciplines of the Christian life. Training provided!

Are you looking for a special ministry with your name on it, but find it has eluded you thus far? Can you describe what you are looking for, or are you not sure where to start? There are many ways to serve that don't get advertised due to space constraints. We would love to talk with you about ways to serve that suit your individual gifts, abilities, time, and interests. For more information call extension 3408.

COVENANT CONNECTIONS

*A Publication of Opportunities to
Serve and Be Served through the
Ministries of Christ Covenant Church*

Contents

Christ Covenant Church, Matthews, North Carolina

"General" Assimilation Process Flow

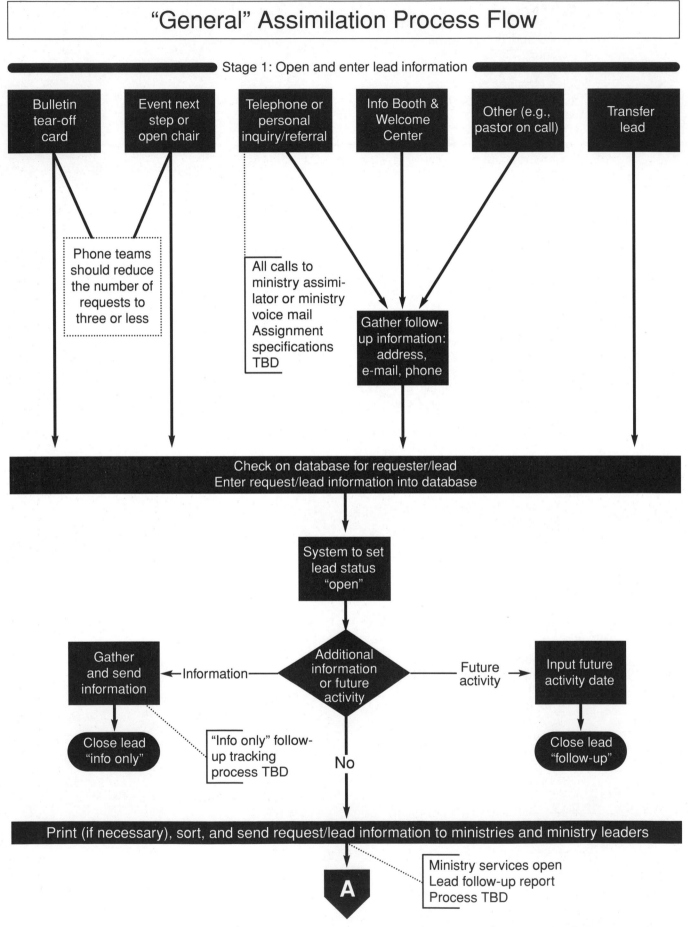

Stage 1: Open and enter lead information

| Bulletin tear-off card | Event next step or open chair | Telephone or personal inquiry/referral | Info Booth & Welcome Center | Other (e.g., pastor on call) | Transfer lead |

Phone teams should reduce the number of requests to three or less

All calls to ministry assimilator or ministry voice mail Assignment specifications TBD

Gather follow-up information: address, e-mail, phone

Check on database for requester/lead
Enter request/lead information into database

System to set lead status "open"

Additional information or future activity

Information → Gather and send information → Close lead "info only"

"Info only" follow-up tracking process TBD

Future activity → Input future activity date → Close lead "follow-up"

No

Print (if necessary), sort, and send request/lead information to ministries and ministry leaders

A

Ministry services open
Lead follow-up report
Process TBD

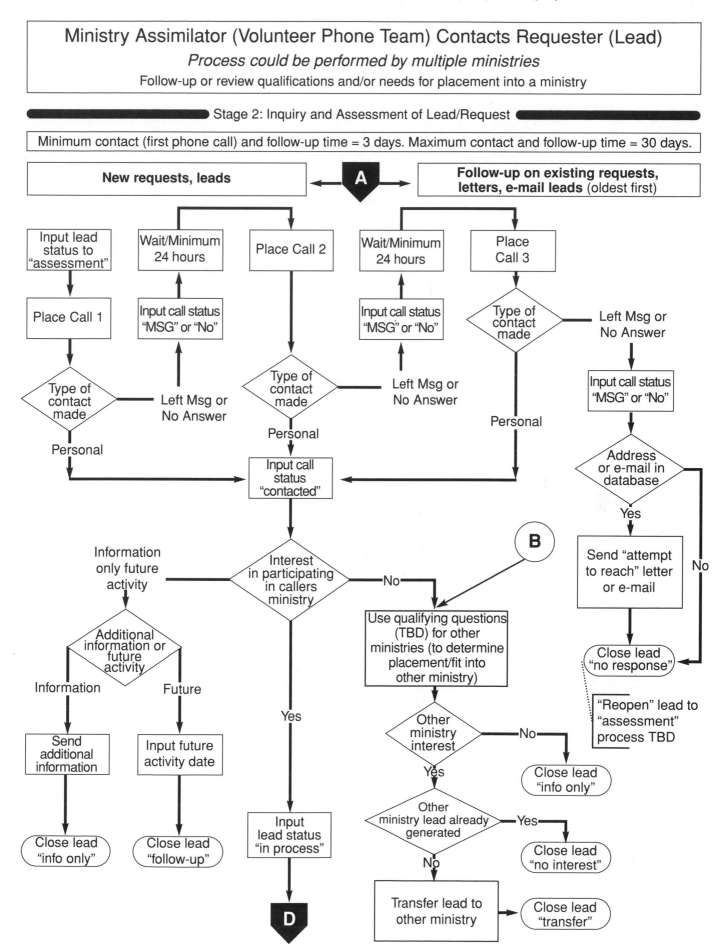

Ministry Assimilator (Volunteer Phone Team) Contacts Requester (Lead)
Process could be performed by multiple ministries
Follow-up or review qualifications and/or needs for placement into a ministry

Stage 2: Inquiry and Assessment of Lead/Request

Minimum contact (first phone call) and follow-up time = 3 days. Maximum contact and follow-up time = 30 days.

Ministry Assimilator Hands Lead/Request to Ministry Leader
Assimilator becomes pipeline manager
Monitor, track, and report on the process to "connected"

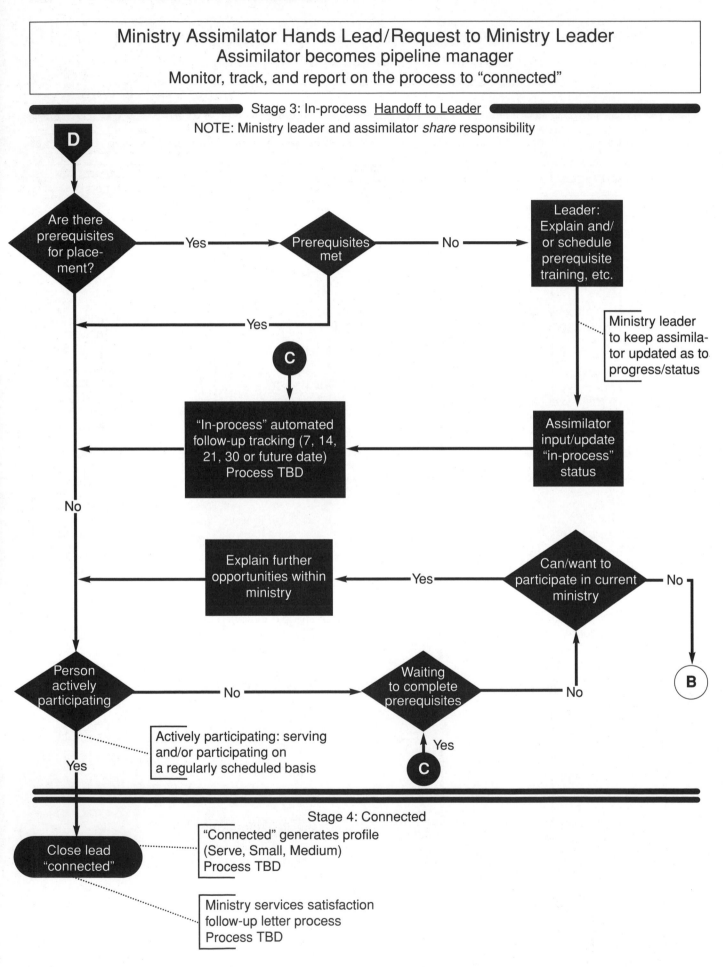

Stage 3: In-process Handoff to Leader

NOTE: Ministry leader and assimilator *share* responsibility

D

Are there prerequisites for placement? — Yes → Prerequisites met — No → Leader: Explain and/or schedule prerequisite training, etc.

Yes

C

Ministry leader to keep assimilator updated as to progress/status

"In-process" automated follow-up tracking (7, 14, 21, 30 or future date) Process TBD

Assimilator input/update "in-process" status

No

Explain further opportunities within ministry — Yes → Can/want to participate in current ministry — No → B

Person actively participating — No → Waiting to complete prerequisites — No

Actively participating: serving and/or participating on a regularly scheduled basis

Yes

C

Yes

Stage 4: Connected

Close lead "connected"

"Connected" generates profile (Serve, Small, Medium) Process TBD

Ministry services satisfaction follow-up letter process Process TBD

Definitions

Assimilation Process Stages:

Stage 1: Open and Enter Lead/Request
Stage 2: Inquiry and Assessment of Lead/Request
Stage 3: In Process
Stage 4: Connected

Lead/Request Status

Open
Assessment
In Process
Closed—by type
    Closed—Information Only
    Closed—Follow-Up
    Closed—No Response
    Closed—Transferred
    Closed—Lost Interest
    Closed—Connected

Call Status

MSG—Left voice mail or message with another person
No—No answer on number provided
Contacted—Talked to individual making request

In-Process Status

CPP1—CPP1 required—CPP2, 3, 4 status will be set by PCP module
Leader—Leadership training required
Front—Frontline training required
Driver—Driver certification required
Train—Orientation/training scheduled
Pend—Connection pending

Processes TBD ("To Be Developed"):

"Telephone inquiry"—develop list of people and extensions for *all* telephone calls to be transferred to.
"Info Only" follow-up—Process to send follow-up letter in attempt to assist those who just asked for information.
"Open Lead" tracking—Process to report leads open by stage, by ministry, assimilator and date, with aging.
"Closed Lead" tracking—Track leads by ministry and assimilator on type of closure.
"Qualifying Questions"—Questions from each ministry for all other ministries to determine other ministry placement.
"Reopen Lead"—Process to allow leads closed with "no response" to be reopened upon response to "attempt to reach" letter or e-mail.
"In-Process" tracking—Track leads that are "in process" by ministry and assimilator with aging.
"In-Process" status tracking—Track leads by ministry and assimilator by "in-process" status with aging.
"Connected" process—Connected process to automatically generate profiles without duplicate data entry.
"Ministry Services Satisfaction"—Letter to connected people to determine ministry and process satisfaction.

Ministries:

Ministries and ministry "source of lead" flags on a separate sheet.

Willow Creek Community Church
ASSIMILATION STEPS
Based on flow-chart model

STAGE 1: OPEN
- **Opportunity is mobilized and individual is moved to connect**

- **INTEREST** is generated by:
  — Telephone call (from an ad in the weekly, ministry hotline, general call)
  — E-mail, Web site, mail, fax, or walk-in to a particular ministry area
  — Information Booth/Welcome Center (general, lobby, and atrium booths)
  — Bulletin tear-off card (from weekend services, from Axis)
  — Events (open house, seminar, class, support group, target weekend, special event, ministry fair, etc.)
  — Small group/serving group
  — Staff referral or volunteer referral
  — Other (rare, random, nonrecurring situations)

- **GATHER** name, address, phone numbers, e-mail of interested person

- **INPUT** information into the database
  — Check database for individual—update if necessary
  — If not found, enter individual's information into database
  — Forward individual to ministry assimilator for action

STAGE 2: ASSESSMENT
- **PHONE CALL** made by staff or volunteer assimilation phone team
  — Call individual for brief assessment
    * First Call—made within 3 days
       Make notes about results of call—make note of date for follow-up call
       Wait at least 24 hours
    * Second Call
       Make notes about results of call—make note of date for follow-up call
       Wait at least 24 hours
    * Third Call
       Make notes about results of call
       All three calls need to be made within 30 days
  — If no response after 30 days, send "attempt to reach" letter or e-mail
    * Close lead in database as NO RESPONSE

- **PERSONAL CONTACT** is successful, there are three possible responses—
No, Maybe, Yes
  — If NO . . . not interested in your ministry
    * Use qualifying questions to determine a fit in another ministry
    * If still no interest, close entry as INFO ONLY
    * If interested in other ministry . . .
        * Transfer information to assimilator for other ministry = Transfer Assimilation
        * Close lead in database as TRANSFER
  — If MAYBE . . . might be interested in your ministry
    * Information only requested
        * Mail requested information
        * Close lead in database as INFO ONLY
    * Future event requested?
        * Input lead in database as FUTURE ACTIVITY
        * Close lead in database as FOLLOW-UP with date
  — If YES . . . person is now in the "in-process" stage
    * Update lead in database to IN PROCESS

continued on next page

STAGE 3: IN PROCESS

- **HANDOFF**—Assimilator hands off information to appropriate ministry leader
  — Automated follow-up tracking system on computer reminds the assimilator to follow up with the ministry leader
- **TRAINING** and/or prerequisites required for placement
  — If YES . . .
    * Leader explains prerequisites and schedules training
    * Leader reports progress to assimilator

  — If ALREADY MET . . .
    * Leader reports progress to assimilator

  — If NO . . .
    * Leader reports progress to assimilator
- **THE BIG QUESTION**—Is this person actively participating?
  Serving and/or participating on a regularly scheduled basis (generally once a month)
  — If YES . . .
    * Go to Stage 4—Connected
    * Close lead in database as CONNECTED

  — If NO . . .
    * Ask questions
      * Is this person waiting for something? ➛ Note follow-up date
      * Has he or she lost interest? ➛ Back to assessment stage
      * Use qualifying questions to determine other ministry interests ➛ Transfer assimilation

STAGE 4: CONNECTED

- Person is **ACTIVELY PARTICIPATING** in a small group or serving opportunity
  — Individual profile is created on computer from lead in database
  — A satisfaction follow-up letter is sent
- Person is pursuing **FULL PARTICIPATION**
  — Membership
  — The Great Commission

> "All authority in heaven and on earth has been given to me. Therefore go and make disciples of all nations, baptizing them in the name of the Father and of the Son and of the Holy Spirit, and teaching them to obey everything I have commanded you. And surely I am with you always, to the very end of the age."
>
> Matthew 28:18–20

Willow Creek Community Church, Barrington, Illinois

Lay Minister Request Form

To be completed by the requester

Requester's name: _____ Date: _____

    Ministry position of the requester: _____

    Phone number: _____ Best time to reach: _____

Ministry Positions in Need of Ministers:

1. Position: _____

    Ministry Description: ❏ attached

                               ❏ being developed—will be available by _____

                               ❏ exploratory area—see description

    Additional information: _____

    _____

2. Position: _____

    Ministry Description: ❏ attached

                               ❏ being developed—will be available by _____

                               ❏ exploratory area—see description

    Additional information: _____

    _____

Response Form

Please return a copy of this form to the lay ministry office.

Responder: _____ Date: _____

Method: ❏ Database review

            ❏ Response to advertisement in _____

            ❏ Other: _____

Position: _____

Potential Ministers:	Contact Number:	Response:
_____	_____	❏ yes ❏ no
_____	_____	❏ yes ❏ no
_____	_____	❏ yes ❏ no
_____	_____	❏ yes ❏ no

source unknown

MEMBER REFERRAL FORM

To be completed by the interviewer

_____ has been interviewed by the lay ministry program. This member has expressed interest and/or experience in your area of ministry. The member has been told that you, or a person you designate, will contact him or her to explore this ministry area in further depth.

Please return the response section of this form to the lay ministry office by _____

Name: _____   Name Called: _____

Address: _____

Date interviewed: _____

Please follow up by: _____

Phone Number: Day _____   Evening _____

Best time to call: _____

Comments: _____

_____

_____

You may request additional information about this member from the lay ministry interviewer:

Interviewer: _____

Phone #: _____   Best time to call: _____

– · –

RESPONSE FORM

Member Referred: _____   Date: _____

Ministry Area: _____   Contact Person: _____

❑ Member placed in service   Position: _____

❑ Member not placed in service   Reason: _____

❑ Other: _____

❑ Member expressed alternative interest: _____

Please return to lay ministry office

Return this response form by _____

source unknown

REFERRAL FOR PERSON SEEKING MINISTRY

Part I (to be completed by small group leader)

Date: _____

Date of Gift Discovery Class: _____ (mo./yr.)

Participant name: _____   Small group leader name: _____

Phone # day: _____   Phone # day: _____

Phone # evening: _____   Phone # evening: _____

Best time to call: _____   Best time to call: _____

Date follow-up meeting took place: _____, or
if participant declined follow-up meeting, check here: ____

PLEASE CHECK AND FILL OUT AS APPROPRIATE:

___**Option 1:** This person has expressed an interest in _____ (name of committee) and in
the following related ministry opportunities: _____

_____

_____

****If there is more than one committee of interest, please attach another paper with the
committee and the ministry opportunities listed.****

___**Option 2:** This person is not interested in pursuing a ministry opportunity at this time. Please contact him
or her at a later date (yes ___ no ___). If yes, approximate date: _____(mo./yr.)

Comments: _____

_____

Part II (to be completed by lay ministry department)

To: _____Committee   Date: _____

Ministry Liaison: _____

_____ has expressed an interest in your committee and the ministry opportunities listed
above. Please contact him or her personally, as soon as possible, to pursue this interest further. Complete the
bottom portion of this form and return this sheet to me by _____. If you have any questions or
need further information, you may call me or the small group leader listed above. Comments: _____

_____

_____

Part III (to be completed by committee liaison to lay ministries)

To: Equipping Ministries   Date of Contact: _____

From: _____   Committee: _____

The following action has been taken regarding the person referred above:

____ **Option A:** Person placed in service. Position: _____

____ **Option B:** Person placed on the "call" list for a later time (within 6 months).

____ **Option C:** Person not placed in service. Reason: _____

____ **Other:** _____

First Presbyterian Church of Bellevue, Bellevue, Washington

GRACE COMMUNITY CHURCH
"Equipping the People of God to Build the Kingdom of God"

MINISTRY REFERRAL FORM

_____ has been interviewed by a gift mobilization consultant. This individual has expressed interest and/or experience in the _____ area of ministry. This individual has been told that you, or a person you designate, will contact him or her to explore your ministry area in further depth.

Please return a ministry response form regarding this individual to the gift mobilization director's office as soon as possible.

Date: _____

Name: _____

Address: _____

Date interviewed: _____

Please follow up by _____

Phone number: Home: _____ Work: _____

Comments: _____

_____

_____

_____

_____

_____

You may request additional information about this individual from the gift mobilization consultant.

Consultant: _____

Phone #: _____

Best time to call: _____

Grace Community Church,
Greensboro, North Carolina

DISCOVERY

Joining God to Make an Eternal Difference!

MINISTRY AREA REFERRAL FORM

Date: _____

To: _____

From: _____ *DISCOVERY* Consultant

The following person is interested in serving in your area of ministry:

Name: _____ ❑ Member   ❑ Nonmember

Home Phone: _____Work Phone: _____

Other #: _____

Servant Profile:

Individual Style: _____

Area of Compassion: _____

Spiritual Gifts: _____

Position/ministry interested in: _____

_____

_____

Consultant Comments: _____

_____

_____

Other ministry areas/positions referred to: _____

_____

_____

PLEASE CONTACT THIS PERSON WITHIN 48 HOURS, AND LET THE INVOLVEMENT MINISTRY KNOW THE RESULTS OF YOUR CONVERSATION.

Date contacted: _____   By: _____

Involvement Potential: _____

_____

Comments: _____

_____

source unknown

Ministries of Care— for each other, for our resources, and for those in need

You're invited to participate in our ministries of care, responding to God's call to grow by using your gifts in an area of ministry that interests you.

Through these ministries we care for each other and for our resources, and we reach out to those beyond our parish, offering compassion, comfort, and warm acceptance.

The shared ministries in this brochure include one-time commitments and long-term opportunities, as well as opportunities to serve as a family. You are welcome and encouraged to participate. We also welcome your initiative in developing new ministries that fulfill our mission.

We appreciate your response. You—and the ministry—are important.

Name _____

Address _____

Phone: Day _____ Evening _____

Please return this form by folding and mailing, bringing it to the parish office, or placing it in the collection plate on a Sunday morning.

source unknown

MATCHING AND PLACEMENT: COMMUNITY CONNECTIONS

CHRIST COMMANDS THAT WE serve in the community (and he models for us how to do so). We must value ministry done outside the walls of the church. Community connections is one way to do this.

For some people the most appropriate ministry for their unique mix of skills, gifts, and passion will be service outside of the church. You may encounter a member whose unique set of abilities falls outside the current mission focus of the congregation. Another person may have a set of gifts and talents that would not be fully challenged through service opportunities currently available in the church. Or yet another may simply feel called to work in the community rather than within the congregation.

Whatever the set of circumstances, each of these situations represents a ministry outreach, and each person deserves the opportunity to have his or her unique contribution utilized, recognized, affirmed, and supported as a valid ministry.

As the director of equipping ministry, you and your team can support people who are seeking or carrying out alternative ministry opportunities:

- Encourage a broad base of ministry outreach. Highlight the service of people currently working in the community. Maintain a bulletin board of significant community concerns. Establish a strong network within your community's nonprofit and public sectors so that you can help people make service contacts.
- During worship, commission people who serve in the community, just as you commission people who carry out ministry within the congregation. Feature their accomplishments in bulletins, newsletters, and other recognition programs.

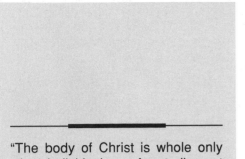

"The body of Christ is whole only when individuals are free to live out their God-given gifts without asking permission."

Bill Easum

- Maintain periodic contact with people who serve in the community. Explore how their ministry is progressing, help them consider the implications of how their service work is integral to their faith development. If the person desires to switch assignments, support this transition in the same way you would support a person who serves within the church.
- Connect the person with others in the congregation who express a similar interest. Provide mentors for their involvement if at all possible. Consider developing small ministry groups for persons who are providing similar types of ministry.
- Above all, don't stifle the creativity and involvement of people who try new things. The fact that something hasn't been done in the past or isn't part of the church's outreach or social ministry plan doesn't diminish its importance. God calls us from all walks of life to all forms of service according to his plan. As we affirm others in service, we all grow as together we spread the Good News.

Some congregations set goals for the percentage of people they hope to connect with ministry opportunities in the community. A church may seek to be a 50/50 congregation, with one person serving in the community for each person serving in the church. Other congregations establish benevolence programs and assign people, as well as dollars, to connect with organizations or groups. Whatever your goal, include "the church scattered" in your vision of equipping people for ministry.

Four Important Tasks in Making Community Connections

1. *Assess what is really needed in your community.* (Refer to volunteer agencies' needs assessments on an annual basis.) What can you be involved in? What do you want to be involved in? How can you provide resources to support what's out there? Do you have the people with the gifts to support this ministry?

Caution: Make sure the church doesn't just do what's comfortable, but that you meet the most pressing needs in the community.

2. *Affirm what people are already doing* outside of the walls of the church. Don't take it for granted that a member doing service in the community is going to connect this service with his or her personal spiritual path. Does the church show that it affirms the "whole" life of the person?

Caution: Make sure the church doesn't give the impression that she is only impressed if a person serves in a "Christian" organization. Do people want to be salt and light just with other Christians, or do they want to be salt and light in the broader community? Where can a person make the greatest difference?

3. *Validate areas of service where people are serving,* and make sure you define what people are doing as "ministry," not just "church work." Validating service outside of the church as ministry contributes to the spiritual connection and growth for the individual. For many people this is an entry point to a meaningful faith journey.

4. *Construct and develop opportunities for community service.* You can do this by modeling this value yourself as you spend some time in service in the community. Work with other ministry leaders and nonprofit leaders to create a special day of service in the community.

The Five Critical Elements of Thoughtful Service

As you begin to build bridges into the community and assist people in making ministry connections, there are key elements of community service worth considering (the following is used with permission of Don Simmons, associate professor of Christian Education at Golden Gate Baptist Theological Seminary in Mill Valley, California):

1. Orientation and Training

- The participant receives orientation about the people, the activities, and the issues that face the service site.
- The participant receives training to act effectively at the service site.
- The participant is aware of why he or she will be working at the service site, what is hoped to be accomplished, and what he or she is expected to do.
- The participant is prepared both to learn and work while at the service site.
- The participant is aware of the emotions he or she may feel doing the service, such as frustration, anger, and uncertainty.

2. Community Voice

- Community agency clients and people of the community are present and work side by side with participants.
- The agency, its staff, and its clients define what they need done as opposed to participants defining it for them.
- The agency and its staff provide supportive learning experiences for the participants.

3. Meaningful Action

- The participant accepts the challenge to participate in as many facets as the organization needs.
- At the same time, the participant understands that even seemingly unimportant or unchallenging work, such as stuffing envelopes, is extremely helpful to the organization's work and overall mission.

4. Reflection

- Participants are given opportunities to think about and discuss what they encounter at the site, what they learn (about themselves, the issues, and the like), and what future actions they can take.
- Participants may link their educational/spiritual/emotional experiences with problem solving to create solutions for root problems.

5. Evaluation

- Participants evaluate their experiences based on the ongoing goals and objectives set forth during their orientation and training.
- Participants help evaluate the overall program.

Why Do People Serve?

1. They do it because they were asked.
2. They do it because it fits with their own sense of mission.
3. They do it because they like a challenge.
4. They do it because they feel connected to God's work.
5. They don't do it for material rewards.
6. They don't do it to meet people.

Marilyn Nelson, Baptist Theological Seminary, Richmond, Virginia

---

Advantages of Church-Based Social Sector Initiatives

While not every church can be characterized as innovative and strongly supportive of social sector initiatives, there is an increasing number in every major city who are. When social sector initiatives are pursued through or in cooperation with these churches, there are some very important advantages:

1. Source of Existing Community
   People who volunteer their time want not only to make a significant impact with their life, but also to have significant relationships in the midst of their work. Healthy churches specialize in creating cultures and programs that emphasize healthy relationships.

2. Source of "Qualified" Volunteers
   There is a fast-growing movement among healthy churches to create ways for people to learn about their natural and spiritual gifts and their areas of interest and skills. With this knowledge, people are matched with appropriate service placements that fit these gifts. Social sector initiatives have a ready source of people who already know how they fit in and who are able to articulate their passion for the cause.

3. Source of Multiple Gifts
   A good social sector initiative requires a team that includes visionaries, implementers, and people who pay attention to the relationships along the way. Many healthy churches provide both the people and the understanding of what makes a healthy team.

4. Source of Ongoing Coaching and Training
   Church-sponsored training provides new skills, churchwide recognition provides avenues of appreciation, and periodic coaching provides a way for the volunteers to evaluate their contribution.

5. Source of Spirituality
   People want their experiences to have both social and spiritual impact. Churches often provide avenues for reflection to help a person understand how involvement in service is creating Christlikeness within themselves and others.

6. Source of Longevity
   Many social sector initiatives lose steam when the charismatic or entrepreneurial founder gets interested in another cause. Connection with a healthy church provides a ready source of successors and apprentices, as well as ownership of the vision from an organization that most likely will remain a strong source of leadership and commitment through many generations.

7. Source of Presence
   In a typical day in the inner city, social workers come in in the morning and return to the suburbs in the evening. Business initiatives bolt their doors at 5 P.M. What is left in the evenings and weekends are people trying to survive their difficult situations . . . and the church on the corner. Churches are always present in the neighborhood.

   Brad Smith, Leadership Network

15

Building the Equipping Ministry System: *Equip*

EQUIP IS THE THIRD of three key processes in your system. The elements of *Equip* deepen the commitment to serve and thus become one of the most important factors in retention. *Growth,* which includes training, affirmation, feedback, evaluation, and ongoing leader development, is the cornerstone of this process. To achieve the goal of whole-life ministry and spiritual development, the encouragement of faith in action is achieved through effective *recognition* and the provision of *reflection* opportunities.

Service involves commitment. People at all levels need to grow in their faith and come to understand the relationship between word and action. Serving God and others by using God-given gifts is the fuel of faith. Like Abraham, many of us have faith (see Galatians 3:6–9). Faith is informed and shaped by the educational programs of the church. But it is Abraham's and our *actions*—the choices in the trials of life, the places of service, and the sacrifices we make for others—that cause faith to grow (see Hebrews 11:8–12).

As people commit to serve, they need the assurance that the church is working with them as they venture into ministry. As the equipping ministry director and team, it is your job to work with staff members and other church leaders and help them grow to understand their role in supporting and affirming people in service. Each of us needs to know that our efforts are appreciated and that we are valued for the ministry we share in Christ. Likewise, informed and effective ministry requires feedback. Without some form of measurement, it is difficult to enhance performance or to grow as servants. TAFE (the acronym for this step)—Training, Affirmation, Feedback, and Evaluation—guides your work of facilitating effective involvement in the church. While your leader development plan began during the building of your relational foundations, ongoing leader development is a vital aspect of the *Equip* process.

> Do you not know that in a race all the runners run, but only one gets the prize? Run in such a way as to get the prize. Everyone who competes in the games goes into strict training. They do it to get a crown that will not last; but we do it to get a crown that will last forever.
>
> 1 CORINTHIANS 9:24–25

> . . . to prepare God's people for works of service, so that the body of Christ may be built up.
>
> EPHESIANS 4:12

325

> [Jesus] appointed twelve—designating them apostles—that they might be with him and that he might send them out to preach.
>
> MARK 3:14

The initial and ongoing equipping of people to serve. The development of competencies and character.

WHEN JESUS APPOINTED the Twelve, he brought his apostles with him in just about all that he did, so that they might learn and be ready to carry on his work. Training and equipping people in ministry service involves a wide range of practical actions—all geared to set people up to be successful.

In order to serve effectively, people must understand the jobs they have accepted. They will need varying levels of support in their ministry positions. Each leader's initial investment of time will pay handsome long-term dividends in dedicated service carried out by the member.

Ways to Prepare and Support People for Ministry

- Orient the person to the work of the team, program, or project.
- Introduce the person to other people working with the team, program, or project.
- Provide the person with an up-to-date ministry description.
- Take time to go over the ministry description and answer questions.
- Describe the connection between the ministry and the mission of the church.
- Provide the person with a roster of others involved in the ministry.
- Sincerely express appreciation to the person for being willing to work in a particular ministry area.
- Provide training for the person.
- Invite the person to attend related meetings, community events, or training opportunities outside of the church.
- Include people in decisions that affect them.
- Provide feedback and encouragement on a regular basis.
- Offer suggestions for improved performance.
- Find out from the person what type of support would be most helpful.
- Offer him or her greater responsibilities as time and performance allow.
- Direct the person back to the equipping ministry office if the ministry is not satisfactory for all concerned.
- Phone to find out why he or she was unable to attend a meeting or meet a commitment.
- Get to know the person and his or her particular life situation, ministry goals, and faith development desires.
- Express interest in the person and his or her family, work situation, or personal life.
- Introduce him or her to other church leaders.
- Take the person on a tour of the facilities if he or she is unfamiliar with the church or program facility.
- Be available to answer questions.
- Take care of details. Be sure he or she knows how to get coffee, where to hang up coats, how to enter or exit a building after hours, and the like.

The Crystal Cathedral in Garden Grove, California, provides a great training resource for those who are being introduced to a new ministry placement.

Volunteer Training Booklet
Crystal Cathedral

Ten Tips for Developing Good Training Programs

1. *Do a needs assessment.* Use surveys, phone calls, and interviews with current and formerly involved people in ministry service to determine what skills and knowledge (information) are essential for success in ministry in your church and in each specific ministry or program.

2. *Define your objectives clearly.* Clearly identify why you need a training program and state specifically what you hope to achieve as a result of the program. Write each objective and share it with your team. It is very important that you are clear about your goals and that all are working toward the same outcomes.

3. *Tailor the program to the people.* Identify specifically what information a person will need in order to succeed with the particular ministry experience. Remember that adults bring a great deal of life experience to their positions. They are interested in practical preparation, not in theoretical lectures. Be sure the training is appropriate to the complexity and duration of the work.

4. *Cover all the bases.* Prepare people to handle emergencies and difficult situations, as well as the more routine aspects of the job.

5. *Facilitate fellowship.* Provide guided opportunities for people to get to know each other. Use name tags and distribute an attendance list with addresses and phone numbers for continuing contact.

6. *Build relationships among staff members and leaders.* Research has shown that people who know where to turn to have their questions answered or to ask for guidance in new or difficult situations stay with the ministry experience far longer and perform more dependably than people who are uncertain about where to go for help. Be sure to provide this information in the training.

7. *Vary your methods of presentation.* We all have different learning styles. As you plan, consider the use of lectures, role playing, video and audio presentations, discussion, observation, demonstration, case studies, simulations, and games. Regardless of technique, be sure people feel comfortable and welcome.

8. *Use other people as trainers.* People are glad to see others succeeding in a particular ministry and being willing to share their experiences.

9. *Train paid and nonpaid personnel together.* In ministry situations where people will be working with paid church staff, joint training helps people to get to know each other and demonstrates the value of their services.

10. *Pay attention to the environment.* Comprehension is directly related to comfort. The chairs, the length of sessions, the ability to see and hear, the temperature of the room, and the seating arrangements—all these things affect learner receptivity. Paying attention to your surroundings pays off!

AFFIRMATION

✐ *Valuing people for who they are, not for what they do. Showing genuine love and compassion to lift up team leaders and team members.*

AFFIRMATION AND RECOGNITION are closely linked, but they are not synonymous. Affirmation is gratitude for and acknowledgment of *who we are* as Christians; recognition is gratitude for and acknowledgment of *what we do* as Christians.

Affirmation is the reassurance that you or a leader of a program provide to people who carry out their ministry. It is the comment, the smile, the word of welcome or thanks that says "we're glad you're here" and "I know you are an important child of God." Affirmation is not the same as recognizing a person for a job well done. Rather, it is the ongoing acknowledgment of the person for who the person is and for being a person involved in ministry for the kingdom. It is a quiet kind of sharing that says to the person, "You are important in the life of this church."

Ways to Affirm

- Listen thoughtfully and respond.
- Call and ask about the ministry experience.
- Make a point of observing and offering feedback.
- Write a note of appreciation.
- Provide guidance, share an article, or invite to a lecture.
- Give a hug.
- Smile.
- Offer help and encouragement.
- Call by name.
- Introduce to others.
- Invite to a staff meeting.
- Ask the person to serve as a mentor or trainer.
- Recognize a disappointment.
- Have a cup of coffee together.
- Ask about the family, the job, the kids, the parents.
- Say thank-you for just being you.
- Sit and talk together over a meal.
- Wait for a person and walk together down a hallway.
- Share a ride.
- Involve a person in a crisis situation.
- Keep candy on your desk.
- Remind a person about a pending meeting.
- Challenge a person to new heights.
- Respect sensitivities.
- Provide child care.
- Share a good joke or a story.
- Maintain a coffee bar complete with decaffeinated and herbal beverages.
- Allow for guilt-free sabbaticals from serving.
- Hold a reflection session or a Bible study.
- Call when a person is absent and express concern.

Think of unique ways to affirm the people who serve in your church. List your ideas and refer to them frequently.

_____

_____

_____

_____

_____

_____

_____

_____

_____

_____

_____

It may be more difficult to affirm and support people who serve in the community. Identify how your church can acknowledge their service and encourage their ministry.

_____

_____

_____

_____

_____

_____

_____

_____

_____

_____

_____

Make affirmation a habit. People need to be acknowledged and to feel needed and special. Affirmation is a key to the retention and continued involvement of your members in ministry.

FEEDBACK

 *Letting people know how they are doing. Providing a compass for reaching goals.*

LETTING THE PERSON know how he or she is doing (what is going well and where a different approach might be more effective) is the essence of feedback. Curiously, feedback or supervision rarely occurs in the church setting. Perhaps it is because we think of it as a formal process with some quantitative end product when, in fact, feedback is the opportunity to share an experience with a thoughtful, informed person who can help us grow and develop into more effective ministers.

Feedback is as simple as telling a person what has happened in his absence, sharing the outcome of a meeting that affects her ministry area, acknowledging a job completed, or providing information about how his service affected another person. Feedback need not be all accolades any more than it need be solely pointing out areas for improvement. It is letting a person know where he or she hit the mark, and where an altered approach might facilitate a more desirable outcome.

Effective feedback . . .

- focuses on the task or the behavior, *not* the person.
- describes to the person what she did and how you felt about the action. Often your interpretation of an event differs from the other person's understanding of the very same event, and you both learn in the process.
- highlights a behavior, increasing the likelihood that positive actions will be repeated.
- demonstrates that you are aware of the person and paying attention to how the ministry is being performed.
- provides an opportunity to learn and grow through service. As you reflect on your behavior and the reasons for an action, you learn much about yourself and how your actions affect others. You have the opportunity to explore your faith and how it is lived out in your daily actions.

Feedback sessions can be conducted privately or in small groups (if you're working on a team project). You may want to organize reflection sessions or Bible studies as an opportunity to offer feedback and to develop more effective ministers who are increasingly becoming grounded in their faith as they serve. As equipping ministry grows, you may want to encourage more formal supervision meetings, especially in situations where people are using ministry experiences to explore career areas or as job reentry points.

EVALUATION

Measuring the results of the ministry. Engaging in reflection on the experience. Asking questions to assess the effectiveness of people and programs.

YOUR YARDSTICK FOR individual success and program improvement is evaluation. Through evaluation you . . .

- learn from your experiences.
- use your experience in planning for the future.
- document program development and service delivery.

Evaluation as a Learning Experience

Evaluating Programs or Events

At the conclusion of a program or event, take time to evaluate the experience. As you meet with all who were involved, ask the questions, "What worked well? What areas need improvement? What changes would enhance this program or event in the future?"

Thoughtful evaluation while the event is fresh in everyone's mind lays the groundwork for future program planning. Look carefully at each work area, analyzing what went well and where problems occurred.

- Was the budget adequate?
- Did planning begin sufficiently in advance?
- Were all the main responsibilities covered, or did certain areas slip between the cracks?
- How did attendance compare with other years? Did it meet your expectations?
- What problems arose this year, and how might they be avoided in the future?
- Review the ministry description. How adequately did it convey the responsibilities?
- Should the project description be revised? If so, how? Who will take charge of that piece of work?

When possible, it's always helpful to ask those who attended the event to offer their opinions and recommendations. You can do this verbally, or through a simple form (see the sample forms on pages 334–35). If you ask for written feedback, be sure to provide a line that allows persons to indicate if they would like to work with you in the future. If a person does offer to help, be sure to keep track of the information and contact the individual when the invitation process begins. Be sure to document your evaluative findings in writing. This information will be invaluable as you plan future events and prepare budgets for the same or a similar event in years to come.

Program and event evaluation need not occur only at the conclusion of the project. It is often a good idea to take time out along the way to assess the progress of a project. Periodic program checkups keep an event on track, serve to remind persons of their responsibilities and timelines, and identify difficulties before they become full-blown problems.

Your yardstick for individual success and program involvement is evaluation.

Evaluating People's Experience

In chapter 14 the exit interview was introduced as a way to discuss a member's experience in service. Exit interviews can be conducted after completion of a ministry experience or when a person leaves the church.

An exit interview is a conversation about a person's experience in ministry. Consider these kinds of questions for your exit interviews:

- How did the ministry utilize your gifts and skills?
- What went especially well during the service venture?
- How might the experience be improved for someone else?
- How accurately did the ministry description reflect the work?
- Do you feel that you grew spiritually through this ministry?
- Could you tell me about the preparation and support you received?
- What did you learn through this ministry?
- Would you recommend this ministry to a friend? If so, how would you describe it?

As your conversation evolves, take time to explore other ministry opportunities. In some situations, he or she may need to take some time off for renewal and reflection. Help him or her feel comfortable with a decision for a sabbatical, and offer suggestions for spiritual renewal and growth. As you discuss together, identify a time when you might reasonably call on him or her to serve again in the future. Maintain a record of your conversation so that you can honor your commitment to each other.

In situations where a person is leaving the church, you may want to work with your pastor or other church leaders to establish a set of questions to evaluate the person's experience in the congregation. Some congregations maintain records of those who transfer to other churches and those who move from the area. Coordinate your efforts with others in the church so that all might benefit from the time spent in a closure discussion.

Regardless of the reason for a person's completion of a ministry experience, be certain to . . .

- evaluate the ministry experience, and not the individual.
- verify with the person what information shared with you may be discussed with others. It is very important not to violate a confidence.
- thank him or her for serving with you.
- learn how you or the equipping ministry system might support or involve this person in the future.

Evaluation as a Development Tool

Releasing people for ministry is what the church is all about. However, doing so through an equipping ministry system is a relatively new development in the life of the church. Accurate records measure your achievements and chart your successes.

Good records . . .

- provide a baseline against which you can measure the success or shortcomings of your efforts.
- help to justify your system in the mind of the trustees and church members or leaders.
- form the basis for future planning.
- help to establish and justify budget requests.
- document your success in expanding the ministry of the church.

> There is a difference between anonymity and confidentiality. So that the church can make improvements based on these evaluations, it is wise to offer anonymity if needed, but to agree that what you have learned together will be shared.

Interviewer: _____   Officer: _____

Brentwood Presbyterian Church
Los Angeles, California

EXIT INTERVIEW

I. **What were the challenges you faced when you first came on board?**

II. **Describe your experiences on the committee(s) on which you served.**

- What were the committee(s)?
- Describe how well the committee(s) were organized—or perhaps not organized.
- What resources were available?
- Describe the degree of staff support and nurturing your committee(s) received.
- What advice did you offer your successor? (If none, what would you like to tell your successor?)

III. **Describe your experiences with your board as an operating body.**

- How did they operate and behave with regard to openness, statesmanship, supportiveness, participation, and ability to set aside committee priorities for a "spiritual leader" point of view?
- What changes would you recommend with regard to structure, length, format, or style of meetings, as well as participation, amount of reading materials required for meeting preparation, officer retreats, and the like?
- How do you think your board is perceived by the congregation, and how is that image conveyed?
- What did you like best about serving?
- What did you like least about serving?
- What training, education, or developmental experiences were helpful to you (for example, retreats, seminars, and leadership development workshops)? Try to be specific about the topics and your impressions.
- What training, education, or developmental experiences do you wish had been available to you? Do you have suggestions for new modes of training?

IV. **Describe your opportunities for personal growth.**

- To what extent were you able to grow personally and develop your leadership abilities? How was this done?
- Do you feel that you made a significant contribution and that your years were well spent? In what ways? What kind of feedback, if any, were you given along the way in this regard?
- Describe your feelings about leaving the board.

V. **You have been in a position to see the "big picture." What advice do you have for Session, the deacons, the pastors, or Brentwood Church as a whole?**

Approaches to Evaluation of Equipping Ministry Processes

The Goals and Objectives Method

In chapter 12 goals and objectives were described as an important planning and evaluation tool. Setting solid goals and objectives allows you to review your progress and determine your successes for the year.

Baseline Measures

In addition to goals and objectives, some churches maintain records on people who are involved in service. Updating these records provides a measure for success and allows you to discern areas where you've made particular gains. If your church has no solid records of people engaged in service, you may want to do your best to establish a baseline figure as you initiate your system. Note areas where involvement is particularly low or high, and then investigate. See how your system might work to assist these areas, or how you can learn from the successes.

Some churches maintain records of people who are involved in ministry in the community as well. The church scattered is every bit as important as the church gathered; bear in mind, however, that this information takes more time to secure. Consider ways to collect information about people involved in service in the community and how you can recognize these persons for their service. This information is valuable in documenting the outreach ministry of the church.

Personal Evaluations or Subjective Measures

Many churches report a change in the "atmosphere" as a result of equipping ministry. People feel more welcome, included, and valued. People benefit from a ministry orientation that guides them to use their gifts and not to just fill slots on an organizational chart. Working with your team or with someone who has research expertise, consider ways to monitor and evaluate the attitude of people toward the church and her mission. Releasing people for ministry is what the church is all about. Persuasive anecdotal information may help the church trustees see equipping ministry as meeting additional objectives for the congregation.

A Word of Caution

- *Discern reasonable and appropriate measures and objectives.* For example, it is doubtful that you would want to set as your goal 100-percent member involvement, even though it does sound impressive! For some, participating in service may be impossible due to age or infirmity. Others who are driven to keep busy may have made a significant spiritual breakthrough with a decision to take a sabbatical. Your goals should stretch you and your team, but not demoralize you. There are seasons of service for all of us, and at any given time gifted members will be serving those in need in your church.

- *Hours only measure time, and not its quality or significance.* To say that 72 people each gave 100 hours worth of service does little to tell us whether their service was in their area of giftedness or whether it met any significant need. Likewise, avoid the temptation to value service in economic terms, such as "minimum wage." For starters, a uniform standard is inappropriate. The service of an attorney evaluating your church's constitution and

> **Each one should use whatever gift he has received to serve others, faithfully administering God's grace in its various forms. If anyone speaks, he should do it as one speaking the very words of God. If anyone serves, he should do it with the strength God provides, so that in all things God may be praised through Jesus Christ.**
>
> **1 Peter 4:10**

SAMPLE FORM

LEVEL 1 INSTITUTE FINAL EVALUATION

LEADERSHIP
training
NETWORK

In reflecting on your week at the Institute, please share the following feedback with us:

1.   Keep doing . . .

_____

_____

_____

_____

_____

2.   I'd like to suggest . . .

_____

_____

_____

_____

_____

3.   I learned . . .

_____

_____

_____

_____

_____

4.   I was reminded . . .

_____

_____

_____

_____

_____

Report and Evaluation of my Volunteer Ministry Experience

Name: _____ Telephone: _____

My Volunteer Position: _____

Assignment Term: From _____ To _____

My Trainer or Supervisor: _____

1. I enjoy this volunteer position because _____
_____

2. I used the following skills in this position: _____
_____

3. The training I received included _____
_____
_____

4. I felt supported in the following ways: _____

5. I received adequate orientation to my work area: yes_____   no_____

6. My supervisor checked my work to ensure it was being done correctly: yes_____   no_____

7. My major frustration with this job was_____
_____
_____

8. I could have done a better job if _____
_____
_____

9. The highlight of this volunteer experience was_____
_____
_____

10. The major accomplishment of this ministry experience was_____
_____
_____

11. The next person to do this job needs to know_____
_____
_____

Please return this evaluation to _____

Crystal Cathedral Volunteer Ministry   Date: _____

> Evaluation can be a very exciting part of system management. It is very rewarding to see progress and to realize that you have made a difference in the life of your church and in the lives of her members.

bylaws on a pro bono basis cannot be compared economically with the work of ushers, even though both are important jobs. Likewise, it's hard to place a monetary value on the time spent counseling and praying with a member who was recently diagnosed with a terminal illness. Select your measures carefully!

- *Keep it simple.* Complex evaluations are difficult to do—and for initial measurement purposes they are unnecessary. Define what you need to know and pilot-test several options for meeting your objectives. Be sure people understand what kind of information you are hunting for, and be sure you know how you will use the information once you have obtained it.

ONGOING LEADER DEVELOPMENT

DISCOVER THE SUPPORT and developmental needs of current leaders by asking them, "Where are you right now in your development as a leader? What do you need in order to be an effective leader?"

Explore the following topics and questions with your core team and staff members as a means of establishing plans for equipping current and future leaders in your church.

Attributes of Leadership

- What do you want your leaders to be about?
- What qualities, attributes, gifts, passion, and level of experience are essential for ministry leaders?
- What will be your process for identifying these attributes in people in your church?
- How and to whom will you communicate this information?

Leadership Roles and Responsibilities

- What are the general responsibilities of a ministry leader in your church?
- Who is responsible for determining this?
- What is the best way to communicate this information to current and future leaders?
- In what ways do you want current leaders to be involved with future leaders?

Staff and Core Team Roles and Responsibilities

- What role will the staff have in developing current leaders?
- What role will the staff have in identifying potential future leaders?
- What role will the core team (equipping ministry team) have in developing current leaders?
- What role will the core team (equipping ministry team) have in identifying potential future leaders?
- What level of support are you willing to give to current leaders (time, resources, and the like)?
- What level of support are you willing to give to potential future leaders?

Systems

- What systems and ongoing practices will you need in order to achieve your long-term goals for equipping future leaders?

- What aspects of your church culture currently support ministry leaders in their ongoing development?
- What aspects of your church culture do you want or need to change in order to provide the level of support you plan to provide to ministry leaders now and in the future?
- How and where do you see new leaders being identified?
- Who is looking for new leaders?
- Who has the permission to ask people to serve in a leadership role?
- Have these people been equipped in how to make "the invitation"?
- How do you enfold potential leaders into a track intentionally designed for developing leaders?

As you determine the best ways to meet these needs, here are some possibilities to consider:

1. *Orientation.* Provide new leaders with information about their role. Be sure to include the basics of how things work in the church office, how to get events scheduled on the church calendar, how to arrange for child care, and the like.

- What information and resources do you want or need to provide to new leaders? Who will be responsible for this?
- What information and resources do you want or need to provide to potential leaders? Consider including information on why someone would want to be a ministry leader; what ministry leaders need to know, be, and do; and how ministry leaders develop and grow in what they know, who they are, and what they do.

2. *Training.* Teach people the skills and knowledge necessary in order to be effective in leadership. Conduct a needs assessment to explore what people need to learn. Determine what information and skills they need to develop in order to be effective in leadership. From this information, determine the content and resource development of the training that should be provided.

> If you address the felt needs of leaders, not what *you* think they need, they will participate in training more willingly.

- What content knowledge and skills are needed for current leaders?
- What content knowledge and skills will be needed for new leaders?
- How will you determine the knowledge level and skills base of your leaders?
- Who will provide training and in what setting(s)?
- How will you evaluate the training? What are your measures for success?
- How will you evaluate the learning? What are your measures for success?

Identify skilled and gifted people who can deliver the training. Look for people who have experience in adult learning technology and who know and support the value of systems in your church. Select the best format option(s) for how to deliver the training:

> Pastors need to be present at training sessions (even if only at the beginning of the meeting) in order to send the message that training is valued and supported.

- workshops
- seminars
- presentations in meetings
- joining in partnership with experienced leaders
- videos
- resource guides
- buddy systems

Ministry leaders are called on to implement the processes of equipping ministry. In supporting them to achieve this goal, the following are skills that can be acquired and utilized in the equipping ministry effort that should become an ongoing part of every leader's experience in ministry service:

- Planning
- Meeting facilitation
- Task management
- Time management
- Invitation into ministry
- Sharing ministry
- Interviewing
- Giving feedback
- Change management
- Vision casting
- Team building
- Spiritual leadership/discipleship

Explore scheduling options to decide when to provide the training. Start with the culture of your church, finding out when meetings occur and what practices have been established for special sessions. Contact other churches to see what they're doing in this area.

3. *Coaching.* Pair up leaders with a coach—someone who will give them the constructive feedback and encouragement that can help them enhance their competence and effectiveness as leaders. Look for former leaders who have a heart for encouraging other leaders and who have the coaching skills to help them grow into their potential. Here are some questions to ask:

- What competencies need to be enhanced in your current leaders? How will you determine this?
- Who will be engaged in this level of support?
- What qualities, attributes, gifts, passion, and level of experience are essential for ministry coaches?
- How will you measure the growth, enhanced competence, and increased confidence of leaders who receive coaching?

4. *Mentoring.* Develop a value for and a process by which leaders are mentored throughout their term of service. Identify and establish a pool of committed leaders who are able and willing to mentor developing leaders by providing them with trustworthy counseling and direction for continuing character development. This is an essential ingredient of a leader development effort. There are many resources and tools available to set up these ministries (visit www.ltn.org for information on resources). Here are some key questions to consider:

- What character qualities need to be developed in current leaders? How will you determine this?

What Is the Best Way to Train?

Deciding on the best method of training is dependent on both your content and your audience. If the content you want to teach involves knowledge, use self-study. If the content involves practical skill and knowledge, use a workshop style with practice opportunities. If the content is an interactive skill, use a skills training seminar with role-play opportunities. The chart below gives some examples:

If the need is . . .	the best method of training is . . .
Biblical foundations of equipping ministry	Lecture Self-study Application: Lead a Bible study with his or her team.
Vision casting	Lecture Workshop
Interviewing skills	Interactive training with role play
Task management	Workshop
Time management	Workshop
Church policy and guidelines	Self-study
Meeting facilitation	Interactive training with role play

- Who will be engaged in this level of support?
- What qualities, attributes, gifts, passions, and level of experience are essential in ministry mentors?
- How will you measure the character development and maturity of leaders who are being mentored?

Receptive, supportive, organized, and enthusiastic ministry leaders are a critical link in a successful program.

Developing a Strategy for Ongoing Support of Your Church Leaders

1. Identify who your leaders are—those individuals who are intentionally leading a group of people to accomplish ministry objectives, learn in a class setting, or experience a small group.
2. Identify who is intentionally giving support to these leaders now. If no one is, identify those who could provide support and coaching for them.
3. Take a complete inventory of what is being asked of your leaders with regard to meetings. How much time a week and how many meetings a month are a part of their ministry involvement? Is it realistic?
4. After reflecting on the current ministry support structure and the regular weekly programming of your church, consider the following questions:

   - What are you currently doing to intentionally develop them as leaders and as Christians?
   - What are the values, truths, processes, and character traits that your church leaders need to be united around and committed to in order for your church to accomplish her mission? Are the current meetings and structures designed to develop and build these things into them in a meaningful and personal way?
   - As you brainstorm with other leaders, what possibilities might there be for a collaborative and unified approach to developing the leaders in your church?

5. Get together with the people identified in #2 and share with them your ideas, hopes, and dreams about the process of developing your leaders, asking them to join with you in prayer regarding this issue.
6. Have these folks consider with you what possibilities exist and how to take the development of your leaders to the next level. Determine which possibility makes the most sense at this time.
7. Begin sharing with the leaders your vision of uniting around a common purpose and building values and character traits into them, as well as the key possibility you've been praying about initiating. Seek their feedback.
8. Pick a start date and carefully think through this development plan. Be sure it hits a felt need of the leaders, encourages them, and challenges them to a higher level of unity and growth.
9. After a season of working this development plan, reassess the needs of the leaders, as well as the structure you've established, and make the necessary adjustments in order to heighten the value of developing leaders and increase your effectiveness in promoting equipping ministry.

"Developing ministers adds to your ministry. Developing leaders multiplies your ministry. Leaders need to be about detecting, developing, and unleashing other leaders."

Alan Nelson,
Leading Your Ministry

GROWTH AND LEADERSHIP TRACK

—We're on Track Helping Individuals Grow and Develop

—We're Becoming Fully Devoted Followers of Jesus Christ

Statement from the pastor

Our goal is to help everyone in our church family become a fully devoted follower of Jesus Christ. The following is a part of how we help you in that process: small group Bible studies, mission projects, and elective study classes are essential in helping each of us understand God's purpose for our lives and how we grow and mature as Christians. Gifted teachers and facilitators lead all of our classes. We will profit greatly from our involvement in these studies.

Growth and Development Opportunities

- Small group Bible studies
- Mission projects
- Windermere U classes

Small Group Bible Studies

Classes are offered Saturday nights at 7:15 and Sunday mornings at 9:45 and 11:00. Other small groups meet throughout the week for specific studies.

Mission Projects

Monthly volunteers help impact lives. Mission projects are planned so that individual classes or families can touch lives in our community, state, and world.

Windermere U

Elective classes are offered throughout the year to help individuals grow and develop.

- 100 Level Classes—designed for personal growth and life management skills
- 200 Level Classes—provides the basics for a maturing faith
- 300 Level Classes—designed for leadership training
- 400 Level Classes—in-depth leadership studies and conferences designed for CORE leaders

continued on next page

Let Us Help Get You on Track

100 Level — MANAGING YOUR LIFE

* Discovering Church Membership
  Parenting
  How to Manage Your Finances
  Marriage Preparation and Enrichment
  Relationship Building
  Support Groups
  Health and Fitness

200 Level — MATURING IN YOUR FAITH

* Discovering Spiritual Maturity
* Discovering Your Spiritual Gifts
* Experiencing God
* Becoming a Contagious Christian
* How to Pray
* How to Study the Bible
* How to Have a Quiet Time
  Prayer
  Bible Studies
  Christian Growth and Maturity
  Developing a Christian Worldview

300 Level — MINISTERING THROUGH SERVICE

* Jesus on Leadership
  Teacher Training
  Leadership Training (T.E.A.M.)

400 Level — MISSION FOR LIFE

* Core Leadership Training
  Special Seminars
  Conferences

Core curriculum course required for leaders
Classes are available on Wednesday nights and on weekends. See a Windermere U brochure
for detailed information on this semester's classes, or call the church office.

Web site: www.fbcwindermere.com

OTHER TRAINING OPPORTUNITIES

Classes are also available for:
Preschoolers
Children
Students

First Baptist Church, Windermere, Florida

> *Valuing the gifts of time and leadership freely given to the church. A celebration of the ministry of God's people.*

CELEBRATING SERVICE IS an integral part of the equipping ministry system. Just as you work to train staff members and key leaders to involve people in ministries that capture their gifts and talents, you need to train your leaders to recognize people for their service to the community. Plan appropriate and frequent celebrations of service to culminate the service cycle.

For most people the decision to serve has nothing to do with a desire for recognition; however, the decisions to return to service and to remain active in the church are strongly influenced by the degree to which people feel their efforts are affirmed, valued, and appreciated. One of the key reasons people drop their church memberships is because no one expressed appreciation for the work expended on behalf of the congregation. While recognition may not bring you new members, it surely helps you retain members who are committed to serving.

As a key component of equipping ministry, recognition needs to be approached as you would any other responsibility area. Working with the equipping ministry team, the senior pastor, your church staff, and key leaders, establish a coordinated, year-round plan to guide your work. Recognition is not something you do alone. Your job is to lift up the value and make sure it is happening. Each ministry area that involves people in service delivery is responsible for *celebrating* service and affirming those who are sharing their gifts and talents—in the same way these leaders are responsible for *inviting* people into ministry and *preparing* them for service positions.

Recognition is more than saying thank-you for a job well done. It is a personalized response to an individual, acknowledging his or her unique contribution to the body of Christ. It is valuing the individual, making his or her service visible, and supporting him or her in both the joys and struggles of working to build the kingdom.

Recognition is important for everyone in every type of position—large and small, short-term and long-term. It tells the young people who agreed to set up tables and prepare the fellowship hall for a congregational event that they, too, are a part of the church. It affirms the months of planning and hours of effort contributed by the director of the Vacation Bible School program. It supports the receptionist and encourages his or her return even when he or she is the recipient of an angry outburst from another person. Recognition promotes growth and continued involvement. It helps to unify all the people of the church as each one makes his or her unique service contribution. It is one of the secrets to retention.

Defining Your Role in Recognition

As the director of equipping ministry, you and your team are responsible for . . .

- lifting up the importance of celebration and recognition events to all persons who involve people in ministry opportunities.
- helping to plan a year-round recognition schedule that leads to affirming the work of people in all forms of ministry.
- modeling recognition through your team interaction and within your office.

Let us hold unswervingly to the hope we profess, for he who promised is faithful. And let us consider how we may spur one another on toward love and good deeds. Let us not give up meeting together. . . .

HEBREWS 10:23–25

Receiving payment for a job does not eliminate the need for thanks. Encourage celebration events that acknowledge the importance of teamwork and focus on the task performed, not on the salary scale.

- including in your annual budget funds for celebration and recognition programs and events and encouraging other ministry areas to do the same.
- training all ministry leaders to recognize the work of people who serve with them, whether on an ongoing or special-event basis.
- working with clergy to recognize people in corporate worship and in the prayers of the church, as well as through Bible study, small group ministry, and other Christian education opportunities.

The Link to Whole-Life Ministry

Implementing and modeling an ongoing value for recognition contribute to the goal of developing whole-life ministry for people who are involved in service. Service in ministry contributes to the spiritual growth and maturity of each person involved, and recognition of their contribution to the body of Christ enables them to make that connection.

Recognize people for what they're doing in ministry *as* ministry. Recognition ties all that people do in service into whole-life ministry. It's why people stay and come back for more; it's often why they leave when they don't receive it. Letting people know how their contributions affect the growth of God's kingdom creates affirmation, which, if continued, will result in spiritual growth and lead to whole-life ministry.

Keys to Effective Service Celebrations

To be effective, recognition must be an ongoing process, not an afterthought. It must be an integral component of ongoing equipping ministry. As you work to develop goals and objectives for a year-round, coordinated, churchwide effort of recognition and celebration, consider these eight suggestions for successful recognition:

1. *Be timely.* Recognize people immediately, or at least in close proximity to the time in which they served. Don't wait to say thank-you on an annual basis or at a big event. Find ways to express thanks all the time—for all levels and types of ministries.

2. *Be consistent.* If you acknowledge some people with a special coffee mug when they rotate off a team, have enough mugs to thank all persons from all teams who are completing their terms of service.

3. *Keep your plans manageable.* It takes time and effort to create meaningful celebration events. Build your teams adequately. Develop your plans well in advance. Pay special attention to details.

4. *Be sincere, honest, and genuine.* Don't give accolades that you don't really mean. Every contribution doesn't have to have been the biggest and the best or the most unusual in order to be acknowledged. It takes lots of people who are doing lots of little things in the background in order for needs to be met and ministry to flow smoothly. Be grateful for all of God's children working in all kinds of different ways.

5. *Be user-oriented.* It is important that the person whose efforts you are acknowledging feels appreciated. Be age-sensitive in your selection of food, the time of day you recognize the group or individual, and the form of gratitude you select.

6. *Keep good records.* Maintain accurate lists of all who have been involved in the ministry—salaried and nonsalaried people alike. When you celebrate accomplishments, include everyone in your expressions of thanks. Feelings are easily hurt when a person's contribution is inadvertently forgotten.

Train staff to say thank-you on an ongoing basis.

7. *Be creative.* Have peers recognize each other. Involve children in the recognition of their teachers. Acknowledge people who have worked together as a team. Have programs outside of the church, as well as on your premises. There are no fixed rules or "right ways" to celebrate, so enjoy brainstorming and coming up with new ideas.

8. *Have fun.* Celebrations are part of the joy of serving. They motivate people to continue in ministry and encourage them to grow through service. So have fun, be whimsical, be upbeat, be lighthearted, and enjoy yourself!

Recognition Ideas

You can recognize service in many ways. This list is not exhaustive, and it is shared to encourage your creativity as you discover the best ways to celebrate service in your church:

- Send letters or notes.
- Create certificates.
- Extend invitations to seminars outside of the church and pay the registration fee.
- Invite a person to participate with you in a community event.
- Ask the person to serve as a mentor or trainer of others.
- Send a thank-you note to the member's family.
- Develop a "gifted servant of the month" program.
- Nominate for a community recognition program.
- Send a birthday card or other seasonal greeting.
- Publish accomplishments in newsletters or bulletins.
- Create a "guardian angel" recognition program, using angel pins.
- Have children recognize their teachers.
- Commission people in worship.
- Recognize kids as they graduate from high school, and support them in their future plans (college, service, work).
- Organize periodic "temple talks," highlighting the work of people in your church.
- In the corporate prayer time pray for members *by name* in their service work.
- Devote an entire Sunday worship service to a "celebration of service."
- Create a "You Are Picture-Perfect" display, with pictures of people in service (choir pictures, kitchen pictures, and so forth).
- Create "You Made a Difference in My Life" buttons, and within twenty-four hours of receipt of the button have people give a button to someone who made a difference in their lives.
- Sponsor a roast for all who are rotating off a committee.
- Send get-well cards.
- Give a pack of Lifesavers with a note that reads, "You saved my life when . . ."
- Send "You Made Me a Shining Star" notes to people who worked with you, especially people who worked in the background on a big project.
- Feature people in news articles in the church paper, as well as in local and metropolitan papers.
- Prepare and distribute trinkets, mugs, pens, and key chains.
- Create a T-shirt.

- Sponsor a trip.
- Plan a party or picnic.
- Take a group photo and reproduce for all people of the group.
- Mount a picture of an important symbol in the church and give to people in recognition of service.
- Shape through calligraphy a meaningful Scripture passage, and put it in a frame.
- Document a person's service in a letter of recommendation.
- Send impromptu cards.
- Purchase newspaper space for a recognition ad.
- Create a recognition edition of the church newsletter or bulletin.
- Attend together a sports event, movie, or play.
- Plan a reception.
- Praise the person to his or her friends and family, publicly and privately.
- Conduct a "team leaders' day" recognizing the leaders of teams, projects, and programs.
- Send a package of tea, with a note that reads, "Since you've joined our group, things are really brewing."
- Send a Thanksgiving card to the person's family, thanking them for sharing their family member.
- Develop an honor roll or alumni association for past leaders.
- Publish a list of all people who serve in the church and community.
- Write thank-you notes—frequently.
- Create rotating recognition programs—January for Sunday school teachers and the education ministry, February for worship and music, March for the board of trustees, and so on.
- Publicize community service recognition received by a person.
- Glue a chocolate kiss or hug to a card that reads, "Take a bow, you deserve a kiss/hug!"

> Marilyn MacKenzie and Gail Moore,
> *The Volunteer Development Toolbox*

> "The reward, the real grace of conscious service, is the opportunity not only to help relieve suffering but to grow in wisdom, experience greater unity, and have a good time while we're doing it."
>
> Ram Dass and Paul Gorman,
> *How Can I Help?*

REFLECTION

🖎 *The framework in which people process and synthesize the information and ideas they have gained through their serving experience and in the learning setting.*

THROUGH THE PROCESS of reflection, people analyze concepts, evaluate experiences, and form opinions and spiritual insights—all within the context of the theological constructs of the church. We need to do what we do by way of service and ministry in a manner that's reflective rather than reactive.

This is a critical element of ministry and should not be overlooked. We want to lead and equip our people to think about what they are doing—that there is a connection between what they are doing in ministry and what God is teaching them through that ministry.

Ministry service, and especially the leadership of an equipping ministry system, is about physical endurance, as well as about emotional and spiritual endurance. Working with people involves them "drawing out of us" continually. Reflection is stepping back, taking a look, and reflecting on what your ministry means in your life. Sometimes we become so

> **But Mary treasured up all these things and pondered them in her heart.**
>
> LUKE 2:19

> After he had dismissed them, he went up on a mountainside by himself to pray. When evening came, he was there alone.
>
> MATTHEW 14:23

involved in an experience that we miss out on the meaning of the experience. As we implement equipping ministry, it's important that we build in "pauses"—times when we reflect on the meaning of the ministry.

It's essential in the act of reflection to ask two key questions:

- So what? (What does this mean? What is God trying to teach me?)
- Now what? (What must I do now as a result of my experience?)

As we mobilize people to use the gifts God has given them, we have to offer them frequent opportunities to ask these two questions. If they are not given the opportunity, it's possible to have the experience and miss the meaning.

Bringing both the meaning and the experience together facilitates conscientious, intentional, and reflective service—not just service you've carried out because somebody asked you to. This is about *spiritualizing* service.

The Mechanics of Reflection

Journals

Keeping a journal is one of the most effective tools of reflection. Journaling is similar to writing a diary—recording what God is doing in your life. It is sometimes helpful to add biblical references when they are meaningful. Remember, this is *not* evaluation—but it is hard to realistically evaluate if you haven't reflected on the experience.

Guided Conversations

A guided conversation is often useful as a reflection tool in a group or mentoring setting. Helping people ask the right questions clarifies the reflection experience.

Creative Activities

Some people find it easier to reflect if they are involved in an activity. The creative activity is normally one that doesn't require much mental attention.

Meditation

Meditation centers on using Scripture to interpret your reflections. It gives you the opportunity to center and focus both on Scripture and the image of Christ. It is important in meditation to make time for "listening" to God.

Prayer

Prayer is another form of quiet time and meditation. Again, the communication is both talking and listening.

JOINING GOD'S WORK IN THE TWENTY-FIRST CENTURY

GOD HAS CREATED A new movement of equipping churches that prepare people according to their calling and gifts to be salt and light in their churches, communities, workplaces, families—in the whole of society. Equipping ministry will always be a work in progress. It is about a process—an intentional way of "doing church." It is a way called out, step by step, in the Scriptures. The end result is that the body of Christ matures; she develops both in breadth and depth. Won't you join what God is doing in this new century?

Bibliography of Sources Quoted
(in order of first appearance)

Cordeiro, Wayne. *Doing Church as a Team.* Honolulu: New Hope Publishers, 1998.

Warren, Rick. *The Purpose-Driven® Church: Growth without Compromising Your Message and Mission.* Grand Rapids: Zondervan, 1995.

Slaughter, Michael. *Real Followers: Beyond Virtual Christianity.* Nashville: Abingdon, 1999.

Bugbee, Bruce. *What You Do Best in the Body of Christ.* Grand Rapids: Zondervan, 1995.

Macchia, Stephen A. *Becoming a Healthy Church: 10 Characteristics.* Grand Rapids: Baker, 1999.

Easum, William M. *Dancing with Dinosaurs: Ministry in a Hostile and Hurting World.* Nashville: Abingdon, 1993.

Mead, Loren B. *The Once and Future Church.* Nashville: Winston-Derek, 1991.

Wilson, Walter P. *The Internet Church.* Nashville: Word, 2000.

Easum, William M. *Sacred Cows Make Gourmet Burgers: Ministry Anytime, Anywhere, by Anyone.* Nashville: Abingdon, 1995.

George, Carl F. *Prepare Your Church for the Future.* Grand Rapids: Revell, 1991.

Schein, Edgar H. *Organizational Culture and Leadership.* San Francisco: Jossey-Bass, 1992.

Nelson, Alan E. *Leading Your Ministry.* Nashville: Abingdon, 1996.

Barna, George. *The Power of Vision: How You Can Apply and Capture God's Vision for Your Ministry.* Ventura, Calif.: Regal, 1992.

Malphurs, Aubrey. *Developing a Vision for Ministry in the 21st Century.* Grand Rapids: Baker, 1992.

Blackaby, Henry, and Claude V. King. *Experiencing God.* Nashville: Lifeway Christian Resources, 1990.

Kouzes, James M., and Barry Z. Posner. *The Leadership Challenge: How to Keep Getting Extraordinary Things Done in Organizations.* San Francisco: Jossey-Bass, 1995.

Weems, Lovett H. Jr. *Church Leadership: Vision, Team, Culture and Integrity.* Nashville: Abingdon, 1993.

Bridges, William. *Managing Transitions: Making the Most of Change.* Reading, Mass.: Addison-Wesley, 1993.

Ogden, Greg. *The New Reformation: Returning the Ministry to the People of God.* Grand Rapids: Zondervan, 1990.

Anderson, Lynn. *They Smell Like Sheep: Spiritual Leadership for the Twenty-First Century.* West Monroe, La.: Howard Publishing, 1997.

McNeal, Reggie. *Revolution in Leadership: Training Apostles for Tomorrow's Church*. Nashville: Abingdon, 1998.

Katzenbach, Jon R., and Douglas K. Smith. *The Wisdom of Teams: Creating the High-Performance Organization*. Boston: Harvard Business School Press, 1992.

Wheatley, Margaret J. *Leadership and the New Science: Learning about Organization from an Orderly Universe*. San Francisco: Berrett-Koehler, 1992.

Miller, Arthur F., and Ralph T. Mattson. *The Truth about You*. Berkeley, Calif.: Ten Speed Press, 1989.

MacKenzie, Marilyn, and Gail Moore. *The Volunteer Development Toolbox*. Darien, Ill.: Heritage Arts, 1993.

Glossary of Terms

Leadership Training Network strives to provide resources to churches from a variety of traditions and cultures. At times, however, there can be confusion over terminology. This glossary provides clarification of the terminology used in this guidebook.

Church Leadership: The governing board of a church—the elders, deacons, vestry, council, session. This team includes pastoral staff members and the senior pastor or head of staff.

Core Team: Usually found in larger churches, these are the core leaders of the various teams who build the equipping ministry system (for example, an assimilation leader who oversees a team of ushers and greeters, the parking lot crew, and the team for the new members class; or a discovery director who oversees the team of interviewers and the team of people cataloging ministry opportunities, and the like).

Culture: The environment and value system of a church that demonstrates core beliefs, spiritual and relational traditions, the vision and mission of a church, and all other aspects that contribute to a church's identity.

Director of Equipping Ministry: Paid or nonpaid staff member who has the gifts and role to facilitate the building of churchwide equipping systems and training for leaders to mobilize ministry. This person identifies, invites into, and leads the core team, committee, or task force. Some variations of the title are volunteer coordinator, director of lay ministry, director of leadership development, or director of assimilation. In many cases it may be an executive pastor, associate pastor, director of Christian education, or children's minister who has been given churchwide equipping ministry responsibility.

Equipping Ministry: Church efforts to build systems and train leaders to identify people's gifts and ministry needs, connect them into service according to their gifts, equip them, and recognize their gifts of service (has also been known as lay mobilization, lay ministry, and gifts ministry).

Equipping Ministry Team: The team or teams of people responsible to create and facilitate the equipping ministry processes and systems.

Key Influencers: Churchwide leaders who determine the overall direction, both formal and informal, of the equipping ministry system.

Laity: A term that generally refers to people who have not necessarily attended seminary, been ordained, or been approved to perform certain sacraments and ceremonies in certain churches.

Ministry Connectors: Those people who serve as the conduit of information between equipping ministry and program ministries. These people serve in the various areas of ministry, but play an additional role of facilitating the ongoing communication with the equipping ministry team in order to ensure effective implementation of equipping ministry systems.

Ministry Leaders (includes the term "congregational leaders"): Those leaders who are responsible for the various areas of ministry and programs within the church (for example, director of children's ministry, adult ministry leader, and missions ministry leader).

Ministry Team Members: Members of teams reporting to their respective core team leaders for such things as assimilation of visitors, administrative and computer support, interviewing, teaching spiritual gift classes, cataloging ministry opportunities, and helping placement/training teams in existing ministries such as children's ministry, youth, adult education, and so forth.

Mobilizing Ministry: Church efforts to build systems and train leaders who cause gift mobilization to occur.

Nonpaid Staff: People who serve the church in a ministerial, staff, or leadership role who do not receive compensation. In many churches this type of service is referred to as "volunteer" service.

Program Ministries: The term to describe the various ministry programs in a church, for example, adult ministry, worship, Sunday school, missions.

Silos: A term used to describe those ministries and departments within churches that gather key people for use in those areas, often at the expense of empowering those people to find their best match in other areas of ministry. This term is analogous to grain silos, not missile silos.

Small groups: A very effective means for team ministry, but not the only means. Many gifts work best in groups larger than ten. Many people learn and grow better in one-on-one situations or in midsize or large groups.

Team Ministry: A way of doing ministry that combines the gifts needed to accomplish the task, the community needed to nurture and encourage its members, and the leadership style required to build respect for each gift in its proper place resulting in maturity and unity of the larger congregation. This is more a value and culture than it is a program, curriculum, or method.

Whole-Life Ministry: People intentionally ministering through their gifts in the church, the marketplace, their communities, and their families.